VIVISECTION IN HISTORICAL PERSPECTIVE

THE WELLCOME INSTITUTE SERIES IN THE HISTORY OF MEDICINE
Edited by W.F. Bynum and Roy Porter,
The Wellcome Institute

VIVISECTION IN HISTORICAL PERSPECTIVE

Edited by
NICOLAAS A. RUPKE

London and New York

First published 1987
by Croom Helm Ltd.

First published in paperback in 1990
by Routledge
11 New Fetter Lane, London EC4P 4EE

Simultaneously published in the USA and Canada
by Routledge
a division of Routledge, Chapman and Hall, Inc.
29 West 35th Street, New York, NY 10001

Printed and bound in Great Britain by
Biddles Ltd, Guildford and King's Lynn

British Library Cataloguing in Publication Data

Vivisection in Historical Perspective. –
   (The Wellcome Institute series in the history of medicine)
   1. Vivisection – history
   I. Rupke, Nicolaas A. II. Series
   619   QP45

Library of Congress Cataloging in Publication Data

   (The Wellcome Institute series in the history of medicine)
   Includes index
   1. Vivisection – history. 2. Animal experimentation – history.
   I. Rupke, Nicolaas A. II. Series.
   HV4915.V58   1987   174'.4'09   87-8992

   ISBN 0-415-05021-9

Contents

Contents

Preface

The place allotted to animals in human society is to a certain extent a mirror of our beliefs and values. Animals have been used for food and clothing, as beasts of burden, for military purposes, in religious ceremonies, for sports, as pets, and increasingly also in scientific experiments. Marked differences in the treatment of animals have traditionally existed between Oriental and Occidental societies; but they have also existed between different groups within a single society.

This collection of essays focuses on the controversy which has arisen within Western society over the use of laboratory animals for scientific purposes. It examines the historical origins of the issue of vivisection in several Western European countries and North America, and places the often vehement arguments of pro- and anti-vivisectionists in the wider conflict over the value of modern science in general.

By bringing our historical account up to date, linking it to the present-day clash between pro-vivisectionists and animal rights campaigners, we situate our volume at the confluence of history with science, ethics and current affairs. This is reflected in the expertise of the authors which includes various branches of history, biomedical science, medicine and animal welfare.

The editor wishes to acknowledge the support in preparing this volume given by the Wellcome Institute, London; the Netherlands Institute for Advanced Study, Wassenaar; and Wolfson College, Oxford. The following individuals have kindly offered encouragement and advice: Professor Ide Anak Agung Gde Agung, Dr William Bynum, Professor Tore Frängsmyr, Professor Gerald Geison, Dr Faye Getz, Professor Margaret Gowing, Raina Haig, Dr Renato Mazzolini and Francis Warner.

Nicolaas A. Rupke
The Wellcome Institute for the History of Medicine

Notes on Contributors

Lennart Bromander studied history of science at the University of Uppsala.

Dr *Paul N. Elliott* studied history of science at the University of Oxford. The title of his DPhil thesis is 'The Social and Intellectual Background to Claude Bernard's Vision of Science' (University of Oxford, 1984).

Mary Ann Elston is Lecturer in Sociology at the Department of Community Medicine, University College, and at Royal Holloway and Bedford New College, London. Her MA thesis is entitled 'Gender, Medicine and Morality in the late Nineteenth Century: a Study of the Anti-Vivisection Movement, 1870-1904' (University of Essex, 1984).

Dr *Patrizia Guarnieri* is Lecturer in Italian at Stanford University in Florence. She recently held a NATO research fellowship at the Wellcome Institute, London. This resulted in her *Individualita Difformi. La Psichiatria Antropologica di Enrico Morselli* (Angeli, Milan, 1986).

Dr *Judith E. Hampson* was, until recently, Chief Animal Experimentation Research Officer, Royal Society for the Prevention of Cruelty to Animals, Causeway, Horsham, West Sussex. She now works as a consultant on laboratory animal welfare. Her PhD thesis deals with 'Animal Experimentation, 1876–1976: Historical and Contemporary Perspectives' (University of Leicester, 1978).

Dr *Christopher J. Lawrence* is Medical Historian (Clinical Medicine) at the Wellcome Institute, London. His PhD thesis is entitled 'Medicine as Culture: Edinburgh and the Scottish Enlightenment' (University of London, 1984).

Dr *Susan E. Lederer* studied history of medicine at the University of Wisconsin, Madison. Her PhD thesis examines 'An Ethical Problem: the Controversy over Human and Animal Experimentation in Late Nineteenth-Century America' (University of Wisconsin, Madison, 1987).

Dr *Andreas-Holger Maehle* is a Senior Research Fellow at the Institute for the History of Medicine, University of Göttingen. An MD of the University of Bonn, he is currently writing a comprehensive history of animal experimentation in Western medicine.

Dr *Diana E. Manuel* is Lecturer in History, School of Education, University of Durham. She is currently writing a book about Marshall Hall based on her PhD thesis.

Sir *William Paton* is Professor Emeritus of Pharmacology in the University of Oxford, and Honorary Director of the Wellcome Institute, London. His many publications include *Man and Mouse: Animals in Medical Research* (Oxford University Press, Oxford, 1984).

Dr *Stewart Richards* is Lecturer in Physiology at Wye College, University of London. His publications include articles on the history of nineteenth-century British physiology and he is the author of *Philosophy and Sociology of Science. An Introduction* (Basil Blackwell, Oxford, 2nd edn, 1987).

Dr *Nicolaas A. Rupke* is a Research Fellow at the Wellcome Institute, London. He is currently working on a scientific biography of Richard Owen, a sequel to his *The Great Chain of History: William Buckland and the English School of Geology, 1814–1849* (Clarendon Press, Oxford, 1983).

William M. Schupbach is Curator of the Iconographic Collections, Wellcome Institute, London. His publications on medical art include *The Paradox of Rembrandt's 'Anatomy of Dr Tulp' (Medical History*, Supplement no. 2, 1982).

Dr *Ulrich Tröhler* is Professor and Head, Institute for the History of Medicine, University of Göttingen. He directs a research programme on the history of vivisection in German-speaking countries. The title of his inaugural lecture is 'Was ist neu'? — Der medizinische Tierversuch im Meinungsstreit', *Swiss Pharma*, vol. 7 (1985), pp. 7–16.

Plates, Figures and Tables

Plates

Figures

Tables

1

Introduction

Nicolaas Rupke

Vivisection: practice and protest

Vivisection is a scientific procedure that is widely used throughout the different fields of study of the living organism. It is practised in virtually all the great research institutions of physiology, pharmacology, biochemistry, microbiology and other biological sciences. Vivisection has also become an essential part of clinical medicine, whether in immunology, pathology, surgery or cancer studies. Techniques such as organ transplants, for example, and other highly interventive therapy are systematically rehearsed on animals before being applied to human patients.

But if the systematic use of vivisection had its origins in laboratories for biological and medical research, it has also found widespread application in the general area of public health. It is routinely used in various laboratories run by the pharmaceutical companies, the food, drinks and tobacco industries, and, most controversially, by the cosmetics industry. Vivisection, in short, has become an integral part of the scientific study of the life processes, be it in pure, medical or veterinary research, or research with a directly commercial motive. To this must be added the widespread use of animals in psychological investigations.

Vivisection is a very old procedure. It has been practised since the beginning of scientific medicine, in ancient Greece and Rome. Through the seventeenth and eighteenth centuries it even acquired a certain degree of popularity. Doubt about vivisection, however, whether of a medical or a moral kind, has been virtually coeval with the existence of the practice. But this doubt did not develop into a major, public controversy until the second half of the nineteenth century. By then, experimentation on living animals had become a quintessential part of physiology as an institutionalised profession.

As a public debate, the vivisection controversy has persisted since it began in 1863, when the first organised agitation against animal experimentation took place in Florence, led by English women. The course of the debate, from its inception till the present day, has shown two major peaks, the first centred on the year 1876 when the earliest law regulating animal experiments was enacted in Britain. The second major peak has emerged recently, in the past decade, related in Britain to the replacement of the Cruelty to Animals Act of 1876 by the Animals (Scientific Procedures) Act of 1986. During this period of 110 years, the intensity of the debate has fluctuated, and its periodicity in different countries has not always been synchronous.

The first anti-vivisection societies originated in England, in 1875, during the year that a Royal Commission looked into the question of laboratory animals. The best known of those was the Society for the Protection of Animals Liable to Vivisection, afterwards called the Victoria Street Society. Among its sensational acts of protest was the issuing of 300 dramatically illustrated placards and 1,700 handbills to be posted in public places. The present wave of debate may be reckoned to begin in 1975 with the publication of literature on animal rights and acts of violence by animal liberation extremists.

Secondary literature

The year 1975 has been something of an *annus mirabilis* of the recent anti-vivisection resurgence. In this year, which marked the centenary of the founding of the first anti-vivisection societies, Peter Singer published his *Animal Liberation*.[1] It spelt out for the first time the philosophy of the animal liberation movement arguing, among other things, that those who oppose racism and support feminism should equally oppose the 'speciesism' of the way in which we use animals for human benefit. Also in 1975, Richard Ryder's publicity-generating *Victims of Science* saw the light.[2] Now, as in the past, the scientists' answer was some years in coming, but with William Paton's *Man and Mouse* (1984) the case for the use of live animals in medical research has been lucidly stated, both with philosophical literacy, rare among defenders of vivisection (Claude Bernard having been one of the exceptions), and with respect for the animal welfare sentiment.[3]

Less well known is the fact that 1975 was also the year in which the first proper historical study was published of the origins of the anti-vivisection movement in England. Several histories of the controversy had appeared before that date, but these were either written with an anti-vivisectionist bias, such as E. Westacott's *A Century of Vivisection and Anti-Vivisection* (1949), or were rather general, such as Hubert Bretschneider's *Der Streit um die Vivisektion im 19. Jahrhundert* (1962).[4] Both books contain a great deal of useful information, but the first definitive study of the origins of anti-vivisectionism was Richard French's *Antivivisection and Medical Science in Victorian Society*.[5]

French's exemplary study focuses on the genesis of the Cruelty to Animals Act of 1876, the passage of which sent shock waves through the biomedical establishments of Europe and North America. French uses the Victorian anti-vivisection movement as a case study of the attitude of society to modern science. He argues that at the heart of the anti-vivisection movement was the public concern over the emergence of science and medicine as leading institutions of Victorian society.

Other recent sources for the history of the vivisection controversy are studies of the origins of the animal protection movement, such as James Turner's *Reckoning with the Beast* (1980) or Brian Harrison's *Peaceable Kingdom* (1982).[6] The animal protection and anti-vivisection societies had, like much else in Victorian society, a strong class bias. Turner argues that the new capitalism of industrialised and urbanised Victorian society went hand in hand with a concern for public morality and work discipline, both flouted by brutality to animals; drunken workers at bull-baiting events had a corrosive effect on factory discipline. Thus animal protection societies appealed to the middle (and upper) classes, and, as Harrison shows, the early RSPCA was certainly timid in its approach to cruel sports such as steeple-chasing and hunting, widely enjoyed by the aristocracy.

Scope of this volume

In the wake of the renewed vigour with which the issue of animal experimentation has been debated since 1975, several projects dealing with the history of the vivisection controversy have been started. This collection of essays represents a 'spring harvest' of the fruits borne thus far by these projects. It adds to the existing secondary literature by both widening and deepening the scope of historical inquiry.

This volume focuses on the second half of the nineteenth century, when the original wave of public debate swept across Europe and North America. The first essay, however, by Maehle and Tröhler, traces the vivisection issue back to pre-Periclean Athens, demonstrating that the basic arguments for and against were formulated long before the Victorian era.

In order fully to comprehend the controversy, we must first learn how and why the scientists resorted in a systematic and increasingly widespread way to experimentation upon animals. The essays by Elliott and Guarnieri explore therefore the culture of science which stimulated the use of vivisectional techniques, while Manuel and Richards deal with specific instances of the experimental work that was carried out on animals.

The scope of this volume extends beyond Britain to include France, the German lands, Italy, Sweden and the United States. Thus a more coherent picture of international comparison is provided by Guarnieri, Tröhler and Maehle, Rupke, Bromander and Lederer, showing, among other things, how very similar the vivisection debates in different countries were. There were differences in when the debates took place; there were differences in personalities and their style; and also in the degree to which anti- or pro-vivisection succeeded. But the arguments for or against were virtually the same everywhere, and till the turn of the century the socio-political colours of the rival parties were similar if not identical. Anti-vivisection tended to be patronised by the upper classes, even by royalty, and it found a sympathetic ear with those who were worried about the secularisation of society. Pro-vivisection, on the other hand, was near-unanimously supported by the leaders of the scientific and medical establishment and by those who continued to believe in the equations 'science is progress' or even 'science is truth'.

Although this volume's emphasis is on the late nineteenth century, two essays connect the historical origins of the debate to the present-day exchanges, mainly by dealing with different aspects of the legislation controlling animal experimentation, how the law works in specific instances (Lawrence), and more comprehensively, what laws are (or are not) on the statute books in the United States and in the twenty-one countries comprising the Council of Europe (Hampson). Furthermore, Schupbach's discussion of five major paintings/engravings of the scientific use of live animals widens our perspective on the cultural landscape in which the vivisection issue has existed. And Paton's epilogue reflects on the contents of this volume, on the issue as it stands today, and on the ultimate objective we are striving for as far as the man-animal relationship is concerned.

One feature of the vivisection controversy which crops up in several different essays is its connection with women or rather with the suffragette movement. Elston's chapter examines why this has been so. Such connections recur from essay to essay, explicitly or implicitly, not only of anti-vivisection with feminism, but also with idealist philosophy, vegetarianism, anti-semitism, alternative medicine, etc. The important point to make is that such links are not spurious, but that they represent the fine-grained socio-political matrix from which anti-vivisectionism sprang. This volume therefore shows to what extent the vivisection question functioned as a catalyst of deeper and wider conflicts in Western society. But this is not just shown with respect to the anti-vivisection movement; the present studies particularly add to the existing literature by also discussing the scientists' side: why, and under what circumstances, did they adopt vivisection as a systematic laboratory technique?

Vivisection and experimental physiology

The first and most important fact, linking the practice of vivisection to its social context, is the connection with the emergence of experimental physiology as a separate academic discipline. In the secondary literature, the vivisection controversy is invariably seen as stemming from the growing animal welfare movement. But the animal protection movement was primarily concerned with the prevention of cruel working-class sports such as bull-baiting, cock-fighting and the like. The middle- and upper-class membership of animal protection societies saw nothing wrong with their own blood sports. The Baroness Burdett Coutts, probably the most influential single voice in the RSPCA in the latter half of the nineteenth century, apparently not only permitted hunting parties on her estates but also the impaling of live bait. Although she spoke out against vivisection, she hosted a famous garden party during the International Medical Congress in London, in 1881, inviting many of Europe's most noted pro-vivisection advocates. Conversely, one might not belong to any animal protection society, like Richard Wagner, and still be active in the anti-vivisection movement.

The practice of vivisection hardly figured among the concerns of the early nineteenth-century animal welfare activists. Animal experimentation became a target for the RSPCA, and separate anti-vivisection societies were founded only after vivisection had become of great methodological and symbolic significance to experimental physiology, and when, during the middle decades of the nineteenth century, the new subject had become institutionalised with new professorial chairs, with laboratories and with handbooks for laboratory experiments. Experimental physiology was used as the horse which drew the cart of the biomedical sciences up close behind the exact sciences of chemistry and physics, and it was animal experimentation that gave physiology the strength to do so.

Thus, in order to understand the emergence of the vivisection controversy, it is crucial not just to examine the growth of the animal protection movement, but above all the meaning which vivisection acquired in the professionalisation and institutionalisation of physiology (as Elliott's essay does). The importance attached to experimentation as a defining feature of proper science meant that animal experimentation could be used as a legitimising factor for the professional and social ambitions of certain scientists. France and Germany led the way.[7] In Britain, physiology remained for a long time anatomical physiology — a physiology based on anatomical observations with anatomy the dominant partner, in such 'anatomy and physiology' courses as had been given by Richard Owen at the Royal College of Surgeons. It was not until the 1870s, as Gerald Geison shows,[8] that experimental physiology became productive in Britain and the *Handbook for the Physiological Laboratory* was published (examined in this volume by Richards) which directed the attention of the RSPCA to the extent of experimental physiology in Britain and abroad.

In other words, when vivisection was attacked, it was not an attack on an isolated laboratory practice, but on all that animal experimentation had come to represent: a new discipline with new career opportunities, a criterion of proper science, a method which raised the status of physiology in the hierarchy of the sciences.

Vivisection and medical reform

In the world of science and medicine, there was more to vivisection, however, than its quintessential significance to the discipline of experimental physiology. Animal experimentation also acquired an essential role in medicine, not just because of medicine's close neighbourly relations with experimental physiology, but equally as a result of the use of laboratory animals in such biomedical subjects as pathology, pharmacology, bacteriology, toxicology, etc.

'Medical Reform' or 'the Progress of Medicine' were major themes of nineteenth-century medical debate. One decisive strategy for improving medicine as a practice and for elevating the status of its practitioners was to turn healing from an 'art' into something more akin to science. 'Scientific medicine' became the shibboleth of the reform movement. Doctors, by adopting the priorities of science, sought to justify and realise their professional ambitions and social aspirations. Thus medical research became an indispensable part of the healing profession, and through the second half of the nineteenth century such research was institutionalised in the form of new university chairs and of new institutes ranging from Virchow's Institut für Pathologie (1856) to the Institut Pasteur (1888) and later also the Rockefeller Institute for Medical Research (1904). Germany was ahead in this respect of both France and England, and the United States too lagged far behind the German example.[9] In 1842 Carl Wunderlich and Wilhelm Roser had founded the *Archiv für physiologische Heilkunde* to make medicine scientific by linking it to physiology. When Rudolph Virchow lectured on 'Die Fortschritte der Kriegsheilkunde' (1874) he boasted that Germany had won the Franco-Prussian War of 1870, in part because of German medical science: 'wir hatten die Deutsche Wissenschaft.'[10]

By taking aboard the scientific spirit and its method, medicine not only acknowledged the sovereignty of observation, but even more that of experiment. The progress of experimental physiology had to be repeated in other auxiliary, biomedical sciences. The scientific aspirations of medicine were the leading theme of the International Medical Congress in London (1881). The President, James Paget, used his opening address to sum up the scientific scope of medicine and to stake out a claim for the biomedical sciences, directly adjacent to the natural sciences. T.H. Huxley, Richard Owen, Virchow and others added their voices to that of Paget in calling for medicine to be made more scientific.[11]

In this context, experimentation upon animals acquired a centre-stage role. As noted above, vivisection met the requirements for recognition as a true experimental science which mere anatomical observations on dead bodies had never been able to do. Claude Bernard's view was widely accepted, namely that scientific medicine can not exist without recourse to animal experimentation, just as physiology would have no foundation without it.[12]

This crucial position occupied by animal experimentation in the biomedical world goes some way to explain the social composition of both anti- and pro-vivisection groups. Vivisection represented the priorities and aspirations of science; and scientists defended the practice, even if they had no direct contact with it. Those who opposed vivisection were people who saw their cultural influence waning as that of science grew, i.e. the aristocracy, the clergy and the judiciary. In England, many of them had, as recently as the first half of the nineteenth century, practised or at least patronised science and scientific societies. The new generation of professional scientists sought neither ecclesiastical preferment nor aristocratic patronage, and thus they represented an encroachment on traditional estates of cultural authority. The new professionals kept their former patrons at bay and moreover threatened to undermine traditional values and beliefs. Zoology had reduced the origin of species to natural causes; now experimental physiology made things worse by driving vitalism into an exile of fringe beliefs, strengthening reductionist materialism.

Lessons from history

In today's altercations between those who condone vivisection and those who detest it, arguments from history are often used. Not infrequently the historical claims are incorrect. Because of this alone, looking at vivisection in historical perspective can be a useful corrective.

But history's lessons can be more profound than the correcting of isolated facts. This volume demonstrates that the controversy over animal experimentation goes much deeper than the surface arguments for or against. The controversy's roots reach deep down into broad, cultural divisions, each stance being inextricably intertwined with other issues. Each is an integral part of a view of society in which science has been assigned a different place. If a meaningful dialogue is to be established between the rival parties, these deeper-seated causes of the difference in attitude towards laboratory animals must be recognised. Today, no less than a century or so ago, vivisection is part of a mechanistic world view and of a scientocratic concept of society; anti-vivisection, on the other hand, ties in to a more Romantic view of nature which emphasises the relational side of existence, giving high priority to conservation, environmental protection and such causes as alternative medicine.

This volume furthermore shows that the self-presentation by the scientists as humanitarian seekers after beneficial truth must be counterbalanced by a picture of science as a profession with self-serving purposes. The claim by scientists that vivisection produces useful results is undoubtedly true; but to say that this has been the motivation for pursuing vivisectional research is at best a half-truth. To the physiologists and to many other biomedical scientists, vivisection meant the experimental legitimation of their career ambitions and social aspirations.

If science were indeed purely a quest for beneficial knowledge, one could respect its claim to freedom from legal interference. But the self-serving aspect of science, which this volume highlights, undercuts any such claim — just as commerce or industry cannot demand exemption from legal restrictions, however beneficial to society at large they may be. If scientists in the various countries where legal measures to regulate vivisectional practices are being discussed, were to recognise this, progress towards solving the vivisection dilemma would have been made.

But is the imposition of regulations from outside really necessary? Are scientists not sufficiently decent and trustworthy to define for themselves their responsibilities towards research animals? Is self-regulation by scientists not possible? The lesson from history is unequivocally clear on this point. Yes, there have been scientists who have drawn up codes of good laboratory behaviour. But no, self-regulation has not worked, in the sense that the profession as a whole has never been led to comply.

In Britain, before the Cruelty to Animals Act was passed in 1876, attempts to introduce voluntary codes failed: Marshall Hall's 'five principles' of 1831, re-enunciated in 1847, were never adopted by his colleagues; and the four rules drawn up by a BAAS committee in 1870 were not even mentioned in the *Handbook for the Physiological Laboratory*. In Florence, in 1874, the idea that the local Society for the Protection of Animals be given the task of supervising Moritz Schiff's laboratory was never put into practice. In the US, Walter Bradford Cannon, chairman of the Council for the Defense of Medical Research, established in 1907, formulated a code of ethics which, however, was never enforced. The more recent NIH *Guide for the Care and Use of Laboratory Animals*, in operation since 1963 for institutions receiving federal funding, has failed to prevent instances of horrific maltreatment of laboratory animals. As Hampson concludes, in Canada, a voluntary system of control in which Institutional Committees play a part, needs legislative back-up in order to be consistently effective. Today, as much as a century or so ago, scientific curiosity and professional ambition easily over-ride concern for animal welfare, if legal enforcement of the latter is not assured.

Speculation and topics for further research

New research not only adds to our stock of learning, it also helps to delineate the unexplored areas on the map of knowledge. This rule fully applies to the present volume. One major, unanswered question raised by the present collection of essays is: why has the anti-vivisection movement been so prominent in mainly northern countries, such as Great Britain, the German lands, Sweden or North America, in contrast to more southern countries, such as France, Italy or Spain? Even today, Spain has no law controlling laboratory experiments on animals. It is true that the first organised anti-vivisection agitation took place in Florence, but as Guarnieri points out in this volume, it was instigated by the English and found very limited sympathy with the Italians. The same was true for France. Is the reason for this difference that vivisectional research was carried out on a larger scale in countries with flourishing anti-vivisection societies? The case of France would seem to belie this.

Or can this north–south contrast be attributed to differences in dominant religious influences? Is there some truth to the old prejudice of the English animal welfare movement that cruelty to animals is something peculiarly Latin and Catholic? It is a fact that Evangelical Protestantism did much to stimulate the animal protection movement, and conversely that Vatican approval of vivisection has been apparent through, for example, the *Catholic Encyclopedia*. But nineteenth-century secularisation diminished direct ecclesiastical influences, in France, Germany or elsewhere. Moreover, some of the German lands were Catholic (*cuius regio, eius religio*). And in Britain Cardinal Manning was an active anti-vivisectionist. If religion has been a major determinant of attitude towards animals, it must have acted to a large extent indirectly by percolating through a society's institutions and its shared cultural values. To establish such a thesis would require extensive further study.

Carrying the question one step further: why was the anti-vivisection movement more successful in Britain than in other predominantly Protestant countries? An answer may be found in the social composition of the rival parties; anti-vivisection societies enjoyed considerable support from the aristocracy, the clergy and also from royalty; pro-vivisection was fronted by prominent university professors. On the Continent, a series of socio-political upheavals ranging from the French Revolutionary Wars to the Revolutions of 1848, had significantly curtailed the power of the Church, the nobility and of royalty. Part of their authority was transferred to the new university professoriate.

None of these upheavals occurred on British soil, where a more traditional balance of cultural authority persisted. The professoriate in particular never acquired the importance it had in some other European countries. These national differences in the relative influence of the traditional estates of cultural authority on the one hand, and the new estate of professional science on the other, may help to explain why anti-vivisection sentiment in Britain could find such early and strong support. But a much more detailed, prosopographical study of anti- and pro-vivisection groups is needed, examining in detail the socio-political allegiances of the individuals.

More specifically, further study is needed of the connection, which existed especially in Continental Europe, between the physiologists and left-wing politics. Sympathy with anarchism, communism, anti-landowner politics, etc. was not uncommon among the parvenu university scientists. To Virchow, for example, socio-political reform and medical reform were inseparable and tied to scientific progress.

In this connection it is important to emphasise that in the course of the past 100 years or so, the socio-political colours of the pro- and anti-vivisection parties have changed radically. Although the basic arguments for or against vivisection have remained the same, the social composition of the opposing groups has become very different. As Tröhler and Maehle show, by the end of the nineteenth century, attempts had already been made by anti-vivisection societies to solicit support from a broader and much larger social layer. Anti-vivisection has since lost much of its upper-class connotation. Conversely, the pro-vivisection scientists have lost their anti-establishmentarian and reformist image. Whereas the Association for the Advancement of Medicine by Research in 1882 was fronted exclusively by prominent professional scientists, the related Research Defence Society, established in 1907, has invited as vice-presidents large numbers of those who had previously fronted the anti-vivisection movement, namely prominent members of the aristocracy, the clergy and men of letters. These and other changes are touched upon in several of this volume's essays, but a more complete documentation of the changes and their causes awaits further research.

Notes

1. P. Singer, *Animal Liberation* (Random House, New York, 1975). See also Singer (ed.), *In Defence of Animals* (Basil Blackwell, Oxford, 1985); T. Regan and P. Singer (eds.), *Animal Rights and Human Obligations* (Prentice Hall, Englewood Cliffs, New Jersey, 1976); S.R.L. Clark, *The Moral Status of Animals* (Oxford University Press, 1977); D. Paterson and R.D. Ryder (eds.), *Animals' Rights — a Symposium* (Centauer Press, Fontwell, Sussex, 1979); B.E. Rollin, *Animal Rights and Human Morality* (Prometheus, Buffalo, New York, 1981); T. Regan, *All that Dwell Therein* (University of California Press, Berkeley, 1982); Regan, *The Case for Animal Rights* (Routledge & Kegan Paul, London, 1984). See also A.N. Rowan and B.E. Rollin, 'Animal Research — For and Against: a Philosophical, Social, and Historical Perspective', *Perspectives in Biology and Medicine*, vol. 27 (1983), pp. 1-17.

2. R.D. Ryder, *Victims of Science. The Use of Animals in Research* (Davis-Poynter, London, 1975).

3. W.D.M. Paton, *Man and Mouse. Animals in Medical Research* (Oxford University Press, Oxford, 1984). See also Paton, 'Animal Experiment and Medical Research: a Study in Evolution', *Conquest* (February 1979), pp. 1-17; Paton, 'Animal Experiment: Benefit, Responsibility, and Legislation', in V. Bogdanor (ed.), *Science and Politics* (Clarendon Press, Oxford, 1984), pp. 90-115.

4. E. Westacott, *A Century of Vivisection and Anti-Vivisection. A Study of their Effect upon Science, Medicine and Human Life During the Past Hundred Years* (C.W. Daniel, Ashingdon, Rochford, Essex, 1949); H. Bretschneider, *Der Streit um die Vivisektion im 19. Jahrhundert* (Gustav Fischer Verlag, Stuttgart, 1962). Another early study was by L. Bromander, 'Vivisektionsdebatten i Sverige under 1880-talet', *Lychnos* (1969-70), pp. 249-91; a shortened translation of this paper appears in this volume.

5. R.D. French, *Antivivisection and Medical Science in Victorian Society* (Princeton University Press, 1975). See also M. Ozer, 'The British Vivisection Controversy', *Bulletin of the History of Medicine*, vol. 40 (1966), pp. 158-67.

6. J. Turner, *Reckoning with the Beast. Animals, Pain, and Humanity in the Victorian Mind* (The Johns Hopkins University Press, Baltimore, 1980); B. Harrison, *Peaceable Kingdom. Stability and Change in Modern Britain* (Clarendon Press, Oxford, 1982), pp. 82-122.

7. See for example W.R. Albury, 'Experiment and Explanation in the Physiology of Bichat and Magendie', *Studies in the History of Biology*, vol. 1 (1977), pp. 47-133; M. Gross, 'The Lessened Locus of Feelings: a Transformation in French Physiology in the Early Nineteenth Century', *Journal of the History of Biology*, vol. 12 (1979), pp. 231-71; J.E. Lesch, *Science and Medicine in France: the Emergence of Experimental Physiology, 1790-1855* (Harvard University Press, Cambridge, Mass., 1984).

8. G.L. Geison, 'Social and Institutional Factors in the Stagnancy of English Physiology, 1840-1870', *Bulletin of the History of Medicine*, vol. 46 (1972), pp. 30-58. See also Geison, *Michael Foster and the Cambridge School of Physiology. The Scientific Enterprise in late Victorian Society* (Princeton University Press, Princeton, 1978); R.D. French, 'Some Problems and Sources in the Foundation of Modern Physiology in Great Britain', *History of Science*, vol. 10

(1971), pp. 28-55; P.M.H. Mazumdar, 'Anatomical Physiology and the Reform of Medical Education; London, 1825-1835', *Bulletin of the History of Medicine*, vol. 57 (1983), pp. 230-46; S. Turner, E. Kerwin and D. Woolwine, 'Careers and Creativity in Nineteenth-Century Physiology: Zloczower Redux', *Isis*, vol. 75 (1984), pp. 523-9.

9. See for example D. von Engelhardt, 'Die Konzeption der Forschung in der Medizin des 19. Jahrhunderts', in A. Diemer (ed.), *Konzeption und Begriff der Forschung in den Wissenschaften des 19. Jahrhunderts* (Hain, Meisenheim am Glan, 1978), pp. 58-103.

10. His address was translated into English: R. Virchow, *Infection-Diseases in the Army. Chiefly Wound Fever, Typhoid, Dysentery and Diphtheria* (H.K. Lewis, London, 1879), p. 13. Virchow had also been principal editor of a weekly, *Die medicinische Reform*, which was published from 10 July 1848 till 29 June 1849; see further E.H. Ackerknecht, 'Beiträge zur Geschichte der Medicinalreform von 1848', *Sudhoffs Archiv für Geschichte der Medizin*, vol. 25 (1932), pp. 61-109, 113-83.

11. See W. Mac Cormac and G.A. Makins (eds.), *Transactions of the International Medical Congress, Seventh Session, London, 1881* (4 vols, J.W. Kolckmann, London, 1881); see also (Ch. Creighton), 'The Progress of Medicine', *Quarterly Review*, vol. 156 (1883), pp. 57-89.

12. See for example the English translation of Bernard's *An Introduction to the Study of Experimental Medicine* (Macmillan, London, 1927); see also J. Schiller, 'Claude Bernard and Vivisection', *Journal of the History of Medicine*, vol. 22 (1967), pp. 246-60.

2

Animal Experimentation from Antiquity to the End of the Eighteenth Century: Attitudes and Arguments

Andreas-Holger Maehle and Ulrich Tröhler

'Vivisection' — a preliminary note on terminology

The term 'vivisection' is a compound, which is derived from the Latin words 'vivus' (living) and 'sectio' (cutting), thus literally meaning 'cutting living bodies'.[1] Its early Latin forerunners were 'incidere vivorum corpora'[2] (cutting the bodies of the living) in Roman Antiquity and 'vivi animantis sectio'[3] (cutting of a living being), 'vivorum sectio'[4] (cutting of the living) or 'viva sectio'[5] (cutting alive) in the Renaissance. Whereas in this period the terms had been used interchangeably for both human and animal vivisection, in the seventeenth century the corresponding general terms for the section or dissection of living beings, 'vivorum anatomia',[6] 'animantium dissectio',[7] 'vivorum dissectio',[8] and 'vivorum sectio',[9] were sometimes differentiated, e.g. by 'vivorum hominum sectio'[10] (cutting of living human beings) and 'vivorum brutorum sectio'[11] (cutting of living animals). The compound 'vivisectio' and its introduction into English[12] and German[13] as 'vivisection' can be traced back to the first half of the eighteenth century.

In this chapter, covering the period from Antiquity to the late eighteenth century, the term 'vivisection' will be consistently used in its original sense, i.e. (partial) dissection of, or surgical intervention on, living animals for the purpose of research. This is distinct from the meaning which the term has widely acquired since the second half of the nineteenth century (partly as a result of its indistinct use by medical laymen opposing animal experiment), i.e. all kinds of animal experimentation including the application of chemical agents, physical stimuli and the inoculation of microorganisms, not necessarily implying surgical procedures.[14]

Because the issue of animal experimentation was (and still is) closely linked with that of pain, it must be remembered that effective anaesthesia became available on a large scale for both animals and human beings only around 1850.[15]

Vivisection by the Ancients

From the very beginning of Western scientific medicine, physicians interested in the anatomical structures as well as in the functions of the human body did not confine themselves to the dissection of corpses, but also occasionally made use of the method of vivisection. Thus about 450 years B.C. Alcmaeon of Croton was able to find the function of the optic nerve by cutting through this structure in the living animal and recording the ensuing blindness.[16] In a similar way the author of the Hippocratic text *On the Heart* (about 300 B.C.) cut the throat of a pig which was drinking coloured water, in order to study the act of swallowing. He also opened the chest of another living animal and described how the auricles and ventricles of the heart were beating alternately.[17] It was in ancient Alexandria that anatomical and physiological research first reached a climax. After Herophilos (about 330–250 B.C.) had shown the functional difference between tendon and nerve, Erasistratos (about 305–240 B.C.) succeeded in making the distinction between sensory and motor nerves by means of vivisection.[18]

It seems to have been obvious to these ancient physicians that knowledge of the bodily functions could best be obtained by studying the interior of *living* organisms. As the Roman writer Celsus (fl. 1st cent. A.D.) reported in his encyclopedia *De Medicina*, some physicians pointed to the example of Herophilos and Erasistratos and furthermore justified vivisection by wanting to see the organs in their natural condition, i.e. free from any post-mortem changes.[19]

In his treatise *De anatomicis administrationibus*, Galen of Pergamon (*c.* 130–210), physician to the Roman emperor Marcus Aurelius, described techniques of dissecting living animals and improved these techniques to an hitherto unknown degree.[20] Using vivisection, he tried to unveil the ever intriguing secrets of respiration and heart action, of the functions of the brain and spinal cord. In this text Galen also expressed his feelings during the performance of such experiments. For the exposure of the brain or the experimental cutting of the recurrent laryngeal nerves he recommended the use of pigs or goats rather than apes, because 'you avoid seeing the unpleasing expression of the ape when it is being vivisected'.[21] As Galen further stated, the 'loathsomeness of the expression in vivisection' was not the same in all animals.[22] Nevertheless, the dissection, once started, should proceed just as with a dead animal, penetrating into the deep tissues without pity or compassion. The physician should not allow himself to be discouraged from repeating the procedure by the frequent outflow of blood.[23]

Galen's attitude was in keeping with the prevailing Stoic philosophy. He held that man was the only being endowed with reason.[24] According to Stoical doctrine, the animal's lack of a rational soul meant that it had no personality or rights. It was therefore a matter of course that Classical Roman law treated animals as mere objects.[25] To Galen, vivisection could be disturbing, but only *aesthetically* so. That is why he refused to dissect the sexual organs of living animals or to dissect even dead animals in an upright, man-like position. In addition, when carrying out public vivisections, he seems to have avoided particularly distasteful operations, although his spectators were surely well accustomed to the even more rousing and cruel fights between gladiators and beasts in the arenas.[26]

Galen's reluctance to vivisect apes or other animals in man-like positions had possibly yet another reason, connected with his reputation as a physician. Celsus had charged Herophilos and Erasistratos with having dissected living criminals, whom they were supposed to have accepted from the prisons of the Ptolemaic Kings. He had condemned this kind of vivisection as cruel and even unnecessary, because the dissection of human corpses and the practice of surgery would suffice to obtain both anatomical and physiological knowledge.[27] Although Galen did not refer to this passage in Celsus, he probably took all possible precautions against any potential accusation of human vivisection. As a matter of fact, Celsus's charge against the two Alexandrian physicians was renewed by the early Fathers of the Christian Church, first by Galen's contemporary Tertullian (about 155–222), who linked the practice with pagan barbarism, and later by Augustine (354–430).[28] From the Renaissance onwards, the horror of human vivisection developed into an important topic in discussions on anatomy and animal experimentation.

Vivisection and the Church: attitudes of Renaissance anatomists

During the Middle Ages experimentation seems to have fallen

almost entirely into disuse. Christianity, more concerned with eternal than worldly life, was hardly motivated to explore human beings or animals in this way. Only toxicological tests on both men and animals, which had been carried out widely since the experiments by King Mithridates (*c.* 132–63 B.C.), were still advocated. Although Galen was generally held in high esteem by the medieval physicians, his experimental method apparently sunk into oblivion.[29] It was for the Renaissance anatomists to rediscover Galenic vivisection.

When Andreas Vesalius (1514–64) performed his anatomical demonstrations at Padua and Bologna, he included the dissection of living animals.[30] Vivisection marked the end and highlight of his public anatomy courses, thus putting 'the finishing touch in the schools to the whole course of anatomical study', as he stated in his *De humani corporis fabrica* (1543).[31] After the students had become acquainted with the structures of the dead body, Vesalius showed them the various functions of its parts, chiefly repeating Galenic experiments. He explained the necessity of vivisection by pointing out its usefulness for acquiring physiological knowledge and surgical practice.[32] In contrast to Galen, Vesalius did not reveal his emotional attitude towards animal experimentation. Lack of free opportunity seems to have prevented him from vivisecting the animal's brain, for he made it clear that the results of such an experiment would probably be inconsistent with ecclesiastical doctrine, and that by doing it he might expose himself to the risk of being accused of heresy. Was it not 'merely out of consideration for our native theologians, [that] we must deprive brute creatures of reason and thought, although their structure is the same as that of men'?[33]

Indeed, the Roman Catholic Church had almost entirely adopted the Stoical notion that animal and man are not related by a common nature. Moreover, because the absence of reason meant also a lack of rights, Church dogma stated that man has no obligations towards animals. Thomas Aquinas (*c.* 1225–74) as well as Augustine underpinned this dogma of a gap between man and animals with the authority of the Bible, teaching that God had given man complete dominion over the animal world. Aquinas commented that passages in the Holy Scriptures forbidding human cruelty towards animals were exclusively intended to remove man's thoughts from being cruel to other men. He obviously feared that cruelty to animals might lead to cruelty to human beings. There was nothing morally objectionable in the animal's suffering as such.[34] In this *anthropocentric* view, the dissection of living animals was entirely acceptable to the Church, unless, as suggested by Vesalius's remark, the experimental results might undermine its doctrines.

Realdo Colombo (1516–59), Vesalius's pupil and successor at the Padua chair of anatomy, reported that high-ranking clergymen took great delight in attending his public vivisections, which he carried out, as his teacher had done before, at the end of an anatomical course.[35] Especially his vivisection of a pregnant bitch commanded the clergy's admiration: Colombo pulled a foetus out of the dog's womb and, hurting the young in front of the bitch's eyes, he provoked the latter's furious barking. But as soon as he held the puppy to the bitch's mouth, the dog started licking it tenderly, being obviously more concerned about the pain of its offspring than about its own suffering. When something other than the puppy was held in front of its mouth, the bitch snapped at it in a rage. The clergymen expressed their pleasure in observing this striking example of motherly love even in the 'brute creation'.[36] The universality of maternal love, embodied in the Christian religion by Mary and Jesus, seems to have impressed them so much that it did not occur to them that this experiment actually appeared to *diminish* the dogmatic gap between man and animal.

Like his teacher Vesalius, Colombo justified vivisection with the argument that it was indispensable for acquiring physiological knowledge. He was anxious, however, to obviate any charge of human vivisection, and stated that the dissection of living human beings, which he believed the ancients had in fact performed, was a crime and a sin in a Christian physician. But he considered *animal* vivisection both permissible and useful.[37] Other sixteenth-century anatomists, such as Colombo's fellow-countrymen Jacob Berengar of Carpi (1470–1530) and Giambattista Canano of Ferrara (1515–79) or the German Volcher Coiter (1534–76), held the same view about human vivisection, but also dissected living animals.[38]

A first type of argumentation in favour of animal experiment began to crystallise. The physician is in urgent need of knowledge about the bodily functions. But the obvious way to obtain this knowledge, human vivisection, would mean a terrible crime and a deadly sin. For this reason the physician has to experiment on living animals.

This argument was put forward in part to avoid being accused of human vivisection, because the old accusation was made anew, now against Vesalius, Berengar of Carpi and Gabriel Fallopius (1523–62), this time by other medical men.[39] But going beyond a mere repetition of Galenic experimentation, Colombo devised new animal experiments, some of which led to his important discovery of the pulmonary blood circulation.[40] Indeed, in the Renaissance, much more than in Antiquity, animal vivisection was used as an heuristic device by men devoted to original research.[41]

In describing his vivisections, Colombo sometimes spoke of 'the poor dog' or 'the unhappy dog', adding in one breath 'or rather the happy dog, because he affords to us a sight suitable for acquiring knowledge of the most beautiful things'.[42] Thus Colombo's tinge of compassion quickly made way for his scientific enthusiasm, which increased even more when he succeeded in correcting or refuting Aristotle or Galen.[43] This type of attitude became yet more prevalent in the next century. In the Christian, anthropocentric world, new scientific findings were clearly more important than the pain and death of animals.

Animal experimentation in the seventeenth century: scientific and moral justification and criticism

At the beginning of the seventeenth century, the British Lord Chancellor and philosopher Francis Bacon (1561–1626) made programmatic suggestions for the improvement of science, which in the case of medicine included vivisection 'in regard of the great use of this observation'.[44] He sided with Celsus in rejecting human vivisection, but thought that this kind of research 'might have been well diverted upon the dissection of beasts alive, which not withstanding the dissimilitude of their parts, may sufficiently satisfy this inquiry'.[45] The predicted utility of animal vivisection soon became reality. In 1627 a remarkable discovery by the Pavia anatomist Gaspare Aselli (1581–1626) was published. By dissecting a living dog, he had discovered the so-called 'lacteals', i.e. the lymphatic vessels in the mesentery.[46] Other vivisecting scientists enlarged our knowledge of what we call today the lymphatic system. In 1647 the French medical student Jean Pecquet (1622–74) of Montpellier discovered the thoracic duct in a dog.[47] The ensuing work on lymphatic vessels, both in living animals and human corpses, by Thomas Bartholinus (1616–80) of Copenhagen and by Olof Rudbeck (1630–1702) of Uppsala, led to a new theory of lymphatic rather than traditional venous resorption of the food, thereby shaking one of the foundations of Galenic physiology.[48] The discovery of the blood circulation by William Harvey (1578–1657), published in 1628, meant a true challenge not only to physiology, but to all fields of medicine.[49] It too was to a large extent based on animal experimentation and in turn caused widespread vivisectional activity, which now was both justified and criticised from scientific as well as moral points of view.

Experimentalists giving reasons for their research

All scientists agreed that human vivisection was a completely unacceptable 'violation of the laws, not only of divinity but humanity'.[50] On the other hand they saw no religious, moral or legal obstacles to the dissection of living animals. This attitude was typical of anatomists and experimentalists throughout Europe in the seventeenth century, e.g. Francis Glisson (1597–1677) and Robert Boyle (1627–91) in England, Ijsbrand van Diemerbroeck (1609–74) and Philippe Verheyen (1648–1710) in the Netherlands, Werner Rolfinck (1599–1673) in Germany, Johann Jakob Wepfer (1620–95) in Switzerland and Gaspare Aselli in Italy.[51] In spite of their unanimous condemnation of the legendary human vivisection in ancient Alexandria, some seventeenth-century scientists did not entirely disapprove of particular experiments on human beings in the more recent past. The Jena anatomist Rolfinck valued the fact that in 1474 Louis XI of France had permitted his physicians to open the abdomen of a living soldier who had been sentenced to death, in order to extract the latter's vesical calculus and to learn at the same time how to perform this operation.[52] Similarly, the Swiss Johann Jakob Wepfer, who carried out toxicological experiments on animals, noted that he had never heard any complaints about the Imperial physicians' studies of the effects of poisons on criminals.[53] After all, if a criminal survived the experiment, he would have been set free.

In the second half of the century, the *success* of the method emerged as a new line of argumentation in favour of animal experiment. Now experimentalists were proud to be able to present the results of this method. Rolfinck argued in 1656 that the lymphatic vessels and the thoracic duct would never have been discovered if Aselli, Pecquet, Bartholinus and Rudbeck had not dissected living animals.[54] Bartholinus himself and Robert Boyle also held this view using the same examples.[55] Boyle, as well as Rolfinck, consistently mentioned the importance of vivisection for the instruction of medical students and young physicians. It was the only way to demonstrate the movements of the heart, lungs and diaphragm, to show Harvey's discovery of the blood circulation or the passing of the chylus through the lymphatic vessels.[56]

Thus in the seventeenth century the term 'usefulness' of animal experiment meant first of all the acquisition of knowledge about our bodily functions. Only a few experimentalists saw immediate *therapeutic* consequences. One of them was the Oxford physiologist Richard Lower (1631–91), who from 1665 carried out blood transfusions from animal to animal, being convinced 'that this discovery . . . will be employed with great profit for the human race, if it is practised with due consideration and care'.[57] About two years later he actually performed a first transfusion from a sheep to a mentally retarded man.[58] Similarly Wepfer, physician in ordinary to several dynasties in southern Germany, wrote in 1679 about his toxicological experiments: 'My sin will be less, if I explore the effects of poisons in animals in order to be of benefit to man.'[59] He declared emphatically that his experiments had been most beneficial for his medical practice.[60]

Wepfer's pupil in toxicology, Johann Jakob Harder (1656–1711), professor of anatomy and botany at Basel, put forward yet another argument in favour of animal experimentation, which in a way characterised seventeenth-century science. He argued that experimental results yielded more *certainty* than the obscure and clashing statements of the Classical authors of Antiquity.[61] Thus experimenting on animals implied casting doubt on the teachings of the ancients. To conservative physicians, on the other hand, this was a reason to criticise animal experimentation.

Medical men criticising the validity of animal experiment

By no means all physicians instantly agreed with the new theories of blood circulation or lymphatic resorption. To cautious, conservative minds the experimental evidence was by no means strong enough to invalidate the rationally coherent teachings which had proved good for hundreds of years. One of these conservatives was Jean Riolan Jr (1580–1657), professor of anatomy and botany at Paris and physician to the kings Henri IV and Louis XIII. Arguing against Harvey's doctrine of blood circulation and Bartholinus' theory of lymphatic resorption, he stressed the significance of the anatomical differences between man and animal. Furthermore, he believed that in the vivisected, dying animal there are completely unnatural conditions, possibly causing the body to behave entirely differently from the healthy human being. In Riolan's opinion animal experimentation was not able to furnish sound evidence.[62]

Exactly the same objections were raised in 1665 by an Irish physician practising medicine in Bristol, Edmund O'Meara (about 1614–81), who opposed both Harvey's and Pecquet's discoveries. He held that 'the miserable torture of vivisection places the body in an unnatural state' and that 'amid the terrible pains of vivisection all the juices are brought to flow together', thus denying the validity of animal experimentation.[63] In the same year Richard Lower replied to this attack, providing both numerous arguments in favour of Harvey's and Pecquet's doctrines as well as polemical comments against his adversary.[64] In 1667 Conlan Cashin, probably an assistant of O'Meara, replied to Lower, stating that 'inferences made from brutes to men are to be considered valid only in those things in which beasts do not differ from men'. But he was convinced that they differed in many respects, 'not least in this, that the souls of brutes are divisible, and of some, at least the more imperfect, co-extensive with their bodies'. By contrast, he thought the souls of men to be 'indivisible and whole in the whole and whole in any part'.[65] Obviously the traditional dogmatic gap between man and animal once again entered the discussion about animal experiment, now raising something which might be called the *transferability problem* in experimental medicine.

Francis Bacon had already been well aware of this difficulty of the 'dissimilitude' of the animal parts when compared with the human ones.[66] For the same reason, Aselli had been anxious to establish that his 'lacteals' could be found not only in living animals but in men too. He argued that Mother Nature would never have denied something to man that she had generously given to animals.[67] Like Aselli before, Johann Jakob Wepfer had to face this transferability question. He stressed that human beings and animals have basically the same anatomical structure, and he argued against his obstinate adversaries: 'If these fine little gentlemen shrank not from staining their hands with blood and mud in an innocent way [i.e. from performing dissections] . . . they would surely find no great difference [between man and animal].'[68]

Dawn of the moral issue: cruelty and compassion

The hitherto mentioned justifications and objections concerning animal experimentation were part of a debate dealing mainly with questions of scientific validity. But through the second half of the seventeenth century the moral issue of cruelty to animals was also gradually introduced. In 1656 Rolfinck still complained that vivisecting anatomists were often victims of unjustified insinuations and insults because of the long-standing confusion between animal and human vivisection.[69] In 1679, however, Wepfer was openly criticised for *cruelty to animals*, after he had poisoned and vivisected animals for the purpose of toxicological research. The Swiss physician was not at a loss for an answer: 'The argument of cruelty is put forward by some men', he said, 'who themselves do not hesitate to fill their stomach with beef, veal, lamb, and fish almost every day.'[70] He thus established, in addition to the argument of human benefit, a new type of argument for experimentation. If people accept the slaughtering of animals for their own needs, they must also grant scientists the essential method of vivisection. We shall refer to this as to the *tu-quoque argument*.[71]

But the cruelty of vivisection also became an issue among some of the seventeenth-century experimentalists themselves. Wepfer and his son-in-law and assistant Johann Conrad Brunner (1653–1727), later professor of medicine at Heidelberg, called the dogs they vivisected 'the martyrs of the anatomists'.[72] The same expression was used by the Leipzig physician Michael Ettmüller (1644–83) in his description of toxicological tests on dogs, for which the new technique of intravenous injection was employed.[73] The term 'martyr of the anatomists', however, did not just imply an attitude of compassion but also a conviction that these animals were *justified* victims of science, so to speak.

Several British authors expressed a kind of 'humanitarian' feeling towards animals.[74] In a letter to Robert Boyle, Richard Lower referred to a blood transfusion from one dog to another as a 'tragedy' because of the donor dog's death.[75] Another English natural philosopher, Robert Hooke (1635–1703), confessed to Boyle that he was unwilling to repeat a particular animal experiment, 'because it was cruel'. He had cut away the thorax and diaphragm of a living dog in order to study the movements of the heart and the lungs. During his observations, which lasted for more than an hour, he had kept the animal's respiration going by pumping a pair of bellows attached to a piece of cane which had been inserted into the windpipe of the dog. 'I shall hardly be induced to make any further trials of this kind, because of the torture of the creature', Hooke later commented. He was convinced that this experiment might be 'very noble', if there could be found a way to stupefy the animal sufficiently. But he doubted that there was 'any opiate' strong enough to render the dog insensible under these conditions.[76] Robert Boyle himself showed some compassion for his animals, when he studied their behaviour in an evacuated glass bowl. One kitten, having survived this 'air-pump experiment' was dismissed from the trial in order 'to allow him the benefit of his good fortune', and another, which also had recovered, was released too, because Boyle thought that it was 'severe to make him undergo the same measure again'.[77]

Clearly, several seventeenth-century scientists felt a certain remorse because of the suffering involved in animal experimentation. The majority of experimentalists, however, never even mentioned the torture and pain of their animals. On the contrary, a new philosophy, the 'beast-machine' theory of René Descartes, encouraged them to perform vivisection in a yet more resolute manner.

Cartesianism and vivisection: studying the beast-machine

The concept of animal machines

In his very influential *Discours de la Méthode* (1637), the French philosopher René Descartes (1596–1650) had stated that the bodies of both animals and human beings could be adequately compared with machines or automata obeying the laws of mechanics. Yet he recognised two important features separating man from the animal world: man's faculty of true speech and his rational, immaterial, imperishable soul. In contrast to the human body, the animal body was supposed to operate without the guidance of a non-corporeal principle. An artificial machine in the shape of an animal would therefore be indistinguishable from the animal itself. In Descartes' view animals differed from man-made machines only in their degree of complexity. Having been created by God, animals were of course infinitely more complex and perfect than — but not fundamentally different from — automata.[78] Descartes argued that the perfection of certain animal actions was not caused by reason, but simply resulted from the appropriate organisation of the animal's parts, just as 'a clock composed only of wheels and weights, can number the hours and measure time more exactly than we with all our skill'.[79]

This concept of a 'beast-machine' was probably both the philosophical extension to the field of physiology of the mathematics and physics of Galilei and Kepler,[80] and the literary response to a view of animals that had been delineated by the sceptic philosopher Michel Eyquem de Montaigne (1533–92) and his disciple Pierre Charron (1541–1603).[81] Unlike Descartes, the latter two had interpreted the perfection of particular animal actions, such as the construction of the spider's web or the organisation of the 'bee-government', as a result of animal intelligence, which in their opinion might even exceed that of man. Consequently, these so-called 'Theriophiles' had actually attributed a rational though perishable soul to animals. While Montaigne's writings on the subject belonged to a genre of paradoxical literature and had a mainly satirical intention, Charron's 'theriophily' was expounded seriously and was taken in just that spirit by its most important opponent, René Descartes.[82]

Although his teaching of animal machines was chiefly speculative, Descartes had made some anatomical and physiological observations of his own. As a young philosopher and mathematician he had often watched the slaughtering of animals, he had even anatomised animals himself and attended public vivisections demonstrating Harveian blood circulation.[83] He agreed with Harvey's theory and, what is more, gave an account of it in his *Discours* before he went on to outline the general nature of man and animal.[84] Just like other scientists of his time, Descartes may, as a result of his anatomical and physiological studies, have become aware that there are no fundamental differences between the structure of human and animal bodies. This fact, however, tended to diminish the ecclesiastical, dogmatic gap between man and the 'brute creation'. Having also studied Thomas Aquinas's *Summa Theologica* under the direction of his Jesuit professors at La Flèche,[85] Descartes may have been conscious of this discrepancy between natural science and theology. His denial that a 'beast-machine' has a rational, immaterial and imperishable soul obviously had a *twofold advantage*. It protected the scientists' mechanistic view of both animals and human beings against the charge of heresy and at the same time reserved immortality exclusively for man, which was to the liking of the Roman Catholic Church.[86] Moreover, even before Descartes, Saint Thomas himself had employed the simile of the watch in his explanation of animal sagacity.[87]

Moral consequences for the treatment of animals

Descartes' 'beast-machine' theory had a crucial implication for the question of animal suffering. His elderly friend, the Minorite Father Marin Mersenne (1588–1648), was probably one of the first to see it, asking him how animals could suffer pain if they had no soul. Descartes answered in a letter of 1640 that in fact animals were unable to feel real pain. They merely went through the external motions which in man were symptomatic of pain, without experiencing its mental sensation. Although Descartes was willing to grant the existence of some inferior kind of feeling in animals, he was convinced that their capacity for sensation was strictly corporeal and mechanical.[88]

Towards the end of his life, Descartes intimated that he had recognised the moral consequences of his theory. In 1649 he wrote: 'Thus my opinion is not so cruel to animals as it is favorable to men . . . , whom it absolves from suspicion of crime when they eat animals.'[89] Descartes may not have conceived, however, that only a few years later his teachings would be abused by some of his disciples for the purpose of reckless vivisection and even intentional callousness towards animals.

Although Cartesianism was bitterly opposed by the Jesuit Order, which in 1663 even succeeded in having the works of Descartes put on the *Index Librorum Prohibitorum*,[90] the attractive theory of animal automatism could not be prevented from entering certain medical and even ecclesiastical circles. Thus among the eminent advocates of the 'beast-machine' we find the medical professors Henricus Regius (1598–1679) of Utrecht and François Bayle (1622–1709) of Toulouse, as well as Father Nicolas Malebranche (1638–1715) of the Paris Oratory and the Jansenist theologian Antoine Arnauld (1612–94).[91] These two clergymen did not hesitate to emphasise their point of view by being ostentatiously cruel to animals. Unlike Descartes himself, they were convinced that animals were devoid of any kind of feeling and absolutely incapable of suffering pain. When the French writer Bernard le Bovier de Fontenelle (1657–1757) visited the Paris Oratory, Malebranche is said to have kicked a pregnant bitch that had rolled at his feet and to have responded coldly to Fontenelle's cry of compassion with the laconic words: 'So what? Don't you know that it has no feeling at all?'[92]

Nicolas Fontaine (1625–1709), a confidant and secretary of several prominent Jansenist Fathers, reported the equally callous behaviour of Arnauld at the monastery Port-Royal. The Jansenist Arnauld had become one of Descartes' most zealous followers and had indoctrinated the Port-Royal solitaries with the concept of animal automata. According to Fontaine, the solitaries beat their dogs 'with the utmost indifference' and laughed at people who still maintained that animals could feel pain. The cries of the dogs were interpreted as the mere creaking of the animal 'clockwork'. This 'Cartesian' callousness also influenced the solitaries' scientific ambitions. As Fontaine compassionately wrote in his eye-witness account, they 'nailed the poor animals to boards by the four paws to dissect them while still alive, in order to watch the circulation of the blood, which was a great subject of discussion'.[93] It was obviously the enthusiasm for both Harvey's discovery of the blood circulation and Descartes' concept of animal machines which had brought about this extreme callousness in vivisection.

Yet there were also experimentalists who, though accepting the Cartesian mechanistic view as a valuable heuristic concept in physiological research, still did not stifle a feeling of compassion for suffering animals. Robert Boyle's inclination to exempt surviving animals from further experimentation has been mentioned above;[94] but he held at the same time that almost all corporeal actions were performed mechanically and that some of these, such as the motions of the limbs and the blood, 'might be by artificial engines . . . not ill represented to our very senses'.[95] Similarly, the Danish anatomist Niels Stensen (1638–86), later Bishop of Titiopolis, was greatly impressed by the accurate method of Cartesian philosophy. Yet, as he wrote in 1661 to his former teacher Thomas Bartholinus, he could not feel convinced that animals had no soul and that there was no difference between touching, cutting or burning the nerves of a living animal and doing the same to the strings of a moving automaton. Stensen's own experience with animal experiments plainly contradicted this Cartesian view. He furthermore admitted that it was only his belief in the methodological necessity of animal experimentation which helped him to overcome his reluctance to perform vivisections.[96] Less responsible and reflective minds, however, had evidently found the Cartesian 'beast-machine' concept a convenient justification for vivisection.

It makes sense that it was a Jesuit, opposed to both Descartes and Arnauld, who as part of his attack on the Cartesians also denounced the popularisation of vivisection. Father Gabriel Daniel (1649–1728), an outstanding member of the Jesuit Order at Paris and historiographer of France by appointment of Louis XIV, ridiculed Cartesianism in his satirical treatise *Voiage du Monde de Descartes*

(1690), which went through several editions, including Latin, English and Spanish translations.[97] Having derided the concept of the body machine[98] he described an imaginary, zealous Cartesian confessing his enthusiasm for vivisection:

> Before my Conversion to Cartesianism, I was so pitiful and tender-hearted, that I could not so much as see a Chicken kill'd: But since I was once persuaded that Beasts were destitute both of Knowledge and Sense, scarce a Dog in all the Town, wherein I was, could escape me, for the making Anatomical Dissections, wherein I myself was Operator, without the least inkling of Compassion or Remorse.[99]

The Cartesian reported that he had invited a group of scholars to his home and delivered an address to them which was 'an Invective against the Ignorance and Injustice of that Senator, the Areopagite, that caus'd a Noble Man's Child to be declar'd for ever Incapacitated from entring on the Publick Government, whom he had observ'd take pleasure in pricking out the Eyes of Jack-Daws, that were given him to play with'.[100]

Daniel's satire is of interest for two reasons. In the first place, the traditional Christian view already referred to in the case of Thomas Aquinas, that cruelty to animals may lead to cruelty to men, was repeated,[101] but now in the context of vivisection. Second, Daniel's attack on vivisection may be seen as reflecting the emergence of a general indignation at the Cartesians' callous animal experiments.[102] In fact, during the seventeenth century, not only the medical student or doctor but also the well-educated gentleman and clergyman was increasingly confronted with animal experimentation. The ensuing awareness of its moral implications was obviously the necessary precondition for an explicit literary attack on it.

The popularisation of animal experiment in the seventeenth and eighteenth centuries and the growth of concern about it

The Boylean 'Air pump experiment' — a paradigm

Besides vivisections demonstrating the blood circulation, Robert

Boyle's animal experiments on respiration in the so-called 'pneu-matick engine' enjoyed great popularity among the educated since the second half of the seventeenth century. John Evelyn (1620–1706), charter member and virtuoso of the Royal Society, repeatedly re-ferred in his *Diary* to the interest in these experiments.[103] The Roman Catholic divine, physician and philosopher Samuel Sorbière (1615–70) paid a great deal of attention to them in his report to Louis XIV about his journey to England in 1663. Moreover, Sorbière pro-mised to inform the king later, in a private conversation, about the details of this 'World of Experiments, that point out to us the In-fluence which the Rarefaction and Compression of the Air have upon Bodies', hoping that 'by this Means we come to know the Cause of Rheumatisms, Contageous Distempers, and several other Indis-positions and Phaenomena's in Nature'.[104]

In view of such expectations, the suffering of experimental animals by withdrawal of air in the pneumatic machine was initially not considered seriously, not even by Evelyn, although he spoke of Hooke's respiration experiment[105] as 'of more cruelty than pleased me' and sharply criticised the popular but cruel blood-sports such as dog-fighting, cock-fighting or bear-, bull- and horse-baiting.[106] In contrast to the cruel pleasures of the common people, the experi-mentalists' similarly cruel actions could be justified by their admir-able scientific purpose. As Isaac Barrow (1630–77) put it, when a student at Cambridge: 'the sanguinary curiosity which has recently ended the life of many a dog or fish or bird [is] a perfectly innocent cruelty and an easily excusable ferocity'.[107]

However, criticism of animal experimentation began to be heard in educated lay-circles in the early eighteenth century. In his widely-read daily paper *The Spectator* (1711–12), the English essayist and statesman Joseph Addison (1672–1719) ridiculed the experimenting physicians, whom he thought to be quite useless in the already over-crowded medical profession:

There are . . . innumerable Retainers to Physick, who, for want of other Patients, amuse themselves with the stifling of Cats in an Air Pump, cutting up Dogs alive, or impailing of Insects upon the point of a Needle for Microscopical Obser-vations; besides those that are employed in the gathering of Weeds, and the Chase of Butterflies: Not to mention the Cockle-shell-Merchants and Spider-catchers.[108]

In 1740 *The Gentleman's Magazine* especially criticised the Boylean air pump experiments. A satirical poem hinted that the torture of animals in this experiment would exceed the morbid cruelty of the Roman emperor Domitian.[109] James Ferguson (1710–76), a public lecturer on astronomy and mechanics and thus an important populariser of natural science,[110] referred in 1760 to the animals' 'agonies of a most bitter and cruel death' in the air pump experiment, which he held to be 'too shocking to every spectator who has the least degree of humanity'.[111] Instead of using an animal, he advocated the use of a mechanical model, in which a bladder represented the animal's lungs.[112]

This example of Boyle's popular respiration experiments clearly shows that around the middle of the eighteenth century a differentiation in attitudes towards animal experiments had developed, ranging from scientific enthusiasm about the method to critical doubt about its usefulness or even to outspoken indignation at the cruelty involved.

Having become acquainted with those Boylean experiments — very probably as a result of Ferguson's lectures — the artist Joseph Wright of Derby (1734–97) recorded in 1767–8 exactly this variety of attitudes in his painting 'The Picture of the Air Pump', showing the different emotions of the spectators at the crucial moment of the experiment (see Plate 1).[113] His painting reflects both the popularity of animal experimentation in the eighteenth century and the range of attitudes towards this method, including clear sensitivity towards animal suffering. This sensitivity can be seen as part of a more general sentimentality towards animals, which had emerged in England together with the rise of Evangelicalism and Humanitarianism.[114] As a result, animal experiments became a target of vehement literary attacks, the issue being closely associated with those of cruelty to human beings, and whether animals have souls.

Men of letters entering the debate

Before his attack on the allegedly useless labours of experimenting physicians in *The Spectator*, Joseph Addison had already ridiculed the efforts of the Royal Society virtuosi in his earlier periodical paper *The Tatler* (1709–11). In two satirical essays of 1710, he warned the virtuosi against becoming too alienated from the world by being permanently occupied with vivisection and the anatomy of minute and low animals:[115] 'They are so little versed in the world, that they scarce know a horse from an ox; but at the same time will tell you, with a great deal of gravity, that a flea is a rhinoceros, and a snail an hermaphrodite.'[116] On the other hand, Addison admired Colombo's experiment on a pregnant bitch,[117] which was becoming a classic for the test of motherly love in animals.[118] The following year he cited it in *The Spectator* as an important example of animal 'instinct'. However, it also horrified him; he called it a 'very barbarous Experiment' and apologised for mentioning 'such an Instance of Cruelty'.[119]

Whereas Addison showed an ambivalent attitude towards animal experimentation, the poet Alexander Pope (1688–1744) proved to be an outright adversary of vivisection. Having moved from Chiswick to Twickenham in 1719, Pope had become a near neighbour and friend of the Reverend Stephen Hales (1677–1761) at Teddington. Although Pope valued Hales as a 'worthy' and 'very good man', he abhorred the Reverend's animal experiments dealing with blood circulation and blood pressure. In 1744, during a private conversation with the Reverend Joseph Spence (1699–1768), Pope expressed his regret that Hales had 'his hands so much imbrued in blood' by cutting up rats and dogs alive. 'Indeed', the poet continued with emphasis and concern, 'he [i.e. Hales] commits most of these barbarities with the thought of its being of use to man; but how do we know that we have a right to kill creatures that we are so little above as dogs, for our curiosity, or even for some use to us?'[120]

Hales himself had temporarily discontinued his animal experiments, 'being discouraged by the disagreeableness of anatomical dissections', as he confessed in his *Haemastaticks* (1733).[121] But being at the same time convinced of the scientific value of the experimental method, he finally overcame his reluctance to vivisect.[122] By contrast, Pope obviously thought that human curiosity or even the possible utility to man were no justification for vivisection. As we know from Pope's further conversation with Spence, the poet's attitude was based on his belief that animals have souls. Well known for his fondness for dogs, Pope was inclined to attribute to them a certain degree of reason and even an unperishable soul.[123] This was why he thought that it was wicked to vivisect dogs.

At Pope's time the majority of English poets, essayists and journalists actually rejected the Cartesian doctrine of the 'beast-machine' and conceded that animals might have feelings and some reason.[124] The radical concept of insensitive animal machines gradually lost its significance. Both Pope and Addison held that animals were guided by 'instinct', which worked infallibly within its narrow limits, and in this respect might be regarded as even superior to human reason.[125] The eighteenth-century discussions of animal soul versus animal automatism thus undoubtedly formed the background to the moral judgement of animal experimentation.

One of the main characters on the English literary scene, Samuel Johnson (1709–84), lexicographer, critic, poet and essayist, also interpreted the seemingly wise actions of animals as instinctive, as Addison and Pope had done before. He disapproved of the Cartesian 'beast-machine' concept, and attributed to animals the ability to suffer pain and to have feelings. Unlike Pope, however, he refused to believe that they had an immortal soul, although he too was known for his fondness for pets.[126] In 1758, Johnson printed in his weekly paper *The Idler* (1758–60) probably the fiercest attack on animal experimentation thus far.[127] Like Addison, Johnson began his essay by deriding the work of the natural scientists. Whilst they were experimenting on inanimate matter he was ready to be indulgent towards them, since he thought that their efforts were at least innocent, albeit useless. But he had no patience whatsoever with physicians experimenting on living animals. Overwhelmed by emotions he wrote: 'Among the inferior Professors of medical knowledge, is a race of wretches, whose lives are only varied by varieties of cruelty.'[128] He further listed some of the cruellest animal experiments. Some had been described long ago, such as nailing dogs to tables and opening them alive, including the mutilation and the excision or laceration of their vital parts.[129] Some were new, such as sensitivity tests using burning irons[130] or specific toxicological trials. Johnson apologised for having offended 'the sensibility of the tender mind with images like these'[131] and went on to outline his main arguments against animal experimentation. First, the physician who had performed experiments on animals as a medical student would be inclined to continue his trials on helpless patients, on children and the old. Second, countering the arguments of the defenders of animal experimentation, he denied that by this method physiological knowledge might be greatly increased. Johnson was convinced 'that by knives, fire, and poison, knowledge is not always sought, and is very seldom attained', thus both emphasising the ineffectiveness of the experimental method and accusing the experimentalists of cruelty. He did not believe 'that by living dissections any discovery has been made by which a single malady is more easily cured'. Whereas Johnson's denial of the therapeutic

32

consequences of animal experiments showed not a shadow of doubt, he was willing to admit that vivisection had led to a small increase of knowledge in physiology, but he maintained that someone 'buys knowledge dear, who learns the use of the lacteals at the expence of his humanity'. Finally he encouraged his readers to express 'universal resentment . . . against these horrid operations, which . . . make the physician more dreadful than the gout or stone'.[132]

Evidently, Johnson was more concerned with the presumed detrimental consequences of animal vivisection to the relationship between physician and patient than with the animal's suffering as such. His view was still clearly *anthropocentric* and corresponded well to his fairly orthodox opinions about the nature and soul of animals. His argument was the logical extension of the ecclesiastical view already expressed by Thomas Aquinas in the thirteenth and by Gabriel Daniel in the late seventeenth century: cruelty towards animals may lead to cruelty towards men.[133]

It was exactly this danger to which the English artist William Hogarth (1697–1764) pointed in the second picture in his moralising series of engravings *The Four Stages of Cruelty* (1751). This picture also reflects his indignation at the maltreatment of domestic animals and at popular blood-sports. Together with the cruelties of hunting, these topics had become prominent in the works of several humanitarian English writers at about the same time.[134] Hogarth himself wrote that he had made the prints 'with the hope of, in some degree correcting that barbarous treatment of animals, the very sight of which renders the streets of our metropolis so distressing to every feeling mind'.[135]

Because outspoken disapproval of cruelty to animals was now also directed against the physicians' vivisections, medical men felt that their professional standing was being jeopardised. They therefore began to formulate their reasons for animal experimentation in greater detail than had their seventeenth-century colleagues.

Eighteenth-century defences of vivisection

In 1745, the Leipzig monthly journal *Belustigungen des Verstandes und des Witzes* published an essay which dealt exclusively with the question ' . . . whether it is allowed to open animals alive for the purpose of physiological experiments'.[136] The author was the talented Christlob Mylius (1722–54), cousin and friend of the writer Gotthold Ephraim Lessing. At this time Mylius was still a medical student at the University of Leipzig, but later he became known as a poet, journalist and natural scientist in Berlin. Following the Christian anthropocentric view, Mylius had already stated in the same journal, in 1744, that animals are created by God solely to serve man.[137] Based on the traditional belief in a gap between man and animals, he considered the infliction of pain in animal vivisection to be a much lesser sin than in human vivisection. He skilfully demonstrated the importance of vivisection for obtaining physiological knowledge, which in his view was absolutely necessary for the practice of medicine. Regarding such benefit as ethically *good* and the inevitable infliction of pain in vivisection as ethically *bad*, he entered into a *moral calculus* to determine the ethical value of animal experiments. The result of this calculus, which he carried out both philosophically and mathematically, was that in *animal* vivisection the good outweighed the evil, whereas *human* vivisection remained a crime, even if its conceivable medical utility was taken into account. Thus Mylius finished his demonstration by stating: ' . . . hence follows that the opening of living animals for the purpose of physiological experiments is not forbidden in the right of nature, but ordered'.[138]

Mylius's point of view must be regarded as fairly moderate, because at this time experiments on criminals were still seriously considered in order to accelerate the progress of medicine. In 1752, the President of the Berlin Academy of Sciences, Pierre-Louis Moreau de Maupertuis (1698–1759), actually suggested in an open letter to King Frederick the Great that physicians should, after previous training on human corpses and living animals, make use of criminals, who had been sentenced to death, for the purpose of carrying out pharmacological and toxicological tests, to try out new surgical techniques and even to study human physiology.[139] This attitude was evidently the result of his high regard for the experimental method, because in another letter concerning human obligations towards animals he had clearly stated that man should not torment or kill unnecessarily any harmless animals. Disagreeing with the theory of animal machines, he believed that animals have souls, which although not capable of reason, do have some form of sensitivity.[140] Like Aquinas, Daniel and Johnson, Maupertuis too feared that cruelty to animals might lead to cruelty among men.[141] But in spite of his general willingness to spare the animal's life wherever this was possible, he was so completely convinced of the methodological necessity of experimentation in medicine that he was prepared to advocate not only animal but also human vivisection.

Whereas the arguments of Mylius and Maupertuis were based on philosophical reflections, which took the problem of animal souls into account, the justifications of eighteenth-century experimental practitioners were more like those of Wepfer in the preceding century.[142] In 1741, when introducing a report about his animal experiments on the healing of fractures to the French Royal Academy of Sciences, Henri Duhamel Dumonceau (1700–82) pointed out that 'each day more animals are dying in order to satisfy our appetite than the scalpel of the anatomists might sacrifice for the purpose of useful research, which is directed to the conservation of our health and the cure of diseases'.[143] In 1752, Albrecht von Haller (1708–77) expressed a similar belief to the Royal Academy of Sciences at Göttingen, when he presented the results of his experiments on the 'sensible and irritable parts' of animals:

> . . . since the beginning of the year 1751, I have examined [in] several different ways, a hundred and ninety animals, a species of cruelty for which I felt such a reluctance, as could only be overcome by the desire of contributing to the benefit of mankind, and excused by that motive which induces persons of the most humane temper, to eat every day the flesh of harmless animals without any scruple.[144]

Thus around the middle of the eighteenth century the reference to medical benefit and the *tu-quoque argument,* i.e. the use of animals for nutritional purposes, seem to have become a kind of standard justification for animal experiments. It was probably used as a stereotype, which was employed in order to calm the possible indignation of sensitive contemporaries. This may well have been necessary, for — although there were no legal provisions to prevent cruelty to animals — as early as 1684 a man had been punished in the Prussian principality of Sagan with two days' exposure at the pillory and an additional fine, because he had severely maltreated his horse. In the second half of the eighteenth century, another German law court prosecuted and convicted two people for ill-treatment of their animals. Based on the notion of natural right, the Leipzig Faculty of Law, in 1765, sentenced a man to six weeks' imprisonment, because he had cut out half the tongue of a living cow. And in 1766 a postillion, who had hounded his horses to death, was sentenced to twelve days' imprisonment by the same faculty, the reasons for this judgement being 'inhumane behaviour'.[145] On the other hand, the law courts of this time would never seriously have considered prosecuting a medical doctor because of animal vivisection. Yet there seems to have been some kind of uncertainty among the experimentalists in this respect. In 1746, Johann August Unzer (1727–99), at this time a medical student at the University of Halle, wrote in the introduction to an anonymous account of his vivisections of dogs: 'Recently I have cut up a dog alive, a murderous deed, which I surely do not confide to you because of your love of discretion. Bring an action against me wherever you want: just listen what I observed on this occasion.'[146]

Of course no legal proceedings were taken against Unzer. However, his publication, being based chiefly on experiments on a decapitated dog and being entitled *A letter to Mr. N.N. in which is shown that it is possible to feel without head*, provoked the sarcasm of a scholar at the nearby University of Leipzig. The mathematician Abraham Gotthelf Kästner (1719–1800), a friend of Mylius, and later professor at Göttingen, read the title of Unzer's essay as ' . . . whether it is possible to *think* without head' and mocked that it clearly showed 'that at least it is possible to *write* without head'.[147]

Kästner's scoff at Unzer was more than a joke, for it was part of an essay in which he attacked animal experimentation in a way that was very similar to that of Johnson. Like the latter, he regarded vivisection as useless and feared its detrimental effects on the character of young physicians. He concluded: 'Least of all it is a proof that someone has the skill to cure people, for he has the heart to torment dogs.'[148]

In the eighteenth century the discussion of animal experimentation had obviously reached a point where the argument of benefit was accepted or rejected depending on a person's subjective view of medical science. In fact, there were no thoroughly convincing examples of immediate *therapeutic* consequences derived from animal experiments. People's respective philosophical views of man's relationship to animals determined attitudes and arguments with respect to animal experimentation and human cruelty.

The old anthropocentric versus the new theriocentric view: two concepts of human obligation towards animals at the end of the eighteenth century

Towards the end of the eighteenth century, the Königsberg philosopher Immanuel Kant (1724–1804) restated the traditional Christian, anthropocentric view of animals. In legal terms, a relationship could exist only between rational beings, i.e. between *human* beings, and it followed that there were neither animal rights nor human obligations towards animals as such.[149] Like the Romans,[150] Kant regarded animals as mere objects, legally speaking. Yet he thought that man should abstain from violence and cruelty to animals, because man's compassion for suffering human beings might be weakened and gradually obliterated. The considerate treatment of animals was therefore *man's duty to himself*.[151] This Kantian argument was evidently determined by the well-known concept that cruelty to animals may lead to cruelty towards men. In fact, Kant is said to have used Hogarth's engravings *The Four Stages of Cruelty* in order to illustrate this view in his lectures.[152]

On these grounds, Kant believed that the slaughtering of animals was permitted, if it was done quickly and without torture, and that man was allowed to make adequate use of an animal's capacity for work. But he also believed that 'the painful physical experiments for the mere sake of speculation are to be abhorred, if the end may be achieved without them'.[153] Thus the notion of medical benefit also entered into Kant's concept, a criterion that was very difficult to evaluate, as we have seen above. But, whereas the problem of whether man would profit therapeutically by animal experimentation remained unsolved, the basic philosophical assumptions, which had hitherto determined the limits of the debate, began to change.

When the English philosopher and theoretical jurist Jeremy Bentham (1748–1832) formulated the principle of utility in his influential *Introduction to the Principles of Morals and Legislation* (1789), it was not without consequences for his view of man's relationship towards animals. Holding that nature had placed mankind 'under the governance of two sovereign masters, *pain* and *pleasure*', he defined utility as 'that property in any object, whereby it tends to produce benefit, advantage, pleasure, good, or happiness, . . . or . . . to prevent the happening of mischief, pain, evil, or unhappiness to the party whose interest is considered.'[154] In Bentham's view, animals form such a party with an interest in the absence of pain and in considerate treatment. He accepted the slaughtering of animals, if it meant a speedier and less painful death than would eventually await the animal in the course of natural life. He supported this view by stating that animals could neither anticipate their future nor their death. Rating legitimate human interests higher than animal interests, he also held that man was permitted to kill animals which do damage.[155] But Bentham, known as a lover of animals just like Pope and Johnson,[156] saw no reason why man should have the right to torment animals. Comparing the status of animals in England with that of human slaves in other countries, he fought for animal rights just as for the abolition of slavery. 'The day *may* come', Bentham prophesied, 'when the rest of the animal creation may acquire those rights which never could have been withholden from them but by the hand of tyranny.' He believed that the orthodox criteria to distinguish between man and animal were now obsolete. He pointed to the French *Code Noir* (issued in 1685), which regulated the status of slaves in the West Indies and forbade the killing of slaves by their masters, giving the royal authorities the power to protect slaves from maltreatment. This law had shown that 'the blackness of the skin is no reason why a human being should be abandoned without redress to the caprice of a tormentor'. Ignoring the Christian dogmatic gap between man and animal, Bentham even speculated that some day 'the number of the legs, the villosity of the skin or the termination of the *os sacrum*' would be equally insufficient for abandoning animals to the fate of torture.[157]

Bentham thought that the traditional 'insuperable line' between man and the animal world had been drawn without valid reasons. The conventional criteria of the faculty of reason and of discourse were inadequate, because in his opinion a full-grown horse or a dog is far more rational and easy to communicate with than a human baby. Bentham defined a new criterion for how to treat animals concluding that 'the question is not, Can they *reason*? nor, Can they *talk*? but, Can they *suffer*?'[158]

Although Bentham did not draw any consequences for the practice of animal experimentation, his statements about the status of animals became of great importance to the modern anti-vivisectionist cause. His was probably the first serious criticism of the Christian, respectively Kantian, doctrine of man's relationship towards animals. From then on, the issue of cruelty to animals was no longer solely seen from an *anthropocentric* point of view, but also from a *theriocentric*[159] one which considered the protection of animals *for their own sake*. Bentham had thrown overboard the old criterion of whether or not animals have a rational soul and replaced it with the criterion of their capacity to suffer pain.

A similar theriocentric viewpoint was taken during the first half of the nineteenth century by the German philosopher Arthur Schopenhauer (1788–1860), who strongly condemned the Christian and Kantian position, pleaded for the restriction of animal experimentation and denounced its abuses.[160] In fact, the English neurologist and physiologist Marshall Hall (1790–1857) made detailed proposals for the professional regulation of physiological experiments as early as 1831, thus evidently reflecting the increasing respect for animal life and consideration of animal suffering in medical science.[161] Whereas Schopenhauer became the idol of some German anti-vivisectionists in the late nineteenth century,[162] Bentham has acquired the same status among Anglo-American adversaries of animal experimentation today.[163] His concept of *animal rights* is now a major issue in philosophical discussions on animal experimentation.[164]

Acknowledgements

The authors thank Mrs Rita Maehle for her help in preparing the notes, Miss Sabine Mildner for her bibliographical assistance, and Mrs Heide Engel and Mrs Monika Tietze for the preparation of the manuscript.

Notes

1. See J.A.H. Murray, H. Bradley, W.A. Craigie and C.T. Onions (eds.), *A New English Dictionary on Historical Principles* (Clarendon Press, Oxford, 1928), vol. 10, p. 272.

2. Celsus, *De medicina*, ed. W.G. Spencer, 3rd edn (3 vols, William Heinemann and Harvard University Press, London and Cambridge, Massachusetts, 1960), vol. 1, p. 40.

3. A. Vesalius, *De humani corporis fabrica libri septem* (Ex Officina Ioannis Oporini, Basileae, 1543, Reprint Culture et Civilisation, Bruxelles, 1964), p. 658.

4. Ibid., p. 658.

5. R. Colombo, *De re anatomica libri XV* (Ex Typographia Nicolai Beuilacquae, Venetiis, 1559, Reprint Culture et Civilisation, Bruxelles, 1983), p. 256.

6. Th. Bartholinus, *Anatome ex omnium veterum recentiorumque observationibus* (Ex Officina Hackiana, Lugduni Batavorum, 1673), p. 2.

7. Ibid., p. 1.

8. F. Glisson, *Anatomia hepatis* (Du-Gardian, Octavian Pullein, London, 1654), p. 4.

9. W. Rolfinck, *Dissertationes anatomicae methodo synthetica exaratae* (Michael Endterus, Noribergae, 1656), p. 30.

10. Ibid., p. 30.

11. Ibid., p. 31.

12. See Murray *et al.*, *New English Dictionary*, vol. 10, p. 272.

13. The term 'vivisection' is used by Albrecht von Haller in a letter dated 'Göttingen. 1751. Jul. 22.' to Georg Th. von Asch, see E.F. Rössler,

Die Gründung der Universität Göttingen (Vandenhoeck and Ruprecht, Göttingen, 1855), p. 337.

14. See also R. Virchow, 'Ueber den Werth des pathologischen Experiments' in W. MacCormac and G.H. Makins (eds.), *Transactions of the International Medical Congress, London 1881* (4 vols, J.W. Kolckmann, London, 1881), vol. 1, pp. 22–37, 34–5.

15. See also U. Tröhler, 'Die Geschichte des wissenschaftlichen Tierversuchs, seiner Begründung und Bekämpfung' in K.J. Ullrich and O.D. Creutzfeld (eds.), *Gesundheit und Tierschutz* (Econ Verlag, Düsseldorf and Wien, 1985), pp. 47–81, 62–3.

16. See J. Hirschberg, 'Alkmaion's Verdienst um die Augenkunde', *Archiv für Ophthalmologie*, vol. 105 (1921), pp. 129–33; H. Erhard, 'Alkmaion, der erste Experimentalbiologe', *Sudhoffs Archiv*, vol. 34 (1941), pp. 77–89.

17. *Oeuvres complètes d'Hippocrate*, ed. E. Littré (10 vols, Paris, 1839–61, reprint Adolf M. Hakkert, Amsterdam, 1962), vol. 9, pp. 80–7; see also G. Senn, 'Über Herkunft und Stil der Beschreibungen von Experimenten im Corpus Hippocraticum', *Sudhoffs Archiv*, vol. 22 (1929), pp. 217–89, 238.

18. See J.F. Dobson, 'Herophilus of Alexandria', *Proceedings of the Royal Society of Medicine*, vol. 18 (1925), pp. 19–32; Dobson, 'Erasistratus', *Proceedings of the Royal Society of Medicine*, vol. 20 (1927), pp. 21–8; G. Senn, *Die Entwicklung der biologischen Forschungsmethode in der Antike und ihre grundsätzliche Förderung durch Theophrast von Eresos* (Verlag von H.R. Sauerländer & Co., Aarau, 1933), pp. 135–51; Ch. Singer, *A Short History of Anatomy from the Greeks to Harvey*, 2nd edn (Dover Publications, New York, 1957), pp. 28–33.

19. Celsus, *De medicina*, vol. 1, p. 14.

20. Galen, *Sieben Bücher Anatomie*, ed. M. Simon, (2 vols, J.C. Hinrichs'sche Buchhandlung, Leipzig, 1906); Galen, *On Anatomical Procedures*, ed. Ch. Singer (Oxford University Press, London, New York and Toronto, 1956); Galen, *On Anatomical Procedures. The Later Books*, ed. W.L.H. Duckworth, M.C. Lyons and B. Towers (Cambridge University Press, Cambridge, 1962).

21. Galen, *Anatomical Procedures. Later Books*, p. 15.

22. Ibid., p. 85.

23. Ibid., pp. 15–16.

24. Galen, 'De usu partium' in C.G. Kühn (ed.), *Opera omnia* (22 vols., Leipzig, 1821–9, reprint Georg Olms Verlagsbuchhandlung, Hildesheim, 1964–5), vol. 3, p. 9.

25. See J. Passmore, 'The Treatment of Animals', *Journal of the History of Ideas*, vol. 36 (1975), pp. 195–218, p. 198; W. Sellert, 'Das Tier in der abendländischen Rechtsauffassung' in Tierärztliche Hochschule Hannover (ed.), *Studium generale. Vorträge zum Thema: Mensch und Tier* (Verlag M. & H. Schaper, Hannover, 1984), pp. 66–84, 72.

26. See Galen, *Anatomie*, vol. 2, p. XIX; Th. Meyer-Steineg, 'Die Vivisektion in der antiken Medizin', *Internationale Monatsschrift für Wissenschaft, Kunst und Technik*, vol. 6 (1912), pp. 1491–1512, 1512.

27. Celsus, *De medicina*, vol. 1, pp. 14, 40.

28. See Dobson, 'Herophilus of Alexandria', pp. 25–6; Singer, *History of Anatomy*, pp. 34–5; L. Glesinger, 'Zur Frage der angeblichen Vivisektionen am Menschen in Alexandria' in *XVIIe Congrès International d'Histoire de la Médecine, Athènes-Cos 1960* (2 vols, Athens, 1960), vol. 1, pp. 287–95;

J. Scarborough, 'Celsus on Human Vivisection at Ptolemaic Alexandria', *Clio Medica*, vol. 11 (1976), pp. 25-38; G. Majno, *The Healing Hand*, 3rd edn (Harvard University Press, Cambridge, Massachusetts and London, 1982), pp. 354-5.

29. See J. Pagel, 'Ueber die Grade der Arzneien', *Pharmaceutische Post*, vol. 28 (1895), pp. 65-7, 131-3, 142-4, 180-2, 221-5, 258-62, p. 143; Pagel, 'Ueber den Versuch am lebenden Menschen', *Deutsche Aerzte-Zeitung*, no. 9-10 (1905), pp. 193-8, 219-28, 194-5; L. Lewin, *Die Gifte in der Weltgeschichte* (Verlag von Julius Springer, Berlin, 1920), pp. 6-7.

30. See M. Roth, *Andreas Vesalius Bruxellensis* (Verlag von Georg Reimer, Berlin, 1892), p. 85; B. Farrington, 'The Last Chapter of the De Fabrica of Vesalius', *Transactions of the Royal Society of South Africa*, vol. 20 (1932), pp. 1-14, 1; N. Mani, 'Vesals erste Anatomie in Bologna 1540', *Gesnerus*, vol. 17 (1960), pp. 42-52, 51.

31. Vesalius, *De humani corporis fabrica*, p. 659 [663], trans. taken from Farrington, 'The Last Chapter of the De Fabrica of Vesalius', p. 14.

32. Vesalius, *De humani corporis fabrica*, pp. 658-9 [663].

33. Ibid., p. 661, trans. taken from Farrington, 'The Last Chapter of the De Fabrica of Vesalius', p. 10; see also Vesalius's similar remark, *De humani corporis fabrica*, p. 636.

34. See I. Bregenzer, *Thier-Ethik. Darstellung der sittlichen und rechtlichen Beziehungen zwischen Mensch und Thier* (C.C. Buchner Verlag, Bamberg, 1894), p. 190; Passmore, 'The Treatment of Animals', pp. 197-8, 200-1; Sellert, 'Das Tier in der abendländischen Rechtsauffassung', p. 76.

35. Colombo, *De re anatomica*, pp. 256-61.

36. Ibid., pp. 258-9.

37. Ibid., p. 256.

38. See Roth, *Andreas Vesalius Bruxellensis*, pp. 47, 209, 473-4; R. Herrlinger, *Volcher Coiter* (M. Edelmann, Nürnberg, 1952), pp. 118-19.

39. See Rolfinck, *Dissertationes anatomicae*, pp. 31-2; Roth, *Andreas Vesalius Bruxellensis*, pp. 274-6, 290-1, 295, 301, 473-85; Singer, *History of Anatomy*, p. 35.

40. Colombo, *De re anatomica*, pp. 175-87, 222-4.

41. Ibid., p. 224; see also U. Tröhler, 'Was ist neu? — Der medizinische Tierversuch im Meinungsstreit', *Swiss Pharma*, vol. 7 (1985), pp. 7-16, p. 10.

42. Colombo, *De re anatomica*, p. 260, trans. by the authors.

43. Ibid., pp. 256-61.

44. F. Bacon, 'The Twoo Bookes . . . of the Proficience and Advancement of Learning Divine and Humane' (1605) in J. Spedding, R.L. Ellis and D.D. Heath (eds.), *The Works of Francis Bacon* (14 vols, Longman and Co., London, 1857-74), vol. 3, p. 374.

45. Ibid., p. 374.

46. G. Aselli, *De lactibus sive lacteis venis*, ed. L. Mendel and S. Schwann (Apud Io. Baptam Bidellium, Mediolani, 1627, reprint edition Leipzig, 1968), pp. 19-21; see also N. Mani, 'Darmresorption und Blutbildung im Lichte der experimentellen Physiologie des 17. Jahrhunderts', *Gesnerus*, vol. 18 (1961), pp. 85-146, 93-100.

47. See N. Mani, 'Darmresorption und Blutbildung', pp. 104-8.

48. Ibid., pp. 110-34.

49. W. Harvey, *An Anatomical Disputation Concerning the Movement of the Heart*

and Blood in Living Creatures, ed. G. Whitteridge (Blackwell, Oxford, London, Edinburgh and Melbourne, 1976).

50. R. Boyle, 'Of the Usefulness of Natural Philosophy' in *The Works of the Honourable Robert Boyle* (5 vols, A. Millar, London, 1744), vol. 1, p. 465.

51. Glisson, *Anatomia hepatis*, pp. 4–5; Boyle, 'Usefulness of Natural Philosophy', p. 465; I. van Diemerbroeck, *Opera omnia, anatomica et medica* (M. v. Dreunen and W. v. Walcheren, Ultrajecti, 1685), p. 2; Ph. Verheyen, *Corporis humani anatomiae liber primus*, 2nd edn (Fratres T'Serstevens, Bruxelles, 1710), p. 1; Rolfinck, *Dissertationes anatomicae*, pp. 30–1; J.J. Wepfer, *Cicutae aquaticae historia et noxae* (J.R. König and J.R. Genathius, Basileae, 1679), p. 132; Aselli, *De lactibus*, p. 20.

52. Rolfinck, *Dissertationes anatomicae*, p. 30.

53. Wepfer, *Cicutae aquaticae historia*, p. 132; see also A.-H. Maehle, 'Zur wissenschaftlichen und moralischen Rechtfertigung toxikologischer Tierversuche im 17. Jahrhundert: Johann Jakob Wepfer und Johann Jakob Harder', *Gesnerus*, vol. 43 (1986), pp. 213–21, 216.

54. Rolfinck, *Dissertationes anatomicae*, p. 31.

55. Bartholinus, *Anatome*, p. 2; see also Mani, 'Darmresorption und Blutbildung', p. 125; Boyle, 'Usefulness of Natural Philosophy', p. 465.

56. Boyle, 'Usefulness of Natural Philosophy', p. 465; Rolfinck, *Dissertationes anatomicae*, p. 31.

57. R. Lower, 'Tractatus de corde' in K.J. Franklin and R.T. Gunther (eds.), *Early Science in Oxford* (14 vols, Printed for the Subscribers, Oxford, 1923–45), vol. 9, p. 189.

58. See W. Shugg, 'Humanitarian Attitudes in the Early Animal Experiments of the Royal Society', *Annals of Science*, vol. 24 (1968), pp. 227–38, 233–4.

59. Wepfer, *Cicutae aquaticae historia*, p. 134, trans. by the authors; see also A.-H. Maehle, 'Johann Jakob Wepfers experimentelle Toxikologie', *Gesnerus*, vol. 42 (1985), pp. 7–18, 16; Maehle, 'Rechtfertigung toxikologischer Tierversuche', pp. 216–17.

60. Wepfer, *Cicutae aquaticae historia*, praefatio.

61. J.J. Harder, *Apiarium observationibus medicis centum* (J. Ph. Richter and J. Bertsch, Basileae, 1687), p. 97; see also Maehle, 'Rechtfertigung toxikologischer Tierversuche', p. 217.

62. See Mani, 'Darmresorption und Blutbildung', pp. 124–5; K.E. Rothschuh, 'Jean Riolan jun. (1580–1657) im Streit mit Paul Marquart Schlegel (1605–1653) um die Blutbewegungslehre Harveys', *Gesnerus*, vol. 21 (1964), pp. 72–82.

63. See K. Dewhurst (ed.), *Richard Lower's Vindicatio. A Defence of the Experimental Method* (Sandford Publ., Oxford, 1983), pp. 229, 231.

64. See Dewhurst, *Lower's Vindicatio*.

65. Ibid., p. 295.

66. See above, p. 19.

67. Aselli, *De lactibus*, p. 20.

68. Wepfer, *Cicutae aquaticae historia*, p. 132, trans. by the authors.

69. Rolfinck, *Dissertationes anatomicae*, p. 30.

70. Wepfer, *Cicutae aquaticae historia*, p. 132, trans. by the authors.

71. See also Tröhler, 'Geschichte des wissenschaftlichen Tierversuchs', pp. 67, 70–1; Maehle, 'Rechtfertigung toxikologischer Tierversuche', p. 216.

72. Wepfer, *Cicutae aquaticae historia*, praefatio; see also Maehle, 'J.J. Wepfers experimentelle Toxikologie', p. 10; J.C. Brunner, *Experimenta nova circa pancreas* (Th. Haak, Lugduni Batavorum, 1709), pp. 10, 14, 54, 57.

73. M. Ettmüller, 'De chirurgia infusoria' in *Opera omnia. Dissertationes academicae* (Sumptibus Johannis Davidis Zunneri, Francofurti ad Moenum, 1688), Diss. XVI, pp. 233–55, p. 236.

74. See also Shugg, 'Humanitarian Attitudes'.

75. Lower, 'Tractatus de corde', p. 183.

76. 'Letter from Hooke to Boyle, 10 Nov. 1664', in Gunther, *Early Science in Oxford*, vol. 6, pp. 216–18, p. 217; see also Shugg, 'Humanitarian Attitudes', p. 232; R.G. Frank Jr., *Harvey and the Oxford Physiologists* (University of California Press, Berkeley, Los Angeles and London, 1980), pp. 159–60.

77. Quoted in Shugg, 'Humanitarian Attitudes', p. 231.

78. R. Descartes, *Discours de la Méthode*, ed. L. Gäbe (Felix Meiner Verlag, Hamburg, 1960), pp. 90–7; see also L.C. Rosenfield, *From Beast-Machine to Man-Machine* (Oxford University Press, New York, 1940), pp. 3–17.

79. Descartes, *Discours de la Méthode*, pp. 96–7, trans. taken from Rosenfield, *Beast-Machine*, p. 7 .

80. See also K.E. Rothschuh, 'René Descartes und die Theorie der Lebenserscheinungen', *Sudhoffs Archiv*, vol. 50 (1966), pp. 25–42, 38.

81. See G. Boas, *The Happy Beast in French Thought of the Seventeenth Century* (Johns Hopkins Press, Baltimore, 1933), p. 2.

82. See ibid., pp. 1–17, 52–117; H. Hastings, *Man and Beast in French Thought of the Eighteenth Century* (Johns Hopkins Press, Baltimore, 1936), pp. 11–13; Rosenfield, *Beast-Machine*, pp. 15, 19.

83. See B. de Saint-Germain, *Descartes Considéré comme Physiologiste et comme Médecin* (Victor Masson et Fils, Paris, 1869), pp. 97–102; Rothschuh, 'René Descartes', p. 39.

84. Descartes, *Discours de la Méthode*, pp. 76–89.

85. See Rosenfield, *Beast-Machine*, p. 19.

86. See also ibid., pp. 20–3.

87. See Boas, *Happy Beast*, pp. 98–9; Rosenfield, *Beast-Machine*, pp. 19–20.

88. See Rosenfield, *Beast-Machine*, pp. 8, 13, 18.

89. Quoted in D. Harwood, *Love for Animals and how it Developed in Great Britain* (Columbia University Press, New York, 1928), p. 84; see also Rosenfield, *Beast-Machine*, pp. 16–17.

90. See Rosenfield, *Beast-Machine*, pp. 181, 282, 287.

91. See ibid., pp. 241–5, 261–9, 281–4.

92. Quoted in Ch.-A. Sainte-Beuve, *Port-Royal* (5 vols, Eugène Renduel, Paris, 1840–59), vol. 2, p. 306, trans. by the authors; see also Rosenfield, *Beast-Machine*, p. 70; Saint-Germain, *Descartes*, p. 435.

93. N. Fontaine, *Mémoires pour Servir à l'Histoire de Port-Royal* (2 vols, Aux dépens de la Compagnie, Cologne, 1738), vol. 2, pp. 52–3; trans. taken from Ch. Beard, *Port Royal. A Contribution to the History of Religion and Literature in France* (2 vols, Longman, Green, Longman and Roberts, London, 1861), vol. 2, pp. 68–9.

94. See above, p. 24.

95. Boyle, 'Usefulness of Natural Philosophy', p. 471.

96. See W. Ebstein, *Der medizinische Versuch mit besonderer Berücksichtigung der 'Vivisektion'* (Verlag von J.F. Bergmann, Wiesbaden, 1907), p. 44; G. Scherz,

Niels Stensen. Denker und Forscher im Barock (Wissenschaftliche Verlagsgesell-schaft, Stuttgart, 1964), p. 194; A. Faller, 'Zur Diskussion um das Stensen-Experiment', *Gesnerus*, vol. 42 (1985), pp. 19–34, 32–3.

97. G. Daniel, *Voiage du Monde de Descartes* (Chez Pierre Mortier, Libraire, Amsterdam, 1700); Daniel, *A Voyage to the World of Cartesius* (Printed and sold by Thomas Bennet, London, 1692); Daniel, *Iter per mundum Cartesii* (Apud Abrahamum Wolfgang, Amstelaedami, 1694); see also Rosenfield, *Beast-Machine*, pp. 86–90.

98. Daniel, *World of Cartesius*, pp. 52–5.

99. Ibid., p. 241.

100. Ibid., pp. 241–2.

101. See above, p. 17.

102. See also Rosenfield, *Beast-Machine*, pp. 89–90.

103. *The Diary of John Evelyn*, ed. E.S. de Beer (6 vols, Clarendon Press, Oxford, 1955), vol. 3, pp. 255, 271.

104. S. Sorbière, *A Voyage to England, Containing many Things relating to the State of Learning, Religion, and other Curiosities of that Kingdom* (Printed and sold by J. Woodward, London, 1709), pp. 34, 47.

105. See above, p. 23.

106. *Diary of John Evelyn*, vol. 3, pp. 491–2, 497–8, 549.

107. Quoted in P.C. Osmond, *Isaac Barrow. His Life and Times* (Richard Clay and Co., Bungay, Suffolk, 1944, Reprint Society for Promoting Christian Knowledge, London, 1976), p. 40.

108. J. Addison, 'The Spectator, no. 21, 24 March 1711' in D.F. Bond (ed.), *The Spectator* (5 vols, Clarendon Press, Oxford, 1965), vol. 1, pp. 88–92, p. 91.

109. Junius, 'The Air-Pump', *Gentleman's Magazine*, vol. 10 (1740), p. 194; see also Shugg, 'Humanitarian Attitudes', p. 230.

110. See E. Henderson, *Life of James Ferguson, F.R.S., in a Brief Autobiographical Account*, 2nd edn (A. Fullarton & Co., Edinburgh, London and Glasgow, 1870).

111. J. Ferguson, *Lectures on Select Subjects in Mechanics, Pneumatics, Hydrostatics, and Optics* (A. Millar, London, 1764), p. 119.

112. Ibid., p. 119.

113. See also B. Nicolson, *Joseph Wright of Derby. Painter of Light* (2 vols, Routledge and Kegan Paul and Pantheon Books, London and New York, 1968), vol. 1, pp. 42–6, 111–22, vol. 2, pp. 35–6.

114. See also R.D. French, *Antivivisection and Medical Science in Victorian Society* (Princeton University Press, Princeton and London, 1975), p. 23. K. Thomas, *Man and the Natural World. Changing Attitudes in England 1500–1800* (Allen Lane, London, 1983).

115. J. Addison, 'The Tatler, no. 119, 12 Jan. 1710, no. 216, 26 Aug. 1710' in G.A. Aitken (ed.), *The Tatler* (4 vols, Duckworth and Co., London, 1898–9, reprint Georg Olms Verlag, Hildesheim and New York, 1970), vol. 3, pp. 27–33, vol. 4, pp. 110–13.

116. Addison, 'The Tatler, no. 216, 26 Aug. 1710', pp. 110–11.

117. See above, p. 18.

118. See Hastings, *Man and Beast*, pp. 270–1. In the nineteenth century the French physiologist François Magendie (1783–1855) repeated Colombo's experiment calling it an 'expérience morale', while at about the same time

the theologians were still occupied with the question either of its vindication or condemnation; see H. Tollin, 'Matteo Realdo Colombo's Sektionen und Vivisektionen', *Archiv für die gesammte Physiologie*, vol. 21 (1880), pp. 349–60; R. Knoche, *Schach den Thürmen!*, 2nd edn (Fr. Culemann, Hannover, 1880); H. Bretschneider, *Der Streit um die Vivisektion im 19. Jahrhundert* (Gustav Fischer Verlag, Stuttgart, 1962), pp. 67–8, 120.

119. Addison, 'The Spectator, no. 120, 18 July 1711' in Bond, *The Spectator*, vol. 1, pp. 489–93, pp. 490–1.

120. See J. Spence, *Observations, Anecdotes, and Characters, of Books and Men*, ed. E. Malone (John Murray, London, 1820), p. 60; see also A.E. Clark-Kennedy, *Stephen Hales, D.D., F.R.S. An Eighteenth Century Biography* (Cambridge University Press, 1929, reprint Gregg Press, Farnborough, Hants., 1965), pp. 55–7; N. Ault, *New Light on Pope with some Additions to his Poetry Hitherto Unknown* (Methuen and Co., London, 1949, Reprint Archon Books, U.S.A. 1967), p. 340.

121. St Hales, 'Statical Essays: Containing Haemastaticks' in A. Ruskin (ed.), *Classics in Arterial Hypertension* (Thomas, Springfield, Ill., 1956), pp. 6–29, p. 7.

122. Ibid., pp. 7–8.

123. See Spence, *Observations*, pp. 60–1; Ault, *New Light on Pope*, pp. 337–50.

124. See W. Shugg, 'The Cartesian Beast-Machine in English Literature (1663–1750)', *Journal of the History of Ideas*, vol. 29 (1968), pp. 279–92.

125. Addison, 'The Spectator, no. 120, 18 July 1711, no. 121, 19 July 1711' in Bond, *The Spectator*, vol. 1, pp. 489–97; see also Shugg, 'Cartesian Beast-Machine', pp. 285, 289.

126. See Harwood, *Love for Animals*, p. 217; Shugg, 'Cartesian Beast-Machine', pp. 291–2.

127. S. Johnson, 'The Idler, no. 17, 5 Aug. 1758' in *The Idler*, 3rd edn (2 vols, Davies, Newbery and Payne, London, 1767), vol. 1, pp. 92–6.

128. Ibid., p. 94.

129. See above, p. 27.

130. E.g. A. von Haller, 'De partibus corporis humani sensilibus et irritabilibus', *Commentarii Societatis Regiae Scientiarum Gottingensis*, vol. 2 (1752), pp. 114–58.

131. Johnson, 'The Idler, no. 17, 5 Aug. 1758', p. 95.

132. Ibid., p. 96.

133. See above, pp. 17, 28.

134. Harwood, *Love for Animals*, ch. 5.

135. Quoted in V. de S. Pinto, 'William Hogarth' in B. Ford (ed.), *The Pelican Guide to English Literature*, 11th edn (7 vols, Penguin Books, Harmondsworth, 1976), vol. 4, pp. 278–92, p. 284; see also Harwood, *Love for Animals*, pp. 242–4; French, *Antivivisection*, p. 23; J. Turner, *Reckoning with the Beast* (Johns Hopkins University Press, Baltimore and London, 1980), pp. 9–10; Tröhler, 'Tierversuch im Meinungsstreit', pp. 12–13.

136. Ch. Mylius, 'Untersuchung, ob man die Thiere, um physiologischer Versuche willen, lebendig eröffnen dürfe?', *Belustigungen des Verstandes und des Witzes*, Aprilmonat 1745, pp. 325–40, title trans. by the authors; for a detailed discussion of this essay see A.-H. Maehle, 'Der Literat Christlob Mylius und seine Verteidigung des medizinischen Tierversuchs im 18. und 19, Jahrhundert, *Medizinhistorisches Journal*, vol. 21 (1986), pp. 269–87.

137. Mylius, 'Untersuchung, ob die Thiere um der Menschen willen geschaffen sind', *Belustigungen des Verstandes und des Witzes*, Weinmonat [Oktober] 1744, pp. 363–81.

138. Mylius, 'Untersuchung, ob man die Thiere . . . eröffnen dürfe?', p. 339, trans. by the authors.

139. P.-L. M. de Maupertuis, 'Sur le Progrès des Sciences' in *Lettres de Mr. de Maupertuis* (Chez George Conrad Walther, Dresden, 1752), pp. 157–228, 198–205, 223–4.

140. Maupertuis, 'Du droit sur les Bêtes' in *Lettres de Mr. de Maupertuis*, pp. 43–7; see also Hastings, *Man and Beast*, pp. 243–4.

141. See above, pp. 17, 28, 33.

142. See above, pp. 21, 23.

143. H. Duhamel Dumonceau, 'Observations sur la Réunion des Fractures des Os', *Histoires (Mémoires) de l'Academie Royale*, 1741, pp. 97–112, p. 98, trans. by the authors; see also U. Tröhler, 'Brève histoire de l'expérimentation animale et des controverses qu'elle a suscitées', *Revue Médicale de la Suisse Romande*, vol. 105 (1985), pp. 817–29, pp. 821–2.

144. Haller, 'De partibus . . . sensilibus et irritabilibus', p. 114, trans. taken from the English edn, *A Dissertation on the Sensible and Irritable Parts of Animals* (J. Nourse, London, 1755), p. 2.

145. See Bregenzer, *Thier-Ethik*, p. 180; see also Sellert, 'Das Tier in der abendländischen Rechtsauffassung', p. 78.

146. J.A. Unzer, 'Sendschreiben an Herrn N.N. worin erwiesen wird, daß man ohne Kopf empfinden könne, ausgefertiget von S.C.I.S.' in *S.C.I.S. Gedancken vom Schlafe und denen Träumen* (Carl Hermann Hemmerde, Halle, 1746), pp. 59–80, 69, trans. by the authors.

147. A.G. Kästner, 'Mahomet II. ein Kunstkenner' in K.W. Justi (ed.), *Sinngedichte und Einfälle*, 2nd edn (Ludwig Schellenberg, Frankfurt and Leipzig, 1800), pp. 221–2, 222, trans. by the authors; see also A.-H. Maehle, 'Christlob Mylius', pp. 281–3.

148. Kästner, 'Mahomet', p. 222, trans. by the authors.

149. I. Kant, 'Grundlegung zur Metaphysik der Sitten' (1785) in Königlich Preußische Akademie der Wissenschaften (ed.), *Kant's gesammelte Schriften. Werke* (9 vols, Georg Reimer, Berlin, 1902–23), vol. 4, pp. 385–464, p. 428; Kant, 'Die Metaphysik der Sitten' (1797), ibid., vol. 6, pp. 203–494, pp. 241, 442; see also H.D. Irmscher (ed.), *Immanuel Kant. Aus den Vorlesungen der Jahre 1762 bis 1764. Auf Grund der Nachschriften Johann Gottfried Herders* (Kölner Universitäts-Verlag, Köln, 1964), p. 173.

150. See above, p. 16.

151. Kant, 'Die Metaphysik der Sitten', vol. 6, pp. 442–3.

152. See Passmore, 'The Treatment of Animals', p. 201.

153. Kant, 'Die Metaphysik der Sitten', vol. 6, p. 443, trans. by the authors.

154. J. Bentham, 'An Introduction to the Principles of Morals and Legislation' (1789) in J.H. Burns and H.L.A. Hart (eds.), *The Collected Works of Jeremy Bentham* (5 vols, Athlone Press, London, 1968–84), vol. 2.1, pp. 11–12.

155. Ibid., p. 282.

156. See Harwood, *Love for Animals*, pp. 168–9, 217–18, 266–7.

157. Bentham, 'Principles of Morals and Legislation', p. 283.

158. Ibid., p. 283.

159. We suggest 'theriocentric' as an opposite term to the widely known 'anthropocentric'. Our new term has been derived from the Greek 'ther', i.e. 'beast'. By using the adjective 'theriocentric' we indicate a specific view of human cruelty towards animals in which the animals' suffering and their (supposed) interest in, or right to, the absence of pain are considered as such, i.e. without a prevalent concern in the possible detrimental effects of cruelty to animals on human morality and society.

160. See below, pp. 150–1.

161. See below, pp. 85–7; see also W. Paton, *Man and Mouse. Animals in Medical Research* (Oxford University Press, Oxford and New York, 1984), pp. 1–2.

162. See below, pp. 161–2, 173, 178.

163. See *The Times*, 21 May 1985, 'Breaking the Cages', p. 10; O.D. Creutzfeld, 'Ethik, Wissenschaft und Tierversuche' in Ullrich and Creutzfeld (eds.), *Gesundheit und Tierschutz*, pp. 11–43, 14–15.

164. See P. Singer, *Animal Liberation. A New Ethics for Our Treatment of Animals* (The New York Review, New York, 1975), pp. 8–9, 222, 229–31; G.M. Teutsch, *Tierversuche und Tierschutz* (Verlag C.H. Beck, München, 1983), pp. 36, 39, 115; Teutsch, 'Tierschutz als Geschichte menschlichen Versagens' in U.M. Händel (ed.), *Tierschutz. Testfall unserer Menschlichkeit* (Fischer Taschenbuch Verlag, Frankfurt a.M., 1984), pp. 39–49, 47–8; A.N. Rowan, *Of Mice, Models, and Men: A Critical Evaluation of Animal Research* (State University of New York Press, Albany, 1984), pp. 256–7; C. Cohen, 'The Case for the Use of Animals in Biomedical Research', *New England Journal of Medicine*, vol. 315 (1986), pp. 865–70.

3

Vivisection and the Emergence of Experimental Physiology in Nineteenth-century France

Paul Elliott

Introduction

Several attempts have been made to produce sketches of the development of physiology in France in the nineteenth century. Perhaps the first of these that ought to be considered is the one put forward by Claude Bernard (1813–78), who was himself one of the most distinguished French physiologists of the period. Bernard's historiography was quite uniquely ethnocentric, not to say egocentric. Reviewing the history of physiological thought as a whole, he identified Albrecht von Haller as an important figure in the eighteenth century and then went on to concentrate exclusively on the contributions made by his fellow Frenchmen. The first of these he singled out was that of Xavier Bichat (1771–1802), who was active at the Paris medical school at the turn of the century. He then went on to discuss at length the role of his master, François Magendie (1783–1855), before culminating his story with details of his own research work, which he seems to have seen, possibly with some justification, as the ultimate expression of contemporary physiology.[1]

Despite the known dangers of following scientists' own versions of the histories of their chosen fields, successive French historians of science have reproduced Bernard's version of the history of French physiology almost without addition. Joseph Schiller in particular was guilty of recycling Bernard's ideas most uncritically. More recently, an American, John Lesch, has produced a book that once more concentrates on the triumvirate of Bichat, Magendie and Bernard, to the virtual exclusion of all other figures active at the time.[2]

Lesch, however, has done more than just recycle the ideas of

Bernard. Following recent historiographical trends in the history of science in the United States and elsewhere, he has sought to find an institutional base out of which French physiology developed. His main thesis is that vivisectional physiology in France grew up as a natural result of the clinical training in surgery given at the Paris school of medicine following its reformation under the Revolution. According to this argument, there emerged from the school a series of young men who were prepared to apply their training in the techniques of human surgery to vivisectional experiments carried out on animals in order to solve problems of vital function. This starting point immediately limits the number of characters available to Lesch for study. Bichat, Magendie and Bernard all neatly fit into his argument, as do Julien Legallois (1770–1814) and Guillaume Dupuytren (1777–1835), figures already brought into the history of French physiology by Schiller and Georges Canguilhem. One can add to this list two further names, those of Nicolas Blondlot (1808–77), another early exponent of animal vivisection in France, who trained in surgery under Dupuytren and went on to practise in Nancy, and Achille Longet (1811–71), whose contribution will be considered further below.

Lesch's case therefore seems, on the surface at least, to be very strong. But closer examination shows that Bichat, Magendie, Legallois and Longet were all physicians, although Magendie did originally study surgery, while Bernard made no attempt to practise medicine of either sort. Of the figures mentioned above, only Longet ever held the chair of physiology at the Paris medical school and he had to wait until 1859 before his final appointment. Bichat's chair was in clinical medicine and Dupuytren's in clinical surgery, while Blondlot was given the chair of chemistry and pharmacy at the considerably less important school of medicine at Nancy. Legallois, Magendie and Bernard were never offered chairs of any sort at any of the medical schools of France. So all that remains of Lesch's argument that the Paris medical shool was the institutional home of French physiology is that several of the most prominent French physiologists of the period received their initial training there.

But this is hardly a surprising conclusion. Table 3.1 lists some of the most distinguished French biologists of the early part of the nineteenth century. As can be seen, with few exceptions, virtually all of them, physiologists, comparative anatomists and botanists alike, received some form of medical training during the early part of their careers. The reason for this is simple: at a time when

Table 3.1: Distinguished French biologists of the first half of the nineteenth century who attended medical school

Name	Speciality	Medical school attended
Alexandre Brongniart (1770–1847)	Paleontology	Paris*
Étienne Geoffroy Saint-Hilaire (1772–1844)	Comparative anatomy	Paris*
Constant Duméril (1774–1860)	Comparative anatomy	Paris
Henri Dutrochet (1774–1847)	Physiology	Paris
Georges Duvernoy (1777–1855)	Comparative anatomy	Strasbourg/Paris
Augustin-Pyrame de Candolle (1778–1841)	Botany	Paris
Henri Ducrotay de Blainville (1778–1850)	Comparative anatomy	Paris
Alire Raffeneau-Delille (1778–1850)	Botany	Paris
François Magendie (1783–1855)	Physiology	Paris
Antoine Desmoulins (1794–1828)	Comparative anatomy	Paris
Pierre Flourens (1794–1867)	Physiology	Montpellier
Henri Milne-Edwards (1800–85)	Comparative anatomy	Paris
Félix Pouchet (1800–72)	Comparative anatomy	Paris
Adolphe Brongniart (1801–76)	Botany	Paris
Henri Lecoq (1802–71)	Botany	Paris
Dominique-Auguste Lereboullet (1804–65)	Comparative anatomy	Strasbourg
Victor Coste (1807–73)	Embryology	Montpellier
Armand de Quatrefages (1810–92)	Comparative anatomy	Strasbourg
Auguste Duméril (1812–70)	Comparative anatomy	Paris
Claude Bernard (1813–78)	Physiology	Paris

*Brongniart and Geoffroy do not appear to have qualified in medicine although they attended courses at the medical school.
Note: Among the few biologists who did not study medicine were Georges Cuvier (1769–1832), who studied law and public administration before entering science, and his close colleague, Achille Valenciennes (1794–1865).

science was still not fully professionalised, medicine was an obvious means of entry into the wider fields of biology, just as pharmacy performed a similar function for so many of the chemists of the period. Of those biologists who did receive a medical training, not all of them did so at the Paris school; some, including the physiologist Pierre Flourens, went to the schools at Montpellier or Strasbourg.

The veterinary schools

Table 3.1 concentrates on the better-known figures of French biology in the first half of the nineteenth century, but there was a group of scientists with an interest in the fields of animal anatomy and physiology who, while of lesser fame, were no less important in the development of the biological sciences in France. These were the professors at the Écoles vétérinaires.

The veterinary schools have been almost completely ignored by historians of French science, although from their first establishment they became important centres for the propagation of a more scientific approach to agriculture. The first of the schools was founded in Lyon in 1761 and was closely followed by the creation of another at Alfort, near Paris, in 1764. These two bodies lasted until the Revolution, during which, like so many other institutions in France, they were completely reformed. It was at this point that they emerged briefly into the mainstream of the history of French science, because such distinguished figures of Parisian scientific excellence as Louis-Jean-Marie Daubenton, Félix Vicq d'Azyr and Antoine Fourcroy were given posts at the school in Alfort.[3]

But, for a variety of reasons, the schools proved unable to hold on to such figures for long. First, the salaries offered to the professors were lower than those at the great educational establishments in Paris, such as the Sorbonne, the school of medicine, the Muséum d'histoire naturelle and the Collège de France. Secondly, even Alfort suffered from being inconveniently outside Paris, while the school at Lyon was completely cut off in the provinces. And thirdly, the students at the veterinary schools, who were not required to have their *baccalauréat*, came from a lower social class than those, say, at the schools of medicine or the École polytechnique, while the professors at the Facultés des sciences, the Muséum and the Collège de France had no formal pupils to bother with at all.

Nevertheless, scientists unfortunate enough to be unable to find suitable posts elsewhere taught at Alfort, usually in cumulation with other posts held in Paris, one such figure being the chemist Pierre-Louis Dulong. Moreover, several of the professors who had received no other scientific training than that given at the veterinary schools themselves, went on to achieve scientific distinction in their own right. There was always at least one professor from the school at Alfort occupying one of the chairs in the Section d'économie rurale at the Académie des sciences, while professors at the school in Lyon often became corresponding members. The professors at Alfort also dominated the six seats given over to veterinary medicine at the Académie de médecine. The veterinary schools were therefore never so far out on the scientific periphery as their subsequent treatment by historians of French science might lead us to suppose.

In terms of experiments on living animals, the professors at these schools had an enormous advantage over everyone else. While the giants of Parisian physiology such as Magendie and Bernard were carrying out their experiments in badly-lit lofts, stairwells and rented rooms in and around the city using such animals, mainly dogs, as they could lay their hands on, the professors of veterinary medicine had free access to almost limitless supplies of animals and horses in particular. It should be remembered that in the nineteenth century the horse was still an essential weapon of war and so governments were always willing to allow scientists to carry out research that was intended to improve their effectiveness. Consequently, old and diseased horses were routinely sent from the army stables to the veterinary schools for use in experiments or anatomical demonstrations. It is therefore no surprise to find that in these schools a tradition of vivisectional experiments on animals arose independently from both the schools of medicine and the direct influence of leading Parisian physiological theorists such as Bichat and Magendie.

Indeed the school at Alfort could claim to have stolen the lead on all of them, for, as early as 1790, Pierre Flandrin (1752–96), director of the school, was systematically applying vivisection in experiments on horses designed to solve the problem of whether absorption from the gut was via the lymphatic system or the bloodstream, experiments which were later repeated by both Magendie and Dupuytren. Unfortunately, Flandrin died just when the scientific elite in Paris was beginning to take notice of his research. But veterinary physiology did not disappear with him. Of his pupils, Alexis-Casimir Dupuy (1775–1849) continued the tradition of applying vivisection to physiological problems, inviting first Guillaume Dupuytren in the 1800s and then François Magendie in the 1820s to join him at Alfort in a series of experiments carried out on horses.[4]

Neither Flandrin nor Dupuy held the chair of anatomy and physiology at Alfort. Thanks in part to the influence of leading medical academics such as François Chaussier and Pierre-Augustin Béclard, who took part in the juries that awarded this chair, this post consistently went to veterinary scientists with a predominant interest in anatomy rather than physiology. Thus when Dupuy was sent to Toulouse in 1828 to take over as director of the newly-founded veterinary school there, animal physiology at Alfort temporarily went into abeyance. Dupuy's two most gifted pupils, Jean-François Bouley

(1787–1855) and Urbain Leblanc (1796–1871) both left Alfort having served in the junior post of *répétiteur* to set themselves up in private practice in Paris.

Although they operated completely outside the academic system, both Bouley and Leblanc carried out research into various problems of animal physiology including the function of the nervous system in horses, the properties of blood and the cause of equine glanders. More importantly, they passed their interest in the scientific aspects of veterinary medicine on to their sons, Henri Bouley (1814–85) and Camille Leblanc, who were both founder members of the Société de biologie. The third vet who appears on the first published membership list of this body was Armand-Charles Goubaux (1819–90), professor of anatomy and physiology at Alfort. Like his predecessors in this post, Goubaux was mainly interested in anatomy and clinical veterinary surgery, but he, like Bouley and Leblanc, carried out a limited amount of vivisectional work.[5]

Apart from the participation of these three figures from veterinary medicine in the foundation of the Société de biologie, the 1840s also saw the emergence of two other figures who perhaps did more than anyone else to establish physiology on the curriculum at the veterinary schools. The first of these was Gabriel-Constant Colin (1825–96), who qualified at the school in Lyon before transferring to Alfort where he spent most of the rest of his career. Right from the start, Colin devoted himself single-mindedly to animal physiology, producing an enormous number of research papers and a manual of physiology. The other was Auguste Chauveau (1827–1917), whose career took the opposite course to that of Colin, since he trained at Alfort before transferring down to Lyon. Although he spent a considerable part of his life carrying out work into the germ theory of disease, Chauveau started and ended his distinguished career performing physiological research. In 1876, the chairs of anatomy and physiology at the Écoles vétérinaires were finally split into two separate posts. Colin was immediately given the chair of physiology at Alfort and Chauveau that at Lyon, while Chauveau's pupil, Saturnin Arloing (1846–1911), took the chair of anatomy at Lyon.[6]

If Colin's abilities as a scientist are open to question, those of Chauveau and Arloing are not. These latter two soon turned Lyon into a centre of physiological research to rival Paris. Chauveau's success was such that, despite his lowly origins as the son of a blacksmith and graduate of the veterinary schools, he was also given, following the intervention of Claude Bernard, the chair of médecine expérimentale at the Faculté mixte de médecine et de pharmacie in Lyon on its foundation in 1876. Later, in 1886, he received the ultimate accolade for a French biologist in being promoted to a chair at the Muséum d'histoire naturelle in Paris, thereby allowing him to take his place among the elite of French science at the Académie des sciences. Arloing remained behind in Lyon, becoming first professor of physiology at the Faculté des sciences, a post that was created specially for him, and then professor of experimental medicine at the Faculté mixte and director of the veterinary school, posts that he inherited from Chauveau. Chauveau and Arloing therefore not only played an important role, along with Colin, in definitely establishing experimental physiology at the Écoles vétérinaires, but also in its introduction into the curriculum at Facultés des sciences and the medical schools.

The important thing to realise about the emergence of experimental physiology at the veterinary schools is that it took place independently of outside influences. True: Dupuy had had contacts with both Dupuytren and Magendie; Bouley *père* served with Magendie on the Commission d'hygiène hippique; Bouley *fils*, Leblanc *fils* and Chauveau were all personal friends of Claude Bernard; and Gabriel Colin collaborated with the medical physiologist Pierre-Honoré Bérard. But it would be hard to argue that these personal relationships served in any way to alter research priorities that were already established. So from Flandrin to Arloing, the veterinary schools formed an institutional basis for the emergence of experimental physiology in France entirely separate from the Paris medical school and the triumvirate of Bichat, Magendie and Bernard.

The medical schools of Paris and Montpellier

The emphasis placed by so many of the historians of French physiology in the nineteenth century on Xavier Bichat is somewhat ironic because, although there had been a chair of anatomy and physiology at the Paris medical school from its reformation in 1794, it was never held by Bichat. His chair was in clinical medicine. Nevertheless, it would still be true to say that Bichat's physiological ideas were to a large degree representative of those of his contemporaries who did hold this chair and, indeed, of medical academics of the time in general.

The beginning of the nineteenth century was in fact a time of considerable activity in the area of medical physiology, as is shown by the appearance of several book-length works on the subject of human physiology published by various leading figures of academic medicine in the early 1800s. These include the publication in 1806 of a new edition of his classic work *Nouveaux éléments de la science de l'homme* by Pierre-Joseph Barthez (1734–1806), a professor of surgery at the medical school in Montpellier; a second edition of the *Table synoptique des propriétés caractéristiques et des principaux phénomènes de la force vitale* published in 1800 by François Chaussier (1746–1828), a surgeon who held the chair of anatomy and physiology at the Paris medical school; an important manual of medical physiology, *Nouveaux éléments de physiologie*, produced in 1801 by Anthelme-Balthasar Richerand (1779–1840), another surgeon active at the Paris medical school; and another great manual of physiology, *Principes de physiologie*, which was published in four volumes between 1800 and 1803 by still another surgeon, Charles-Louis Dumas (1765–1813), professor of anatomy and physiology at the medical school in Montpellier. Bichat's own *Recherches physiologiques sur la vie et la mort*, published shortly before his death in 1802, was therefore just one of a considerable output of such works at the time.[7]

It would be wrong to suggest that the ideas put forward in these works were merely different versions of the same thing. There were in fact frequent lively controversies between their authors as to whose version of human physiology was the correct one. More importantly, it became customary later in the nineteenth century to attribute the supposed opposition between the medical schools of Paris and Montpellier to the divergence between the ideas of Barthez and Bichat. Barthez had insisted on the essential unity of the living being and was inclined to attribute this to the action of a single agent or vital force, while Bichat emphasised more the different vital properties of the various organs of the body.[8] Still, Bichat no less than Barthez was adamant that vital phenomena were to be distinguished absolutely from those of inorganic matter.

Apart from this tendency to resort to some form of vitalism, there was another clear line of similarity in the physiology of these medical academics. They all operated within the traditions of eighteenth-century biology and medicine. As has been pointed out by Michel Foucault among others, knowledge in this so-called classical period consisted of classification, i.e. the analysis and identification of differences, followed by the application of names to the different categories thus produced. Among Parisian medical academics who clearly followed this programme of research were Xavier Bichat, who produced a classification of tissues based on direct observation and various rudimentary chemical tests; François Chaussier, who developed a convoluted anatomical system involving the application of complex names, derived from ancient Greek, to the parts of the body; and Philippe Pinel, who produced an equally 'complexed' classificatory system of diseases or *Nosographie philosophique* as he called it.

Physiology was approached by these men and their contemporaries in much the same way. Pierre Flourens argued that Bichat lifted his physiological theories straight from the great natural historian, Georges Buffon, but possibly a more important influence was Théophile de Bordeu (1722–76). In the hands of men such as Buffon, Bordeu and, outside France, Albrecht von Haller, physiology was reduced to the analysis of the properties of the components of the living body. Following on from the work of these men, Barthez, Chaussier, Richerand, Dumas and Bichat all gave the world subtly different, intricately argued classifications of the vital properties of irritability, sensibility and contractility.[9]

But, over and above these more philosophical considerations, one thing above all determined the approach to the problems of physiology adopted by these men and this was the fact that they were medical men first and scientists only secondarily. This meant that they confined their outlook almost exclusively to the human organism and were therefore forced to draw their conclusions solely from anatomical and clinical observations. Of the figures mentioned above, only Bichat attempted to use vivisectional experiments on animals in any sort of systematic manner and, as has been pointed out by William Albury, this reliance on vivisection was only limited. Bichat's experiments consisted of injuring a specific organ in an animal and then observing the process of death. From this he hoped to support deductions he had already made from anatomical and clinical observation on his human patients. There was thus a distinct hierarchy of evidence in Bichat's physiology. At the top stood anatomical observations made on normal tissue, followed by similar observation of pathological tissue; vivisection was confined to his studies of death and came below the other two forms of evidence.[10]

Bichat died at the very early age of thirty-one, just after the turn of the century, but already he had attracted a considerable following at the medical school in Paris. One of those who adopted his ideas was Pierre-Hubert Nysten (1771–1818), a Belgian active in the Paris medical community. More than anyone else, Nysten kept alive Bichat's research programme in physiology and continued to perform vivisectional experiments to examine the process of dying in order to draw physiological conclusions.[11] But Nysten too died relatively young. The influence of Chaussier and Richerand at the Paris medical school was to be longer lasting. Chaussier held onto his position there until 1822 when the school was closed down by the government following a series of student disturbances. Unlike the atheist Chaussier, Richerand was re-appointed to his chair when the school was reformed several months later, and continued to be a major influence on the instruction given for many years afterwards.

One of the effects of the reformation of the Paris medical school in 1822 was to increase significantly the number of chairs. Among the new posts created was a separate chair of physiology. Previously, there had only been a joint chair of anatomy and physiology, a situation which only encouraged the tendency of Chaussier and others to reduce physiology to the level of deductions drawn from anatomy. But it was to take more than the inauguration of a new chair to alter the approach to physiology taken by medical academics.

In 1831, the chair of physiology fell vacant and the two leading applicants for the post were Pierre-Nicolas Gerdy (1797–1856) and Pierre-Honoré Bérard (1797–1858). Gerdy had already held the post of *prosecteur* in anatomy at the medical school and, at the age of nineteen, been authorised to give a course in anatomy and physiology at the Charité, one of the major hospitals of Paris attached to the medical school. This course had been a brilliant success and drawn the attention of several of the leading figures of the medical faculty including Dupuytren. But, despite this, Gerdy was not to be honoured with the chair of physiology; he had to wait another two years for his professorship, which was in the subject of *pathologie externe*. The chair of physiology went instead to Bérard.

The *curricula vitarum* of Gerdy and Bérard clearly illustrate the situation of physiology in the French medical schools in the first half of the nineteenth century. In the first place, both men were surgeons and not scientists as such. Secondly, despite Lesch's contention that the use of vivisection in physiology arose out of the teaching of clinical surgery at the Paris medical school, Gerdy was a resolute opponent of its use. For his application, in 1824, for the position of *agrégé* in anatomy and physiology at the Paris medical school, he had produced a thesis which attempted to demonstrate that vivisectional experiments on animals were of no significance whatsoever for the purposes of medical physiology.[12] The fact that this application had been successful would strongly imply that some at least of the professors at the school agreed with his point of view.

Unlike his rival Gerdy, Bérard did not openly oppose vivisection;

indeed, late in his life, he came round to its use in physiological research carried out in collaboration with the veterinary scientist, Gabriel Colin. But during the early part of his career he ignored it completely and, like his predecessors, drew his conclusions entirely from anatomical and clinical observations. This was only natural, given his training. He had been a pupil of Richerand and Pierre-Augustin Béclard (1785–1825), another surgeon who had held the chair of anatomy and physiology at the Paris medical school and who, although he had collaborated with Legallois in research into the mechanism of vomiting, later concentrated almost exclusively on anatomy and histology, seeing himself as continuing the work in these fields inaugurated by Bichat. One of the first things that Bérard did as professor of physiology was to edit another edition, the tenth, of Richerand's great manual of physiology.[13]

Bérard held on to the chair of physiology until his death in 1858, although he gave up active teaching following a stroke in 1853. Thus physiology at the Paris school of medicine remained right up until the middle of the century in the hands of medical practitioners, usually surgeons, who resisted the temptation to use animal vivisection to draw general conclusions in human physiology.

The same was true, only more so, at the medical school of Montpellier. On the death of Charles-Louis Dumas in 1813, the chair of anatomy and physiology was passed on to another surgeon, Jacques Lordat (1773–1862). When this chair was divided in 1824, Lordat, who was at this time also dean of the school, chose to retain the subject of physiology under his control and continued to dominate physiological teaching at Montpellier until his retirement in 1860. Lordat had been a close friend of and literary executor to Pierre-Joseph Barthez and spent the entire length of his exceptionally long academic career attempting to keep Barthez's physiological doctrines — or, rather, his own version of them — alive. Although fairly advanced in their own time, Barthez's ideas belonged firmly to the eighteenth century. Like Bordeu before him and Bichat after him, he had espoused apparently positivistic views on the nature of science, but still left room in his physiology for the concept of a vital force. It was this more than anything else in his work that Lordat seized on and, since Barthez had distinguished the vital force from the human soul, Lordat called this version of human physiology *double dynamisme*.

Lordat's claim to be the rightful heir to Barthez and his appointment as dean of the school during the Bourbon Restoration put him in a position to establish double dynamism as more or less the official doctrine of Montpellier medical school. Throughout the first half of the nineteenth century, he and his fellow professors advocated this doctrine with considerable energy. The tendency always in their arguments was to insist on the right-thinking spiritualist basis of this theory and to raise it up in opposition to what they perceived as the fundamentally materialist nature of the teaching given at the Paris school, which they were inclined to attribute to the bad influence of Xavier Bichat.

There was almost certainly a political undercurrent here. Lordat and the academic community in Montpellier generally seem to have been conservative. Their open hostility towards the medical academics of Paris may therefore have arisen from the tendency among the reactionary bourgeoisie on the south coast to blame Paris and its advanced ideas for the Revolution and all subsequent political upheavals. Bichat was a natural target for such feelings as he was clearly a man of the Revolution who had risen to prominence as a direct result of it. No doubt this highly vocal campaign, conducted in medical journals and elsewhere, was successful in attracting the children of more conservative parents away from the Paris medical school and down to Montpellier, thereby reinforcing the division between the two schools.[14]

But right-thinking conservative and good Catholic though he was, when Lordat's doctrine finally came under systematic attack, it was not from the materialists of Paris that the assault came but, of all places, from the Catholic Church. The reason for this lies deep within the history of Catholic theology. Towards the middle of the nineteenth century and developing rapidly from then, leading Catholic theologians in Rome and elsewhere were attempting to reframe and unify their doctrine. This was presumably in an attempt to set up a consistent philosophy, covering all areas of human knowledge, with which to fight off the rise of secularism, caused in part by the enormous advances that were being made in the natural sciences. As the basis of their ideas, they turned to the works of Thomas Aquinas, and the neo-Thomism they produced was to become a major force for renewal in Catholic thought throughout the second half of the nineteenth century.[15] One of the first indications of the emergence of these new ideas, in France at least, was a somewhat arcane argument that developed in the 1850s between the Montpellier medical school and one of the leading advocates of the new theology, Gioacchina Ventura de Raulica.

The problem was that neo-Thomist animism implied that there was only one metaphysical entity underlying both the phenomena of life and the intellectual phenomena of the mind. This was in direct contradiction with the doctrine of double dynamism. Thus when Ventura put his ideas forward in a well-publicised lecture given in Paris, Lordat felt obliged to rush into print to defend his doctrine using arguments drawn from his medical observations and quotations from Holy authorities of the past. He soon received support from the Bishop of Montpellier; from some of his fellow professors at Montpellier, who produced a new French translation of the works of the great eighteenth-century animist, Georg-Ernst Stahl; and from some of his ex-pupils at the medical school. But all this was to no avail; in 1860, Lordat lost his battles on all fronts. He lost his debate with the neo-Thomists when the Pope himself came down firmly on their side in a dogmatic statement issued from Rome. But worse still, Lordat could only watch helplessly when, following his retirement, the government in an unusual step chose as his replacement in the chair of physiology an *agrégé* from the hated medical school of Paris.[16]

Possibly the best way to consider the situation of physiology in the medical schools of France during the first half of the nineteenth century is to look at it within the context of the teaching at these schools as a whole. Historians of academic medicine in France have rightly dwelt on the tradition of clinical training that was established in the three great schools of medicine following their reorganisation during the Revolution.[17] The importance of this emphasis on clinical instruction cannot be over-estimated. Its influence was felt not only by the students but also by the professors themselves. The great stars (and stars is the right word, since there was a strong element of theatricality in the lectures of leading French academics of the period) of the Faculté de médecine in Paris were all those who gave clinical courses. Such was the force of the clinical prerogative that supplementary sciences such as anatomy and physiology became subordinated to it. Chairs in these subjects consistently went to surgeons who would have been happier in one of the major clinical posts. The result was inevitable. These men turned their lectures into an adjunct of the clinical courses, drawing their ideas almost exclusively from their experiences in the dissecting room and the hospital.

The consequence of this was that medical physiology became almost entirely divorced from animal physiology and from science in general. The situation in Montpellier was perhaps extreme, where, in the hands of Lordat, physiological research came to consist of the production of critical editions of the works of major eighteenth-century medical theorists, the issuing of pamphlets of complex theological exegesis and the intervention of bishops. But the situation in Paris was not so very different. Gerdy was by no means a lone voice at the Académie de médecine in denying that a science of life based on vivisection was possible, given the innate uncertainty of vital phenomena. Indeed, so complete was the isolation of medical physiology from contemporary biology that even the so-called advanced thinkers of academic medicine showed an almost complete ignorance of the activities of the experimental physiologists. François Broussais (1772–1838) is a case in point. During his time as professor of pathologie et thérapeutique générales at the Paris school of medicine from 1824 until his death, he attracted a considerable following among the medical students of the capital, who were drawn to him largely on account of his open advocacy of materialist ideas. But for all his radicalism, his great system of pathology bore a much closer resemblance to the ideas of the eighteenth-century Scottish physician, John Brown, than it did to contemporary French experimental physiology.[18]

Legallois, Magendie and Flourens, and the intervention of the Académie des sciences

Experimental physiology had therefore to grow up beneath the shadow of the clinical prerogative in acacemic medicine and against the open hostility of certain leading surgeons. Consequently, in order to seek out the origins of the discipline, one must divert one's attention away from the medical schools and towards other institutions. The role of the veterinary schools has already been discussed. Of equal importance were the careers of two Parisian physicians, Julien Legallois and François Magendie, and a biologist, Pierre Flourens.

Of these, Magendie is the most important to the historian, because, unlike the other two, he made a very early attempt to synthesise his ideas in the form of a paper entitled 'Quelques idées générales sur les phénomènes particuliers aux corps vivans'. This so-called manifesto of the new physiology is interesting in a number of ways: first because it appeared in the journal of the Société médicale d'émulation, which was a publication largely given over at that time to the propagation of the ideas of Bichat; secondly, because it did not contain any references to the use of vivisection; and thirdly, because its author made no attempt to overturn the doctrine of vitalism, but concentrated his criticism on the concept of vital properties. In fact, Magendie only began the systematic use of vivisection in the years immediately after the publication of this paper, following on the lead already provided by Flandrin, Dupuy, Legallois and Dupuytren, and, like Flourens, Bernard and Longet after him, never openly denounced the doctrine of vitalism unless it was used to question the meaningfulness of the results of experiments carried out on live animals.

Quite possibly, at this early stage when he still hoped to pursue a career in academic medicine at the Paris medical school, Magendie saw himself as making a contribution to the debates that were taking place within medical physiology and his paper was less a statement of intent than a critical review. Nevertheless, it showed remarkable self-confidence in such a young man to publish an article which criticised by name the work of all the established figures of French medical physiology, including Bichat, Barthez, Chaussier, Richerand and Dumas.[19] But this iconoclasm appears much less audacious if one considers that one year prior to the appearance of Magendie's article, Georges Cuvier, who was a figure of no little influence in scientific circles in Paris, had already expressed very similar reservations over the scientific status of the vital properties put forward by Bichat and others. Cuvier's concern was that the postulation of these properties was not the result of proper scientific observation.[20]

The intervention of Cuvier at this point puts a new perspective on the emergence of experimental physiology in France. The large number of publications concerning human physiology produced by leading medical academics in the first decade of the nineteenth century has already been mentioned. But physiology was not an area that affected medicine alone. Biologists, such as Cuvier himself, and even chemists and physicists could also claim an interest in the subject. After all, had not Antoine Lavoisier and his co-worker, Pierre Laplace, set the crucial precedent of chemical research into the phenomenon of animal heat, research which, of course, involved the use of experiments on live animals?

At the turn of the nineteenth century, French science was entering a critical stage in its development. Following on from the advances made during the Revolution and before, academic science was becoming fully professionalised and, under the guidance of figures such as Cuvier and Laplace, this step was being taken on the basis of the establishment of the research ideal and the experimental imperative. Physiology was therefore brought to the attention of these figures at an important moment and, if the attitude adopted by Cuvier is anything to go by, the state of the science seems to have given them some cause for concern. The urgency of the situation can only have been heightened by the fact that there was no section at the Académie des sciences given over to the subject, presenting the leaders of science in Paris with the problem of an area of science that might slip from their control.[21] As if to compensate for this, when, in 1818, Pierre Laplace was consulted in his capacity as secrétaire perpétuel of the Académie by a rich benefactor, the Baron de Montyon, about the donation of money for a new prize to be awarded by the Académie, he thought not of his own area of research, but suggested that the prize should be awarded for a contribution to research into what he called *physiologie expérimentale*.[22]

The title chosen by Laplace for this new prize was no accident. The word *physiologie* could take on a variety of interpretations during the first half of the nineteenth century. It could mean the exclusively human physiology of the medical academics; it could mean the study of the physiology of the higher animals using vivisection, as practised by Legallois, Magendie and Flourens; it could mean the use of the methods of comparative anatomy applied across the whole animal kingdom in order to uncover the functions of the various parts of the organism; it could mean the physiologie générale of Henri Dutrochet (1776–1847), i.e. the application of the scientific methods of observation and experiment to both plant and animal systems; or it could mean the chimie physiologique of various chemists, such as Pierre-Louis Dulong, Jean-Baptiste Dumas and Anselme Payen. The term physiologie expérimentale could be applied to all of these with one exception, that of medical physiology. Thus, in the years following its establishment, the prix Montyon de physiologie expérimentale was awarded to vivisectors, natural historians, plant physiologists and chemists, but never to any of the medical physiologists.

Following on as it did from Cuvier's direct criticism, in the name of the scientific method, of the direction taken by medical physiology, the foundation by Laplace of the prix Montyon was a clear attempt by the established elite of Parisian science to alter the alignment of French physiology. Leading French scientists, particularly those involved in the physical sciences such as Laplace, were trying to establish scientific practice on a strict programme of experimentation. It was therefore natural that they, in conjunction with prominent biologists such as Cuvier, should attempt to extend this to the biological sciences. Possibly because they themselves lacked the proper knowledge or technical skills to carry out their own research in the area of experimental physiology, what they did was effectively to issue a challenge to the younger generation of scientists to come up with the ideas.

This was no empty intellectual challenge. Given the powers of patronage that resulted from membership of the Académie des sciences, Laplace and Cuvier were in a position to offer very real incentives for young men aspiring to enter into the elite of French science to conform to their view of proper scientific practice. By no means the least of these incentives was the existence of the developing prize system of the Académie. In the absence of proper government funding for scientific research, the availability of cash prizes was an important influence over the areas of research entered into by scientists who had still not established themselves.[23] Neither Flourens nor Magendie had academic posts at the time of the foundation of the prix Montyon and so the prospect of this award must have given them considerable encouragement. It may even be that Laplace had one or both of them in mind when he first proposed the prize.[24]

Magendie had started his academic career well enough. In 1807, before he had qualified as a doctor, he was employed as an assistant in anatomy in the Paris medical school and was giving a course in physiology. By 1811, he had his full medical qualification and was a demonstrator in anatomy, teaching surgery as well as physiology. However, he soon fell out with the powerful professor of anatomy and physiology, François Chaussier, and resigned from his post at the Faculté de médecine in 1813. Forced to find the means to support himself, he began a career as a physician and continued to practise medicine for the remainder of his life. In addition, he published books aimed at the large market of medical students and doctors. Included in his publications at this time was a manual of physiology, the first edition of which appeared in 1816, and a pioneering work on the preparation and use of purified drugs, which also went into several editions. But most importantly so far as the history of French physiology is concerned, he ran a series of private courses in experimental physiology for those medical students and others who were prepared to pay for the privilege of observing demonstrations of his vivisectional experiments.[25] It was presumably in his private laboratory that he carried out the bulk of his research.

Unlike Magendie, Flourens made no attempt to start a career in medical practice or academic medicine. On the contrary, he seems to have had his sights firmly set on a career in science from a very early stage. On receipt of his degree from the Montpellier medical school in 1814, he went straight to Paris carrying with him a letter of introduction addressed to Georges Cuvier. Once in the capital, however, his career went along very similar lines to that of Magendie. He too taught at the Athénée de Paris, a private teaching establishment on the fringe of the academic circuit, and accepted various commissions to produce books and articles for dictionaries. It is not clear where he carried out his experimental work: possibly he had a private laboratory or alternatively he may have been able to find research facilities at the Muséum d'histoire naturelle through his patron Cuvier.[26]

But if neither Magendie nor Flourens could penetrate into the academic system that was not yet ready to accommodate their form of experimental physiology, they did manage to attract the attention of the members of the Académie des sciences. Magendie in fact never won a prix Montyon, but this was for a very good reason. The first of these prizes was awarded in 1821 and was shared by Henri Dutrochet and William Edwards, who was at that time working in Magendie's laboratory; Magendie himself received an honourable mention. Later that same year, Magendie was elected to the Académie, an event which disqualified him from further entry for the prize and, more importantly, placed him on the committee responsible for its award. Flourens followed him into the Académie in 1828, by which time he had won the prize on two separate occasions. Legallois died before the instauration of the prize and before he was well enough established to gain election to the Académie, but he too had received considerable encouragement from members of the Académie, including both Laplace and Cuvier.[27]

But in spite of this support and encouragement coming from the Académie des sciences, experimental physiology was still in a precarious position in 1830. The lack of career prospects in the subject meant that researchers were being attracted away towards other areas of science and medicine that offered better opportunities. Dupuytren had been exceptional among the surgeons at the medical school of Paris in that he showed an early interest in vivisection and had started a programme of physiological research of a type very similar to that later carried out by Magendie. However, following his appointment in 1812 to the chair of surgery at the medical school, he abandoned physiology altogether in order to concentrate on his clinical teaching.

Jean-Baptiste Dumas (1800–84) arrived in Paris in 1821. As a student in Geneva, he had already attracted a considerable amount of attention with his researches in both chemistry and vivisectional physiology. It was therefore touch and go at this early stage whether he pursued a career as a chemist or a physiologist. But, once in Paris, the opportunities for advancement presented themselves only in the field of chemistry and this was the direction his career took. William Edwards (1772–1842), Magendie's early pupil who shared the first prix Montyon awarded in 1821, eventually gave up physiology in favour of another research field that occupied an equally precarious position on the periphery of the academic system in France, that of ethnology. Another of Magendie's early pupils, Gabriel Andral (1797–1876), went on, like Dupuytren, to take up a clinical post at the Faculté de médecine and, although he continued to carry out research of direct medical interest, never went back to vivisectional work. Edwards's brother, Henri Milne-Edwards (1800–85), also carried out a small amount of vivisectional work in the 1820s. But he too quickly gave this up in favour of the methods of comparative anatomy, this presumably in an attempt to gain a post at the Muséum d'histoire naturelle, which was at the time the centre of biological research in France and was dominated by natural historians trained in comparative anatomy.

Given the complete dominance of the chairs of physiology at the medical schools by surgeons who were much more interested in problems of anatomy and clinical medicine and given also the power that these men had over the appointments to the chairs of anatomy and physiology at the Écoles vétérinaires, experimental physiology in the 1820s gave every appearance of being a career dead-end. The subject badly needed a chair of its own to stand any chance of becoming a research discipline in its own right and prevent the leakage of talent to other fields.

The story of Magendie's eventual success in obtaining an academic post reveals clearly from where the support came for his approach to physiology. It also shows the importance of factors from outside science in the insertion of new ideas into the academic curriculum. The chair of medicine at the Collège de France had always been held by a distinguished medical practitioner of the time. In the two previous centuries, it had usually gone to one of the King's own medical advisers. This tradition lasted into the nineteenth century, although the system was by this time for the Académie des sciences to recommend to the monarch the candidate they felt most deserving of the honour. Following the death of Jean-Noel Hallé in 1822, the chair became vacant for the second time during the Bourbon Restoration. At this time Magendie had only recently been elected to the medical section of the Académie and so, following a vote, the Académie had no hesitation in putting him at the top of their list of recommended candidates above Réné Laennec. Louis XVIII however had other ideas, and Laennec was given the chair. The reason for this is not hard to find: Laennec was a known supporter of the monarchy, whereas Magendie was a liberal.

Four years later, Laennec was dead and the Académie again took the opportunity to put forward Magendie at the head of their list, this time voting by fifty-five votes to five in his favour over the distinguished surgeon Joseph Récamier. This time the King hesitated. Abbé Fraysinnous, who at the time had almost complete authority over the education system and was an uncompromising defender of the Catholic Church, interviewed Magendie. It is not known what was said during the course of this interview, but it was Récamier who was given the chair. Like Laennec, Récamier was a Royalist and a member of the King's medical staff. Fraysinnous was under considerable pressure from the liberal party at this time and the liberal press turned Magendie's treatment into something of a *cause célèbre*, but to no avail. Then finally political events came down on Magendie's side. On the collapse of the Bourbon Restoration in 1830 and its replacement by the house of Orléans, Récamier refused to serve under the new dynasty and resigned from his chair. Magendie, now supported by both the Académie des sciences and the liberal party, had an irresistible claim to the chair.[28]

Like all the previous incumbents of his chair, including Laennec and Récamier, Magendie continued to practise medicine, but from then on he had a position of some authority from which to expound his views and demonstrate his discoveries. The professors at the Collège had no formal students and were not obliged to stick to any officially laid down curriculum for their public lectures. Magendie was therefore free to alter slightly the title of his chair, calling it the chair of médecine expérimentale. This enabled him to justify his almost exclusive concentration on experimental physiology in all but the very first course that he gave.

At the time that Magendie entered the Collège de France as full professor, Flourens was already meeting with some success at the same institution. Thanks to his contacts with Cuvier, he was giving a course of natural history there. But it was at the equally distinguished Muséum d'histoire naturelle that he eventually succeeded in gaining a permanent post. Following the death of Antoine Portal in 1832, he was immediately nominated to the chair of anatomie humaine, although, after the death of his close friend

Frédéric Cuvier in 1837, he later transferred to the more suitably named chair of physiologie comparée.

Through Magendie and Flourens, experimental physiology had succeeded in penetrating not only the Académie des sciences but also two of the most prestigious academic institutions in France. As has been pointed out by several historians of the period, government support for science was especially poor during the Bourbon Restoration and July Monarchy. Consequently, it was inevitable that the arrival of these two men and their science of experimental physiology was at the expense of another area of science. In both cases, it was medical science that suffered and, as it turned out, the loss was to be permanent.

Magendie had taken over a course normally reserved exclusively for the presentation of purely medical ideas and had radically altered it to enable him to give public demonstrations of vivisectional experiments. The chair taken over by Flourens was similar. It did not have quite the history of the chair of medicine at the Collège de France, but the previous incumbent, Portal, had been a medical anatomist who had taught in the medical schools of Paris before being awarded a chair at the Muséum or Jardin du Roi as it was then known. Flourens's transfer to the chair of physiologie comparée in 1838 did not bring about the reversion of this chair to medical anatomy; the comparative anatomists, who were the dominant force at the Muséum, gave the chair a new name, that of anthropology, thereby enabling them to appoint one of their own kind to this post. It therefore appears that the scientists at the Académie des sciences and the Muséum saw medicine as expendable in their attempt to place men with their own attitude as to the importance of experimental research in biology in posts at the great institutions of academic science in Paris.

The role of Claude Bernard

The establishment of Magendie and Flourens in chairs at the Collège de France and Muséum was by no means the final step in the professionalisation of experimental physiology in France. This was left to the generation that followed. The outstanding member of this generation was unquestionably Magendie's last and most famous pupil, Claude Bernard. Bernard's early career showed pronounced similarities to those of Magendie and Flourens. Like them he trained in medicine, but soon became more interested in a career in science.

His first attempts in this direction were singularly unsuccessful. He had never been a particularly brilliant student and in 1844 he lost out in the competition for the *agrégation* in anatomy and physiology at the Paris medical school to Jules Béclard. Shortly after this, following the example of Magendie, Achille Longet and a character by the name of Martin-Magron (1810–71), he tried to set up his own private teaching laboratory of physiology, but this enterprise soon collapsed when he and his partner, Charles Lasègue, found that the fees they were collecting were barely covering the cost of the animals on which they carried out their experimental demonstrations.

Thus excluded from a career in academic medicine, Bernard was forced, like Magendie and Flourens before him, to rely on the good-will of the community of scientists in Paris to help him get established. Pride of place must, of course, go to Magendie, who employed Bernard first as *préparateur* and then *suppléant* attached to his chair at the Collège de France. But equally important were the chemist, Jules Pelouze, and the medical scientist, Pierre Rayer. Pelouze provided Bernard with space in his private teaching laboratory in which to carry out experiments into the process of sugar metabolism. Rayer meanwhile helped Bernard find commissions for the production of a surgical textbook and invited him to take part in the formation of the Société de biologie.

With three such influential patrons, Bernard's success at the Académie des sciences was assured. Between 1845 and 1853, he won the prix Montyon on no less than four separate occasions. This by itself represented a considerable source of income. The quality of his work undoubtedly fully merited this unprecedented run of success, but it cannot have hindered his chances that Magendie chaired the committee that awarded the prize and that, besides Flourens, Milne-Edwards and others, Pelouze and Rayer also often served on the committee. Bernard's tenure on the prix Montyon ended in 1854 with his election as full member of the Académie. That same year, Rayer, who as personal physician to the Emperor possessed considerable influence over government policy towards the medical sciences, secured for Bernard a chair at the Sorbonne. This new chair, which replaced one that had formerly been given over to the subject of botany, received the title of physiologie générale and was the first such chair established at any of the French Facultés des sciences. Magendie died one year later and Bernard took over the chair of médecine expérimentale at the Collège de France. As the possessor of two chairs and member of the Académie des sciences, Bernard had finally arrived at the very top of the scientific tree in France.[29]

Recently, it has become the custom to depict Bernard as an archetypal discipline builder.[30] However, the proposition that Bernard 'built' the discipline of physiology in France is far from proved. The quite exceptional success of his research career and the way in which he rose to a position of prominence in the scientific community of Paris has made it all too easy to exaggerate his role in the development of experimental physiology. If one were to follow the arguments presented in two recent papers by Gross and Albury, it was the generation of Legallois, Magendie and Flourens who gave French physiology its conceptual base.[31] They redefined the object of the science, turning it away from the analysis of vital properties towards the experimental determination of the mechanism of the vital functions; they, along with Flandrin, Dupuy and Dupuytren, established vivisection as the means to achieve this; and they provided their successors with paradigms or model experiments in the form of their classic work into the functions of the nervous system. Following this argument to its logical conclusion, Bernard becomes less of an innovator and more a brilliant pupil of Magendie. He added little to the basic methodology of experimental physiology. His genius was to enlist the aid of the advances made in chemistry and microscopical histology in order to refine and adapt techniques already used by others, thereby enabling him to produce some of the most important discoveries made in physiology in the nineteenth century.

Moreover, Bernard, like Magendie, spent his entire career outside the medical schools. His influence on the eventual establishment of scientific physiology within the three great schools of French medicine was therefore at most only peripheral. This achievement belonged to another group of men including Achille Longet, Jules Béclard (1818–87), Alfred Vulpian (1826–87) and Charles-Édouard Brown-Séquard (1817–94) in Paris, Charles Rouget (1824–1904) in Montpellier, and Émile Küss (1815–71) and Henri Beaunis (1830–1921) in Strasbourg and Nancy.

Of these Longet was perhaps the most important, if only because he was the first advocate of vivisectional animal physiology to take over a chair of physiology at one of the medical schools. Having given a popular semi-official course of experimental physiology at the École pratique attached to the Faculté de médecine in Paris throughout the 1840s, he eventually took over as *chargé du cours* in the chair of physiology in 1853, following Bérard's promotion to inspecteur général de l'enseignement de la médecine. He became professeur titulaire a year after Bérard's death in 1858. Meanwhile, Béclard, another experimentalist, had been appointed *agrégé* in anatomy and physiology at the same school in 1844, and Vulpian and Brown-Séquard were learning the techniques of vivisection in the laboratories of Flourens and Martin-Magron respectively. Vulpian and Brown-Séquard went on to take up posts at the Faculté de médecine in the 1860s and Béclard took over the chair of physiology in 1871.[32]

All these men entered successful careers in physiology independently of both Bernard and his master, Magendie. The tendency of Schiller, Lesch and others to concentrate on these latter two figures has therefore considerably distorted our picture of the emergence of physiology in France, allowing subsequent commentators to imply that French physiology was constructed single-handedly by Bernard. Similarly, the role of Magendie and Bernard in the development of the tradition of vivisection in the veterinary schools was even less significant. As has been discussed above, experimental physiology emerged within these schools independently of activities elsewhere and according to its own precedents. Even within the community of scientists in Paris, men such as Étienne-Jules Marey (1830–1904) and Louis-Émile Javal (1839–1907) entered into careers in physiology and established their own research schools without being directly influenced by Bernard or his master, although in the case of Marey, Bernard played no small role in his appointment to a chair at the Collège de France.

Nevertheless, Bernard's role in the formation of the academic discipline of experimental physiology in France is important to historians of science in at least one respect. Following the production of his early paper 'Quelques idées générales sur les phénomènes particuliers aux corps vivans', neither Magendie nor his contemporaries made any further attempt to synthesise their ideas as to the nature of the science of physiology. Bernard, on the other hand, was always highly attuned to the importance of defining fully the exact position occupied by physiology within the context of science as a whole. Yet it took the accident of a prolonged period of illness in the early 1860s to drag him away from the workbench long enough to produce a book-length statement of his ideas. This book, the *Introduction à l'étude de la médecine expérimentale*, like his subsequent work, *Rapport sur les progrès et la marche de la physiologie générale en France* and the series of articles that he published in the leading bourgeois review of the day, the *Revue des deux mondes*, can be read as an extended argument on behalf of the status of physiology as an independent academic research discipline in its own right.[33]

Bernard was a writer of enviable clarity and consistently managed to distil his propositions down to simple, easily memorable formulae. The presentation of his case for the independence of physiology is one such example. On the one hand, so the argument ran, there were the experimental sciences, represented at the top by physics and chemistry, and on the other, there were the life sciences. The latter traditionally depended on observation rather than experiment from which to draw conclusions, albeit that such observation was comparative thereby allowing genuinely scientific conclusions to be reached. Physiology was placed at the juncture between these two broad categories of science. It belonged to the first in that it was experimental and not merely observational, and it belonged to the second in that it had as its object the phenomena of life. The all-important aspect that gave physiology this unique status was that it was based on the practice of vivisection, which was the only way, so far as Bernard was concerned, for the biological sciences to become experimental.[34]

Bernard's arguments might not have been so contentious had he not then gone on to say that only the experimental sciences could give man power over natural phenomena, while the observational sciences merely allowed the prediction of their course. This attempt to raise the status of physiology to the level of a fully developed science alongside physics and chemistry, at the expense of the other biological sciences, provoked two leading natural historians, Victor Coste and Henri de Lacaze-Duthiers, to publish replies defending the position of zoology as a science. Coste's arguments in particular were highly persuasive. He pointed out that his own observational work on the life-cycle of fish had been of considerable use to the fishery industries in France and left the reader to draw his own conclusions about the actual advances in medicine produced by the use of vivisection.[35]

But contentious or not, the drift of Bernard's argument was quite clear. In bringing the speculations of previous generations of physiologists under some form of experimental control, vivisection had, according to Bernard, raised the subject to the level of a true science. It is therefore but one small step from Cuvier's intervention in the debates over contemporary physiology in the 1800s and 1810s to Bernard's great campaign on behalf of physiology as an independent scientific discipline based on experimentation. Cuvier had questioned the scientific status of the vital properties put forward by medical theorists such as Bichat on the grounds that they were not the result of proper scientific observation. Legallois, Magendie and Flourens had all resorted to vivisection in an attempt to answer these criticisms and, in doing so, had received considerable support and encouragement from Cuvier and other members of the Académie des sciences. Now some fifty or so years later Bernard was trying to give their decision some form of intellectual justification.

In the meantime, experimentation had been raised almost to the level of a fetish among the elite of French scientists at the Académie des sciences. Leading French biologists, such as Bernard himself and Charles Robin, were resistant to the Darwinian theory of evolution and showed a disinclination to accept the cell theory in its totality; leading French chemists, such as Bernard's close friends Marcellin Berthelot and Henri Sainte-Claire Deville, were unwilling to adopt the atomic theory; and another of Bernard's close friends, the physicist Victor Regnault, devoted a large part of his research career to the collection of data on heat exchange without ever showing the desire to step back and make out the laws of thermodynamics.[36] In each case, these giants of French science resisted these ideas because they saw them as the result of speculation unsupported by proper experimental evidence. The emergence of experimental physiology based on vivisection was therefore an integral part of a general trend in French science away from anything that could be interpreted as speculation towards a science based rigidly, too rigidly perhaps, on laboratory work and experiment.

Conclusion

The fact that some of the greatest French physiologists of the nineteenth century studied at the Paris medical school should not necessarily be taken as proof that this institution played a central role in the emergence of experimental physiology in France. The lack of a fully developed career structure in academic scientific research meant that almost all of the most distinguished French biologists of the period passed through one or other of the three great medical schools before going on to specialise in one of the many areas of biological research.

Moreover, of all the different areas of biological research, experimental physiology was possibly the least dependent on the medical schools, because the veterinary schools were also producing scientifically trained individuals interested in research in this speciality.

This was particularly so right at the beginning of the century, when, through the work of Pierre Flandrin and Alexis-Casimir Dupuy, veterinary scientists were among the pioneers of experimental physiology, and again in the middle of the century, when Auguste Chauveau and his pupil Saturnin Arloing emerged as research physiologists of the highest calibre.

The medical schools were in fact a late conversion to the cause of experimental physiology. Throughout the first half of the century, physiological teaching at these schools was in the hands of surgeons and other clinicians who preferred an approach to physiology based on anatomical and clinical observations on human patients to one founded on animal experiments. This situation did not change until the 1840s, when Achille Longet was allowed to run a semi-official course of experimental physiology at the Paris medical school and Jules Béclard was appointed *agrégé* in anatomy and physiology at the same institution. Even then, it was not until 1859 that Longet was made full professor and experimental physiology became definitively established at the Paris medical school.

In its early stages, therefore, experimental physiology had to grow up entirely separately from the medical schools. The first wave of vivisectors included the veterinary scientist, Pierre Flandrin, and the independent physician, Julien Legallois. These were closely followed by Guillaume Dupuytren, Alexis-Casimir Dupuy, François Magendie and Pierre Flourens. With the exception of Dupuytren, none of these men remained attached to a medical school long after their initial training and the support for their activities came from scientists rather than medical academics. The institution at the centre of this support was the Académie des sciences. It is this body, and not the Paris school of medicine, that must be seen as the institution responsible for the initial establishment of experimental physiology in France.

Among the scientists who were most active in encouraging the experimental physiologists were Georges Cuvier and Pierre Laplace. It was Cuvier who first expressed dissatisfaction with the ideas put forward by medical physiologists and called for a more scientific approach to the subject. Responding to this call, Legallois, Magendie and Flourens significantly altered the direction of physiological research in France. In their hands, physiology became the determination of the mechanism of the functions of the organism by means of experiments on live animals, instead of the analysis of the so-called vital properties favoured by Xavier Bichat and other medical physiologists. It was left to Magendie's pupil Claude Bernard to bring this new approach to full fruition. Using refinements of techniques that he had learnt directly from his master, Bernard made four of the most important discoveries attributed to physiologists in the nineteenth century and established himself as the most distinguished French man of science of his day.

If his great research achievement was little more than the culmination of a research programme already initiated by Flandrin, Magendie and others, then similarly Bernard's propositions on the nature of science were a synthesis of the ideas pervading the elite of Parisian science at the time. The general idea was that the highest form of science was that which was based directly on experiment. Bernard's main contribution to the debate was to insist that, in adopting the practice of vivisection, physiologists had caused their discipline to make the all-important transition to the level of full experimental status.

This anxiety to demonstrate the uncompromisingly experimental nature of his chosen speciality underlines clearly the impulse behind the use of vivisection by French physiologists. It did not arise out of medicine and the search for the explanation of disease, although Magendie and Bernard in particular always used this as a justification for their work. On the contrary, vivisection had its origins deep within science. The adoption of the experimental prerogative by French scientists around the turn of the nineteenth century made it inevitable that physiologists such as Magendie and Flourens, and later Bernard, would attempt to found their science on experiments on living animals and, in doing so, receive the unquestioning support of the elite of scientists at the Académie des sciences. Experimental physiology, and with it vivisection, only entered French medicine later, when through figures such as Achille Longet, Jules Béclard, Alfred Vulpian and the Positivist, Charles Robin, leading medical academics began to adopt sytematically the priorities of the scientists.

Notes

1. Cl. Bernard, *Leçons sur les phénomènes de la vie communs aux animaux et aux végétaux* (Paris, 1879), vol. 2, pp. 438–45, and *Rapport sur les progrès et la marche de la physiologie générale en France* (Paris, 1867), pp. 1–7.

2. J. Schiller, 'Physiology's Struggle for Independence in the First Half of the Nineteenth Century', *History of Science*, vol. 7 (1968), pp. 68–89; G. Canguilhem, 'La Constitution de la physiologie comme science', in G. Canguilhem, *Études d'histoire et de philosophie des sciences* (Paris, 1970),

pp. 226–73; and J.E. Lesch, *Science and Medicine in France: the Emergence of Experimental Physiology, 1790–1855* (Harvard University Press, Cambridge, Mass., 1984).

3. *Journal officiel de la République française*, 19 Feb. 1874, pp. 1366–8.

4. J.E. Lesch, *Science and Medicine*, pp. 86–7 and 168.

5. H. Bouley, 'De l'action de la section des pneumo-gastriques sur l'empoisonnement par le noix-vomique', *Comptes rendues des séances de la Société de biologie*, ser. 1, vol. 2 (1850), p. 195: C. Leblanc and E. Faivre, 'Mémoire sur l'action physiologique de la vératrine', ibid., ser. 2, vol. 1 (1854), pp. 143–62; A.-C. Goubaux and J.A. Giraldès, 'Expériences sur les injections de la perchlorure de fer dans les artères', ibid., ser. 2, vol. 1 (1854), pp. 50–2; and M.D. Grmek, *Catalogue des manuscrits de Claude Bernard* (Paris, 1967), p. 182.

6. L.-L. Trasbot, 'Obsèques de M. G. Colin (d'Alfort)', *Bulletin de l'Académie de médecine*, ser. 3, vol. 35 (1896), pp. 704–6; and V.A. McKusick, 'Chauveau, Jean-Baptiste Auguste', in C.C. Gillispie (ed.), *Dictionary of Scientific Biography* (Charles Scribner's Sons, New York, 1970–6), vol. 3, pp. 219–20.

7. W.R. Albury, 'Experiment and Explanation in the Physiology of Bichat and Magendie', *Studies in the History of Biology*, vol. 1 (1977), pp. 47–131.

8. Article entitled 'Barthésrien' in P. Larousse (ed.), *Grand Dictionnaire universel du dix-neuvième siècle*, reprint (Slatkine, Paris, 1982), vol. 2, p. 281.

9. W.R. Albury, 'Experiment and Explanation', pp. 75–80.

10. Ibid., pp. 67–70.

11. P.-H. Nysten, *Recherches de physiologie et de chimie pathologique pour suite à celles de Bichat sur la vie et la mort* (Paris, 1811).

12. P.-N. Gerdy, *Quid medicinae profuerent vivorum animalium sectiones?* (Paris, 1824).

13. A.-B. Richerand, *Nouveaux éléments de physiologie*, 10th edn (Paris, 1833).

14. J. Lordat, *Réponses à des objections faites contre le principe de la Dualité du dynamisme humain* (Montpellier, 1854), pp. ix–xcii; Ch. Dupin in 'Délibérations au Sénat sur une pétition relative à l'enseignement supérieur', *Moniteur universel* (20 May 1868), p. 689; and Ev. Bertulus, 'De la Théophobie scientifique et médicale', *Marseille médical*, vol. 9 (1872), pp. 40–7.

15. G.A. McCosh, *Catholic Theology in the Nineteenth Century: the Search for a Unitary Method* (New York, 1977).

16. P.N. Elliott, 'The Social and Intellectual Background to Claude Bernard's Vision of Science', unpublished DPhil thesis, University of Oxford, 1984, pp. 255–6.

17. E.H. Ackerknecht, *Medicine at the Paris Hospital, 1794–1848* (Baltimore, 1967).

18. Fr. Broussais, *Traité de physiologie appliquée à la pathologie* (Paris, 1822–3).

19. Fr. Magendie, 'Quelques idées générales sur les phénomènes particuliers aux corps vivans', trans. W.R. Albury in W.R. Albury, 'Experiment and Explanation', pp. 107–15; and W.R. Albury, 'Physiological Explanation in Magendie's Manifesto of 1809', *Bulletin of the History of Medicine*, vol. 48 (1974), pp. 90–9.

20. M. Gross, 'The Lessened Locus of Feelings: A Transformation in French Physiology in the Early Nineteenth Century', *Journal of the History of Biology*, vol. 12 (1979), pp. 241–2.

21. Et. Geoffroy Saint-Hilaire, La Zoologie a-t-elle dans l'Académie des sciences une représentation suffisante? La physiologie n'y a-t-elle pas été entièrement oubliée?', *Revue encylopédique ou analyses et annonces raisonnées*, vol. 13 (1822), pp. 501–11.

22. J.M.D. Olmsted, *François Magendie. Pioneer in Experimental Physiology and Scientific Medicine in Nineteenth Century France* (Schuman, New York, 1944), pp. 81–2.

23. E. Crawford, 'The Prize System of the Academy of Sciences 1850–1914', in R. Fox and G. Weisz (eds.), *The Organisation of Science and Technology in France 1808–1914* (Cambridge University Press, 1980), pp. 283–307; and M.P. Crosland, 'From Prizes to Grants in the Support of Scientific Research in France in the Nineteenth Century: the Montyon Legacy', *Minerva*, vol. 17 (1979), pp. 365–80.

24. J.M.D. Olmsted, *François Magendie*, p. 87.

25. Ibid., pp. 45–81.

26. J.M.D. Olmsted, 'Pierre Flourens', in E.A. Underwood (ed.), *Science, Medicine and History. Essays on the Evolution of Scientific Thought and Medical Practice Written in Honour of Charles Singer* (Oxford University Press, 1953), vol. 2, pp. 290–302.

27. O. Temkin, 'The Philosophical Background to Magendie's Physiology', *Bulletin of the History of Medicine*, vol. 20 (1946), p. 20; and M. Gross, 'The Lessened Locus', p. 255.

28. J.M.D. Olmsted, *François Magendie*, pp. 91 and 158–9.

29. J.M.D. Olmsted and E.H. Olmsted, *Claude Bernard and the Experimental Method in Medicine* (Henry Schuman, New York, 1952), pp. 37–91.

30. W.R. Albury, 'Going Beyond the "Introduction": Claude Bernard Scholarship in the 1970s. An Essay Review', *Bulletin of the History of Medicine*, vol. 56 (1982), pp. 271–5; and W. Coleman, 'The Cognitive Basis of the Discipline. Claude Bernard and Physiology', *Isis*, vol. 76 (1985), pp. 49–70.

31. W.R. Albury, 'Experiment and Explanation', and M. Gross, 'The Lessened Locus'.

32. H. Larrey, 'Discours prononcé aux obsèques de M. Longet', *Bulletin de l'Académie de médecine*, vol. 36 (1871), pp. 1063–77; J.M.D. Olmsted, *Charles-Édouard Brown-Séquard. A Nineteenth Century Neurologist and Endocrinologist* (Baltimore, 1946); and J.-M. Charcot, 'Discours prononcé aux funérailles de M. Vulpian', *Archives de la physiologie normale et pathologique*, ser. 3, vol. 9 (1887), pp. 345–52.

33. Cl. Bernard, *Introduction à l'étude de la médecine expérimentale* (Paris, 1865), *Rapport sur les progrès*, and *La Science expérimentale* (Paris, 1878).

34. Cl. Bernard, 'Le Problème de la physiologie générale', in Cl. Bernard, *La Science expérimentale*, pp. 101–8.

35 V. Coste, 'Note sur le rôle de l'observation et de l'expérimentation en physiologie', *Comptes rendues de l'Académie des sciences*, vol. 66 (1868), pp. 1278–84; and H. de Lacaze Duthiers, 'Direction des études zoologiques', *Archives de zoologie générale et expérimentale*, vol. 1 (1872), pp. 1–64.

36. R.E. Stebbins, 'France', in T.F. Glick (ed.), *The Comparative Reception of Darwinism* (Austin, Texas, 1972), pp. 117–67; M.J. Nye, 'Anti-Atomism: A "Matter of Taste"'', *Annals of Science*, vol. 38 (1981), pp. 585–90; T. Shinn, 'Orthodoxy and Innovation in Science. The Atomist Controversy in French Chemistry', *Minerva*, vol. 18 (1980), pp. 539–55; and R. Fox, 'Regnault, Henri-Victor', in C.C. Gillipsie (ed.), *Dictionary of Scientific Biography*, vol. 11, p. 353.

4

Marshall Hall (1790–1857): Vivisection and the Development of Experimental Physiology

Diana Manuel

According to R.D. French in his *Antivivisection and Medical Science in Victorian Society*,[1] Marshall Hall probably became the main target for the opprobrium of the anti-vivisectionists in the first half of the nineteenth century. Hall indeed carried out vivisection procedures as a means of pursuing his physiological research. Through this work Hall — and a few other individuals working mainly in isolation like Hall himself — was seeking to establish a scientific, experimental research basis to medicine. He was questioning and seeking to undermine traditional medicine, that is, its explanations of sickness and disease, to modify its corresponding therapies including bleeding and purging and to reform diagnostic and clinical procedures. However, Hall was active in a cultural, social and political environment which was by and large inimical to science. The period, according to Matthew Arnold, was a dangerous interval for Britain, which was a society with 'a working class not educated at all, a middle class educated on the second plane, and the idea of science absent from the whole course and design of our education'.[2]

Edinburgh training and other early influences on Hall's attitude to experimentation

As the son of a Nottingham cotton manufacturer and bleacher who was a religious dissenter and had been personally acquainted with John Wesley, Hall studied at the University of Edinburgh, which he entered in 1809. It is not surprising that Marshall Hall received his university education in Edinburgh rather than Oxford or Cambridge, which were less accessible to the families of dissenters. Nevertheless, at this time Edinburgh attracted students from all over

Europe and America to attend courses in what was regarded as the best medical school in the English-speaking world. According to Hall's wife, her husband's favourite study as a student was at first chemistry and already at that period he had published in *Nicholson's Journal* a paper 'On the Combinations of Oxygen'.[3] At the same time Hall was a member of the student Royal Medical Society in Edinburgh at which students read and discussed papers, thus providing themselves with an opportunity for rehearsing one of the exercises demanded of candidates for medical degrees in Edinburgh, namely the defence of a thesis. Hall, who became a vice-president of the society, presented and defended papers 'On Chemical Attraction' and 'On the Application of the Analytical and Synthetical Methods in the Prosecution of Medical Science',[4] thus indicating his empirical and philosophical interest in science and its application to medicine.

It seems that a great stimulus to chemical investigation at Edinburgh — reflecting the vigorous development of chemistry on the Continent — was given by the successful large-scale experiments which Thomas Charles Hope (1766–1844), Professor of Chemistry at Edinburgh, performed before his classes which in 1823 numbered 575 students. Although a great experimenter himself, Hope did not provide his students with the opportunity of carrying out experiments. This practice was introduced by his assistant only in 1823, a decade after Hall's departure, but his Edinburgh training had already inclined Hall towards a scientific and experimental approach to medicine.

Hall's attitude also derived from his admiration of France and French institutions, including French medicine in which experimental physiology was already developing apace in the early decades of the nineteenth century. The earliest independent chair of physiology was established in the Paris Faculty of Medicine in 1823 and André Dumeril was its first holder. It was not until the 1830s that chairs in physiology, combined with anatomy, were established in London. Robert Todd held the first chair in physiology and general and morbid anatomy at King's College, whilst William Sharpey was appointed to the first chair of anatomy and physiology at University College.

On leaving Edinburgh, Hall travelled on the Continent and eventually returned to Nottingham where he practised as a physician between 1816 and 1826. Already in Nottingham Marshall Hall established what his neighbour, the Archdeacon of Nottingham George Wilkins, described as 'his laboratory' where he pursued 'experimental studies'. After Hall's death Wilkins recalled that Marshall Hall would step into the vicarage late in the evening 'for conversation on some experiment that he had made or was making'.[5] Similarly when he moved to London in 1826 Hall set aside part of his house as a laboratory for carrying out experiments and for much of this work he was assisted by a member of the Royal College of Surgeons, Henry Smith, to whom he dedicated his work, *A Critical and Experimental Essay on the Circulation of the Blood.* Hall wrote of Smith: 'There is no one to whom I can with so much propriety, or so much pleasure, inscribe this little volume, as to you, who have aided me throughout the whole series of experiments which it details, with such talent and patience.'[6]

Hall's wife sometimes wrote out the articles which he submitted for publication and so she would have been familiar with the details of some of her husband's work. In her *Memoirs* she refers, for example, to the apparatus which he designed for recording the temperature of bats when in a state of hibernation, the subject of an early paper by Hall read to the Royal Society in 1832. She also gives details of the animals Hall used and of the accommodation provided: 'The animals required for all these investigations formed a little ménagerie in a room in our house devoted to that special purpose. There were assembled mice, hedgehogs, bats, birds, fishes, frogs, toads, tritons [newts], snakes etc.'[7] Revealing her awareness of a certain sensitivity on the issue of the use of animals for experimental purposes she added: 'Perhaps some of my readers may think the collection not a very choice one; but they were subservient to useful scientific purposes, were well cared for, and humanely treated.'[8] She also had a due sense of the relative status of physicians compared to surgeons at the time, for she observed: 'Marshall Hall devised the experiments and Mr. Smith assisted in their performance with admirable dexterity. The one furnished the head, the other the hands.'[9]

Animal experimentation by Hall's contemporaries

Whilst Hall was establishing himself as a young physician in Nottingham, A.P. Wilson Philip, a physician and physiologist who, like Hall, had been educated in Edinburgh, settled in London. He had already indicated that physiologists needed to give public assurance of the care and concern with which they carried out experiments on animals. Nevertheless, Philip made it clear that he ascribed lack of progress in gaining knowledge about the nature of internal diseases at least in part to the prevailing reluctance to do experiments on living animals. However, in an account of certain of his experiments in which he was investigating Legallois's work, Philip clearly wished to defend his own practices and deflect criticism from himself. He revealed that he had already made attempts to use alternatives to living animals:

> I have endeavoured as much as possible to avoid experiments on living animals. Most of those related in the following Inquiry were made on the newly dead animal; and it will appear, I think, from what I am about to lay before the reader, that for many experiments, for which the living animal has been thought necessary the newly dead animal may be used with equal, and sometimes with greater advantage.[10]

Nevertheless Philip found himself unavoidably using some living animals to investigate Legallois's work and, defending himself on the grounds of using responsible criteria, he pointed out:

> When it was necessary to experiment on the living animal, I uniformly observed the following rules; to destroy the sensibility previous to the experiment when this could be done without influencing the result; when several animals were equally fit for the experiment to choose the one which would suffer least from it; when there were several ways of performing the experiment, to choose the way which would occasion least suffering; if the experiment was necessarily fatal to destroy the animal as soon as the purpose in view was answered; and to take such precautions as rendered as few repetitions as possible requisite.[11]

Another contemporary of Hall who became a target of public criticism was James Blundell. Born in the same year as Hall, Blundell was keenly interested in the problem of blood transfusions. He carried out research on dogs, bleeding them almost to death and then trying to revive them by means of blood transfusions. He was an uncompromising advocate of liberty in physiological experimentation and his reply to opponents of this attitude was:

> Those who object to the putting to death of animals for a scientific purpose, do not reflect that the death of an animal is a very different thing from that of a man . . . Is not pain daily and hourly inflicted upon the inferior animals to contribute

to the support and pleasure of man; and shall it be particularly objected to when inflicted for the purpose of advancing physiological and medical knowledge? Shall it be said that the objects of physiological science are not worth the sacrifice of a few animals? . . . We defend the sacrifice of animals in so far as it is calculated to contribute to the improvement of science; we maintain that such a sacrifice is not only justifiable but a sacred duty.[12]

Hall's work on blood-letting

A large part of medical practice — gynaecology, obstetrics and paediatrics — relates to woman and it is not surprising that Hall initially but briefly considered these topics. Thus he wrote on the effects of loss of blood including the incidence of haemorrhage during childbirth and on child-rearing. But seeing the fruits of research as a possible route to a fellowship of the Royal Society, Hall turned his attention to an experimental study of the blood system which became the first major area of his research. According to his wife, Hall's change of interest from women's diseases to experimental investigations was accompanied by a diminution in his practice. She attributed this to the public knowledge that he was devoting himself to physiology. Hall had made reference to the effects of haemorrhage in publications in 1820 and 1822, but in 1824 he submitted a paper, 'On the Effects of Loss of Blood',[13] to the Medico-Chirurgical Society of which he later became a member and office-holder. In view of the frequency both of haemorrhage as a disease and blood-letting as a remedy, Hall considered it important that the effects of blood loss should be investigated experimentally in order to establish a more informed use of the lancet and a more efficacious treatment for haemorrhage.

In his 1824 paper, which did not contain details of any animal experiments, Hall presented his observations on the effects on patients of loss of blood and he discussed the immediate effects such as syncope (or fainting), as well as the cumulative effects of repeated or protracted loss of blood which lead to conditions such as exhaustion, sinking and dissolution. He also made brief reference to the effects of age and the presence of disease, and noted that more observations were needed on the effects of blood loss on the internal organs.

Hall illustrated the principles of his exposition by reference to six clinical cases, five of which concerned women in childbirth and the sixth a robust man of forty whose horse had reared up and then fallen upon the thrown man, fracturing some of his ribs. He, like the women, had been treated by bleeding but was among the three patients who died. Hall completed his essay with the claim that he had not included reference to any circumstances which were not amply substantiated by well-observed facts and he announced his intention to investigate the remedies of loss of blood, by means of a series of experiments.

Although details of his experiments on animals did not appear until 1831 and 1832, Hall had already, during the late 1820s, been carrying out experiments similar to those which he published in the *Medico-Chirurgical Transactions* in 1832.[14] A major aim of these experiments, which involved the use of dogs, was the investigation of the most appropriate conditions under which to carry out blood-letting as a remedy. The same aim was already embodied in Hall's publication of two years earlier, *Researches Principally Relative to the Morbid and Curative Effects of Loss of Blood* (1830).[15] This work was an extension of the 1824 paper and is clearly a handbook especially for the in-experienced physician handling cases of blood loss and needing guidance on the appropriate use and methodology of blood-letting as a therapeutic measure.

In *Effects of Loss of Blood* Hall presents further clinical case studies of his own patients as well as those of other well-known individuals from the contemporary London medical scene such as Abercrombie, Copeland and Brodie, to provide an unbiased testimony to the truth of the general principles he wished to present. In this treatise Hall provides details of some of the unexpected phenomena arising from loss of blood, of the remarkable difference in the degree of tolerance or intolerance to loss of blood which exists in different diseases. He warns of the equal danger accompanying either an inefficient or an undue use of the lancet and seeks to eliminate this by what he rightly sees as a unique contribution, his proposal of a rule for good procedures to ensure safety in the use of blood-letting.

According to Hall's recommendation the patient is placed sitting perfectly upright, the arm being previously prepared and the blood is allowed to flow from a *free* opening, to the point of incipient syncope:

> The quantity of blood which flows when a patient requiring full bloodletting is placed upright and bled to deliquium [sinking feeling], seems accurately proportionate to the exigencies of the case. In inflammation much blood should

be taken; and much blood will flow before deliquium is induced: in irritation, little blood should be drawn; and there is early syncope from blood-letting. The quantities are even accurately suited, not only to the exigencies of the disease, but to the powers of the system; at least so it appears to me from considerable experience.[16]

Some of the details of this rule, especially the importance of the position of the subject, seem to derive from the dog experiments published in 1832, for in that paper Hall noted:

From observations made on the human subject, and in the course of these experiments, I am alike persuaded that blood-letting ought never to be employed in the horizontal position. The quantity of blood taken, although apparently moderate, may be beyond the powers of the system to bear. But if the erect position be adopted, the occurrence of syncope limits the flow of blood, and the change to the horizontal position affords a prompt refuge from danger.[17]

These experiments had involved investigations during November and December 1830 on seven adult terrier or mongrel dogs whose type, age and weight were recorded. They were subjected to a series of episodes of blood-letting, the details of which were also recorded, to various conditions from syncope to death. For instance: 'Experiment 1. Nov 2d, 1830. The first experiment was performed on a terrier dog, aged 18 months, weighing 17 pounds, lively and muscular. It was bled to syncope; nearly 16 ounces of blood were taken.'[18]

Throughout this series of experiments the positions of the dogs, horizontal or vertical, head held high or low, were altered at different stages of the experiment and the condition of each animal — deterioration or improvement — was recorded as each experiment progressed. Underlining his emphasis on the importance of the subject's position during blood-letting, Hall continued:

The influence of position upon the action of the heart, in cases of syncope, is one of the most interesting facts, ascertained, and repeatedly verified in the course of the subsequent experiments. It was at once marked and decided. The erect position subdued the action of the heart; the inverted position restored it, even still more promptly.[19]

Hall, who had clearly used the findings from these experiments in the designing of his rule on blood-letting, produced a table for physicians to record just such data on their patients, including for example, age and strength of patient, disease, its stage and complications, quantity of blood taken and repetitions of the blood-letting.

According to D'Arcy Power, Hall's work on blood-letting was highly significant in clinical practice, because it helped to wean the profession 'from the pernicious habit of bloodletting, not because he disbelieved in its efficiency but because he endeavoured to lay down rules for its rational employment'.[20]

Appeal for a research institute

Hall's clinical observations and experimental work during the late 1820s and early 1830s had not been confined to events associated with blood loss. He was also interested in the physiology of the blood circulatory system and the influence on it of the nervous system, the areas he explored in *A Critical and Experimental Essay on the Circulation of the Blood*.[21]

From an early stage in his own career, Hall had been aware of and sensitive to expressions of disapproval about animal experimentation and, in the Introduction to his *Essay on the Circulation* he urgently appealed for the formation of 'a society of physiological research'. Hall claimed that it was not experiments *per se* which could be objected to but the conditions of their performance. Revealing his genuine concern for animals used in experimentation, Hall began the Introduction with:

> Unhappily for the physiologist, the subjects of the principal department of his science, that of animal physiology, are sentient beings; and every experiment, every new or unusual situation of such a being, is necessarily attended by pain or suffering of a bodily or mental kind.[22]

Because of the developing antipathy towards physiological experimentation, Hall felt that 'Investigations in this science should, therefore, being exposed to peculiar difficulties, be regulated by peculiar laws.' Without these laws, or principles as he called them, Hall believed that physiologists would scarcely escape the imputation of cruelty. He therefore put forward five principles which the Society might use a the basis of discussions among its fellow members in coming to decisions on support for or rejection of proposed experiments on animals.

Hall's first principle was that experiment should never be resorted to if the necessary information could be gained by observation, and he reminded his readers of the value of cases of monstrosity, such as acephalous infants which provided 'a sort of natural experiment'. In Hall's opinion such cases present less equivocal phenomena than any which could result from an actual operation involving the infliction of violence or pain. As a second principle Hall advanced the view that without a clearly defined and attainable objective no experiment should be performed. Hall was well aware of the extreme difficulty in physiology of devising an unequivocal and unexceptional experiment and that not a few physiologists had on occasion erroneously attributed a simple effect to one particular cause when in fact it was associated with one or more other quite different causes.

To these Hall added a third principle, that of the need to avoid unwarranted repetition of an experiment, especially if already performed by physiologists of reputation. Only if there arose real doubt about the accuracy of the earlier experiments was repetition justifiable. This principle implied that physiologists should be aware of what their predecessors had done, an interesting point in view of the unjustified accusations made against Hall from time to time concerning his ignorance of the work of his predecessors. Hall's fourth principle concerned the need to carry out any justifiable experiment with the least possible infliction of suffering and he recommended the use of lower, less sentient animals such as batrachian reptiles (amphibia). He praised Philip for his discovery that the newly dead animal might be substituted for the living one without disadvantage to the results, yet with the great advantage of inflicting no pain.

Hall's final principle was that every physiological experiment should be performed 'under such circumstances as will secure a due observation and attestation of its results, and so obviate, as much as possible, the necessity for its repetition'. To his five main principles Hall added the further recommendation that the publication of investigations be done under the aegis of the Society he was proposing which would, he felt, enhance the prestige of the subject. Hall was concerned that in London, as in the provinces, animal physiology was not recognised as an essential and separate branch of the study of 'physic and surgery'. He therefore proposed that the results of experimentation should be laid before the public in the simplest, plainest terms.

In his *Memoirs on the Nervous System*, published some years later, Hall was at pains to protect himself from charges of cruelty, by showing that he had been following his own proposed principles. At the same time he questioned the propriety of a common practice which probably caused little or no concern among the public at large, namely the skinning of live eels. Hall for his part called for a more humane method of handling the eels. Referring to his own experiments and basing his claim to be an humane experimenter on his disputed belief that a spinal cord animal, that is a decapitated or decerebrated one, is not capable of sensation, Hall claimed:

> It is gratifying to me to state that no part of these experiments has inflicted pain, beyond that of prompt decapitation, or division of the spinal marrow. This is true, at least, if the conclusion be correct, that when the head is removed from the body, sensation and volition cease . . . This fact will suggest the propriety, as well as the means, of avoiding such monstrous cruelty as that of skinning eels alive. This will be effectually done by first removing the head, however the animal may afterwards move on the application of stimuli and *appear to feel*.[23]

No such Society as Hall called for was immediately forthcoming and the criticism and accusations of cruelty continued and increased in many quarters including the medical journals in which Hall himself was attacked, especially in the late 1840s.

Hall's physiological experiments

Hall's *Essay on the Circulation* embodied a paper 'On the Anatomy and Physiology of the Minute and Capillary Vessels' which had been unsuccessfully submitted for publication in the *Philosophical Transactions*. As its title suggests, the essay contains details of numerous experiments which, Hall declared, he had repeated in the presence of some of the leading physiologists in the country. These experiments included the investigation of the blood circulation in external structures such as fins and in internal structures such as the lungs. He also investigated the effect of alcohol and opium on the heart and the circulation, applied both externally and to the exposed brain and spinal cord. In addition, and revealing a shift of interest towards the nervous system, Hall considered a problem which had already interested earlier physiologists, namely the inter-relationship between the blood circulatory system and the nervous system. To this end he investigated the effect of destruction of different parts of the nervous system on the circulatory system and he compared the effect of crushing the brain and spinal cord, as well as other parts of the body, on the heart and circulation.

Hall chose fish and amphibia as his experimental animals be-cause, with their capillary systems visible in the fins and webbed feet, these animals provide an opportunity for observing the blood system in an intact animal and without the need for vivisection pro-cedures. Vivisection was however necessary for investigations on the blood circulation within the lungs, and Hall provided some beautiful illustrations of blood vessels in the fins of fish and in the web and lung mesentery of amphibia.

Hall was well aware that the lower the animal in the zoological scale 'the more capable it is of submitting to division, and of yielding, in each part, the phenomena of life',[24] before death over-comes it. This characteristic thus provided Hall with another important rationale for using lower vertebrates such as fish and amphibia and he emphasised the need to use considerable caution in extending the facts observed in these groups to higher animals. He cautioned: 'It will be necessary to exercise a just degree of reserve in passing from mere facts observed in one order of animals, to general conclusions in regard to others.'[25]

By the early 1830s, Hall's research interest had definitively moved towards an emphasis on the nervous system and in particular to a study of the phenomenon of reflex action on which he concentrated for the rest of his life. He later, but erroneously, claimed that he had demonstrated the existence of a separate anatomical system within the nervous system associated exclusively with reflex action. He named this system the excito-motory system. Hall's extensive repertoire of experiments, for which he used animals from the major vertebrate phyla, reveal his comparative approach. Hall's shift of emphasis from the blood to the nervous system had arisen from an experimental observation which he published in the *Memoir* (1833). He described what he had noticed in the behaviour of a recently separated newt's tail, during an investigation of the animal's capillary system:

> I was first struck with the phenomenon of the reflex function
> of the spinal marrow in the separated tail of an eft [newt].

On being excited by the point of a needle passed lightly over
its surface, it contracted and moved as if it still formed part
of an entire animal.[26]

Hall had already included a reference to this observation, and related
ones on reflex action, in a paper to the Zoological Society in the
previous year.[27] In his *Memoir* (1833) he provided details of further
vivisection procedures and his subsequent observations on the
behaviour of a turtle:

This (live) animal was decapitated in the manner usual with
cooks, by means of a knife, which divided the second or third
vertebra. The head being placed upon the table for observation, it was first remarked that the mouth opened and shut,
and that the submaxillary integuments descended and
ascended, alternately, from time to time, replacing the acts
of respiration. I now touched the eye or eyelid with a probe.
It was immediately closed: . . . I then touched the nostril with
the probe. The mouth was immediately opened widely, . . .[28]

Hall explained that having repeated his procedures and made the
same observations, he finally withdrew the medulla and brain and
observed that 'All the phenomena ceased from that moment.'

An important feature of Hall's theory of reflex action was his
insistence on its involuntary nature, that is, its independence of sensation and volition, which meant that no pain could be involved
where the animal was decapitated or decerebrated. Thus, referring
to investigations on a series of decapitated animals, including those
in which he was investigating the relationship between the blood
circulatory system and the nervous system, Hall emphasised that
there was no question of any sensation of pain being involved, despite
appearances to the contrary created by movements in the animals'
limbs and trunks. This aspect of Hall's theory provoked a controversy concerning the properties of the spinal cord.[29] Hall's
opponents, including George Paton, who published a paper 'On
the Perceptive Power of the Spinal Cord',[30] claimed that the soul
extended to the spinal cord, and persisted even in headless
organisms. Thus according to this group, decapitated creatures were
still sentient and experienced pain. And, in their eyes, Hall and his
fellow experimental physiologists were guilty of inflicting pain on
animals used in experiments. Hall linked his own assertion to the
contrary to the very persuasive, naturally occurring, pathological

conditions such as those of paraplegia and hemiplegia where the victims experience no sensations even when, for example, they can see their paralysed limbs being stimulated.

Concerning the influence of the brain and spinal marrow on the circulation, Hall was aware that this issue had intrigued a number of earlier physiologists including Spallanzani, Haller, Fontana and Whytt as well as some of his own contemporaries including Legallois, Philip and Flourens. He was familiar with the details of earlier and contemporary experimental work for which large numbers of frogs and salamanders had been used and in which the brain and sometimes the spinal cord had been removed or crushed. Robert Whytt, an eighteenth-century neurophysiologist from Edinburgh, had frequently used the methods of decapitation illustrated by Alexander Stuart in his Croonian Lecture of 1737, with its classical account of the effects of stimulating the spinal cord of a decapitated frog.[31] Legallois used this technique, being careful to tie a ligature around the neck to prevent loss of blood since, as he observed, copious bleeding destroys the circulation in the extremities. Revealing his greater admiration for some of the earlier experimental work, Hall commented:

> The experiment of removing the brain and spinal marrow, and of watching the effect on the heart and capillary circulation, belongs to a former day, and especially to Whytt and Spallanzani; . . . The repetitions of this experiment by Legallois, Dr. Philip and M. Flourens, and M. Brachet are, in my opinion, less satisfactory than the original experiments of Whytt and Spallanzani, having occupied less time, and consequently afforded less scope for observation; . . . [32]

Wilson Philip considered that the circulatory system was independent of the nervous system whilst Legallois adopted the opposite view. Flourens believed that the power of the heart and circulation was only impaired by the destruction of that part of the nervous system upon which respiration depended. By way of investigating for himself the fundamental question 'What maintains the circulation of the blood?' Hall, in one of his experiments, gently tied a ligature around the limb of a frog and observed the effect on the pulsatory movements on the globules of blood in the web capillaries. He noticed that 'The pulsatory, and the retarded or arrested movements, of the globules of blood, may be varied, in an infinite manner, by increasing or diminishing the degree of tightness of the ligature'.[33] Such observations persuaded Hall that it was the pulsatory power of the heart itself which immediately maintains the blood flow throughout the circulatory system of arteries, capillaries and veins. The details of one of his experiments on the relationship between the circulatory and nervous systems included:

> The brain and spinal marrow of a frog were removed with the utmost precaution to avoid the effect of shock. The circulation in the web which had been vigourous, was observed to become very gradually slower; it was lost in the capillaries in five minutes, in the veins in ten, and in the arteries in between fifteen and twenty. The whole of these changes were slow and progressive. Some interval elapsed before we examined the lung, — and its circulation had ceased. The heart still beat feebly thirty six times in a minute. Scarcely any blood was lost.[34]

And the details of another experiment, this time using a live eel, were as follows: 'An eel was placed so that the circulation in the tail could be observed. It proceeded rapidly. A fine wire was passed down the spinal canal. From this moment the circulation, without being at all immediately arrested, became gradually slower.'[35]

Hall speculated that if in the experiments of removing the brain and spinal marrow of a frog, a stream of air could be continually directed into the cavities of the lungs it was probable the animal would live indefinitely.[36] In any case Hall felt that his deduction about the brain not being necessary for the immediate functioning of the blood circulation was supported by the 'natural experiments' of acephalous infants who, despite being born without a brain survive for some time after birth, even suckling in some cases. Nevertheless Hall was of the opinion that 'It cannot . . . by any means, be said that the circulation is independent of the brain and spinal marrow.'[37] He saw in this relationship a further manifestation of reflex action in which the spinal cord and the special excito-motor system he envisaged, played an important role.

Hall expressed considerable scepticism over deductions about the relationship between the nervous system and the circulatory system based on investigations in which regions of the brain and spinal cord were crushed rather than neatly and speedily removed. As Hall asked:

> Were the results observed, the effects of crushing these organs

specially, or the mere effect of violence and injury inflicted generally? What would be the comparative results of crushing other parts or organs, as the stomach, a limb etc? And lastly does the experiment of crushing the brain and spinal marrow really lead to any accurate knowledge of the peculiar functions of these individual organs?[38]

Hall was convinced that whatever may be the character of the connection between the brain and spinal marrow on the one hand and the heart and circulation on the other, the same basic relationship, or sympathy as earlier physiologists had called it, exists between other organs and parts and the organs of circulation even though there may be a difference of degree. He illustrated the point by referring to the case of a healthy wagoner who fell down and suffered the passage over him of the wheel of his heavy wagon. His heartbeat was so enfeebled that his pulse could hardly be felt. The effect on him was similar to that of crushing a portion of the brain and spinal marrow and on examination his ileum was found to be lacerated in two places. Hall asserted that crushing the brain no more teaches us the function of the brain than crushing the stomach or the hand teaches us the functions of the stomach or the hand. In his opinion: 'I confess that I think no physiological deduction can be drawn from the experiment of crushing the brain and spinal marrow, in regard to the functions of those organs.'[39]

Views of contemporary medical journals

In general the medical journals carried correspondence both condemning and condoning vivisection and in their editorials revealed their own stance on the issue. Magendie's lectures on physiology, delivered in London in 1824 and published in the *Lancet*, fuelled the deep anti-French feelings in this country and provoked vehement accusations of cruelty. Such feelings were widely publicised in the press, including the medical journals. Five years later, in 1829, when Warburton's anatomical bill was seeking to legalise and facilitate the practice of dissection on human cadavers,[40] an editorial in the *London Medical Gazette* recalled the strength of feeling provoked by Magendie's work, as a vehicle for criticising individuals such as Hall:

We recollect, some few years ago, a violent clamour was raised against the practice of experimenting upon living animals; indeed we believe the ferment has not yet subsided. Certain lecturers were represented in the most odious light as unnecessarily torturing and sacrificing the lives of rabbits, frogs, dogs and cats. The attention of Parliament was called to the subject; the infliction of pain and penalties was threatened; and conviction, under a special statute, was with difficulty evaded. The appalling experiments of Magendie were the topic of the day; and the correspondence of Mr. Abernethy, Sir Everard Home, and others, with various members of parliament, excited a strong sensation.[41]

However, the journal was generally sympathetic to the need for vivisection in medical research and the object of the editorial was to inform people that if dissection of cadavers were prevented then the only recourse open to surgeons would be to practise and learn surgery by taking the opportunity of dissecting patients who were on the point of death. If such clamour had been produced by the issue of experimentation on living animals, what should be the public response to this prospect of dissecting living human beings? In the event the Anatomy Bill was eventually passed in 1832 and it made available certain classes of cadaver for medical education.

In 1836, and indicating the still relatively small amount of vivisection being carried out in Britain, the *Lancet* responded to a letter protesting about the cruelty and immorality of experiments on animals with:

> This expostulation is partly directed against a 'practice' which does not exist. Our correspondent is not justified by facts in connecting this word with 'experiments on living animals'. British professors of medicine *very rarely* prove by such experiments that they feel themselves warranted in testing theories which hold forth a promise of ulterior benefit to man.[42]

In reviewing Grainger's work *On the Structure and Functions of the Spinal Cord*,[43] the *Medico-Chirurgical Review* in 1838 took up certain of his critical remarks and itself referred to 'some of the recent vivisections' and to 'Magendie the arch-vivisector of modern times'.[44] Both Grainger and the reviewer revealed the still prevalent influence of anatomy on physiology. Nevertheless, as the reviewer noted, Grainger displayed a cautious, almost ambivalent, attitude towards the practice of vivisection. On the one hand he could say 'success, when it is to be obtained by experimental inquiry, . . . when judiciously applied is a very important means of discovery . . .'[45]

On the other hand, an extract in the review revealed Grainger as understandably reluctant to give credit to vivisection as a useful method of inquiry into the mental operations of animals. The extract ran:

> It is acknowledged by all parties, that the results of vivisec-
> tions, particularly those which relate to the mental operations
> of animals, in which it is so difficult justly to interpret the
> effects produced on their feelings, must be received with the
> greatest caution.[46]

Magendie's experimental work was described by Grainger as 'most objectionable'.

However, closer attention to Grainger's work reveals that with the multitude of experiments cited and commended, he could not have been an anti-vivisectionist. And since he was a supporter of Marshall Hall and could be said to have received impetus for his own anatomical approach to physiology through Hall's speculation on the existence of a distinct nervous system associated with reflex action, one would not expect to find Grainger completely anti-pathetic to animal experimentation. He was certainly a harsh critic of Magendie but since he dwelt admiringly and at length on the experimental work of Flourens, which involved the decerebration of hens and salamanders, Grainger's attitude towards Magendie could not have been motivated exclusively by xenophobia.

It would seem that Grainger genuinely, and understandably, believed that Magendie went too far and unjustifiably inflicted pain on his animals. Hall's silence on the subject of Magendie was prob-ably due to the fact that being himself a target for attacks, he was in no position to criticise a fellow vivisector. The *Medico-Chirurgical Review* had in fact quoted sections of Grainger's work in order to provide a vehicle for an attack on Magendie and other experi-menters, and the reference to dogs suggests that Hall could be an unnamed target. The reviewer declared:

> Experimental vivisections are so cruel, so opposed to the best
> feelings of our nature, that they should ever be undertaken
> with reluctance, and prosecuted in the most sparing manner.
> If a chemist consumes uselessly some bottles full of gas, the

only mischief is a little loss of time and material. But if a dozen dogs or pigeons are physiologically tortured to death, with the vague expectation of some curious fact turning up during the process, there is a great wrong done to humanity and probably no great good to science. In the case of M. Magendie both results have taken place. His experiments, not being philosophically instituted or directed, have tended to confuse the plainest truths, and to establish the most extravagant fancies.[47]

There is sound criticism here in the injunction, an echo of Hall's earlier recommendation, about the need to be sparing in carrying out vivisections. But the dismissive manner in which Magendie's work, which undoubtedly contained contributions of real worth to physiology, was dealt with called into question the impartiality of the reviewer.

In 1837 and again in 1839 editorials of the *London Medical Gazette* appeared under the title 'Experiments on Living Animals'.[48] The first editorial singled out Magendie as 'the most deservedly notorious' of modern vivisectors. Displaying the persisting, marked anti-French feelings, it alleged that Magendie 'presents, in his single practice, a compendium of all that is odious in this mode of investigation . . . ' and went on to describe some of Magendie's experiments the better to show his cruelty. The journal even recalled an incident from one of his lectures delivered more than a decade earlier at the Windmill Street School of Anatomy. Magendie was alleged to have criticised a hapless dog which was operated upon and which would not calm down with the dismissive comment: 'Ah! Mon Dieu, il n'entend pas Français.'[49]

Nevertheless, the aim of both editorials was to lend support to properly conducted experimentation. The journal, without referring to Hall's appeal in 1831, proposed certain restrictions which ought to guide and control animal experimentation procedures. In proposing such measures as the condemnation of needless repetition of experiments whose outcome was already well known, the journal could well have used Hall's work as a source for the views put forward. Furthermore it called for section of the spinal cord just below the medulla oblongata, to deprive animals to be experimented on of sensation at least below the wound. This step too had been one of Hall's principles as had the suggestion that use be made of frogs rather than warm-blooded animals. At the same time, the journal displayed a certain ambivalence and could have been criticising

Hall by asking for cessation of the practice of some 'leading members of the scientific part of the profession' who popularly and unnecessarily perform vivisections.

The 1837 editorial revealed an anti-sport bias in pointing out that animal experimentation was no more cruel than 'those manly sports of fishing or shooting, or those punily philosophical occupations, entomology and its congeners'. The reason for the bias was contained in the final sentences of the editorial: 'Yet the majority of these destroyers of life for their own pleasure, are loud declaimers against those who commit only similar cruelties for the profit of others.'[50] Two years later, the 1839 editorial stressed more positively the gains which would follow observance of the restrictions it had proposed; in its opinion, 'If these and similar restrictions be carefuly and kindly observed, a man may experiment on living matter with as good a conscience as he can on the dead.'[51]

In the early 1840s the *London Medical Gazette* had provided a forum for an attack by R.M. Hull and George Macilwain, both medical men, against painful animal experiments, and by implication against the experimenters, including Hall, as immoral and unenlightening. Macilwain, a Fellow of the Royal College of Surgeons, remained an active anti-vivisectionist for many years. In 1847 he prepared a pamphlet for the Royal Society for the Prevention of Cruelty to Animals in which he attempted to refute the claim that vivisection was useful and necessary to medical practice.[52] This he did through a number of case studies asserting that experiments on living animals had led to failures in the hands of Hunter, who had wrongly claimed improvements in the treatment of aneurysm; of Orfila, who was accused of torturing and sacrificing thousands of animals; and of Astley Cooper, whose erroneous deductions about fractured hips, made as a result of experiments, had led to needless but permanent lameness among many of Cooper's patients and those of generations of his students.

Charles Bell was cited as a medical investigator who was considered to vindicate claims regarding 'the successful application of experiments, on living animals to the study of Physiology'. On the contrary, alleged Macilwain, this was a misinterpretation. Bell, it was claimed, had arrived at his discoveries on nerves as a result of comparing his anatomical observations made on cadavers and other dead animals with observations of the functions of the same parts in the living animal. Macilwain quoted Bell as acknowledging that 'experiments have never been the means of discovery', and that his own findings were based on deductions from anatomy.

It is perhaps not surprising that Bell and Hall made few references to each other's work. They were both interested in the nervous system but their mode of investigation differed. In a paper to the Anatomy and Physiology Section of the British Association at Edinburgh in 1834[53] — and it was not until the 1870s that the British Association produced a set of guidelines on animal experimentation — Bell had listed the modes of investigating the nervous system. He clearly indicated his preference for anatomical study and his lesser enthusiasm for experimental investigations, Hall's preferred method and which in any case, in Bell's opinion, depended on anatomical findings.

The allegedly widespread anti-vivisection sentiment expressed by Macilwain in his publication in 1847 affected Hall in the same year. In January 1847 he became the victim of an attack, in the *Medico-Chirurgical Review,*[54] based on his description of an experiment on a dog in his *Practical Observations and Suggestions in Medicine.*[55] In this detailed chapter by chapter review of Hall's work, there is undoubted admiration but also a degree of hostility towards physiology (and towards science and the French). The reviewer observed: 'Physiology can't put things right, in spite of all that Dr Hall says in its praise: nay, there may be empiricism and charlatanerie in it as well as in other departments of science; witness the doings of more than one of the French school in the present day.'[56] But the author's real condemnation was reserved for experimental work and in particular for the experiment which Hall and Smith — 'these *gentle*men' as the reviewer scornfully calls them — performed on a dog with the view of ascertaining whether the Dura Mater membrane surrounding the brain, which is supplied by the trifacial nerve, is itself excitory. The reviewer provided details of the experiment which involved the removal of the dog's cranium over the left hemisphere of the cerebrum and application of pressure, which led to damage of the brain. It was observed that the dog behaved as if it were sleepy, then had convulsions. The sense organs were stimulated and showed responses and, as the reviewer noted, 'the poor tortured animal continued to breathe until the medulla oblongata and upper part of the spinal marrow were removed'.[57]

The reviewer dismissed Hall's findings and declared that if this kind of physiology is the only foundation for practical medicine then it would be better if physiology were buried in 'the oblivion of Alchemy and Astrology'. He continued his tirade:

Have we learned to treat any of the diseases of the nervous system more successfully, after all the horrible butcheries that have been committed within the course of the last five-and-thirty years, than did the wise and able men of last century, the Boerhaaves, the Cullens or the Heberdens? Was Sydenham, may we ask, educated in the school of blood and torture? Was Mead a vivisector? Did Jenner's great thought originate in mutilating experiments on animals?[58]

The reviewer referred to several other individuals and even doubted if the French physician Louis, for whom Hall had such admiration, had carried out Hall's type of animal experimentation rather than relying on what Hall had often somewhat slightingly referred to as 'crude and *post-mortem* morbid anatomy'. It is significant that the reviewer did not make favourable mention of either Whytt or Charles Bell, both of whom, and especially Whytt, did perform vivisections.

Hall replied to this attack on his experimental work through a letter to the *Lancet* whose editor Thomas Wakley was one of his supporters. Hall's letter appeared under the heading 'On Experiments in Physiology, as a Question of Medical Ethics'.[59] Revealing the effects of the hostility towards and pressure on him and speaking of the 'difficult and painful career' of the physiologist, Hall asserted: 'We are greatly in need of a code of medical ethics.' And, reminding readers of his attempts in 1831 to establish such a code, Hall re-enunciated the five principles which he had presented then for the guidance and control of experiments in physiology. At the same time he questioned what he saw as the illogicality of those who saw fit to kill and eat animals to preserve strength and health but sought to prevent experiments which, observing the precautions he had advocated in his principles, could 'promote that very science, on which not only the preservation but the restoration, of strength and health depend'.

Hall's letter provoked a reply which was also published in the *Lancet*.[60] Hall was accused of 'unjustifiable cruelty in the performance of experiments upon living animals'. His opponent decided to provide *Lancet* readers with some further deails of the experiment to which he had originally objected. These details of the trepanning of the skull and subsequent destruction of the brain of the spaniel — a favoured domestic breed of dog — copious loss of blood, paralysis on one side and the struggling efforts of the animal to raise itself by its unparalysed side were, like the original criticism, designed to provoke revulsion. The reviewer was however on this occasion particularly at pains to stress that, whilst following the complete destruction of the cerebrum 'the animal lost all *sensation*', it was nevertheless 'quite sensible at the commencement of the experiment'. The reviewer, who was right about the dog's condition, asked: 'Can it be conceived that the infliction of such horrible suffering is necessary for the elucidation of any important truth' or for the advancement of physiology? Hall's critic then displayed contempt for what he perceived as misuse of fundamentalist Christianity, with a jibe and his own Scriptural retort:

> To base the justifiableness of vivisections on the permission or injunction 'to kill and eat', is, to say the least of it, a strange misapplication of scriptural language. He who gave that permission, hath also told us — and how startling is the announcement — that 'not even a sparrow falleth to the ground without His knowledge'.[61]

In the reviewer's opinion, the spaniel experiment actually opposed the very principles laid down by Hall in 1831 as did 'some other experiments described or hinted at in *Practical Observations*'.

At this point in the correspondence, Wakley added a footnote in which he asserted that the main questions to be answered concerned the justification of experiments on living animals or 'vivisections, as they have been nicknamed'. In Wakley's view, the reply had to be in the affirmative, otherwise the whole science of physiology fell to the ground. Wakley's second question referred specifically to Hall since he asked if Hall had ever devised and performed an operation without justification. His answer revealed unequivocal support for Hall: 'We believe not. We have ourselves seen Dr. Hall perform a great number of his experiments, and we have even seen him follow the humane principles laid down by himself in the introduction to the Physiology of the Circulation. — Ed. L.'[62]

Hall again replied[63] and whilst he could not deny that some pain was involved in cutting the integuments and removing a portion of the cranium, he explained that the reviewer was ignorant if he supposed that the cerebrum and other nervous tissues are endowed with sensation. Hall presented the results of his experiment which, he claimed, had important bearing on the diagnosis of diseases of the nervous system. He asked why he had been singled out for special attack among a host of other experimental physiologists including Hope, Addison, Morgan, Brodie and Travers. He again pleaded for the institution of a Physiological Society to promote physiological science and to prevent cruelty. He also appealed for a Court Medical which would determine the ethics not only of physiological experiments but also of anonymous and calumnious medical reviewing such as that to which he was being subjected.

In the same issue of the *Lancet*, Hall received support from 'A Fellow of the Royal Medico-Chirurgical Society'[64] mentioning Benjamin Brodie, who always illustrated his lectures with 'well-devised experiments'. In his view Brodie was a more able practitioner 'than if he were ignorant of the results of physiological experiments, as performed by himself'. The writer then went on to discuss the experiments of Bell and Shaw to whom 'we owe the distinction between mere facial and cerebral paralysis' and he claimed that their experiments were 'tenfold more severe than that by Dr. Marshall Hall, on which the reviewer in the *Medico-Chirurgical Review* has commented'. To reinforce this point he explained that it is more difficult and inflictive of pain and suffering to lay bare a nerve deeply seated in the tissues of the neck, such as Bell and Shaw did, than to denude the cerebrum — Hall's procedure. And there, for a time, the matter rested.

In another British medical journal, the restrictive atmosphere in Britain was held responsible for inhibiting research developments which were progressing in France. Thus, in the year following Hall's death an anonymous reviewer, seeking to defend Bell's reputation and writing on Claude Bernard's work, for the *Glasgow Medical Journal*, claimed:

> In this country, experimental physiology labours under peculiar disadvantages. There still exists some of that feeling of repugnance to vivisections which prevented Sir Charles Bell from discovering those functions of the spinal cord which M. Brown-Sequard is now elucidating. Those tender feelings touching the sufferings of animals, embodied in acts of parliament and incorporated in societies for the prevention of cruelty to animals, not to speak of our innate sympathies, stand in the way of our prosecuting inquiries which demand vivisections for their elucidation . . . Practically and legally, then, we may consider ourselves as quite *hors de combat* respecting these physiological 'nouveautés' which we see issuing from time to time from the Parisian press.[65]

Two years later the same journal was repeating its claim that it was the repugnance of British physiologists to vivisection which had prevented certain discoveries from being made, whereas in France there appeared to be less scruple in this matter. The journal reflected on this situation and, in a manner which would have increased Hall's feeling of despair, concluded: ' . . . we could almost go to the length of saying, that we should feel content that the status quo should remain as it is, even though our continental brethren should continue in advance of us in matters pertaining to experimental physiology.'[66]

Conclusion

Thus the activities and pressures which eventually culminated in the anti-vivisectionist movement, active in England from about 1870 onwards, were already beginning to manifest themselves much earlier in the century. These influences grew in strength during the period when Hall was carrying out his main research and it was inevitable that Hall would be subjected to criticism for his experimental work involving vivisection. The criticism against Hall was reinforced by his wider pursuit and promotion of science within medicine and by his admiration of France in particular and of Continental science in general. In addition, Hall's religious background and its association with Dissenters rather than with the Established Church, seems to have increased the hostility towards him. It certainly played some part in the lack of enthusiasm for Hall displayed within the Royal Society. These factors, combined with, it must be acknowledged, Hall's somewhat confrontational attitude to any criticism or opposition to his views, deprived him of any established post within the London teaching hospitals. With these disadvantages it is not surprising that Hall, in spite of his great skill as an experimenter and as a clinician, had no following of students and founded no important school of physiology. To a great extent experimental physiology had, even by the middle of the nineteenth century, made few real advances in Britain.

Notes

1. R.D. French, *Antivivisection and Medical Science in Victorian Society* (Princeton University Press, Princeton and London, 1975), p. 21.

2. M. Arnold, *Schools and Universities on the Continent* (Macmillan, London, 1868).

3. M. Hall, 'On the Combination of Oxygen. In a Letter from the Author', *Journal of Natural Philosophy, Chemistry and the Arts*, vol. 27 (London, 1810), pp. 213–17. (The journal was popularly known as *Nicholson's Journal* after its editor W. Nicholson.)

4. MS, *Records of the Royal Medical Society Commencing in 1811, Dissertations,*

1811-1813, vol. 66, pp. 193–209 and vol. 68, pp. 84–94, University of Edinburgh.

5. C. Hall, *Memoirs of Marshall Hall* (Richard Bentley, London, 1861), p. 58 in a letter from the Archdeacon. Hereafter in text and notes this work will be referred to as *Memoirs*.

6. M. Hall, *A Critical and Experimental Essay on the Circulation of the Blood; Especially as Observed in the Minute and Capillary Vessels of the Batrachia and of Fishes* (London, 1831), p. iii. Hereafter in text and notes this work will be referred to as *Essay on the Circulation*.

7. C. Hall, *Memoirs*, p. 82.

8. Ibid.

9. Ibid.

10. A.P. Wilson Philip, *An Experimental Inquiry Into the Laws of the Vital Functions, With Some Observations on the Nature and Treatment of Internal Diseases . . . in Part Republished by Means of the President of the Royal Society, From the Philosophical Transactions of 1815 and 1817, With the Report of the National Institute of France on the Experiments of M. Le Gallois and Observations On that Report* (London, 1817), p. xi.

11. Ibid.

12. J.H. Young, 'James Blundell (1790-1878). Experimental Physiologist and Obstetrician', *Medical History*, vol. 8 (London, 1964), p. 164.

13. M. Hall, 'On the Effects of Loss of Blood', *Medico-Chirurgical Transactions*, vol. 13 (1824), pp. 121–51.

14. M. Hall, 'An Experimental Investigation of the Effects of Loss of Blood', *Medico-Chirurgical Transactions*, vol. 17 (1832), pp. 250-99.

15. M. Hall, *Researches Principally Relative to the Morbid and Curative Effects of Loss of Blood* (London, 1830). Hereafter in text and notes this work will be referred to as *Effects of Loss of Blood*.

16. Ibid., p. 179.

17. M. Hall, 'Experimental Investigation', *Medico-Chirurgical Transactions*, vol. 17 (1832), p. 267.

18. Ibid., p. 265.

19. Ibid., pp. 253–4.

20. D'Arcy Power, 'Dr Marshall Hall and the Decay of Blood Letting', *Practitioner* (London, 1909), p. 3.

21. See note 6 above.

22. M. Hall, 'Introduction. Of the Principles of Investigation in Physiology', p. 1.

23. M. Hall, *Memoirs on the Nervous System* (London, 1837), pp. 37–8. Hereafter in text and notes this work will be referred to as *Memoirs* (1837). This work consists of two papers which were read before the Royal Society in 1833 and 1837. The first was published by the Royal Society, M. Hall, 'On the Reflex Function of the Medulla Oblongata and Medulla Spinalis', *Philosophical Transactions*, vol. 123 (1833), pp. 635–65. This paper will be referred to in the text as *Memoir* (1833) but reference to it in the notes will be from *Memoirs* (1837). The second paper was rejected by the Royal Society.

24. Hall, *Essay on the Circulation*, p. xi.

25. Ibid., p. xii.

26. Hall, *Memoir* (1837), p. 14.

27. M. Hall, '27th November, 1832, A Brief Account of a Particular Function on the Nervous System', Proceedings of the Committee of Science and

Correspondence of the Zoological Society of London, part ii (1830-32), pp. 190–2.

28 Hall, *Memoir* (1837), p. 12.

29. The Pflüger-Lotze controversy between Pflüger, Professor and Director of the Physiological Institute at Bonn, and Lotze, Professor of Philosophy at Göttingen. Pflüger attacked Hall's views by questioning his assertion that the brain was the exclusive organ of consciousness. According to Lotze the actions of the spinal animal were not due to intelligence and sensation but to traces within the nervous system which had survived decapitation. F.Fearing, *Reflex Action: A Study in the History of Physiological Psychology* (Baillière, Tindall and Cox, London, 1930), pp. 161–86.

30. G. Paton, 'On the Perceptive Power of the Spinal Cord as Manifested by Cold-Blooded Animals', *Edinburgh Medical and Surgical Journal*, vol. 65 (1846), pp. 256–7.

31. A. Stuart, 'Three lectures on Muscular Motion read before the Royal Society in the year MDCCXXXVIII', Supplement to vol. 40 of *Philosophical Transactions of the Royal Society* (London, 1741).

32. Hall, *Essay on the Circulation*, pp. 186–7.

33. Ibid., p. 76.

34. Ibid., p. 124.

35. Ibid., p. 126.

36. Ibid., p. xiii.

37. Ibid., p. 140-1.

38. Ibid., p. 152.

39. Ibid., p. 158.

40. Henry Warburton MP, was chairperson of the parliamentary committee on the study of anatomy which began its sittings on 28 April 1828, and after one failure through the action of the House of Lords succeeded in 1832 in carrying an Anatomy Bill which is still essentially the law of the land. *Dictionary of National Biography*, vol. 59 (1899), p. 297.

41. 'Dissection of the Living', *London Medical Gazette*, vol. 3 (London, 1829), p. 644.

42. J.D.P., 'Experiments on Living Animals', *Lancet*, vol. ii (1835-36), pp. 390-1.

43. R.D. Grainger, *Observations on the Structure and Functions of the Spinal Cord* (London, 1837). Hereafter referred to as *The Spinal Cord*.

44. Review in *Medico-Chirurgical Review and Journal of Practical Medicine*, new series, vol. 28 (London, 1838), pp. 132–3.

45. Grainger, *The Spinal Cord*, p. 68.

46. Ibid., p. 67.

47. Ibid., p. 68.

48. 'On Experiments on Living Animals', *Medical Gazette*, vol. 20 (1837), pp. 804–8. 'Experiments on Living Animals', *Medical Gazette*, new series, vol. 2 (1839), pp. 212–15.

49. Ibid., vol. 20, p. 806.

50. Ibid., pp. 807–8.

51. Ibid., n.s. vol. 2, p. 215.

52. G. Macilwain, *Remarks on Vivisection, and on Certain Allegations as to its Utility, and Necessity, in the Study and Application of Physiology*. Published by the Desire of some Medical and other Supporters of the Royal Society for the

Prevention of Cruelty to Animals (London, 1847).

53. C. Bell, 'Observations on the Proper Method of Studying the Nervous System', *Report of the Fourth Meeting of the British Association for the Advancement of Science Held at Edinburgh in 1834* (London, 1835), pp. 667–70.

54. *Medico-Chirurgical Review and Journal of Practical Medicine*, new series, vol. 5 (1847), pp. 151–66.

55. M. Hall, *Practical Observations and Suggestions in Medicine*, second series (London, 1846).

56. *Medico-Chirurgical Review* (1847), p. 152.

57. Ibid., p. 156.

58. Ibid., p. 157.

59. M. Hall, 'On Experiments in Physiology, as a Question of Medical Ethics', *Lancet*, vol. 1 (1847), pp. 58–60.

60. Reply to Dr Hall, ibid., p. 135.

61. Ibid.

62. Ibid.

63. M. Hall, 'On Experiments in Physiology as a Question of Medical Ethics', ibid., p. 161.

64. 'On Physiological Experiments', ibid., pp. 161–2.

65. 'The Salivary Glands and Pancreas, Their Physiological Actions and Uses in Digestion: Being a Review of the Doctrines Taught by M. Claude Bernard', *Glasgow Medical Journal*, vol. 21 (Glasgow, 1858), pp. 1–2.

66. Ibid., vol. 22 (1860), pp. 244–5.

5

Moritz Schiff (1823–96): Experimental Physiology and Noble Sentiment in Florence

*Patrizia Guarnieri**

Man's relationships to animals

Shortly after he moved to Florence, in 1863, Professor Moritz Schiff decided to have a couple of house-dogs. Or perhaps three. One was probably called Fido; a fairly common name in Italy for examples of the canine race, since fidelity is certainly one of their most appreciated merits. It is not certain, however, that the dogs whose company the physiologist enjoyed were Italian; or whether he might have preferred dogs from Frankfurt on Main, his native city. Perhaps he brought them from Berne, where he had taught comparative anatomy. Unfortunately, not much is known about them.

To tell the truth, I have no idea — as you may have guessed — whether Schiff ever owned a dog or any pet. But, without making the reader impatient, some effort of imagination is necessary for a discussion of the theme of this chapter. It certainly must not be forgotten, however, that the German physiologist did carry out vivisection experiments, and that he was accused of inflicting the most horrible cruelties on hundreds of animals each year in his Florentine laboratory. Knowing this, is it a plausible hypothesis that he might have been the owner, and an affectionate one, of house-dogs? Or, more to the point, would this have seemed plausible to those who took part in, or witnessed, the dispute which involved him in Florence, in 1863 and 1873-4?[1] How would the anti-vivisectionists and protectors of animals have thought he would treat his own dogs? Through asking such questions we can seek something more from this dispute than the attacks and the belligerent defence which succeeded them. Since the vivisectionist Schiff naturally

*Translated from the Italian by Jane Bridgeman and Catherine Crawford.

retorted that in so far as those who accused him of cruelty were lying, they impugned not only his personal morality but also his scientific reputation.

Miss Frances Power Cobbe (1822–1904), the tireless champion of anti-vivisection, was not very concerned with establishing what the German researcher did, nor whether his experiments upon animals might or might not have scientific value. Schiff challenged his adversaries on these grounds; but according to the English *signorina*, any discussion of the scientific and utilitarian aspects of the problem was secondary. Vivisection in itself 'was an *evil thing* which she must oppose to the death and with which no compromise was possible'.[2] No matter how distinguished, Schiff, who had dealings with 'the demon of vivisection', could not be a man sensitive to the qualities of animals. The good Miss Cobbe deemed him absolutely incapable of perceiving, and of reciprocating, the love that so strongly emanated from pets. If an unfortunate dog had happened to come near Professor Schiff, he would have maltreated it, in one way or another.

And yet the physiologist gave assurances that he believed in 'the holy cause of protecting animals'; he swore that he was a good friend to animals, and that he very much cared for them. Those who worked with him in the laboratory testified in his favour: his assistants Alexander Herzen Jr (1839–1906) at Florence and Hillel Yofé (1864–1936) at Geneva.[3] But even some amongst those who protested against his experiments admitted that he behaved with 'scrupulous humanity'. Fabio Uccelli of Pisa University, wrote in *L'Italiano*, 15 January 1864: 'I recall with real pleasure seeing some puppies whose spleens had been removed running happily to brush affectionately against the distinguished scientist's feet.'[4]

According to these statements, therefore, the activity of the vivisectionist did not necessarily preclude a caring attitude towards animals, or a reciprocal relationship of good-will. On the one hand, the white-coated scientist who tied down an etherised dog on the operating table who, in order to study changes in motor function, opened its skull and removed the cranial lobes.[5] On the other, the gentleman who always had some delicacy in his pockets for the animals, and made sure that they lacked neither food nor affection. A sort of Dr Jekyll and Mr Hyde perhaps.

It is worth mentioning Biagio Miraglia (1823–85), a psychiatrist at the Aversa mental hospital near Naples and, on the national scene, an isolated admirer of phrenological theories.[6] His chief queries were these: did vivisection advance knowledge? Was the experimental method correct? Was it necessary? And above all, was there only one way of carrying out vivisection? Or was it possible to make a distinction between a 'bad' experiment, that is, one which was unnecessarily cruel, and one which attempted to spare animals any pain? And who would have determined this distinction, or whether the unavoidable pain might be justified by foreseeable results? Uncompromising anti-vivisectionists would not accept so much speculation: no progress could compensate the cost paid by the innocent victims.

But even those who were open to the demands of science could be dissatisfied with the above-mentioned separation of scientific conduct and man's natural inclination. The unity of the two could be insisted upon. But not from a priority like that of Cobbe, who inferred insensitivity or moral wickedness from the practice of vivisection. Rather than continuing to pay heed only to itself, science ought to listen to humanitarianism and ethical sentiment. These should not control research, Fabio Uccelli argued; but a dialogue between the two demands was necessary. This would have been certainly more advantageous than each continuing to defend its own position.[7]

Because, really, no one was talking about animals as such. Each antagonist referred rather to a specific man–animal relationship. Miss Cobbe always had in mind her personal attachment to her adored lap-dogs; it was they who filled her spinster life with a love and devotion that she had not found abundant in men. Indeed she and her female friends fussed over dogs and cats, sometimes also cage-birds and horses. But what about frogs? Schiff argumentatively noted that no one took pity on them.[8] And yet they, in even larger numbers than rabbits, were the 'martyrs of science', however difficult the Englishwomen might have found it to care for them, pet them, to hold them on their laps as they did their dogs. Naturally, everyone was free to love pets in their own way, and to discover in them a sensitivity which not only Miss Cobbe judged to be 'more really and intensely human' than in men.[9] Those who did not share such a sentiment (or a belief in a future paradise for good cats and dogs) did not need to deny it to others. The opposite happened however: this 'purely personal' sentiment manifested itself as intolerant, exclusive, based on a superior truth. From this standpoint, other interests seemed inconceivable; even when, tacitly and contradictorily, they were admitted in practice.

Schiff on the other hand, held that man maintained a plurality of relationships with animals; he evaluated these according to the needs they had to fulfil. There was the tie of affection — unique and particular — between a person and his own pet; but there were also various relationships of utility which provided work, food and other goods for members of society. Not least were the benefits, even if not immediate, sought by science when it subjected guinea-pigs to experiments. According to Schiff, many dispositions not only could co-exist, even in the same individual, but were perfectly reconcilable. He asserted many times that everyone ought to be inspired by respect, by 'compassion and love' for the creatures man took into his service.[10]

It was noted how difficult — although not impossible — it was for the scientist to exchange one attitude for another. The vivisectionist had to assume an appropriate role in relation to the dog upon which he operated, he had to distance himself from the emotions which might be aroused by the condition of his patient: self-control was necessary, like that of a surgeon with a patient.[11] Probably, Schiff would never have carried out vivisection on his own pet dog. He insisted that the animals used for his experiments were strays, lacking ties of affection with man. They all came from the municipal dog-pound, where they soon would have been put down, without even gaining the merit of having been useful to science. If this declaration had been untrue it would have been easy to demonstrate; but it was contradicted by no one. Today, unfortunately, it is almost impossible to discover the truth of the matter, although it remains legitimate to doubt the complete good faith of both sides.

Schiff was certainly the principal enemy, then and later, of the sparse Italian anti-vivisectionist literature. Sometimes Paolo Mantegazza (1823–1910), an anthropologist in Florence, was also attacked; but others were seldom mentioned.[12] Not only this. The 'agitation against the experiments of Moritz Schiff proved the starting point of a lengthy discussion of the rights and wrongs of vivisection in British periodicals'.[13] Evidently, then, the 'case' on which this chapter focused is important, even omitting further ramifications that would also be of interest.

I should point out, however, that the dispute caused by Schiff's experiments on animals was not as lengthy and intense in Florence, where it took place, as in Victoria's England. The fact that the British press gave space, from 1863, to news originating in Florence could have led, and perhaps still leads, to an over-estimation of the importance of this dispute in Italy itself.

The recent references made in English and non-English histories to the Schiff affair at the Specola Museum of Natural History and the Istituto di Studi Superiori, have been based on secondary sources. Moreover, Italian historians have never concerned themselves with vivisection, or with what was thought about it by 'the Italians' (as they had just, and only officially, become in 1861).[14] It is necessary to keep all these points in mind, because the history of this debate is also the story of a cultural confrontation. It can reveal a great deal about different values and mentalities; these caused various misunderstandings precisely because they either took little cognizance of reciprocal differences or had no respect for them.

The dispute of 1863

In 1863, the first to agitate against Moritz Schiff was Frances Power Cobbe, who at the time was enjoying a sojourn in the hills of Florence. She herself related how it happened: one day, whilst she was giving one of her usual weekly receptions at Villa Brichieri, at Bellosguardo, her guests passed on some worrying rumours.[15] Dogs, pigeons and other animals were being kept in distressing circumstances behind the Specola Museum, near Piazza Pitti, before undergoing who knew how many painful experiments. A certain Dr Appleton from Boston, a friend of and doctor to Theodore Parker (1810–60), had even seen them there. Miss Cobbe, who only a few months before had defined the 'Rights of Man and Claims of Brutes', lost no time. That same evening she wrote a petition to Schiff, requesting him to cease vivisection; and on 21 December she also sent a protest letter to the *Daily News*. Only the following day did the Florentine daily *La Nazione* mention, briefly and polemically, the unpublished petition which had been supported by some 783 signatures.

In the same newspaper, a week later, the accused physiology professor thanked the signatories with cold courtesy and assured them that their appeal was 'absolutely useless' because he performed experiments according to humanitarian requirements. And a more detailed reply to the accusations was written by the Russian physiologist Alexander Herzen, Schiff's assistant at the Istituto di Studi Superiori. The caustic editor of the *Zenzero*, another daily newspaper, had ironically asked for explanations of the mysterious business. Herzen wrote to him as 'a true friend of animals, especially of dogs'; and he described, as an eye-witness over the past two months, what went on in the laboratory at the Specola. Most research was carried out on dead animals immediately after having been killed; every experiment with live dogs, cats, rabbits and frogs was painless, because the physiologists gave them the requisite ether. There was no need, Herzen said, to remind his readers of the importance of these studies to medicine, and of the need for the life sciences to carry out research upon living animals.[16]

Finally, Schiff himself sent a long, harsh letter to *La Nazione*. An anonymous correspondent in the *Daily News* of 29 December had attacked the professors of physiology at Florence and at other universities with accusations which, Schiff maintained, were untrue. It was false: (1) that he kept unfortunate dogs 'in a state of continuous pain, subject to horrible tortures — some having their intestines or internal organs on display'; (2) that the howls of agony resulting from the presumed 'cruel operations' were heard throughout the neighbourhood; (3) that he had moved the laboratory to an internal room in the building, so that 'the noise of the maltreated animals' would not be heard in the street. The tale of a Florentine who had found his dog expiring at Schiff's hands 'after lengthy tortures had been inflicted upon it' was a 'fraudulent fiction'.

Elsewhere Schiff gave his own, somewhat coloured, version of the barking which had been heard from inside the Specola. This had been caused not by pain, but by jealousy, which the dogs felt every time the researcher paid attention to only one of them. In any case, the offended Schiff challenged the anonymous author of the English article to name the eye-witness for a public confrontation.[17]

Miss Cobbe immediately revealed, as she tells in her autobiography, that the article in the *Daily News* was hers; and she enclosed the statement of reported facts endorsed by her informant Appleton. She sent Appleton to the editor of *La Nazione* who, however, not very interested in the issue, would only accept the letter as 'paid advertisement', and in certain columns where 'no decent reader would look for it'. Disgusted by the newspaper, which Miss Cobbe considered filled 'by the help of that class of notices which are declined by every reputable English newspaper', the Boston physician directly requested Schiff 'to compel the editor to put our answer. The learned and scientific gentleman', Miss Cobbe recalled thirty years later, 'shrugged his shoulders and laughed in the face of the American'. There was indeed rather too much arrogance in the whole business. The Englishwoman, therefore, 'left Florence soon after this first brush with the demon of vivisection'.[18]

She did not say, in her memoirs, that in fact Appleton's statement appeared in the *Gazzetta del Popolo* on 14 January 1864; nor that Schiff's reply followed, the next day, in the same newspaper. He himself had been the guide during the visit that the American gentleman (and a colleague) had made to his laboratory the previous May; and he now showed that the animals thought to be dying were instead, eight months later, enjoying good health.[19]

The dispute had by now acquired a pedantic tone; not sufficiently sensational for public opinion, nor rigorous enough for a scientific debate. Schiff then decided to write a series of articles *On the Method Followed in Experiments with Living Animals at the Florence Museum of Natural History*.[20] He remained silent about the dispute which involved him, but recalled the far more famous one at Alfort in France, provoked in 1863 by 'an association of English ladies and gentlemen'. After a long debate, also reported in the Italian periodicals, the French Academy of Medicine had refused their request; vivisection experiments should not be abolished, because they aided progress. The real problem was therefore how 'to reconcile the needs of science with the most refined humanitarian sentiment'.

Schiff proposed to improve the experimental method in order to achieve a double objective: 'to remove the slightest possibility of pain'; to leave 'always intact the vital properties that are the special focus of the experiment'.[21] These could survive for a certain period (longer in frogs than in mammals) if the animal were killed instantaneously by inserting a needle into the spinal cord; it was then necessary to maintain the excitability of the organ under examination, by a kind of artificial respiration and other suitable means. In these instances, the avoidance of pain, of muscle spasms and of blood loss aided correct scientific observation, and were not merely an optional noble gesture. For the same reason, when, less often, the physiologist made use of live animals, he had to suspend their sensitivity, by means of opium, ether or chloroform, depending on which vital functions he wanted to examine and thus to maintain as normal.

Schiff did not conceal that there were many difficulties in such research. These were caused above all by the purpose and method peculiar to physiology, as another foreigner who worked in Italy had emphasised. The Dutch physician Jacob Moleschott (1822–93), at the University of Turin from 1861, warned against the temptation of approaching the investigation of life teleologically rather than experimentally. He cautioned that one could not expect from physiology the same strong certainties offered by physics. Physiology was still trying to find its way.[22] And Schiff was pointing out the best one, most of his colleagues believed. The positivist Pietro Siciliani (1835–85), for example, teaching at Florence, praised him as the 'true scientist' who therefore did not stop at mere observation, but had finally provided physiology with a theoretical foundation. His courses were models to imitate, which the students of the Florentine Institute considered themselves fortunate to attend.[23] In the *Lectures on the Experimental Physiology of the Encephalic Nervous System*, given at the Museum in 1864–5, Schiff again posed the above-mentioned problem and various possible solutions.[24] In every case it was necessary to prevent the physiological phenomenon to be observed from being altered directly or indirectly. Serious disruptions would arise from the prolonged pain which anti-vivisectionist abhorred and which vivisectionists should try to avoid.

An English view of Florence

'To justify the accusation . . . of going beyond the needs of science . . . one must naturally *know* those needs.' Schiff strongly doubted that there was anyone amongst his critics who was competent to judge, or who was at least not ignorant of the way experiments were carried out — except for two doctors, one of whom changed his opinion immediately after visiting the physiological laboratory.[25] Who were the signatories to Miss Cobbe's petition? They were the English and the other foreigners, extraneous to the life of the city, who frequented the Florentine villas; together with 'almost the whole historic aristocracy of old Florence'. A list of names that 'recalled Medicean times', exclaimed the satisfied Miss Cobbe. 'Very few of them were of the *mezzo-ceto* class and *none* belonged to the (Red) Republican party. Schiff was himself a Red, and as such he might, apparently, commit any cruelty he thought fit'.[26] To prevent this danger, Protestant priests in Florence and even children had signed.

It certainly could not be said that the group was very representative of the Florentine people at whom, nevertheless, the appeal was directed. Nor was it really able to influence them, Schiff noted sarcastically. Yet the English *signorina* and her female friends, perhaps a little ingenuously, believed they could; but this was explained by the fact that they did not know much about the people of Florence. Luckily, not all Miss Cobbe's fellow-countrymen who visited and lived in Florence, or elsewhere on the peninsula, shared her opinions and attitudes. 'The only interest' that she found in her stays abroad, was certainly 'the social life of Italy'; but she did not mean 'the society of Italians themselves. Into the actual native circles a foreigner rarely enters, and, when he does so, seems to find few topics of common interest.'[27] The sole non-foreigner on her long list of 'remarkable people one meets in Florence' was Massimo D'Azeglio (1798–1866), depicted as 'a fallen Statesman, an almost forgotten Author, a general on the shelf, a Prime Minister reduced to living in a single room at a hotel, without a secretary or even a valet'.

Apart from her 'maid and a man servant . . . always clean and respectably dressed', Miss Cobbe must have noticed indigenous Italians; but none worthy enough to attract her attention. Besides, her special reason 'for visiting Florence' was to meet the poetess Elizabeth Browning, who talked to her about Tuscan art; a topic about which Cobbe 'knew little and, perhaps, cared less'.[28] She had no interest in the company of Italian women: they always seemed married and always young because, observed the no-longer youthful spinster, they had dowries sufficient 'to secure a husband, the only question being, whether he is a little younger or older, richer or poorer'. After which, they all shut themselves up in families which were 'enormously large . . . under the same roof', the English concept of a house for every nuclear family being completely unknown to them.

On the other hand she knew these facts well, even before her arrival in Florence. Perhaps she did not bother to look around her, even when she chose to write a weighty tome actually entitled, *Italics: Brief Notes on Politics, People and Places in Italy in 1864*. In this, furthermore, the author explained why the educational level of the Italians was lower than that of other peoples; how the Church monopolised education (she made no mention of the laws establishing compulsory public education) despite the Italians' hatred of papal government and their religious apathy. And indeed, the most backward European countries were none other than those which were the most Catholic: the two Sicilies, Ireland and Spain. Fortunately, Italy was at least a country favourable to 'literary and artistic people': 'some French, many more German, still greater numbers of English and Americans'; to all except Italians, apparently. Through her foreign friends, Miss Cobbe made herself an expert on the defects of Italian politics and culture, and thus in her book provided very detailed information on the universities. It was therefore possible to learn such grotesque myths that at Naples, a major cultural centre, there were no more than two students; and that at Florence university-level education (to which Schiff contributed) did not exist at all.[29]

Scientific versus traditional culture

Tuscany boasted an ancient and exemplary tradition of schools, study and research; in 1859, the government had founded there the Istituto di Studi Superiori Pratici e di Perfezionamento — the Institute of Higher Practical Studies and Post-graduate Research, arranged in four departments: law, philology and philosophy, medicine and surgery, natural sciences. It drew students and lecturers from every part of Italy and from abroad.[30] At this institute in Florence, a city which became the capital of the Kingdom of Italy in 1865, commitment to social reform was closely tied to the programme of scientific research; it is sufficient to cite the 1865 inaugural lecture — the manifesto of Italian positivism — given there by Pasquale Villari (1827–1917).[31] Before anywhere else in Italy, Florence had a chair and a museum of anthropology, held by Paolo Mantegazza, the founder of the *Archive for Anthropology and Ethnography*; and the psychiatrist and philosopher Francesco De Sarlo (1864–1937) later established the laboratory of experimental psychology there. Historians and sociologists, researchers in the natural sciences and students of Far Eastern civilisations at the Institute habitually debated with philosophers of various schools of thought.

Not always without disagreement. The evolutionary theories publicised also by Schiff and by Herzen Jr, son of Ivanovic, friend of the anarchist Michael Bakunin and the republican Giuseppe Mazzini; their democratic ideals in science and education; the experimental method itself, seemed too liberal for moderate Catholic members of the older generation. On 24 March 1863, *La Nazione* reported the public lecture 'On the relationship between man and monkeys' given by Alexander Herzen at the Museum of Natural History. A few days later Abbot Raffaello Lambruschini (1788–1873) wrote a concerned letter to the editor; 'I do not really understand what can be the use of informing ordinary people that their ancestors were monkeys.'[32] Was this a fact ascertained by science? He wished to believe not; but he thought in any event that it would be more properly discussed, and then with caution, only by those persons qualified to do so (amongst whom, however, he would not have been included).

Lambruschini asserted that scientific disclosure was permissible only if it did not provoke worrisome moral and civil consequences. The unwelcome revelation of man's relationship with monkeys, however, diminished 'the ordinary people's respect for the sacred scriptures'. All beings had their origin in divine creation: this belief was 'the only one which would not *perturb* the minds of the devout, the only one people could be told. For whatever the truths of science, they must remain silent before superior truths flowing from the sanctuary of the conscience which is a study of a higher physics, a higher chemistry and a higher physiology than the study in which the senses speak.'

In his reply, Herzen did not restrict himself to defending evolutionary theories and scientific independence from the claims of a theology with which he saw no possibility of accord. He declared himself as concerned for the ordinary people as the Abbot, but his social ethics differed. He did not deny that scientific disclosure might have moral consequences; it was as a result of these that he hoped to free Italians of superstition. Descent from animals might not be a flattering concept; but it encouraged the prospect of a future 'boundless perfecting of humanity'. Moreover, when he and his colleagues had circulated the theory of evolution, society had not actually collapsed, nor had there been any increase in the number of criminals; nor, still less, had the ordinary people been offended. Herzen the Russian knew the Florentines fairly well; he appreciated their humour enough to smile when they had joked about him; 'He's the one who says his dad was born to a monkey . . . But who knows, suppose it's true?'[33]

Lambruschini's criticism is only one example, among many, of the attacks on naturalism which pervaded Italian culture of this period until the neo-idealistic hegemony of Benedetto Croce (1866–1952) and Giovanni Gentile (1875–1944). Often the controversy degenerated into belittlement of the natural sciences themselves and of psychology; to compound the difficulties, during this difficult period of transition, few topics were left undisturbed by the critics, especially by those in the most reactionary Catholic circles; a glance at the pages of *Civiltà Cattolica* from 1860 onwards is enough to confirm this.[34] Nevertheless it contains no articles opposing vivisection: this did not become either a motive or a pretext for another crusade against the dreaded positivism. The Jesuits were probably aware that public opinion was not particularly sensitive about the issue; and the Church moreover maintained its own notions regarding animals and man's relationship with them.

According to natural and revealed ethics, 'animals cannot be subjected to any law'. This in fact would presuppose free will and a knowledge of good: exactly what they lack. The *Summa Theologica* stated that animals do not have a rational life, by which they direct and move themselves; but are always impelled as by another, natural impulse; and that this is a sign that they are by nature servile and created for use. Following the example of Adam, and of Noah, man must relate to animals according to the divine intention which destined them to serve and therefore he ought to use them for a purpose. He would sin only if he makes them suffer through mere caprice.

Such prescriptions contrasted less, in Italy, with the general mentality and with the scientific vision of naturalism, than with the anthropomorphism of certain anti-vivisectionists, particularly the English ones. In fact the massive *Catholic Encyclopedia*, published by the Vatican, later declared that vivisection (the accomplishment, that is, of *painful experiments*) is permissible whenever it has scientific purposes; and thus is useful. On the other hand, the activities of the animal protection societies were also approved, providing they did not adopt erroneous principles, such as the rights of animals; a duty of charity towards them cannot exist in the Christian sense nor a sentimental love for inferior creatures.[35]

The edifying discussions about Christ, cats, dogs or flowers, which took place between Miss Cobbe and her female friends, really did sound sentimental, even amazing, to the inhabitants of the country which gave them hospitality. The Italians, for the most part, maintained direct relations with animals; relationships of work, of use but also a very different kind of affection; a familiarity which had disappeared in large cities and was unknown in certain social classes. Most people would not have been able to believe that Mrs Mary Somerville could be distressed because she might not find her 'own roses and mignolette' again in Heaven. They would have found it odd that she consoled herself by saying: 'dear animals, I believe *we shall* meet. They suffer so often here, they must live again!' When Lord Shaftesbury, in a letter to Cobbe, theoretically justified the same conviction — 'love so manifested by dogs especially is an emanation from the Divine essence and as such, it can or rather it will never be extinguished' — he most decidedly shocked a Catholic priest.

Many people protested that it would have been better to help one's neighbour, rather than animals. Not a few insinuated that the exaggerated love of pets was too great and the capacity to love men too little. But Miss Cobbe insisted on having known many people who, thank God, 'have all a dog's merits of honesty and single-hearted devotion plus all the virtues which can only flourish on the high level of humanity'. By this she meant 'intellectual ability', which in four-legged creatures is not boundless, although they did not lack a 'quite unlimited Love'. She did not, moreover, appreciate all dogs indiscriminately, only those endowed with a 'true Dog-character'; for the possession of which mere membership of the canine race was certainly not sufficient.[36]

If the criteria for this definition had been made clear, some possibility of a compromise with the physiologists might have resulted. Those dogs which were not supremely good and responsive, those which in fact did not have the 'right character', would have been perfectly suitable for their experiments. But no one sufficiently appreciated Miss Cobbe's subtle distinctions, if only because, when she talked, it was not always clear whether she referred to dogs or to people. The anthropomorphism she applied to her pets related exclusively to goodness, found in an ideal person or rather in a child, 'in the sense in which a child is human'. But to the 'Italian mind' — if one can use such a generalization — neither children nor animals are particularly good. The talking cats and dogs in fairy-tales and proverbs, from Piedmont to Sicily, do not speak in the way that Beatrix Potter (1866–1943) would have made her little rabbits talk.

The abortive trial of 1873

Misfortunes did not entirely end, for Moritz Schiff, with the energetic Englishwoman's departure from the Tuscan capital. Another dispute, again more publicised in British than in Italian journals, hit him in 1873. In this year, the Society for the Protection of Animals in Florence was founded, supported chiefly by the aristocracy and a high percentage of foreign, especially English, members. Miss Cobbe, in 1894, confided that they had 'led the agitation there against vivisection ever since'.[37] She would have been less content, had she known more: for example, that one of the founder members was actually the dauntless vivisectionist Schiff, who entirely approved of the principles of the Society's constitution. The lawyer member Ottavio Andreucci, of the Istituto di Studi Superiori, explained that the aim of the Society 'is not exclusively humanitarian', but the protection of those lesser creatures of which man ought to consider himself master, without indulging in excessive love for them.[38] Defending animals against cruelty, improving their conditions in order to make 'the best use of the same'. This was stipulated in article 1 of the Constitution.

The three-word slogan, 'Justice, Humanity, Profit', inspired well-meaning activities: inspection of markets and slaughter-houses, re-organisation of the transport of horses, a watch over the city's zoos, creation of courses in veterinary science, legislative schemes to regulate hunting and fishing and opposing the maltreatment of animals. Working on these were suitably qualified persons in each area, politicians and university lecturers. The ladies were assigned to the ethical commission, entrusted with 'refining the minds' of the less educated public and particularly of children; for which purpose the protection of animals was only one of many possible means. Moral appeals were made indefatigably to parish priests and priors, to masters and ministers, to carters even; perhaps without much success. The Director of Public Education in Florence reacted by praising Countess Baldelli's noble sentiments but he rejected her request. The government did not deem it necessary to adopt measures such as teaching school children duties towards animals, which seemed more suitably done privately.[39]

Undoubtedly the Florentine Society was very heterogeneous, combining people of different social class, culture and ideology. Sometimes members expressed views in public in the name of the Society which conflicted with its official policy. 'The executive council ought to forbid such a thing', protested Signor Amico at the general meeting of 31 March 1875. It was not proper that a translation of a strongly anti-vivisectionist English book should state on the frontispiece that it was 'printed by the Society for the Protection of Animals in Florence'. Being hostile to the autonomy of scientific research, this book by George Fleming contradicted the official position expressed by the Society.[40]

In April 1874, its President A. Magliani (1825–91), adviser to the Corte de' Conti, an administrative organ of the civil magistrature, had in fact nominated an internal commission of doctors and lawyers to examine vivisection and other problems. They confirmed their support for the decisions taken by the Medical Academy in Paris in 1863, on behalf of freedom for practitioners in physiology and also in opposition to any form of control. This declaration of agreement also implied a clear statement of position regarding a trial which had begun some months before. The chief plaintiffs, their lawyer Giacomo Pimpinelli and the defendants were all founder members of the Society.

In September 1873, three aristocratic residents of the neighbourhood to which the physiological laboratory was being moved had instituted legal proceedings against Moritz Schiff and the Mayor of Florence, Ubaldino Peruzzi (1822–91), superintendent of the Istituto di Studi Superiori. They were held responsible for the disturbance occasioned by the heart-rending howls of animals in pain, caused by the operations to which they were subjected night and day. The trial in the civil court did not then continue because one of the plaintiffs, the Marquis Gino Capponi (1792–1896), a cultured man and a friend of Lambruschini, withdrew his statement before the trial began.

In the meantime, Professor Schiff considered himself insulted, as usual, and he insisted in vain upon the trial at all costs, to demonstrate the baselessness of the attack upon his scientific integrity and upon his humanity. He clarified his position in a letter of 30 December 1873, sent to *La Nazione* and to *The Times*. The latter newspaper's fulminations against Italian barbarity and cruelty to animals were answered two days later by Alexander Herzen.[41] After all the uproar, it seemed that the barking had come from guard-dogs, belonging to Schiff and to the owners of neighbouring villas, which had been particularly excited by the bustle of setting up the new laboratory.

If there had been a misunderstanding, the professor nevertheless demanded a formal apology. The Marquis, senator Gino Capponi, had to declare his 'love for Science . . . , his esteem for its distinguished practitioners'. But the unnamed Schiff requested and obtained, thanks to Herzen's mediation, more than this. The Marquis endorsed the following declaration: 'I have never believed, nor do I believe now, that the howling which disturbed me was caused by his methods of experimentation.'[42] On publication of this retraction, Schiff might have felt satisfied. But he was not.

He had just dedicated the second edition of his book *On the Method Followed in Experiments with Living Animals* . . . 'To the Florentine Society for the protection of animals, in full acknowledgement of its high aims'; Schiff then took to deploring the ambiguities within the Society itself. In his opinion, the executive council had contradicted the aims mentioned above, favouring the absolute autonomy of physiological research, already voiced earlier by Magliani's internal commission. At the general meeting of 31 March 1875, two members of the latter, the physician Amerigo Borgiotti and the lawyer Andreucci requested that their report on vivisection of 10 September the previous year be published in its entirety. It was, after a long delay and a dramatic debate.[43] The split within the Society was already obvious when on 14 September 1874, a majority of the executive council — some Italian aristocrats and a few

Englishmen (a composition very different to that of the special commission) had decided to have physiological experiments carried out in Florence under the control of a committee.

Moritz Schiff had himself invited members of the Society to visit his laboratory, but he denied that those authorised to do so — all of whom were unacquainted with physiology — had the 'right to supervise the procedures'. He therefore declared that he would have felt it dishonourable to continue supporting a Society 'whose management protects libel . . . neglects and discredits its own duties, and . . . is a tool for the blind fanaticism of a minority of its members'.[44] He consequently tendered his resignation, and so did the members who worked at the Istituto di Studi Superiori: it was a serious loss, both for the Florentine Society and for the cultural and reforming movement which animated the city.

The relations between Schiff and the Société pour la protection des animaux de Genève were, in contrast, very calm. From 1876, when Carl Vogt (1817–95) invited him to teach at the Genevan university, Schiff was able to pursue his teaching and research in peace, even though he once more came across an anti-vivisectionist Englishwoman. Anna Kingsford openly said: 'I do not love men and women. I dislike them too much to do them any good.' She dedicated all her efforts to rescuing animals from human cruelty, even to the extent of offering herself as a subject for vivisection. She founded an anti-vivisectionist society at Geneva in 1883; but this never succeeded, stated J.J. Dreifuss, in having a lasting influence upon public opinion.[45]

Acknowledgement

Thanks are due to Dr Renato Mazzolini for various helpful suggestions.

This chapter examines Moritz Schiff's role in a major episode of the vivisection debate. It does not deal, therefore, with the actual physiological research which Schiff carried out — which would, however, be worth a separate study.

Notes

1. The original documentation for the two disputes was collected by A. Herzen, together with his own ironic commentary, *Gli Animali Martiri e i loro Protettori e la Fisiologia. Udienza Pubblica del Tribunale Civile della Ragione. Rapporto Stenografico* (A. Bettini, Florence, 1874), pp. 47–105.

2. B. Atkinson, 'Introduction', in *Life of Frances Power Cobbe as Told by Herself, with Additions by the Author,*, posthumous edn (Swan, Sonnenschem & Co., London, 1904), p. ix (italics mine). See also F.P. Cobbe, *Meeting at Stoke Bishop* (London, 1883) p. 4: 'as an Intuitive Moralist . . . I decline, for my own part to entertain the question of the possible usefulness of vivisection.'

3. See for example, M. Schiff, 'Dichiarazione', *La Nazione*, 6 January 1864, and Herzen, *Animali Martiri*, p. 60. The memoirs of H. Yofé are cited by H. Friedenwald,'Notes on Moritz Schiff', *Bulletin of the Institute of the History of Medicine*, 5 (1937), pp. 589–602.

4. Also in Herzen, *Animali Martiri*, p. 71.

5. On the scientific and teaching activity of the German physiologist at Florence, see P. Siciliani, *Della Fisiologia e delle Lezioni Fisiologiche Sperimentali del Prof. Maurizio Schiff* (Pieraccini Printers, Pisa, 1863); M. Schiff, *Lezione di Fisiologia Sperimentale sul Sistema Nervoso Encefalico date dal Prof. M.S. nel Museo di Firenze l'anno 1864–65*, 2nd edn (Cammelli, Florence, 1893); 'Relazione Generale sugli Esperimenti Fatti nel Primo Trimestre dell'Anno 1866 nel Laboratorio Fisiologico del Museo di Firenze', *Nuovo Cimento*, 21–2 (1865–6), pp. 307–36; *Sunto dei Lavori Fatti nel Laboratorio Fisiologico di Firenze nell'Anno 1869* (Florence, 1870).

6. B. Miraglia, *Contro la vivisezione degli animali*, lectures published and financed by the Victoria Street Society (L. Gargiulo printers, Naples, 1884). On Miraglia, see V.D. Catapano, *Le Reali Case de' Matti nel Regno di Napoli* (Liguori, Naples, 1986), in particular ch. xi.

7. In Herzen, *Animali Martiri*, p. 72.

8. M. Schiff, *Sopra il Metodo Seguito negli Esperimenti sugli Animali Viventi nel Museo di Storia Naturale di Firenze. Cenni.* (Barbera, Florence, 1864), p. 37.

9. *Life of F.P. Cobbe*, p. 616.

10. M. Schiff, 'Dichiarazione', *La Nazione*, 6 January 1864 in Herzen, *Animali Martiri*, p. 60.

11. Also in defence of Schiff, see the medical journal *Imparziale*, for example 4 (1864), pp. 21–32 and 5 (1865), p. 254.

12. *Grida della Civiltà e dell'Umanità contro le vivisezioni. Agli Uomini di Cuore*, 4th edn (Borgarelli printers, Turin, 1881), p. 46; N. Licò (pseud.), *La Protezione degli Animali* (Hoepli, Milan, 1902); *La Vivisezione. Suoi Errori e sua Inutilità* (Bucolo, Paternó, 1907), p. 13; A. Agabiti, *Il Problema della Vivisezione* (Voghera, Roma, 1911), opposing only painful experiments which could not be justified by useful results; G. Ciaburri, *La Vivisezione* (Bocca, Turin, 1938). The accusations against the anthropologist referred to experiments he himself reported, P. Mantegazza, *La Fisiologia del Dolore* (Paggi, Florence, 1880), opposing which L. Scocia, *Se Sia l'Anima o il Cervello che Sente e Pensa*, 2nd edn (Ricci printers, Florence, 1887). Since such research into pain necessarily excluded anaesthesia, Schiff declared that 'for the moment science would do better not to pose such questions', *Sopra il Metodo*, 2nd edn, enlarged (Bettini, Florence, 1874), p. 71n. It should be noted that much of the anti-vivisectionist literature published in Italy consisted of translations of British writings.

13. R.D. French, *Anti-vivisection and Medical Science in Victorian Society* (Princeton University Press, Princeton and London, 1975), p. 50.

14. An inaccurate reference to the dispute with Schiff occurs in G.

Landucci, *Darwinismo a Firenze. Tra Scienza e Ideologia (1860–1900)* (Olschki, Florence, 1977), pp. 32–3 which provides a picture of the Florentine culture of the time.

15. *Life of F.P. Cobbe*, pp. 622–3.

16. See *Zenzero*, 23 December and 31 December 1863; and similar arguments made by Herzen, 'Lettera al Direttore', *Gazzetta del Popolo*, 31 December 1863, all in *Animali Martiri*, pp. 48–9, 52–8.

17. Ibid., pp. 59–62.

18. *Life of F.P. Cobbe*, pp. 623–4.

19. Also in Herzen, *Animali Martiri*, pp. 67–71. Previous advertisements paid for by the accusers had appeared anonymously in the *Gazzetta del Popolo*, 28 December, 31 December 1863, 8 January 1864. Three Italian signatories to Cobbe's petition declared that they were withdrawing their support 'having verified that the accusations were false', *La Nazione*, 9 January 1864.

20. They appeared first as a supplement in *La Nazione*, then in book form (see note 8 above).

21. Schiff, *Sopra il Metodo*, 1st edn, p. 4, and pp. 9–35.

22. See J. Moleschott, *Del Metodo nella Investigazione della Vita. Prima Prolusione al Corso di Fisologia Sperimentale, nella Reale Università di Torino* (Loescher, Turin, 1862), p. 28; *L'Unità della Vita. Terza Prolusione* (Loescher, Turin, 1864), p. 52; *Fisiologia e Medicina. Quarta Prolusione* (Loescher, Turin, 1865), p. 43.

23. The specificity attained in physiological research resulted precisely from 'being entirely based on vivisection, the principal method guaranteed by direct experiment'. P. Siciliani, *Della Fisiologia*, p. 9.

24. See note 5 above.

25. *La Nazione*, 11 January 1864, and Herzen, *Animali Martiri*, p. 65.

26. *Life of F.P. Cobbe*, p. 623. The first to sign was Mrs Somerville; Walter Savage Landor added such furious words that Cobbe herself thought it better to omit them.

27. F.P. Cobbe, *Italics: Brief Notes on Politics, People and Places in Italy in 1864* (Trubner & Co., London, 1864), p. 373 and ch. xvii. She was not, however, displeased by D'Azeglio's company, 'considering the common-places to which even clever Italians are fond of limiting their subjects' (p. 388). Other references pp. 137–8.

28. *Life of F.P. Cobbe*, p. 378 and pp. 366–9.

29. Cobbe, *Italics*, pp. 57–8, 49, 52, 375.

30. E. Garin, 'L'Istituo di Studi Superiori di Firenze', in his anthology, *La Cultura Italiana tra '800 e '900* (Laterza, Rome-Bari, 1976), pp. 29–69; G. Gentile, *Gino Capponi e la Cultura Toscana nel Secolo Decimonono* (Vallecchi, Florence, 1922); A. Olivieri, 'L'Insegnamento della Filosofia nell 'Istituto di Studi Superiori di Firenze 1859-1924', *Annali dell'Istituto di Filosofia*, Florence University (publishers), 4 (1982), pp. 100–46.

31. P. Villari, 'La Filosofia Positiva e il Metodo Storico', *Politecnico*, serie IV, scientific lit., 1 (1866), pp. 1–29. On Mantegazza, see Landucci, *Darwinismo*, pp. 107–27; for De Sarlo, P. Guarnieri, 'Il Morale e il Normale: sull'Antideterminismo di F. De Sarlo', *Rivista di Filosofia*, 75 (1984), pp. 251–71; and also by the same author, '"La Volpe e l'uva". Cultura Scientifica e Filosofia nel Positivismo Italiano', *Physis*, 25 (1983), pp. 601–36.

32. R. Lambruschini's letter, *La Nazione*, 4 April 1869, is reprinted together with the reply in A. Herzen, *Sulla Parentela fra l'Uomo e le Scimmie*,

2nd edn (Bettini, Florence, 1869), p. 5.

33. Herzen, *Animali Martiri*, p. 24.

34. For example, all in *Civiltà Cattolica*: 'Conseguenze Sociali del Naturalismo Politico', 16, vol. 2 (1985), pp. 641–57; 'I Meriti dei Liberi Pensatori', 16, vol. 1 (1865), pp. 290–305; 'Non Può un Cattolico Fare Onore ai Liberi Pensatori', 16, vol. 1 (1965), pp. 522–36.

35. See entry, 'animal' (vivisection does not exist) in *Enciclopedia Cattolica*, published by the Ente per l'Encic. Catt., Vatican City, 1948, vol. 1 (my italics).

36. *Life of F.P. Cobbe*, pp. 384, 573 and 616.

37. Ibid., p. 623.

38. See O. Andreucci, *Della Società Fiorentina Protettrice degli Animali. Esposizione Storico-Igienico-Economica* (Gazzetta d'Italia printers, Florence, 1873), pp. 4, 8, 10. SPAF (Società Prottetrice degli Animali in Firenze), *Resoconto dell'Assemblea Generale tenuta in Firenze il 15 Gennaio 1873* (Claudiana Printers, Florence, 1873), 'Statuto Organico', pp. 17–18; this also contains the list of 529 members, pp. 31–46. Honorary members were: Countess G. Baldelli, A. Bankes, Esq., A. De Noe Walker, H. Oxford, Lady Paget. Donor members: P. Amphoux, Monna M. Della Torre, H. Th. Graham, R.G. Shaw, C. Shinkwin, M. Shinkwin, Lord Sinclair, E. Vernon, Lady Willoughby.

39. See various letters from SPAF to ecclesiastic and state authorities, together with G. Cammarota's reply, 7 July 1874 in SPAF, *Resoconto dell'Assemblea Generale, tenuta in Firenze il 31 Marzo 1875* (Gazzetta d'Italia printers, Florence, 1875), pp. 76–81, and the letter from the Ministry of Public Education, 28 November 1876 in *Resoconto dell'Assemblea Generale, tenuta in Firenze il 24 Marzo 1877* (Galletti & Cocci Printers, Florence, 1877), pp. 72–5. The Sardinian Penal Code of 20 November 1859, extended to the entire kingdom, did not consider maltreatment of animals as a crime in itself but a crime against property and public order (art. 675–7, 681, 683–5). Tuscany retained its own penal code, which was sufficiently progressive, treating cruelty to animals as an offence against public morality, punishable by Police Regulations. In 1889 when all legislation was completely unified, the Zanardelli Code penalised cruelty to any species of animal, even when it was 'solely for scientific or educational purposes, but outside institutions intended for teaching . . . and experiments such as to arouse revulsion' (art. 491). The first comprehensive law regulating the Societies for the Protection of Animals was promoted by L. Luzzati, on 12 June 1913 (n. 611) and remained in force until the legislation passed 11 April 1938. The first law concerning vivisection was that of 12 June 1931 (n. 924), modified in 1941, but still binding today: 'Vivisection and all other experiments upon warm-blooded vertebrates (mammals and birds) are prohibited when not having the purpose of furthering progress in biology and experimental medicine' (art. 1). See under entry 'Animals', *Enciclopedia del Diritto* (Giuffré, Milan, 1958), vol. 2. A careful consideration and comparison with the contemporary British situation was provided by F.S. Arabia, *Della Leggi intorno alle Sevizie verso le Bestie* (printed by the Reale Università, Naples, 1874).

40. For the whole debate, SPAF, *Resoconto 31 Marzo 1875*, pp. 37–60 (Amico's intervention, pp. 47–50).

41. The above-mentioned letters, other news in the *Corriere* and *Gazzetta*

d'Italia, and translated articles in British journals (including a defence of Schiff by R.E. Lankester) are published, with an ironic commentary by Herzen, in *Animali Martiri*, pp. 73–105.

42 G. Capponi's letters of 30 January and 5 February 1874, together with the entire report are in Schiff, *Sopra il Metodo*, 2nd edn, reprinted with a double preface especially for this dispute, pp. v–vii and 72–6.

43. The Report 'Della Vivisezione' and deliberations of the Executive Council in SPAF, *Resoconto 31 Marzo 1875*, pp. 63–73 and 43. At the first Congress of the Italian Societies for the Protection of Animals (Rome, May 1878) it was the President of the Florentine Society who persuaded the delegates that a request to parliament for a special anti-vivisection law would have been inopportune; see SPAF, *Resoconto della (6a) Assemblea Generale* (printed by Galletti and Cocci, Florence, 1878), pp. 13–15. The *Resoconto*, then the *Bollettino* of SPAF, which I have examined as far as 1915, contain no other relevant discussions on vivisection, but only news and translations of the proceedings of other societies, especially those in Great Britain.

44. M. Schiff explained what the Society had done and, on the other hand, what it ought to have done, in his 'Prefazione' to the Italian translation of a work on anti-vivisectionist errors and prejudices written by a New York Professor of physiology, J.C. Dalton, *Esperimenti sugli Animali come Mezzo di Conoscenza nella Fisiologia, nella Patologia, e nella Medicina Pratica* (Bettini, Florence, 1875), pp. 5–24.

45. J.J. Dreifuss, 'Moritz Schiff et la Vivisection', *Gesnerus*, 42 (1985), pp. 289–303, focuses on the time at Geneva. See also E. Maitland, *A. Kingsford, Her Life, Letters, Diary and Work* (London, 1896), 1, p. 48, also cited in French, *Anti-vivisection*. See also Tröhler and Maehle, this volume, p. 153.

6

Vicarious Suffering, Necessary Pain: Physiological Method in Late Nineteenth-century Britain

Stewart Richards

Introduction

The historian of physiology faces unusual problems which spring directly from the nature of physiological research. In recent years we have grown accustomed to public (and increasingly to scientific) disquiet over the destructive potential of the physical sciences, despite their employment of a method that is still widely regarded as intrinsically 'neutral'. With physiology, however, there is a more immediate problem, for anxiety here centres on the moral status, not of its ultimate ends, but of its essential means. Again in our own time, the orthodox defence of 'vivisection' has most often been made in terms of therapeutic necessity, the suffering of animals being justified by the benefits to humankind. But how much more difficult of resolution was this equation in the 1870s, when the vivisection controversy in Britain was reaching its peak, and the number of animal experiments beginning to rise steeply on its now-familiar exponential course.[1] Claude Bernard himself, writing towards the end of his life's work, could apparently cite few cases of clinical application in concrete support of experimental medicine, while Michael Foster, near the beginning of his career, named as specific benefits of vivisection only the 'scientific ligature', and Bernard's own work on the glycogenic function of the liver (although diabetes remained untreatable for another fifty years).[2]

Even by 1900 the clinical benefits of experimental physiology (as distinct from those of bacteriology, pharmacology and pathology) were few indeed, and it was just this problem that made the ethical conundrum so challenging. All the actors in the vivisectional drama performed as if they accepted the hypothesis of medical utility in advance of the evidence to support it, doubtless realising that it would do no harm to their strategy of establishing physiology as an independent science justified by the pursuit of knowledge for its own sake. However, it is not sufficient for the historian merely to justify their work on grounds of perspicacity or foresight. At the time, it seemed to their critics that physiologists in Britain were guilty of perpetrating under the *protection* of the Cruelty to Animals Act (1876) wanton yet premeditated cruelties of just the kind that other Acts had already been introduced to proscribe.[3] In these circumstances, therefore, it was inevitable that physiological experimentation should have to proceed in an atmosphere of intense and undiminishing controversy.

The nature of the anti-vivisection movement in Britain has, of course, been the subject of a certain amount of historical scholarship,[4] although little attention has yet been given to the dilemma faced by the physiologists themselves. What I have referred to elsewhere as the 'inescapable element of personal morality' in their work represents a dimension for physiologists which few other natural scientists have been obliged to confront.[5] In the present chapter I shall concentrate upon the methods of nineteenth-century experimental physiology, with particular reference to John Scott Burdon Sanderson's *Handbook for the Physiological Laboratory* of 1873,[6] and in so doing, examine something of the attitude of its practitioners to the vexing problem of pain.

Sanderson's *Handbook*: scenes of laboratory life

When Gerald Geison remarked that the history of physiological techniques has been 'pitifully neglected',[7] it is clear that he had chiefly in mind the mechanical, electrical and chemical methods pioneered most notably by the Germans in the mid-nineteenth century, methods (and instruments) that soon found their way to laboratories around the world. Geison was concerned to show that the very interest of historians in ideological, institutional, economic and even 'national' factors influencing the direction of physiology, might have exaggerated the impression of different 'schools' and different 'styles'. If we concentrated more on what French and German physiologists actually did in their laboratories and less on their programmatic and retrospective statements, then we might be surprised at the degree of similarity between their approaches.[8] Certainly, there is one technique that has always been universal — as well as a prerequisite for the others — and that is vivisection itself, even though it has been associated particularly with the French, perhaps because their measuring and recording instrumentation was inferior to that of the Germans,[9] and because antivivisection agitation in France was never comparable to that in Britain.[10]

Publication of Sanderson's *Handbook* marked a watershed in the transmission of Continental methods to British laboratories, and from its 725 pages we can gain the closest approximation available of what it was like actually to do physiology at the time. Although it was the first book of its kind in any language, its perusal reveals the enormous debt which resurgent British (and particularly English) physiology owed to the French and German schools. By its didactic style, moreover, it takes us into the minds of the very men who, bringing the methods of their teachers to Britain, were to transform the status of British physiology within a generation.

But before examining the *Handbook* itself, we must first encounter its editor and his co-authors. John Scott Burdon Sanderson was an Edinburgh-trained physician, profoundly influenced by a postgraduate sojourn in Paris, where he had studied organic chemistry under Gerhardt and Wurtz, embryology with Coste and physiology under Claude Bernard.[11] From 1856 to 1867 he had been Medical Officer of Health for Paddington, and thereafter, until his appointment in 1870 as Professor of Practical Physiology and Histology at University College, London (under William Sharpey), had devoted himself increasingly to pathological investigations at his own private laboratory in Queen Anne Street, collaborating there with the pioneer neurologist David Ferrier, and with Thomas Lauder Brunton, lecturer in Materia Medica at St Bartholomew's Hospital. Even after assuming his initial university post, and then subsequently after Sharpey's retirement in 1874, when the two chairs were merged into the single Jodrell Professorship of Human Physiology (the first independent chair of physiology in the country), Sanderson actively continued the study of infectious processes at the newly-established Brown (Sanitary) Institution (1871), of which he became the first Superintendent.[12]

A short testimonial by Bernard indicates that he had been well satisfied with his student's progress and thought favourably of his future prospects: 'Très souvent, dans le laboratoire, en travaillant avec M. le Dr Sanderson, j'ai été à même d'apprécier toute l'entendue et la solidité de ses connaissances dans les sciences médicales . . . Je souhaite qu'un esprit aussi distingué ne reste pas perdu pour la science.'[13]

Sanderson's able and ambitious collaborators (all medically

trained) were Michael Foster, his predecessor at University College and now praelector in physiology at Trinity College, Cambridge, the individual who, probably more than any other, advanced the reputation of British physiology in the last quarter of the century;[14] the histologist Emanuel Klein, whom Sanderson had brought from Vienna as Assistant Professor of Pathology at the Brown Institution;[15] and his research colleague Lauder Brunton, who was soon to become the country's leading pharmacologist.[16] Together, they produced an enormously impressive summary of the micro-anatomical, vivisectional and experimental bases of the physiology of their day, specifically as a stimulus and guide for those wishing to gain the experience necessary to undertake original research of their own. As Sanderson's preface put it:

> This book is intended for beginners in physiological work. It is a book of methods, not a compendium of the science of physiology, and consequently claims a place rather in the laboratory than in the study . . . The practical purpose of the book has been strictly kept in view . . . [and] many subjects are omitted . . . either because they do not admit of experimental demonstration or because the experiments required are of too difficult or complicated a character to be either shown to a class or performed by a beginner.[17]

The book itself was in two volumes, one of almost 600 pages of text, and another devoted entirely to some 353 illustrations divided between 123 plates. A fully comprehensive description of its contents would be a more lengthy undertaking than is here possible, but for present purposes a brief, selective, but representative summary will suffice. Klein's histology required rather more than a quarter of the text for a systematic account of the microscopic morphology of the tisssues, copiously illustrated by 189 engravings made from the author's own original drawings. The methods for obtaining and preparing tissues from the living animal and from preserved material, with or without the various reagents, stains and hardening materials, and for cutting either frozen or wax-embedded sections, were described at length, and their particular cellular features exemplified in considerable detail. Dealing comprehensively with characteristic structures from all over the body, from the simplest blood corpuscles and epithelia to the compound tissues of the great organ systems and even to the phenomenon of inflammation, it was, as *Nature*'s reviewer expressed it, 'far superior to any existing work'.[18] In view of this, it was all the more surprising that there was no proper illustration of the microscope — for the use of which all the other methods were but a preparation — nor any discussion of the principles of its use. 'Beginners' in physiology could not, at this time, have been expected to enjoy familiarity with such an instrument, especially in view of the book's indication that the distributors were all to be found in Germany and France (whereas the other histological apparatus, such as syringes, cannulae, injecting equipment, warm stages, ovens, surgical items and the like, were evidently available in London).[19]

If the proportion of an experimental handbook that was devoted to structure appears excessive, we must remember that physiology in Britain, while actively throwing off the fetters of gross, morbid anatomy, was for many years to continue a close and fruitful relationship with histology.[20] This is clear at the beginning of Sanderson's first chapter, on blood, although any duplication of Klein's work is here skilfully avoided by his concentrating on the plasma, on coagulation, the chemical and optical properties of haemoglobin and its quantitative determination in whole blood, and finally upon the methods of analysing the blood gases. Here, and indeed throughout his section of the book, Sanderson draws overtly on the instruments and experimental methods of his Continental peers (later estimating that the whole subject of physiology at this time was 'founded to the extent of about perhaps nine parts out of ten upon experiments conducted in foreign countries').[21] From Hoppe-Seyler's simple bottle for preparing fibrin and Heynsius's method for isolating its source of origin, he passed to the experiment of Max Schultze on the action of heat and then to consideration of the various pumps designed to extract the gases from blood (for example Geissler and Sprengel's in Germany and Alvergniat's in France). Finally, there were the procedures used for blood gas analysis, namely, the volumetric method of Bunsen and Pflüger, and that by replacement with carbonic oxide (CO) devised by Bernard.

When, in his second chapter, Sanderson turned to the circulation of the blood, his debt to French and German physiology remained overwhelming. For the measurement of systemic pressure, Poiseuille had connected one branch of an ordinary mercury manometer to an artery and designated his device the haemadynamometer; in all probability the method had originated in the crude experiments of Stephen Hales. This technique had been used until Ludwig, in 1846, invented the recording drum kymograph, an instrument of the greatest importance in many branches of physiology and one, according to Sanderson, that was probably 'suggested by a contrivance of Watt's for registering the pressure of the steam engine'.[22] However this may be, it was Ludwig's clockwork instrument (and, for some purposes, the spring kymograph of Fick) that revolutionised experimental work by yielding a permanent record on a smoked drum of functional events against a constant time base. For work of a more clinical character, i.e. where direct pressure measurements could not be made, Marey's sphymograph worked on much the same principle. Sanderson improved this by providing graduation marks and a calibration procedure so that a reliable indirect estimate of changes in pressure could be obtained, and had himself published a *Handbook for the Sphymograph* in 1867.

For many experiments on the circulation, the recording kymograph was to be used in conjunction with the induction apparatus and key of Du Bois Reymond, an assembly that was indispensable for many of Sanderson's demonstrations of nervous control. In both frogs and rabbits he repeated the classical experiments of Brown-Séquard, Ludwig, Cyon and others, designed to clarify the role of the spinal cord, medulla oblongata and autonomic nervous system, experiments that often required delicate surgery and artificial respiration (by means of Sprengel's blow pipe). On the heart itself, he described the methods for examining its contraction *in situ*, also in both amphibia and mammals, and again related these observations to clinical practice by the use of Marey's cardiograph and tympanum on the human chest and by the analysis of heart sounds. One method for measuring endocardial pressure had been developed by Joseph Coats of Glasgow (though in Ludwig's laboratory), another by Chauveau in France, while the experiments on the intrinsic cardiac nerves, and on the vagal and accelerator functions, drew upon work by Bernstein, Blasius, Cyon, Czermak, Goltz, Marey and Stannius, with illustrated physiological dissections by Ludwig and Schmiedeberg.

Sanderson's chapter on the respiratory system began with simple observations of external thoracic movements, using Bert's modification of Marey's recording stethograph. It then proceeded to an investigation of the muscles responsible, together with their innervation and influence upon the circulation, and finished with an experimental study of apnoea. The reader was referred to Ludwig's *Arbeiten* of 1869 for the most accurate (closed circuit) method of determining expired carbonic acid gas (CO_2), but the more convenient, if somewhat less exact, open-circuit apparatus designed by Petten-kofer was considered satisfactory for most purposes. Some of the experiments on the vagus nerves were of a chronic character, simply involving observations over the few days prior to death of animals subjected to bilateral cervical vagotomy, but others demanded careful surgery (performed on Czermak's rabbit support) and a full range of stimulating and recording apparatus. Of the latter kind were those designed to repeat the celebrated work of Hering and Traube on the effects of respiration on the arterial pressure. Sanderson closed this chapter with some of his own research (drawing also on experiments by Pflüger and Rosenthal) on the patho-physiological consequences of dyspnoea and terminal asphyxia. His section as a whole ended with a brief account of the principles and practice of calorimetry, using a whole-body instrument little changed from that of Lavoisier and Laplace, and with a description of thermometry in the context of physiology which recommended the use of 'thermo-electric needles' and Sir William Thomson's galvanometer.

To Michael Foster fell the task of investigating the functions of muscle and nerve. Where Sanderson had struggled with a diverse and derivative field which drew extensively not only on more basic areas within physiology, but also on physics and chemistry, Foster's topic was a clearly-circumscribed unity, the very stuff, we might say, of first principles. Of this subject he was unmistakably the master: though elementary in essence, it was of absolutely fundamental importance to the new quantitative physiology and Foster had the refreshing confidence to keep his treatment simple. In just seventy-eight pages, divided into no less than sixteen easily-comprehended chapters, he succeeded in covering his whole field in one compelling sequence. First there was a short introduction on the intentionally limited scope of his section, followed by clear general instructions for preparing the necessary apparatus and materials. There followed chapters on the general properties of muscles at rest, on the laws of contraction and tetanus, the electrical currents in nerves and muscles, on electrotonus, and on the nature of the nervous impulse. The problem of 'urari poisoning' and independent muscular irritability was given a separate chapter, and the section ended with more complex experiments investigating the spinal nerves (including the phenomenon of recurrent sensibility), reflex action and selected functions of the encephalon investigated by surgical ablation. Foster's instruments for exploiting the frog muscle and nerve-muscle preparations were almost all based on the myograph and associated apparatus devised by Marey, Helmholtz and Pflüger, on Du Bois

Reymond's induction equipment and accessories, and on various versions of the kymograph, calibrated quantitatively by means of the recording tuning fork of König. All of these instruments were clearly illustrated in use. One surprising omission from Foster's sequence was the experiment which measured the velocity of the nerve impulse, which had been performed both by Helmholtz and Bernstein during the previous two decades.[23] But overall his section was undeniably impressive, in part for the remarkable clarity of style which was soon to distinguish his famous *Textbook of Physiology* (1877), and in part for his particular device of summarising, clearly and logically, the theoretical principles that were to be derived from his practical results.

The final section of the *Handbook*, by Brunton, was on digestion and secretion, together with two introductory chapters on the properties of albuminous compounds and the methods for their analysis, and on the chemistry of the tissues (nicely complementing Klein's work on structure). Throughout, the author adopted the wise and useful expedient of classifying his experiments by asterisks to indicate the 'most important and best suited for demonstration', the 'less important' and the 'unimportant or . . . difficult to perform' (though these last two categories were not separated). The chapter on digestion proper commenced with an investigation of the properties and constituents of saliva and proceeded to a long series of complex experiments for the study of its secretion. These involved the surgical preparation of permanent parotid and submaxillary fistulae, employing realistic illustrations of typical dissections by Bernard. Fistulae were also used to study digestion in the stomach (Bernard), the secretions of pancreatic juice (Ludwig and Bernstein) and intestinal juice (Thiry and Paschutin) and the secretion of bile by a technique developed in Edinburgh by William Rutherford.[24] Overall, this chapter was unusual in that its many straightforward methods of clinical chemistry (for examining the properties of materials such as ptyalin, pepsin, the bile acids and pigments, and glycogen) could be performed only after elaborate surgery, there being no better example than the simple test for glycosuria, which followed upon Bernard's (illustrated) method for discretely puncturing the floor of the fourth cerebral ventricle.

Brunton's section ended, however, with a chapter on two secretions, milk and urine, that could be easily collected without surgical intervention. Here reference was made to recent work by Hoppe-Seyler and Lubavin on the digestion of casein, and to the long-established methods of Liebig for determination of chlorine and urea in urine, even Davy's for the latter, and to Fehling's method for detecting sugar. Finally, there was a short appendix on such useful ancillary techniques as the manipulation of glass tubing, the prevention of water loss by evaporation (using Liebig's condenser), precipitation, filtration (Bunsen's water air pump), dialysis, ignition, weighing, the determination of specific gravity and the use of measuring flasks, pipettes, burettes and the like, in volumetric analysis.

Despite its occasional omissions, the *Handbook* thus provided a detailed overview of the major experiments performed during the preceding generation. All of the contemporary reviews recognised it as a major landmark which signified the arrival of an new *kind* of physiology in Britain. Indeed, the *Medical Times and Gazette* went further, claiming that it represented a 'new era in the history of physiology . . . throughout the world'.[25] For the *Lancet* it was 'perfectly unique', providing the adequately prepared student with 'so thorough a knowledge of physiology as shall stand him in good stead in whatever branch of medical practice he shall afterwards be engaged'.[26] This, however, is not to say that the book escaped criticism, in particular the misleading nature of its editor's opening prefatory sentence concerning 'beginners in physiological work'. By any standard, it was not for the uninitiated; rather, it was an advanced companion, the *British Medical Journal* considering it 'of much service to teachers and to those who may desire to prosecute some research', but also remarking that it was difficult to see 'where Dr Sanderson would have the "beginner" begin'.[27] E.A. Schafer, Sanderson's assistant and colleague at University College, his eventual successor in the Jodrell Chair, and the youngest of the 'great triumvirate' (with Foster and Sanderson)[28] responsible for the regeneration of British physiology, was too young himself to contribute directly to the *Handbook*, but he too considered it to be the earliest sign of revival.[29]

Yet the *Handbook*'s remarkable impact, both on physiology itself and on its public image, can have had little to do with any commercial success, for there is nothing to indicate that it sold in significant numbers. Indeed, it could hardly have done so, for Sanderson estimated in 1875 that there were still only fifteen or sixteen individuals 'currently engaged in physiological investigations' in the country, and he claimed pointedly to have recommended to his own medical students that they not buy the book.[30] No second edition ever appeared in Britain (although a single-volume French translation — omitting Klein's work — was published in 1884), and it is tempting to wonder whether a good proportion of the print run was not given away. Evidence for such speculation comes in the shape of a 'memorandum' on courtesy copies in Sanderson's private diary for 19 March 1873. This consists of a list of some forty-four names of eminent British and Continental colleagues (though not including Bernard and Ludwig, who were perhaps too obvious to need any reminder), among whom the best known were Bennett, Bernstein, Brown-Séquard, Brucke, Chauveau, Darwin, Fick, Goltz, Hering, Hermann, Humphrey, Huxley, Marey, Murchison, Pflüger, Ranvier, Rutherford, Sharpey (to whom the book was dedicated), Schiff and Simon.[31] With such generosity, it is difficult to see how the publishers (J. & A. Churchill) could have anticipated a market sufficient to cover their costs. At all events, while it may indicate Sanderson's concern to repay his professional debts and to ensure the propagation of his cause, it also suggests that the infamous reputation so rapidly acquired by so specialised a book was the result, not of its wide public distribution, but rather of its particularly sensitive theme.

Justification: ethics and anaesthetics

Nowhere in the *Handbook* did Sanderson or his co-authors specify a coherent policy on anaesthesia, an omission severely criticised in the review by *Nature*, which said that a whole chapter devoted to the issue was desirable.[32] This is a matter of critical importance in connection with the vivisection controversy because the fear and loathing of the physiologists' critics was directed against what they alleged to be experiments causing unjustifiable pain. If it could be shown that anaesthetics were effectively applied, then any criticism of experimental physiology would be restricted (except for the slight pain of induction itself) to the question of taking life — which very few opposed on principle — or to more peripheral issues such as how and from where the animals were obtained and under what conditions they were kept while awaiting experimentation or for the duration of chronic experiments.

From his evidence before the Royal Commission in 1875, it is clear that Sanderson regretted his weak editorial policy on this question, suggesting that the report of the British Association's biology committee of 1870 should be circulated or prefixed in the book. In this report (which he had signed) it had been stated that anaesthetics should always be used when practicable and never omitted for purposes of teaching known facts; that physiological truths should be sought only by experienced investigators in properly equipped laboratories; and that living animals should never be used in veterinary education in the mere pursuit of manual dexterity.[33] The fact that the report, or something like it, had not been used in the book, suggests either a generally lackadaisical approach, or a naive unawareness that any ethical problem might conceivably exist. The 'beginners' for whom the *Handbook* had been written were not, claimed Sanderson retrospectively, 'ordinary [medical] students . . . [but] persons who are engaged in physiological study . . . requiring a knowledge of what has been done before and the way in which it has been done'. '[We] had not in view', he continued,

> the criticism of people who did not belong to our craft in writing it, and we did not guard against all possible misunderstanding of that sort. It is generally understood that we use anaesthetics when ever we possibly can, and consequently that is a thing taken for granted. That ought to have been stated much more distinctly at the beginning in a general way, but it was not stated for the reasons I have given.[34]

But of course this comment could carry little weight, for the uncomfortable reality was that the only persons who 'generally understood' what really went on in the laboratory were the very ones whom the anti-vivisectionists most suspected of cruel actions.

Following the storm that by this time had broken, Foster also acknowledged that if he 'had to write the book over again, [he would] be more careful'. But he reiterated Sanderson's claim that it was intended for students working under experienced supervision, rather as a book on surgery, without mentioning anaesthetics but assuming that they would be used.[35] It was unfortunate that the whole position had not been properly clarified, but the furore, he implied, was out of all proportion to the realities of laboratory life, being the result not of something genuinely sinister, but simply of misunderstanding, misrepresentation and oversight.

Klein's evidence, however, was of a different order. Many of his experiments in the *Handbook* were, he said, necessarily painful, but he never used anaesthetics, except for teaching purposes or for his own convenience (that is, to keep his animals still, to eliminate their cries and to prevent his being scratched or bitten). Asked about his attitude to the suffering of animals, Klein answered at once: 'No regard at all.' He employed anaesthetics for demonstrations because 'there is a great deal of feeling against [cruelty] in this country' and it was appropriate to have regard for the opinions of others.[36] The physiologists were horrified at his outspokenness, which did great damage to their cause and undoubtedly contributed to the legislative action that followed the Royal Commission. Yet it has been claimed that Klein was well known as an animal lover and he was, of course, employed in an institution dedicated to their well-being.[37] In this context, it is therefore important to realise that he appeared explicitly to reject any utilitarian arguments based on the balance of animal and human suffering or gain, simply disregarding anaesthetics or animal suffering when engaged in research.

Not that the matter of anaesthesia was clear-cut. We must appreciate that the state of the art was then hardly one of sophistication, such that it could by no means be assumed that 'anaesthetised' animals were necessarily free of pain. Genuine volatile anaesthetics, such as ether and chloroform (both in use since the 1840s) were applied only by means of a sponge soaked in the liquid, while other materials, such as opium and its derivatives, were narcotic agents rather than true anaesthetics; in any case, the degree of insensibility could have been assessed only by wilfully inflicting pain and observing the reactions.

The doubt over anaesthesia was further exacerbated by the problem of curare. This substance (also known as 'urari' and 'woorari', variously spelt) was a bitter resinous material obtained from plants of the genus *Strychnos*. It had long been known as a South American Indian arrow poison and had been shown by Bernard to produce motor paralysis but not afferent insensibility, such that a victim might experience 'the most atrocious suffering which the imagination of man can conceive'.[38] Where it was used in addition to some analgesic agent, the latter was typically withdrawn after initial surgery, and respiratory movements — paralysed by the former — then maintained by a reciprocating pump. The function of the curare was therefore to eliminate any residual whole-body movements still permitted by the restraining apparatus and which otherwise would be a source of inaccuracy during the experiment. It was partly for this reason that curare exerted a special fascination over physiologists, because the autonomic functions of the body appeared to continue operating normally under its influence. Such was by no means always the case with the then-conventional anaesthetics which, for example, tended to lower the body temperature and blood pressure in mammals, were liable to produce effects that varied widely between species (making extrapolation to the clinical situation the more dangerous), and were not unknown even to reverse an other-wise 'normal' physiological response.[39] It is perhaps significant that the index to the *Handbook*, while omitting any reference to anaesthesia or to specific agents, included both curare and urari and referred the reader to Foster's section where he said that, if given sub-cutaneously, 'the frog will be perfectly motionless, with respiration arrested, but its heart still beating'.[40] For some purposes this would have been an ideal preparation indeed.

Painful dissections advocated in the *Handbook* for the unanaesthetised frog included the following:

To investigate the histology of the eye (p. 38):
> The centre of the cornea of a frog . . . is firmly cauterized with a pointed stick of lunar caustic [silver nitrate] [and about an hour later] the cornea is excised . . . [A similar result could be achieved by] first scraping the cornea of a living frog . . . with a sharp cataract knife, so as to remove the epithelium completely.

To demonstrate the influence of afferent nerves and the vagus on the heart (p. 272):
> A frog is secured in the supine position [by pinning to a board]. The pleuro-peritoneal cavity is then opened, and the intestines and other viscera are removed, great care being taken not to injure the mesentery. Nothing now remains excepting the heart resting upon the oesophagus.

To prepare for an examination of the roots of the spinal nerves chloroform should be used for initial operative procedure, but not for the experiments themselves (p. 400):
> The results are most clear and distinct when the organs of consciousness are intact, and the ordinary tokens of sensa-tion are used to determine whether the impulses caused by [electrical] stimulation of the peripheral termination reach the conscious central nervous system or not.

The casualness of these, and countless other instructions, would seem to indicate that the status of the frog as a sentient vertebrate was submerged in the exigencies of laboratory life by its contingent suitability as a 'preparation' for demonstrating simple physiological laws. (Note, for example, that the instruction to use 'care', unfail-ingly refers to the operative procedure, never to the animal itself.). Such detachment, however, was not confined to lowly amphibia, as the following extracts from experiments on rabbits illustrate:

To produce inflammatory changes in liver cells (p. 160):

> Inflammation of the tissues of the liver may be induced by passing a needle into the organ. Twenty-four to forty-eight hours after the injury, the animal must be killed.

To prepare for kymographic recordings of arterial blood pressure (p. 212):

> The animal having been secured on Czermak's rabbit board [which incorporated a 'kind of forceps' . . . which . . . seize upon the head . . . and . . . convenient attachments for the extremities'] and the fur clipped, the skin is pinched up . . . on either side of the . . . trachea [and opened] vertically . . . The opening having been enlarged . . . the sterno-mastoid is slightly drawn aside, so as to bring the [carotid] artery, with its three accompanying nerves . . . into view . . . the distal end [of the artery] is tied, and the proximal end closed by a clip. Finally . . . the cannula is inserted, and the ligature tightened around the constriction.

For excitation of the nerves of the ear (p. 245):

> The animal having been curarized, the apparatus for artificial respiration is connected with the trachea, and the manometer of the kymograph with the carotid artery. The great auricular nerve is then carefully exposed . . .

Even where anaesthesia was recommended during massive surgery, as for the extirpation of the cerebral hemispheres after removal of the root of the skull, 'the amount of ether or chloroform should be no more than is absolutely necessary just to send the animal off' (p. 418).

With dogs — one of the species most likely to elicit outrage from the opposition — there was equally little evidence of sentiment or compassion. Thus asphyxia could be produced by complete occlusion of the trachea and the consequences clinically described up to the final spasms which precede death in three to four minutes.

> In these spasms . . . the head is thrown back, the trunk straightened or arched backwards, and the limbs are extended, while the mouth gapes and the nostrils dilate. They are called by physiologists stretching convulsions, and must be carefully distinguished by the student from the expiratory convulsions previously described. (p. 320)

Finally, there were those experiments which could, in any case, be witnessed only in the absence of anaesthesia. For example, the reflex excitation of the chorda tympani (nerve) could cause an increased secretion of saliva only after the animal had been 'allowed to recover from the chloroform' (p. 473), whilst Bernard's method for demonstrating 'recurrent sensibility' in the spinal roots could succeed only after complete 'recovery' because it depended on the contraction of muscles in response to (presumably severe) pain.

> If the animal be strong, and have thoroughly recovered from chloroform . . . irritation of the *peripheral* stump of the anterior root causes not only contraction in the muscles supplied by the nerve, but also movements in other parts of the body indicative of pain or of sensation. (p. 403)

The *Handbook*, then, by overtly encouraging young physiologists to adopt the 'new' methods, also exposed these methods to wider critical scrutiny. In particular, by taking the vivisectional approach for granted, and hence by implying the necessity for some pain, it provided essential ammunition for the anti-vivisectionist case. Yet in an extraordinary way, that is surely symptomatic of the nature of the dilemma encapsulated by the book, it showed that some of those very experiments which were clearly more difficult to justify than the physiologists claimed, were at the same time often a good deal less objectionable than the anti-vivisectionists supposed.

The paradox here represented is perhaps best illustrated in a general way by a quantitative analysis of the *Handbook*'s contents designed to identify the proportion of all experiments that were, in the terms of the 1876 Act, 'calculated to give pain'. Whether or not pain resulted would then have depended upon the anaesthetic precautions taken. Needless to say, any such approach is fraught with difficulty, for to remain manageable, it cannot avoid the crude reduction of a very wide range of procedures — from elementary observations to complex investigative research — to the single term 'experiment'; nor can it distinguish different degrees or durations of pain. The figures that appear in Table 6.1, therefore, provide no more than a makeshift summary of the book as a whole, although they do give a relatively accurate estimate of the number and proportions of painful vivisections. They are maximum figures, based upon the authors' failure to specify anaesthesia; if, as they claimed, anaesthetics were nevertheless often applied, the table may significantly exaggerate the numbers of painful experiments.

For present purposes, what emerges most strikingly from Table 6.1 is that some 22 per cent of all experiments described in the

Table 6.1: An analysis of the Handbook for the Physiological Laboratory *in terms of its authors and the experiments they described*

Author	Number of experiments	Number calculated to give pain[a]	Number with anaesthetics or 'pithing'	Number causing pain[b] Under curare	No precautions specified
Klein	179	32	0	6	26(10)
Sanderson	120	66	20	19(8)	27(21)
Foster	118	14	7	7	0
Brunton	205	25	19	0	6(6)
Totals	622	137	46	32(8)	59(37)
Percentages	100	22	7	15	

[a]Note that the 1876 Act concerns vertebrate animals only.

[b]In these columns, the first figures refer to total numbers of experiments, those in parentheses to experiments on mammals only (mostly rabbits and dogs).

Handbook were potentially painful, but (at most) only 15 per cent actually caused pain. In a minority of cases the pain was 'necessary' (in the sense that meaningful results could not be obtained under deep anaesthesia), and in some of these there is no doubt that it must have been prolonged and severe. It can also be seen that Klein and Sanderson, the individuals who took the brunt of the anti-vivisectionists' criticism, were also those who described the great majority of painful experiments; on the other hand, Foster (who has sometimes been regarded as ruthless)[41] advocated only seven, and none of these was on mammals.

It is obviously no easy matter to assess the attitude of the *Handbook*'s authors to the problem of pain. Such evidence as we have on Sanderson, for instance, does suggest that he was indelibly influenced by Claude Bernard, whom he considered to be 'the most inspiring teacher, the most profound scientific thinker, the most remarkable experimental physiologist that he had ever known'.[42] 'A physiologist', wrote Bernard himself, ' . . . no longer hears the cry of animals, he no longer sees the blood that flows, he sees only his idea and perceives only organisms, concealing problems which he intends to solve.' 'The science of life [moreover] is a superb and dazzlingly lighted hall which may be reached only by passing through a long and ghastly kitchen.'[43] If Bernard's matter-of-fact attitude towards vivisection was promoted by his early experience in the notorious veterinary school at Alfort,[44] it seems equally possible that Sanderson's exposure to the 'ghastly kitchen' in Paris left him marked for life. Or, we might say with greater accuracy, unmarked, for in his extensive laboratory notebook, taken down at the master's lecture-demonstrations, there is no hint of any misgivings; perhaps his feelings really were 'blunted', or at least inhibited by fear of 'professional ruin', as another of Bernard's British students maintained.[45] At any rate, there was no mention of a place for anaesthetics in Bernard's experiments that included, in rabbits, cutting the sympathetic nerves to influence peripheral blood flow, or the vagi to observe the (chronic) accumulation of food in the oesophagus; in dogs, the injection of saliva into the circulation, and the dissection out and cannulation of the pancreatic duct to collect secretions; in the horse, division of the ducts of the parotid glands to demonstrate the effect on mastication time; and in species unnamed, the injection of coffee into the circulation to increase the blood pressure, or air into a vein to cause death by asphyxia. Bernard did, it is true, stress the difficulties of experimentation, and illustrated them by reference to the great number of contradictory results which, he said, were occasioned chiefly by the use of different species under different conditions — a point, incidentally, that had always been made by the anti-vivisectionists in their critique of the supposed relevance of animal experiments to human medicine. Even without these problems, successful replication was difficult, for when 'about 40 grammes' of saliva were injected into the jugular vein of a 'moderate sized dog', the creature displayed 'symptoms like those of narcotic poisoning almost immediately', despite Bernard's assurance that on previous occasions 'no bad consequences' had followed.[46]

Sanderson's records of his own subsequent researches indicate that he brought back from France something of the atmosphere of his master's laboratory. They clearly show that he sometimes experimented without anaesthetics (or with curare), but on other occasions used them (though not always with conspicuous success). Thus one of his experiments on asphyxia involved an unanaesthetised dog that was 'much excited . . . and struggled much while it was being secured'. Sanderson was irritated because 'much time was lost in readjusting the arterial tube', but when this had been done he casually recorded that 'the thoracic cavity was opened by two large incisions in each flank . . . and artificial respiration was maintained for about 20 minutes', before producing asphyxia. In other, similar, experiments, 'anaesthesia' was induced by morphine (but 'the animal never fell asleep or became insensible') or by 'burning a puff ball in a metal box' (but 'before the usual operation had been completed the effect had passed off — and the animal was excited . . . ').[47] Any explanation for his inconsistent policy is not apparent. What is clear is Sanderson's conviction that he was exercising the 'sharp compassion of the healer's art';[48] painful experiments on asphyxia were justified by their ultimate consequences for the benefit of mankind.

Evidence on the other authors is scant and somewhat contradictory. Klein always maintained that while public attitudes to vivisection on the Continent and in England differed substantially, this distinction did not extend to the physiologists themselves.[49] Foster, however, thought that 'physiologists abroad [were] not so tender . . . as are the English physiologists', although (practically alone among the latter) he had had no direct acquaintance with their laboratories.[50] Finally, Brunton maintained that his concern for the welfare of experimental animals was nurtured during his spell with Ludwig in Leipzig, where the master 'would not allow anything that approached to cruelty in his laboratory'. So great, indeed, had been Brunton's own wish to resolve the doubts about curare that, while in Germany, he had volunteered to be put under its influence and burned with a hot iron so as to experience for himself whether or not he felt the pain. It would have been a critical test for those who still clung to the belief that curare did have analgesic properties, but in the event Ludwig had vetoed the experiment as too dangerous.[51]

As is well known, the government, in the wake of the *Handbook*'s influence, tried to codify the now-manifest problems of laboratory ethics in its Cruelty to Animals Act of 1876. It will therefore be of interest to close this section with a brief examination of how the Act could influence the day-to-day activities of a working physiologist. E.A. Schafer, for example, had been granted the third licence to be issued by the Home Office, in October 1876, although his research activities were restricted not merely to his employing institution (University College), but to five named rooms within it, 'viz, The Physiological Theatre, The Microscope Room with Ante-room, the Jodrell Laboratory, the Physiological Laboratory and the Curator's Room'.[52] Somewhat ominously, he may have felt, he was also subject to any 'such conditions as the Secretary of State may hereafter think fit to press in the event of . . . becoming possessed of a Certificate exempting him from the operation of any of the provisions of the said Act as to the use of Anaesthetics'. When the licence was extended for a year some fourteen months later Schafer was restricted to a maximum of twenty experiments only under Certificate B (permitting recovery from anaesthesia);

this condition was applied until 1884, when the number was raised to fifty, although he was then obliged to report to the Home Office after each ten. In 1887 and 1889 came official reminders that if 'severe pain' had been induced as a result of the Certificate B experiments, the animal was to be immediately killed under anaesthesia; that all wounds were to be dressed antiseptically; and that a copy of any work published was to be sent to the Home Secretary.

By the 1890s, Schafer's research under Certificate A (without anaesthesia) involved 'subcutaneous injections of extracts of suprarenal capsules and other organs' in rodents, cats, dogs (both requiring Certificate E also) and monkeys, while that under Certificate B included 'removal of the whole or part of certain organs . . . with the view of determining what if any changes in nutrition result therefrom', and it had to be performed on cats and dogs because 'all previous experiments on nutrition [had] been', and because 'these animals also bear such operations better than rodents'. Other investigations required lesions to be made in the central nervous system and in various glands of cats, dogs, horses and monkeys. In January 1898 came a warning letter from the Home Office.

> It appears that you have exceeded by three the ten experiments allowed on cats and dogs under Certificates B7 and EE1 . . . The Secretary of State is willing to consider that the three unauthorized experiments were performed through inadvertence in failing to remember the limitations, but he must impress upon you the obligation of making yourself fully acquainted with the Conditions of your licence.

On this evidence it would seem that the system of licences and certificates introduced by the Act was implemented effectively by the Home Office and scrutinised with care. It was a genuine attempt to allay public misgivings by being seen to regulate vivisectional activities, an attempt that was sufficiently rigorous to irritate and even sometimes to impede the physiologists,[53] yet at the same time one that continued to allow the great majority of experiments to proceed unhindered. In consequence, of course, the Act — a fine example of British compromise — proved to be one that satisfied nobody; the scientists, while grudgingly admitting that it protected them from malicious persecution, resented being identified by the stigma of legal restriction, while the anti-vivisectionists, who seldom bothered to distinguish one type of experiment from another, were wholly dissatisfied by the governmentr's unwillingness to abolish them all.

Conclusion

The late nineteenth century saw the emergence in Britain of a new kind of physiology which explicitly accepted the need for vivisectional techniques. There is little evidence of wanton cruelty on the part of individual physiologists, but sufficient to indicate that they were engaged in a profession that might necessarily prescribe the infliction of pain. Such pain as was unavoidable was justified however because it was construed as the indispensable condition for medical advance.

It would be altogether too simplistic to pretend that the contradictions inherent in the vivisection debate can be resolved merely by unrelenting exposure to the physiological techniques employed. Yet none of the conflicting implications that arise from these methods can be fairly assessed without a detailed awareness of the methods themselves. Empathetic entry to the physiological laboratory is the only reliable ground from which worthwhile discussion can proceed, but the present chapter, in helping to create this minimal basis, makes no attempt to establish the case for one side in the debate or the other. Indeed, its essential point is that dispassionate examination of physiological method reveals the overall ethical issue as altogether more ambiguous than any thesis of simple polarity might suggest. In advocating a more 'committed' historiography, it aims merely to redress a balance which hitherto has weighed heavily in favour of a naive and dismissive positivism, and which accordingly has provided only a partial impression of what physiology *must* be like. A properly balanced appraisal, on the other hand, should represent physiology, not as a special case of physics or chemistry, but as a science whose instrumental norms are inseparable both from its public and its private ethics.

Acknowledgements

I am grateful to Maurice Crosland and Nicholas Rupke for helpful suggestions, and to the Archivists at Edinburgh University Library, the National Library of Scotland and University College Library, London, for permission to consult papers in their care, and to quote from them where appropriate. The work was supported by a grant for research in the history of science from the Royal Society.

Notes

1. R.D. French, *Antivivisection and Medical Science in Victorian Society* (Princeton University Press, Princeton, 1975), ch. 12.

2. C. Bernard, *An Introduction to the Study of Experimental Medicine*, trans. H.C. Green (Macmillan, New York, 1927), pp. 214–15; M. Foster, 'Vivisection', *MacMillan's Magazine*, vol. 29 (1874), pp. 367–76 (p. 272). The evidence for the utility and necessity of animal experimentation that was considered by the *Second Royal Commission on Vivisection* (1906–12) — which had been set up to review the working of the Act of 1876 — is usefully summarised by J.E. Hampson, 'Animal Experimentation 1876–1976: Historical and Contemporary Perspectives' (unpublished PhD thesis, University of Leicester, 1978), ch. 2, Tables I and II. The case was made strongly in connection with work that was undeniably 'applied' (e.g. bacteriology, and research into cancer and other diseases), but it was still remote and indirect with respect to most 'pure' physiology. See, for example, the *Final Report* (Cd. 6114), *Parliamentary Papers* (1912/13), XLVIII, 401, paragraphs 39–49.

3. See B. Harrison, 'Animals and the State in Nineteenth Century England', *English Historical Review*, vol. 88 (1973), pp. 786–820 (esp. pp. 787–99). The Act of 1876 was certainly unusual, for not only did its system of certificates make legal some procedures already prohibited by other laws, but also permitted the licensee to breach the basic provisions of the Act itself.

4. The standard reference on the British anti-vivisection movement is French, *Antivivisection*. The movement's influence on the growth of physiology is discussed in G.L. Geison, *Michael Foster and the Cambridge School of Physiology* (Princeton University Press, Princeton, 1978), esp. ch. 2; E.S. Turner, *All Heaven in a Rage* (Michael Joseph, London, 1964), ch. 15; J. Turner, *Reckoning with the Beast. Pain and Humanity in the Victorian Mind* (Johns Hopkins University Press, Baltimore and London, 1980), esp. ch. 6; L.G. Stevenson, 'Science down the Drain: On the Hostility of Certain Sanitarians to Animal Experimentation, Bacteriology and Immunology', *Bulletin of the History of Medicine*, vol. 29 (1955), pp. 1–26; and L.G. Stevenson, 'Religious Elements in the Background to the British Antivivisection Movement', *Yale Journal of Biology and Medicine*, vol. 29 (1956), pp. 125–57.

5. S. Richards, 'Drawing the Life-Blood of Physiology: Vivisection and the Physiologists' Dilemma, 1870–1900', *Annals of Science*, vol. 43 (1986), pp. 27–56 (p. 29). In this paper I have explored these problems more fully, and offered a defence of my 'committed' historiographical approach.

6. E. Klein, J. Burdon Sanderson, M. Foster and T. Lauder Brunton, *Handbook for the Physiological Laboratory*, ed. J. Burdon Sanderson (2 vols, Churchill, London, 1873).

7. Geison, *Michael Foster*, p. 34.

8. Ibid., p. 17.

9. Bernard, *Experimental Medicine*, pp. 147–8. See also K.E. Rothschuh, *History of Physiology*, trans. and ed. G.B. Risse (Krieger, Huntington, New

York, 1973), p. 271.

10. For a comparative study of the movements in different countries see H. Bretschneider, *Der Streit um die Vivisektion im 19. Jahrhundert* (Gustav Fischer, Stuttgart, 1962). The Société française contre la vivisection was founded in 1882 with Victor Hugo as its Honorary Chairman. See J. Schiller, 'Claude Bernard and Vivisection', *Journal of the History of Medicine*, vol. 22 (1967), pp 246–60 (p. 253).

11. A.S. McNalty, 'Sir John Burdon Sanderson', *Proceedings of the Royal Society of Medicine*, vol. 47 (1954), pp. 28–32 (p. 29). For the fullest account of Sanderson's life and work, see Lady G. Burdon Sanderson, *Sir John Burdon Sanderson. A Memoir* (Clarendon Press, Oxford, 1911).

12. The foundation of which was greeted by the *Lancet* as 'one of the most important scientific events that have ever happened in this country'. *Lancet*, vol. 2 (1873), p. 238.

13. Testimonial by Bernard in connection with Sanderson's application for the post of physician at the Western General Dispensary, dated 24 June 1853. National Library of Scotland, Edinburgh, MS 20501/5.

14. See Geison, *Michael Foster*, and *Dictionary of Scientific Biography* (Scribner's, New York, 1972), vol. 5, pp. 79–84.

15. W. Bulloch, 'Emanuel Klein (1844–1925)', *Journal of Pathology and Bacteriology*, vol. 27 (1925), pp. 684–97.

16. *Dictionary of Scientific Biography* (Scribner's, New York, 1970), vol. 2, pp. 547–8.

17. *Handbook*, p. vii.

18. *Nature*, vol. 7 (1873), pp. 438–41 (p. 439).

19. *Handbook*, p. 573.

20. See K.J. Franklin, 'Physiology and Histology', in H. Dingle (ed.), *A Century of Science* (Hutchinson, London, 1951), pp. 222–38; and L.G. Stevenson, 'Anatomical Reasoning in Physiological Thought', in C. McC. Brooks and P.F. Cranefield (eds.), *The Historical Development of Physiological Thought* (Hafner, New York, 1959), pp. 27–38.

21. *Report of the Royal Commission on the Practice of Subjecting Live Animals to Experiments for Scientific Purposes* (C. 1397), *Parliamentary Papers* (1876), XLI, Q. 2211.

22. *Handbook*, p. 209.

23. See M.A.B. Brazier, 'The Historical Development of Neurophysiology', in *Handbook of Physiology*, Section 1, *Neurophysiology*, 1 (American Physiological Society, Washington D.C., 1960), pp. 1–58 (pp. 22–3).

24. See J.H. Bennett, 'Report of the Edinburgh Committee on the Action of Mercury on the Biliary Secretion', *Report of the British Association for the Advancement of Science* (Norwich, 1868), pp. 187–232. Bennett noted that the method involved 'loathsome manipulations' (p. 232). For Rutherford's own difficulties on the vivisection problem, see S. Richards, 'Conan Doyle's "Challenger" Unchampioned: William Rutherford, FRS (1839–99), and the Origins of Practical Physiology in Britain', *Notes and Records of the Royal Society*, vol. 40 (1986), pp. 193–217.

25. *Medical Times and Gazette*, vol. 1 (1873), p. 433.

26. *Lancet*, vol. 1 (1873), p. 632.

27. *British Medical Journal*, vol. 1 (1873), pp. 490–1. That Foster soon

realised the absurdity of the Preface is shown by his publishing *A Course of Elementary Practical Physiology* in 1876, which was described as 'an introduction to the *Handbook*' (p. ix). He was careful here to mention the use of anaesthetics and to describe the method of 'pithing' a frog under ether. Sanderson also produced his elementary *University College Course of Practical Physiology* in 1882 and stated that frogs should be pithed and mammals anaesthetised (pp. 2 and 33).

28. See Geison, *Michael Foster*, p. 6.

29. E.A. Schafer in Burdon Sanderson, *Sir John Burdon Sanderson*, p. 97.

30. *Royal Commission*, Q. 2607 and 2239.

31. Burdon Sanderson Papers, University College Library, London, MS Add. 179/29. The book was also sent to several scientific institutions, including the Royal Society, and the Royal Colleges of Physicians and Surgeons.

32. *Nature*, vol. 7 (1873), p. 441. None of the medical journals, however, made this point or showed any awareness that there might be an ethical dilemma.

33. *Report of the British Association for the Advancement of Science* (Edinburgh, 1872), p. 144; and *Royal Commission*, Q. 2369.

34. *Royal Commission*, Q. 2239.

35. Ibid., Q. 2333.

36. Ibid., Q. 3531–43. Klein's remarkable testimony has been discussed at greater length elsewhere, for example by French, *Antivivisection*, pp. 103–7 and L.G. Stevenson, 'Physiology, General Education and the Antivivisection Movement', *Clio Medica*, vol. 12 (1977), pp. 17–31 (pp. 29–30).

37. Bulloch, 'Emanuel Klein', pp. 688 and 686.

38. J.M.D. Olmsted, *Claude Bernard, Physiologist* (Cassell, London, 1939), pp. 233–9 (p. 226).

39. See, for instance, *British Medical Journal*, vol. 1 (1899), p. 94, for the stimulating effect of morphine in dogs, and the *Handbook* itself (pp. 311–12) for the reversal of a response by chloral. More than thirty years later, the *Report of the Second Royal Commission on Vivisection* seemingly acknowledged the difficulties inherent in the use of anaesthetics by its failure to make specific recommendations on this most sensitive of points. It was aware that the genuine anaesthetics then available could produce full insensibility and preferred simply to assume that they were always used effectively. See *Final Report*, para. 81.

40. *Handbook*, p. 395.

41. The novelist George Eliot, for example, who knew Foster through her common law husband George Henry Lewes (an amateur physiologist), wrote (to Mrs Charles Bray, 3 February 1876) that Foster was 'in many ways an admirable man — but men, like societies, have strange patches of barbarism in the midst of their "civilisation" '. See G.S. Haight, *The George Eliot Letters* (7 vols, Oxford University Press, London, 1956), vol. 6, p. 221.

42. See F. Gotch (obituary notice on Sanderson), *Proceedings of the Royal Society*, vol. 2 (1905), p. 3.

43. C. Bernard, *Experimental Medicine*, pp. 103 and 15.

44. On Alfort, see Olmsted, *Claude Bernard*, p. 26; also *British Medical Journal*, vol. 1 (1861), pp. 502–3; and *Lancet*, vol. 2 (1860), pp. 143–4 and vol. 2 (1863), pp. 224–5, for British complaints.

45. See the letter by George Hoggan, *Spectator*, vol. 48 (1875), pp. 177–8. Sanderson's notebook of Bernard's Course in Experimental Physiology (1852–3) is in the National Library of Scotland, MS 20504/1–55.

46. Sanderson's 'Bernard' notebook, National Library of Scotland, MS 20504/4.

47. Sanderson's own experimental notebooks of 1866–7, National Library of Scotland, MS 20505/4/13/18.

48. T.S. Eliot, 'East Coker', IV, 1.4.

49. *Royal Commission*, Q. 3543 et seq.

50. Ibid., Q. 2410.

51. *Second Royal Commission, 3rd Report, Evidence, Parliamentary Papers* 1908 (Cd. 3757), LVII, 283, Q. 7106 and 6918.

52. The licence is in the University of Edinburgh Library, GEN. 2007/5. All of the following details are taken from this source.

53. See French, *Antivivisection*, pp. 186–7.

7

Anti-vivisection in Nineteenth-century Germany and Switzerland: Motives and Methods

Ulrich Tröhler and Andreas-Holger Maehle

The antecedents: man and animals from 1830 to 1870

The gradual perception of cruelty to animals

The rise of sentimental feelings towards animals displayed by the eighteenth-century reading public[1] took on organisational form around 1840 with the foundation of the first animal protection societies in both Germany and Switzerland. They were the 'Vaterländischer Verein zur Verhütung der Tierquälerei' in Stuttgart (1837) and the 'Tierschutzverein' in Berne (1844), respectively. In Germany, societies in Dresden and Nürnberg (1839), Berlin, Hamburg and Frankfurt (1841), and in other main cities such as Munich (1842) and Hanover (1844) followed. Some of these had their own periodicals. By 1881 over 150 societies belonged to the nation-wide organisation 'Verband der Tierschutzvereine des Deutschen Reiches'.[2]

In Switzerland, where no towns of comparable size existed, societies were formed in those cities which, as was the case with Berne, had a medical faculty, i.e. Basle (1849) and Zurich (1856), and in towns with a major contingent of foreign residents such as Lausanne (1860), Lucerne (1866) and Geneva (1868). In 1861, an assembly uniting the deputies of these and of agricultural societies started the 'Schweizerischer Thierschutzverein' which by 1877 had thirteen local branches. Its animator was the Protestant clergyman Philip Heinrich Wolff (1822–1903), the founder of the Zurich society. As of 1864, he edited the periodicals of this all-Swiss society, first the *Schweizer Thierschutzblätter*, then the *Thierfreund*.[3] It is noteworthy that another Protestant clergyman, Albert Knapp (1798–1864), is likewise considered 'father' of the German animal protection movement. Indeed, he founded the Stuttgart Society in 1837.[4]

Besides the annual national congresses, there were also international meetings of animal protection societies during the nineteenth century. The first took place in Dresden in 1860, the thirteenth in Paris in 1900.[5]

The main purpose of these societies was the abolition of cruel treatment of domestic animals in agriculture, slaughtering and in other parts of the economy, e.g. by striving for adequate conditions for horses and mules in transport, thereby safeguarding the optimal use of animals for people.[6]

Animal protection was also realised on the legal level. It is true that as early as the seventeenth century, even in the absence of any formal regulations, particular acts of cruelty had been condemned by certain German courts as an offence against public feelings.[7] Now, one after the other, the German and Swiss states introduced laws into their penal codes against cruelty to domestic animals. The first states to do this were the kingdom of Saxony (1838) and the Swiss canton of Schaffhausen (1842). By 1871 all German states except the city of Lübeck, and by 1885 all Swiss cantons had legal regulations or police orders against cruelty to animals. Many of these, as for example those introduced in 1839 in Württemberg, 1851 in Prussia, or 1858 in Oldenburg, stipulated that cruelty was condemnable only if it had occurred in public.[8]

This criterion of publicness illustrates the *anthropocentric* orientation given to the relationship between man and animals by the animal protection societies; for it was man they intended to protect from the sight of brutal acts rather than the animals from the ensuing suffering. The unilateral outlook also featured in the penal code of the new German Empire (1871), modelled upon its Prussian forerunner.[9] It was congruent with the religious and philosophical traditions prevailing in the Occident since Antiquity, which emphasised the differences between man and animals rather than their similarities.[10]

The idea of protection of animals for their own sake, however, had already been expressed by Jeremy Bentham half a century earlier and was now developed for the first time on the Continent by Arthur Schopenhauer (1788–1860). In his *Basis of Morality* (1841) he characterised as 'revolting and abominable' Immanuel Kant's view that cruelty to animals was to be condemned only because it might weaken our compassion towards human beings.[11] This essay was not very successful. Schopenhauer began to acquire fame only in the early 1850s with *Parerga and Paralipomena*, a collection of sarcastic essays on various topics, in which he took issue with Kant again and with what he called the Judo-Christian, hierarchical view of the relationship between man and animals. He believed in the metaphysical identity of all living beings based on their will to exist, and he elevated compassion to the central moral principle.[12]

In Schopenhauer's opinion the great benefit of the railways was that they were saving millions of draught-horses from a miserable existence, and he suggested that slaughtering — albeit unavoidable in the northern countries — should be made painless by prior 'chloroformisation'.[13] It was time that the 'Jewish' view regarding animals came to an end in Europe so that animals would cease to be creatures without rights. With respect to animal experimentation this would mean 'that every medicaster [i.e. unqualified medical man] would no longer be at leasure to test each . . . whim of his ignorance by the most horrid torture of an immense number of animals, as happens nowadays'.[14]

Schopenhauer in fact meant to criticise the abuses of animal experimentation, of which he quoted some examples, for elsewhere he acknowledged the use of anaesthesia and conceded that there had been progress in physiology from René Descartes' 'spiritus animales' to Charles Bell's sensory and motor spinal roots and Marshall Hall's reflexes.[15] Yet agreeing with the Göttingen professor of medicine Johann Friedrich Blumenbach (1752-1840), whose lectures he had attended earlier in the century, he insisted on a restriction of animal experimentation to well-defined purposes promising results of immediate utility.[16]

Animal experimentation and the public: reactions to a seemingly new phenomenon

There had been discussions on animal experiments among educated laymen in the eighteenth century. But as indicated by Figures 1 and 2 of this chapter[17] which only show four references to the subject prior to 1875, neither the general public nor the animal protection societies took much notice of the issue. On particular occasions, however, one could now see, read and hear that hitherto unfamiliar things took place behind the walls of newly-created university institutes, namely living animals were being used for the purpose of human medicine. In Zurich and Berne for instance, where the new radical governments had founded universities in the early 1830s, this use of animals seemed something new.

In Berne in 1834, the department of physiology directed by Professor Gabriel Valentin (1810-83) occupied five rooms in the centre of the old town. It was at that time the best equipped in the German-speaking lands.[18] When in 1838 a dog prepared for the measurement of blood volume escaped from the laboratories and strayed around town in that state, it caused angry reactions in the press. Valentin was accused of being an animal torturer. He sought and obtained the protection of the government.[19] Four years later, the professor of anatomy, Friedrich Wilhelm Theile (1801-79), who worked under the same roof as Valentin, addressed the public in his annual oration as rector of the university 'on the utility of physiological experiments with animals for medicine and on the preconceived ideas against such experiments'. Theile did not mention the source of the 'preconceived' objections such as the problem of transferability of results from animals to humans.[20] But he rejected them with the by then familiar reference to the usefulness of animal experiments which he competently illustrated.[21]

In Göttingen, just as in Florence, neighbours complained about the noise and the sight of the dogs in the physiological institutes situated in the centre of the old town. The rumours ceased, however, after some alterations had been made in the building.[22]

As Schopenhauer had foreseen, the use of animals in experiments at some stage had to become of interest to animal protection societies. In Switzerland the discussion started, avowedly upon instigation from London and Paris,[23] when in 1860 the Basle society questioned the medical faculty. The reassuring answer it received seems to have satisfied its members. The Zurich society, however, went directly into the daily press and in 1862 petitioned the government, which, in turn, approached the medical faculty. In its report, the Zurich faculty unanimously insisted on the necessity of experiments. As in Berne twenty years earlier, the government in Zurich supported the faculty by refusing to consider the petition which asked for the regulation and supervision of animal experimentation. In its answer to the Animal Protection Society the administration followed the faculty's argumentation, citing the small number of experiments, the use of anaesthetics and the incompetence of the general public to judge scientific questions.[24]

Although the two animal protection societies did not wish to drop the issue, their annual reports do not show any anti-vivisection activities during the following fourteen years.[25] Yet this was the period during which an extremely strong movement originated in Great Britain. It led in the summer of 1876 to the Cruelty to Animals Act which was the world's first legislation regulating animal experimentation.[26] The Continental daily press reported on it, and some of the English propaganda literature, such as George Fleming's *Vivisection*[27] — *is it Necessary or Excusable?*, was translated into German.[28] In the spring of 1876, i.e. before the British Act had been passed, animal experimentation was discussed at the annual meeting of the 'Schweizerische Thierschutzverein'. The delegates adopted five moderate proposals, which were entirely along the Blumenbach-Schopenhauer line, although neither of the two was mentioned. They agreed that 'vivisection (i.e. the surgical experiments on living animals) should not be opposed on principle, in order not to deprive medical science of one of its most important aids. This Society should repress the *abuses* . . .'[29] As a consequence it once more asked the Zurich medical faculty to explain their practices. The faculty's answer, stressing the potential health care benefits of experiments, calmed the majority of the delegates at the meeting of the following year. Somewhat grumblingly they realised that 'at this moment it is not possible to introduce legislation on this matter'.[30]

In 1876, the appointment of Moritz Schiff (1823-96) to the newly created chair of physiology at Geneva was accompanied by some public irritation in western Switzerland, because of his allegedly cruel experiments. Schiff, previously professor of physiology at Florence, had been, since 1863, the main target of the world's first anti-vivisection agitation directed by Frances Power Cobbe.[31] *Pro* and *con* were discussed in the Geneva press, but when he arrived and in December 1876 met the representatives of the local animal protection society, the question was settled to the satisfaction of both parties.[32]

Animal experimentation and the public: the scientists' view

These repercussions of foreign events were seen in a different light by the Swiss scientists directly concerned. On the whole, the Zurich faculty considered the controversy as imported from abroad and therefore of little consequence to Switzerland.[33] However, the rector of the University of Geneva, the zoologist and geologist Carl Vogt (1817-95), and the Zurich professor of physiology, Ludimar

Hermann (1838-1914), did not take the issue lightly. Their experience with local animal protection sentiment and their knowledge of the British agitation made them take up the pen preventively. In 1877, they published three essays in defence of animal experiments.[34] Hermann wrote:

> The preparations for an agitation against vivisection are already well under way in Germany and Switzerland. Science would be badly advised if it nobly ignored the threatening danger, and — as was the case in England — raised its voice only at the last moment — too late.

Analysing the English campaign he further realised that the vivisection issue 'too readily led to the unintentioned or deliberate propagation of incorrect or exaggerated assertions, for the truth to ever stand a chance to make its way by itself'.[35]

In a monograph entitled *Die Vivisectionsfrage für das grössere Publicum beleuchtet* Hermann contested that any well-known physician, surgeon or physiologist had ever doubted the necessity of vivisection. There were too many examples demonstrating its usefulness. His comment that 'by reducing vivisection one would save the life of a number of animals . . . only by paying in human lives'[36] became a cliché in the later debates.[37] Hermann also maintained that well-chosen experiments are indispensable in lectures to students. Their elimination would lead to less well-qualified doctors in the future, because students needed direct experience, not merely textbook knowledge.[38]

Yet Hermann felt that to defend vivisection with the sole argument of diminishing human suffering might be considered ignoble and egoistic. What really counted was the increase of knowledge. He agreed, however, that the moral justification needed discussion. There was certainly no straightforward solution, for while there were moral laws implanted in each man's heart concerning the relationship between men, this was not the case for his comportment towards animals: 'Where killing, i.e. an act that among humans would be a felony, is generally permitted [as in slaughtering], the limits of admissibility cannot be considered as clearly established', Hermann wrote.[39] He further cited warfare and many examples of animal torture common in food preparation and in agriculture such as cutting off ears and tails and particularly castration. Did these cruel acts not condemn animals to a sad life for the mere satisfaction of human appetite and economic profit?[40]

Yet Hermann insisted that he did not list these examples with a recriminative purpose, so to speak to justify little sins by the impunity of greater ones. This would have been the *tu-quoque argument* known since the seventeenth century.[41] He made it clear that a general guideline had to be agreed upon for the relationship between man and animals, rather than dealing separately with one issue simply because it is easier to campaign against fifty physiologists than against 100,000 farmers.[42]

The most crucial issues, namely the infliction of pain and the use of curare, were not evaded. Hermann conceded that, although most laboratory animals were by now anaesthetised, this could not always be done for experimental reasons. He wondered, however, whether animals were able to realise pain *qua* pain, in the same way as man. Even if they showed symptoms of suffering, it was not possible to transfer the human sensation of pain to animals, since they lacked the psychological background of man. He also was of the opinion that the intensity of pain sensation increased with an animal's phylogenetic position, i.e. with the development of an increase in the central nervous system. As for curare, which paralysed muscles without being an anaesthetic, it could not be used without an additional anaesthetic. Furthermore, by calming the animal, curare allowed control of the experiment in order to avoid artefacts so that both duration and number of experiments could be kept to a minimum.[43]

Vogt's view was far less sophisticated. He knew the political arena well since he had been a member of the first German Parliament in Frankfurt after the revolutions of 1848 and of its short-lived remnant in Stuttgart. That is why he had been obliged to exile himself to Switzerland, where in 1868 he became a member of the Swiss Federal Parliament in Berne. For him the question of vivisection was just one battle in the long-standing war between science and faith, the origin of which lay in Pietistic sentimentalism. In his pamphlets Vogt defended the scientific importance of vivisection, but he also indulged in citing recriminative examples. His style was sarcastic and bluntly inflammatory. He justified this by saying that he had to respond to insulting aspersions just as he had received them.[44]

The publications by Hermann and Vogt illustrate the two levels at which the discussions took place. Hermann's considered view, although sophisticated, was much more difficult to understand than a simple enumeration of advances in diagnostics and therapeutics would have been. It had less of an echo with the 'larger public', for which it was meant, than Vogt's emotional argument. Indeed, Hermann's assessment of the situation proved correct, for behind the apparently pacified public scene, and with governments entirely on the side of the scientists, horses were being saddled for a major campaign.

Preparing a campaign: the motivated and their motives

Two minds come together

In Germany, around 1878, less than a handful of people had come together with the clear-cut intention of fighting vivisection.

The first to be mentioned is Marie-Espérance von Schwartz (1818–99). Daughter of a wealthy Hamburg banker, she was born in Britain and educated chiefly in Geneva and Rome. A widow at sixteen, the talented and independent young lady settled in Rome. With her second husband, Ferdinand von Schwartz (1813–83), she travelled on horseback to Egypt through Greece, Turkey and the Near East and published her diary of this trip in 1849. She again took up residence in Rome, where her 'salon' attracted foreign aristocrats and artists, but also continued travelling after her divorce in 1852. She became close to Giuseppe Garibaldi (1807–82), whom she visited repeatedly on his island of Caprera. She translated the manuscript of his memoirs into German in 1860 and wrote about him in 1864 and 1884. In 1865 she moved to Crete, where she became a greatly esteemed benefactress by founding asylums and schools, as well as hospitals for people and for animals. She continued writing under the pseudonym 'Elpis Melena', chiefly about her travel experiences.[45]

Early in 1875, Mrs von Schwartz chanced to read the German translation of Fleming's essay on vivisection. Deeply impressed by it and by articles in the British press,[46] she 'felt as though convicted of a crime' had she not done 'everything in her feeble forces to oppose the ruthless acts of vivisectors'.[47] Thus she wrote an anti-vivisection novel entitled *Gemma or Virtue and Vice*. In the spring of 1877, on one of her periodic tours of Europe, she submitted the manuscript for criticism to an old friend of hers, Dr med. et phil. Ernst Grysanowski (1824–88).[48] They had first met in Rome in 1848 just after her return from Egypt. Soon the young attaché to the Prussian embassy had become an intimate friend of the Schwartzs. In her biography of Grysanowski, Espérance von Schwartz warmly described him as having been for them 'a true fount of new interests and stimulations, a sparkling fire of brilliant insights'.[49]

Of modest origin, Grysanowski had studied mathematics, astronomy and Oriental languages in his native Königsberg. Disenchanted with diplomacy and finally dismissed by his aristocratic ambassador, he had become preceptor to an Italian prince. The help of the Schwartzs then enabled him to take up medical studies in Pisa, Montpellier, Heidelberg and Naples. In 1855, he was promoted MD in Heidelberg and took up practice among the foreign residents in Pisa and later in Florence. Grysanowski was on terms of intimate friendship with the Brownings, the Trollopes and many other celebrities then residing in the Tuscan capital, including Mrs von Schwartz's sister. In 1865, he married the daughter of a British vicar. He was also in close contact with Frances Power Cobbe, who since her campaign against Schiff in Florence regularly sojourned in Italy. Grysanowski had quietly thought and corresponded about the usefulness and morality of animal experimentation. He had not, however, considered 'a public apostolate' for himself. It was Mrs von Schwartz who changed his mind in the spring of 1877 on the day they met in Livorno to discuss her *Gemma* manuscript.[50]

Grysanowski's long-standing preoccupation with vivisection came to her as a great surprise. With tears in her eyes she convinced him to act, and promised him financial help. Grysanowski sealed their mutual vows: 'Your *Gemma* which goes right to the heart and my essay which I shall entitle *Vivisection, its scientific value and ethical justification* together shall undertake a crusade . . . against the most outrageous cruelty of our century.'[51]

Being people of action, Grysanowski and Espérance von Schwartz travelled to Germany to complete their literary projects. As a result, *Vivisection* and *Gemma* were published in the same year under the pseudonyms 'Iatros' (i.e. the doctor) and 'Elpis Melena', respectively.[52]

Anti-vivisectionists' arguments

Grysanowski's argumentation followed one main line. Vivisection had to be abolished because it exemplified the wrong track on which medicine was engaged and because of this it was morally wrong.

The future of medicine lay in using the healing forces of nature, the *vis medicatrix naturae*, and in prevention rather than in intervention: 'The progress of medicine neither lies in an increase of diagnostic wisdom nor in the discovery and testing of new remedies, but . . . in hygiene, i.e. in its own superfluousness.'[53]

Even if this option meant medical 'suicide' it was a 'salutary suicide', because with the exception of surgery and toxicology, where (animal) experiments might be tolerated, 'medicine is neither a science nor will it ever be one'.[54] It had to adhere to its own methodology, i.e. to its empirical tradition, to bedside observation and necroscopy — and to natural experiments occurring by accident. 'Knowledge at any cost' was to be rejected. Morality had priority over science.[55]

This double standard — the recognition of the epistemological superiority of the experiment on the one hand, and the negation of its applicability to medicine on the other — was the fundamental position of the non-polemical anti-vivisectionists. In Grysanowski's case it was based on a misinterpretation of the past importance of animal experimentation, e.g. when he called the discovery of the blood circulation 'a superfluous tautology', or when he ignored the potential of the method, e.g. for the treatment of diabetes.[56] Despite his philosophical erudition Grysanowsky refused to look beyond his own time. Even if future biological science and therapeutics were to become impossible without vivisection he, as a doctor, would remain steadfast — and fatalistic:

> We are absolutely ready to renounce all medical treatment and to depend entirely on the old *vis medicatrix naturae*, which, . . . [while] indeed so often replacing us at the bedside . . . still grants us the appearance of having the merit [of a cure]. 'Our days are numbered', says Frances Power Cobbe, 'and . . . medicine . . . cannot after all do much to prolong them. Are these few things really proportionate to the torments of thousands of animals? Who would want to pay such a price for a cure or an alleviation'?[57]

Clearly there was no compromise possible: one had to choose between older methods of observation and newer ones of experimentation.

While *Vivisection* was intended for academics, above all for doctors, *Gemma* was meant to exert influence in high circles via the ladies. It was dedicated by Espérance von Schwartz with eighteenth-century obsequiousness to a prince of Sachsen-Meiningen. The characters of the novel were stereotypes. There was Gemma, the heroine, a nineteen-year-old, charming, charitable, pious, animal-loving girl, living in the country with her father, a cynical, licentious, alcoholic, animal-hating doctor indulging in vivisection parties in London. Her lover was a chivalrous young foreigner who in the end turned out to be her lost brother, ready to sacrifice his life for her, just as she was for anti-vivisection. The plot was poor and grossly tendentious. Among others, it featured a dog which saved the lives of both daughter and father — how, one is not told — but which still ended up being vivisected in this materialist world. Gemma actually died as a result of her father's brutality.[58] The old topic of brutality against animals leading to ruthlessness against people,[59] especially against women, was revived. Despite its shortcomings, the novel was turned into a play some years later.[60]

The two inner circles

Mrs von Schwartz translated her own novel into English, French and Italian and found publishers for them. Grysanowski's work had little success despite the fact that it was, internationally, the first book-length discussion of the subject by a medical author and was written in elegant and non-polemical prose. In July 1879, only 430 copies had been sold, 200 of these to Espérance von Schwartz. 'This sheds light on the true state of public opinion', Grysanowski wrote to her,[61] whilst working on his next manuscript. This was to be published by an anti-vivisectionist society, newly founded by a third key figure, Ernst von Weber (1830–1902). In fact, *Gemma* had meanwhile attracted the attention of this energetic gentleman, and influenced by it he had decided to enter the arena. As Espérance von Schwartz wrote later, it was this 'outcry of my tortured heart that was instrumental in making this "zoophile" inspired by the "feu sacré" of purest humanity initiate a general agitation against the scientific cruelty to animals'.[62]

Born in Dresden, von Weber belonged to the landed gentry. He was a man of the world who sojourned regularly in London and spent his winters in southern climates. He had travelled in most circum-Mediterranean countries, the Middle East and the United States. At the age of twenty-five he had been involved in a Balkan conflict and imprisoned in Turkey.[63] His wealth, travels and activities as a writer made him the perfect male counterpart of Mrs von

Schwartz. In the spring of 1876, upon his return to his German home after a five years' absence spent travelling to the diamond mines in South Africa and back through Russia to Dresden, he wrote to Emperor William I and to Chancellor Bismarck urging them to acquire the German colonies in order to strengthen the Empire's economic basis, a subject on which he had a brochure printed in 1878.[64] A report of his African trip was published in the same year.

These two volumes on Africa show him to be a fervent opponent of slavery, yet also a critic of the overly indulgent treatment of blacks in British Africa.[65] The vivisection debates in Britain had also left their mark on this Anglophile. He extolled the British humanity towards negroes and believed that it was exemplified also by the new British legislation to control animal experimentation. Had a German Parliament proposed and elaborated legislation like the British? Closely following Grysanowski — whose booklet he warmly recommended — he pointed to the role in this achievement played by the clergy and by the educated ladies 'who both enjoy uncomparably more esteem, recognition and influence there than in Germany'. In an appendix he enlarged on the subject by reference to the literature including the Report of the British Royal Commission,[66] Hermann's monograph and *Gemma*, and urged German ladies to agitate through the animal protection societies.[67] As of 1878 von Weber actively joined von Schwartz and Grysanowski. Already in April 1878 he lectured to the Dresden Animal Protection Society of which he was a vice-president. In early 1879, this address was published as a 77-page pamphlet, entitled *Die Folterkammern der Wissenschaft* (*The Torture Chambers of Science*).[68]

Unlike Grysanowksi's, von Weber's brochure was an immediate success. It imitated Frances Power Cobbe's pamphlet *Light in Dark Places* as it included quotations and pictures from the scientific literature taken out of context and by its restriction to poorly described but cruel experiments — some old and without anaesthesia, some more recent. They constituted for him an example of 'the intellectual disorder and the moral licentiousness of our age' particularly in Germany.[69] But more was to follow. Soon von Weber succeeded in winning the support of the majority of the Dresden Animal Protection Society[70] and, most important, of a man much inclined to deplore the contemporary intellectual, moral and artistic state of Germany, the composer Richard Wagner (1813–83).

It was Wagner who on 11 August 1879 took the initiative. He wrote to the Dresden Society asking for the by-laws as he wished to become a member. In the ensuing correspondence with von

Weber, Mrs von Schwartz and Grysanowski were kept posted.[71] A month later von Weber invited himself to Wagner's residence in Bayreuth.[72] He took anti-vivisectionist literature along which immediately captivated Wagner and his wife. By the end of von Weber's stay, Wagner had made up his mind to publish an enlarged version of one of his letters to his new friend as his own contribution to the agitation against vivisection. It was published in the autumn of 1879 in the *Bayreuther Blätter* which had a circulation of 1,700 copies. A further 2,000 offprints, paid for by Wagner, were distributed by von Weber's Society.[73]

On the medical issues, Wagner relied on Grysanowski and agreed with him that the uselessness of animal experimentation would soon be obvious to everybody. The type of doctor who acquired his expertise from physiology could only be 'a man entirely incapable of compassion, even a bungler in his profession' and would soon belong to the past.[74] It would have been 'cowardice', however, if vivisection were to be abandoned merely for medical reasons. Wagner had in mind a more lasting improvement of the human mind. It was called 'regeneration' in other writings of these years.[75] Wagner entirely agreed with Arthur Schopenhauer, who had been one of his favourite authors since 1854,[76] in explaining why he had never joined an animal protection society but had immediately supported the anti-vivisection ones: the former were guided by the 'dogma of utility to mankind' whereas the latter were motivated by compassion and by the metaphysical unity of man and animals. Compassion should direct doctors, too, rather than the 'anxiety of their own ignorance' which made them climb 'on the tree of knowledge like apes'.[77]

In October 1879, Wagner wrote about the vivisection question to his royal friend, King Louis II of Bavaria. Later that month von Weber informed him that the conservative party might support the movement.[78] From then on Wagner, his family and, after his death in 1883, his circle, publicly supported the 'cause' for decades to come using the *Bayreuther Blätter*.[79] Thus, during 1879 the anti-vivisection cause was boosted not only by several successful publications but also by political and institutional momentum, when, with remarkable skill, von Weber took the organisational reins of the campaign firmly in his own hands.

In August 1879, the German Animal Protection Congress met at Gotha. Moderate protectionists and radical anti-vivisectionists clashed. The president Dr Bruno Marquardt, a teacher, who sat on the committee of the Dresden Society, belonged to the moderates.

They were of the opinion that laymen were not competent to decide about the need for vivisection and they did not aim at abolition but at restriction under state control, at the obligatory use of anaesthesia and at immediate killing of animals after the experiments. The moderates carried the vote on the first congress day, and von Weber promptly retaliated on the second day. With his loyalists — among them Mrs von Schwartz, freshly arrived from Crete — he founded the 'Internationale Gesellschaft zur Bekämpfung der wissenschaftlichen Thierfolter' ('International Society for Combat Against Scientific Torture of Animals') and had himself elected president. The Society was housed at von Weber's address in Dresden and as of 1881 edited a radical monthly periodical called *Thier- und Menschenfreund*. The Society's committee included Espérance von Schwartz. It immediately benefited from Richard Wagner's financial support and became the centre of what as of then can be called the German anti-vivisection movement.[80]

In Switzerland a similar group was formed in Berne during the same period, 1878–9, around the aristocratic businessman Anton von Steiger (1840–84) and the writer Jules Charles Scholl (1850–86). In 1880, von Steiger made an important speech, drawn from Grysanowski and Schopenhauer, at an all-Swiss meeting of animal protection societies. The Berne group did not, however, succeed in persuading the majority of delegates to stand up for the abolition of vivisection. Thence this group, which called itself 'Schweizerische Antivivisektionsgesellschaft' ('Swiss Anti-Vivisection Society') between 1883 and 1888, had no political impact.[81]

This was not the case for the German societies. Once the inner circle had formed, the campaign took off according to the programme that von Weber had outlined in his *Torture Chambers of Science*.

Action and reaction, 1879–85

The strategy of the adversaries

Consciously trying to imitate the British example, von Weber had stipulated in 1879:

1. Physiological articles and books must be scrutinised for cruel experiments to be presented to the public out of context.
2. Anti-vivisectionist literature, pamphlets and journal advertise-

ments were to be distributed free of charge. Von Weber stressed that they should include illustrations. Articles could be written by a single author under various pseudonyms.

3. Once public awareness had been raised by this literary warfare, agitation could be carried to the political arena by petitions to parliaments. Picture posters should be used to attract attention and stimulate the public to sign the petitions. It did not matter if idlers contributed. The end justified the means.

4. Animal protection societies with their existing organisational structure had a crucial role to play in the distribution of literature and the collection of signatures. They therefore had to become either anti-vivisectionist or the anti-vivisectionists had to leave them and found their own societies.

5. The only logical and effective way to oppose cruelty once and for all would be the complete abolition of vivisection. For tactical reasons, however, one might have to proceed step by step and first plead for severe restrictions.

6. Von Weber particularly appealed to ladies, 'the noble keepers of moral law' to join the vivisection front and not to forget their children as potential fighters.[82]

The literary warfare

Von Weber's *Torture Chambers of Science* was a perfect example of this programme in practice. The booklet was widely distributed in coffee houses, train stations, public transport facilities and schools all over German-speaking Europe. It was soon translated into French and Italian by Mrs von Schwartz, but they could not dispose of the translations even by giving them away. Their reaction was that the Italian public was 'hard to interest in real scientific reading'.[83] Henceforth, they concentrated their efforts on northern countries.

North of the Alps von Weber's pamphlet could be found even in such remote regions as the small county of Appenzell in Switzerland.[84] Its echo was remarkably loud. Many newspapers reviewed it, enabling von Weber to add to later editions an appendix with thirty-two favourable reviews.[85] He published one more pamphlet in 1883 consisting of letters by Richard Wagner and Chancellor Bismarck.[86]

Figure 7.1 gives an overview of the literary *pro* and *con* up to the First World War (but without the articles in the daily press). It shows two peaks. The first and major one was between 1879 and 1885. It involved both advocates and adversaries of animal experimentation. The second peak, between 1895 and 1900, concerned only the anti-vivisectionists; from 1888 the advocates published new pamphlets at regular intervals. The twenty-two pamphlets in favour of animal experimentation printed between 1877 and 1883 were written by twenty-one different authors, most of them medically qualified. Besides Hermann, eleven university professors of non-clinical disciplines (seven in physiology, two in pathology, one in anatomy, and one in experimental pharmacology) contributed, as well as five clinicians (three university professors and two medical practitioners). But there were also Carl Vogt, Robert Marty (1843–1906), a Jesuit, and Henri Tollin (1833–1902), a Protestant clergyman, as well as the writer Wilhelm Jensen (1837–1911).

Figure 7.1: Anti- (upper panel) and pro-vivisection (lower panel) pamphlets published in German-speaking lands, 1870–1914. Only separate publications and major articles available as offprints are included

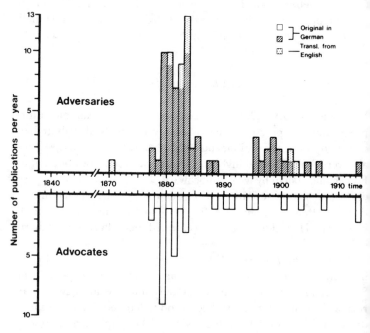

The fifty original German pamphlets against vivisection published between 1877 and 1885 were written by only twenty-one authors. There were six multiple authors, the most productive of them being Grysanowski. He alone wrote no fewer than fifteen pamphlets, initially under the pseudonyms 'Iatros' and 'E.G. Hammer'. Some of these were more than fifty pages long. He was the recognised literary champion of anti-vivisection in Germany. Among the others there were two general practitioners, Richard Nagel (died 1895), a vegetarian, and Gustav Voigt, author of a book on nature cures.[87] The rest were lay speakers such as Dr Paul Förster (1844–1925), a professor at a Berlin Gymnasium, Richard Knoche (1822–92) and Emil Knodt (1852–1924), Catholic and Protestant clergymen, respectively, Alfred von Seefeld (1825–93), an editor, Anton von Steiger, a Swiss businessman, or Adolf von Zedtwitz (1823–95), an Austrian count, who ensured that many walks of middle and upper-class society were represented. Their contributions, however, never reached the standing of Grysanowski's. They were largely based on them, but given a polemical turn. There were also six German translations of English pamphlets and open letters by high-ranking persons such as Lord Coleridge and Cardinal Manning, or by the surgeon Robert Lawson Tait (1845–99).[88] The latter, who was internationally famed for his operations on the ovaries and the appendix, became an often-quoted medical authority against vivisection.[89]

These German authors formed the outposts, so to say, of the Dresden action centre with which they were in close contact, as von Weber's plan to bring animal protection societies on the anti-vivisection track succeeded in a few places only. In his native Dresden at first this tactic was successful,[90] but it failed in the long run. In 1881, von Weber was excluded from the Animal Protection Society because of his radical views, whereupon he founded the New Animal Protection Society, entirely devoted to anti-vivisection.[91] This pattern was followed for example in Hanover (under Knoche), Leipzig, Berlin (under Nagel) and Hamburg, in Lausanne and Geneva. Von Weber himself was present at the foundation of the New Leipzig Society; a terrible fracas occurred caused by intruding students, defending vivisection. On the other hand, animal protectionists burgled the Leipzig Physiological Institute. All these events were keenly discussed in the Leipzig and Dresden press[92] and in turn taken up in pamphlets.[93]

No wonder that the advocates of vivisection reacted. In 1879, the Leipzig physiologist Carl Ludwig (1816–95) wrote two short papers. Another defender of experimentation who came out with two publications was his Breslau colleague Rudolf Heidenhain (1834–97), and in the following year an anonymous re-edition of Mylius's eighteenth-century essay appeared.[94] Ludwig, whose model department attracted scientists from all over the world, was concerned for two reasons. First, he had been unfairly criticised by von Weber, who had 'inspected' his institute in his absence, and second, he was a vice-president of the Old Leipzig Animal Protection Society.

It was probably Ludwig who in February 1879 motivated his faculty colleagues to send out a copy of the *Torture Chambers* together with a circular letter asking the twenty-six other German-speaking medical faculties to sign a declaration outlining the necessity of vivisection for the progress of medical science. This declaration was to be published in the daily press.[95] Within a month sixteen sister faculties, including the three Swiss ones, signed this letter, but some refused, among them Göttingen, Berlin and Würzburg. It was not that they disagreed with the contents of the declaration, but they thought it either untimely, formally too weak or altogether inappropriate.[96]

The Zurich attitude of the mid-1870s persisted in Göttingen where the whole agitation was seen as imported from abroad and therefore as factitious: 'Don't paint the devil on the wall!', commented the gynaecologist Jakob H.H. von Schwartz (1821–90).[97] In Berlin it was felt that any statement by the faculties would only help anti-vivisection by attracting the attention of the public. As for any denunciations or petitions to the government, one was confident that the Prussian Ministry of Culture, being well informed about the questions, would handle these efficiently and protect the interests of science.[98] Würzburg held that, by entering the arena at the onset of the agitation, the medical faculties deprived themselves of the possibility of being expert arbiters if the quarrel ever achieved greater political impact.[99]

All these arguments show a feeling of supremacy among the learned professors *vis-à-vis* the lay public, and a confidence in their connection with the government. This confidence was put to a tough test during the course of the parliamentary deliberations to come.

Parliamentary debates

On the political level the anti-vivisection controversy started in 1879 in Saxony. The government had been induced by it to inquire into the conditions at the Dresden Veterinary School and at Leipzig University. It reported to Parliament that no legal measures were required.[100]

The question was then debated in the Bavarian Parliament after it had been dealt with extensively in the Council of Ministers. It is conceivable that King Louis II exerted some influence.[101] An administrative regulation was introduced in 1880, the first of its kind in Germany. It restricted animal experiments to state institutions; made it compulsory to anaesthetise animals whenever possible; limited experiments in lectures; and required the use of the lowest possible class of animals.[102]

Up to early 1880 four petitions asking for complete abolition of vivisection were also addressed to the Reichstag, the German national Parliament. Two of them were by the New Leipzig and Dresden Societies. They were dealt with on 30 April 1880 by the petition commission which asked the well-known pathologist Rudolf Virchow (1821-1902), also a liberal member of Parliament, to act as an expert. The commission then recommended the plenum not to enter the matter, and because of shortage of time it was not debated in the House.[103]

This lack of success did not prevent the agitators from continuing in 1881. They attributed the failure partly to the fact that Virchow, himself a 'vivisector', had been put in a position to judge his own case. Again the New Leipzig Society and the Dresden International Committees deposited radical petitions supported by a pamphlet by Grysanowski. The parliamentary commission this time discussed the issue using reports from the Imperial Health Department and the Scientific Deputation of Medical Affairs, which had been requested by Chancellor Bismarck and by the Ministry of Culture. The commission voted not to recommend any legislation but accepted a debate in the plenum.[104]

Thus on 23 January 1882, the representatives of science had to defend vivisection against the views held by the conservative and centre parties.[105] Spokesmen for the abolitionists were Baron Wilhelm von Minnigerode (1840-1913), a conservative, and Ludwig Windthorst (1812-91), the leader of the centre party. Being laymen they basically presented the arguments contained in the anti-vivisectionist pamphlets. The best speakers in favour of vivisection were the Greifswald surgeon Karl Hüter (1838-82) and Rudolf Virchow, who meanwhile had made his fervent plea in favour of animal experimentation at the 1881 International Medical Congress in London. His main point there had been that killing was worse than torturing.[106] Virchow now aptly used the weakness of von Minnigerode's speech to deride his confusing cell theory with materialism. He exclaimed that if one wanted to speak on these issues to the House one ought to study them more seriously beforehand. Gustav von Gossler (1838–1902), the Prussian Minister of Education, was decidedly on the side of the physiologists, but he made an effort to reconcile the two camps. Finally, the recommendation of the commission, i.e. no legislation, was accepted with the support of all the liberals, some conservatives and some members of the centre. Their majority was not overwhelming but, nevertheless, this result meant a defeat of the anti-vivisectionists on the national level.[107]

Further debate now followed in the Prussian Parliament, engineered by von Weber who continued his 'action of enlightenment'. In February 1882 he wrote a circular letter to all Church authorities in Germany, Protestant, Catholic and Jewish alike, asking for support and explaining that the lack of success so far had to be attributed to lack of ecclesiastical help. In 1882, Reverend Knoche's Hanoverian anti-vivisection society sent a petition to the Prussian Landtag, the Prussian House of Commons. In agreement with the Dresden International Committee, this petition once more asked polemically for complete abolition of vivisection. It was accompanied by the expert judgement of a Dresden lawyer attempting to show that animal experimentation did not fall under the cruelty to animal laws, wherefore appropriate legislation was necessary.[108]

Von Weber tried to influence the government's treatment of this new petition by writing directly to Bismarck on 20 February 1883. In his answer, dated 23 February, the Chancellor condemned abuses of animals, for which he referred to the cruelty to animals paragraph of the civil court, but diplomatically he did not support outlawing all vivisection. Von Weber, however, alleged that he did and published Bismarck's letter together with letters from Richard Wagner, who had just died, thus claiming that two of the most revered heroes of modern Germany were against vivisection.[109]

When the petition was discussed in Parliament, the Petition Commission was unable to reach agreement on the need for legislation. On 16 April 1883 the question was debated in the House. Commissary for Higher Education Friedrich Althoff (1839–1918), speaking for the government, considered such petitions as a vote of no confidence in the doctors. Otherwise the same speakers as the year before once more entered the debate. This time, von Minnigerode delivered a very well prepared speech. Windthorst maintained that there was no fire without smoke. An agitation as constant and lasting as the present had to mean that not everything was as clean as von Gossler tried to suggest. With a quite clear-cut majority produced by the conservatives and the centre parties the House voted to pass on the petition to the government.[110]

Governmental measures did not automatically follow, because Prussia had no parliamentary government. Yet in December 1883, Education Minister von Gossler started an inquiry with all medical faculties in Prussia as to the extent to which animal experimentation was needed and used in lectures and research and whether existing animal protection legislation was sufficient to prevent abuse.[111]

The Prussian debate of 1883 provoked a large number of reactions on both sides, as can also be seen in Figure 7.1.[112] In 1884, von Gossler received another petition signed by thirteen animal protection societies, among these the notorious new ones in Leipzig, Dresden, Berlin, and Hamburg. The Old Berlin Society, however, declared publicly that it did not approve of abolition or of the distribution of pamphlets aimed at restricting free research. The majority of the 140 German societies followed this moderate line.[113] This enabled von Gossler to stick to his unilateral inquiry, despite von Minnigerode's parliamentary interpellation asking to hear von Weber's International Society.[114] In early 1885, the result of this inquiry[115] was presented to the Prussian Parliament together with a new monograph completed by Rudolf Heidenhain at the request of von Gossler.[116] These two documents put in perspective the claims by anti-vivisectionists and the exaggerations which had occurred on both sides. The minister had to choose to drop the issue, or to take administrative steps, or even to propose legislation to Parliament. The fact that only five to six out of 140 German animal protection societies had publicly supported the petition[117] and that he was not convinced of any abuses, made him decide to issue a decree (Erlass) on 2 February 1885. It included neither the requirement of registration nor any penal threat and was couched in general terms like the Bavarian one. It in fact sanctioned the existing situation.[118] On 25 February 1885, an angry reaction in the Prussian Parliament followed, but von Gossler, assisted by Virchow, once more firmly defended his decision. He asked whether the members of the House could really consider men like Drs Tait, Grysanowski and Nagel as medical authorities? It would have been hard to correspond with such gentlemen and, added Virchow, if one had allowed them to speak, their own absurdities would soon have silenced them.[119]

Thus the Prussian minister rehabilitated the scientists and at the same time took the grist from the agitators' mill. In fact the result of the Prussian debate marked the political defeat for decades to come of Ernst von Weber and his group. They continued petitioning the Prussian *Landtag* in 1886 and 1891 and the German *Reichstag* in 1887, 1888 and 1891, but were refused by the parliamentary commissions on the grounds that the effectiveness of the 1885 decree would only become clear with time.[120] This decree was the second in Germany after the Bavarian one. Before the turn of the century it was adopted by the other states of the German Empire.[121]

The trust of the scientists in the governments to protect scientific interests had proved justified in the end. This was above all due to Gustav von Gossler who stimulated medical research and admired its outstanding representatives such as Koch, Virchow and Ehrlich. Another person, in his place, might have used the vote of the Prussian *Landtag* as a lever to introduce severe restrictions on research. And obviously Bismarck, who otherwise intervened frequently in social and cultural policies, did not object — despite his wife's support for anti-vivisection and von Weber's direct intervention.[122] Von Gossler's successor under Emperor William II, Count Robert von Zedlitz-Trützschler (1837–1914), seemed in fact more inclined towards anti-vivisection. In February 1892 at least, he personally received Alfred von Seefeld and Dr Paul Förster and promised them further talks once he had studied their writings.[123] Unfortunately for anti-vivisection, perhaps, he had to resign a month later, leaving the anti-vivisectionists to fight for themselves.

Fighting on, 1886–1900: old and new ways and motives

The old family in 1888

The year 1885 was a turning point for the anti-vivisectionist movement. Disillusion set in among such leaders as Grysanowski and von Weber as well as among members such as Princess Bismarck.[124] Death reduced the leadership, too. In 1884 von Steiger and in 1886 Scholl died in Berne, and in 1888 Grysanowski himself died in Italy. While in 1888 the most important Swiss anti-vivisection society in Berne reunited with the Animal Protection Society,[125] von Weber in Dresden and his younger friend Paul Förster in Berlin did not give up. Förster was now president of the New Berlin Animal Protection Society.[126] He had already written an anti-vivisection pamphlet in 1885, then a book on vegetarianism in 1886. Now he tarted to publish articles on vivisection, animal protection and mallpox vaccination.[127] Otherwise the personalities, tactics and ome of the cited materials were the same as before. Espérance von Schwartz published a book-length biography of Grysanowski in 1890, vhich contained extracts of his writings with a comment by Knodt. She also paid for an edition of the collected anti-vivisectionist works of the revered man prepared by Knodt in 1897.[128] Von Weber still presided over the International Society, but Förster edited the *Thier- und Menschenfreund*, which was also the official organ of the new Animal Protection Societies of Berlin, Dresden, Hamburg and Leipzig. The journal offers a representative insight into the social background, the finances and the intellectual ramifications of anti-vivisectionism in these years.

Table 7.1 summarises some of the results of an analysis of the twelve issues for the year 1888. They comprise 100 pages and allow the identification of 898 individual members, their gender and social categories as well as their financial contributions. Over one third of the members were women. Their financial contribution was proportionally comparable to that of men. Women were considered as particularly suited to disseminating noble feeling and morality, as their high position in the educated classes seemed to give them much influence.[129] 'A great womanly mind has disappeared', wrote in 1888 Ernst von Weber in the obituary of Anna Kingsford,[130] who, together with Frances Power Cobbe, had been the most active British anti-vivisectionist internationally.[131] Likewise, as the example of Espérance von Schwartz shows, women had been instrumental in organising anti-vivisection in Germany from the start. Among them, Countess Auguste Eleonore Agnes von Egloffstein (died 1888) must be mentioned. She translated Cobbe's *Light in Dark Places* into German.[132] On the other hand, anti-vivisection was important to some women because they clearly saw it as a means of emancipation.[133]

Table 7.1 also shows that the male categories listed under Property owners' proportionally contributed much more than those termed 'The educated'. This holds particularly true for the nobility. They represented less than one fourth of the membership but contributed over 40 per cent of the total budget. Noblemen were also important as organisers. Besides von Weber, Count Adolf von Zedtwitz, a convinced vegetarian and an adept of nature cures, member of the International Committee, was a prime mover of anti-vivisection in Vienna.[134] Another member of the International Committee and yet another vegetarian received a Prussian knighthood in 1890, namely Alfred von Seefeld, who owned a publishing house in Hanover and edited much of the anti-vivisectionist literature.[135]

Table 7.1 further shows that only two medical doctors could be indentified among the society's members, who, however, made higher than average financial contributions. It is possible that the category 'Other academics' comprised some doctors, for it was stated that in 1885 the Society counted '17 M.D.s among approximately 1,500 members'. But very few doctors actually joined. Förster and Grysanowski admitted that leading members of the medical profession were supporters of vivisection,[136] and that the average doctor followed them just as the average citizen did not carry 'his centre of gravitation within himself but saw it in the gods and half-gods around him', in front of which he bowed without will of his own, particularly if these deities were the miracles of natural science.[137]

This lack of a will of one's own in most people explained, according to Grysanowski and Förster, the general decline of interest in the anti-vivisection campaign once the initial outcry of moral indignation had faded.[138] It became apparent therefore that the solution would take time and presupposed a 'change of philosophical conscience', which would clearly perceive that medicine, based on natural science, produced 'maggoty, rotten fruits'.[139] Was the death in 1888 of Emperor Frederick III of a carcinoma of the larynx not the best proof, Förster asked? He believed that even this disease could have been checked by nature remedies rather than by modern 'medical superstition'.[140]

Accordingly *Thier- und Menschenfreund* opposed compulsory vaccination against smallpox (introduced in 1874) and tetanus. These preventive measures were rejected in long articles as dangerous and superfluous.[141] Not surprisingly, therefore, the Dresden Anti-Vaccination Society was partly composed of members from the Anti-Vivisection Society.[142]

On the other hand there were no direct references to vegetarianism in the 1888 editions of *Thier- und Menschenfreund*. Certainly, a number of anti-vivisection leaders were vegetarians from the outset, or became so during the campaign, like Mrs von Schwartz and Grysanowski. Yet Grysanowski warned against too close a connection with vegetarianism. He believed that the achievement of the precise scope of anti-vivisection, i.e. of the legal abolition of a single practice, might be endangered if the public associated it with the fundamental cultural change implicit in vegetarianism.[143]

This example shows that the question of the links of early anti-vivisection with contemporaneous reformist movements is difficult to answer. In a formal sense, *Thier- und Menschenfreund* in 1888 opened its columns to anti-vaccination and to advertisers of all sorts of nature cures. There were personal connections also with representatives of 'alternative medicine' such as air, water and sun cures, yet none of the persons concerned seems to have been a leader in any of these reformist movements.[144] Anti-vivisection at this stage was steadily following Grysanowski's medical argumentation and used von Weber's methods. Not even Schopenhauer was quoted by Grysanowski. This was left to an unknown philologist, Victor Gützlaff (born in 1839), who in 1879 published a mixture of Schopenhauer, von Weber, 'Iatros', 'Hammer' and Grysanowski, subtitled *A Contribution to the Ethical Aspect of the Vivisection Question*.[145]

Reading the 1888 issues of *Thier- und Menschenfreund* also shows that anti-vivisection had become something of a closed circle, the tone of its message growing ever more moralising and bewailing. It was 'our' Grysanowski and 'our' Anna Kingsford who both died in 1888. And it was 'our' Ernst von Weber who announced his engagement and for whom 2,500 Marks were collected as a wedding present in the form of a fund bearing his name and to be used as he saw fit.[146] The annual meeting of the New Berlin Society was a social event held in the elegant rooms of the 'Philharmonie' with 'music, living pictures, dinner and dancing'.[147]

It is clear from Table 7.1 that the upper classes were strongly represented even if we assume that among the unidentified members (i.e. one third of the male and female members taken together) there were some commoners. The International Society prided itself on its aristocratic patrons such as HRH the Princess Eugénie, sister of the King of Sweden, or Princess Bismarck, the wife of the Chancellor.[148] Napoleon and Emperor Frederick III were quoted as indirect supporters.[149] Accordingly the deaths of the Emperor, of HRH the Dutchess of Hamilton, née Princess Marie of Baden, and of the Countess Egloffstein, were prominently announced.[150] Ernst von Weber proudly and in detail reported that during his 1888 journey to Sweden he had been entertained by 'high-ranking personalities from the nobility and from the world of learning, who for the greatest part constitute the Scandinavian Anti-Vivisection Society'.[151]

The 1888 issues of *Thier- und Menschenfreund* thus give an impression of a somewhat stagnant old family of anti-vivisectionists, drawing more than half of its members from the educated and/or

Table 7.1: *Social origins and financial contributions of the members of the International Society for the Combat Against Scientific Torture of Animals, in 1888*

Social categories	Members		Contributions	
	Number	%	Marks	%
All members	898	100	5479	100
Male				
Officials with academic education	68	7.6	386	6.7
Medical doctors	2	0.2	44	0.8
Clergymen	59	6.6	188	3.8
Other academics	57	6.3	341	6.2
Military officers	41	4.6	217	4.0
'The educated'	227	25.3	1176	21.5
Industrialists, men of private means	38	4.2	185	3.4
Nobility	109	12.1	1296	23.6
'Property owners'	147	16.4	1481	27.0
Unidentified	198	22.0	959	17.5
Total	572	63.7	3616	66.0
Female				
Nobility	95	10.6	999	18.2
Others	231	25.7	864	15.8
Total	326	36.3	1863	34.0

Note: Only individual, not corporate members were counted. When allocation to two social categories was possible (e.g. nobleman and officer), the choice was made at random.

Source: 'Quittungen', i.e. receipts of annual subscriptions (minimum was 2 Marks) as published monthly in *Thier- und Menschenfreund*.

wealthy classes of society. There was, however, the possibility of opening a door to a new class of members, for, also in 1888, a member of the New Berlin Society lectured to a group of craftsmen.[152] This can be seen as an indication that the movement had become aware of its isolation and had attempted to broaden its basis.

Broadening the basis and unveiling new motives

At the onset of the agitation, the fight against 'materialist medicine' as well as against 'materialist socialism' had been part of von

Weber's programme, which addressed itself to a 'moral elite' of the German nation.[153] Ten years later, his friend Paul Förster could not understand why the social democrats had voted in favour of free research both in the *Reichstag* and in the Prussian *Landtag*[154] and why they continued to oppose the anti-vivisection movement. Was it just because freedom meant so much to them?[155] By 1890 Förster, although vice-president of the International Society, had become the movement's effective leader, as von Weber now, in his sixties, was often absent or ill.[156] After addressing a meeting on nature cures attended by 'over 1,000 men and women' he wrote with some satisfaction:

> The [vivisection] question ought to be brought more often before a greater public forum, for more comprehension and a greater treasure of intact feelings for this sad moral question can be found in general there, rather than in the higher classes where the numbers of our supporters is still but a few . . . And still fewer among these possess the true courage necessary to push our concerns through regardless of the circumstances . . . It is necessary to bring the great mass of the population into a salutary agitation.[157]

This broader approach was needed all the more as by 1896 the membership of the International Society stagnated at around 1,150 members — as many as in 1881.[158] And there were some indications that the social composition was changing, meaning that a few wealthy subscribers could only be replaced by many less well-to-do members. At the death of the Duke Elimar von Oldenburg, Förster commented: 'Death incessantly leaves greater breaches in our ranks, breaches for which we have in general no proper substitution'.[159] In autumn 1900, new popular meetings were organised in Berlin. And the accountant Hermann Stenz, a committee member of the International Society for more than a decade, started weekly lectures to the members of the 'fourth' class.[160] The explicit argument for the mobilisation of the workers was the allegation that the poor were used in public hospitals as human guinea pigs. This reason, already expressed in Britain in the eighteenth century by Samuel Johnson, and again in the 1870 anti-vivisection debates,[161] was not new in the German context but from this time on was used frequently.[162]

The hope for more success on this broader social basis was also nourished by events in Switzerland. First, in 1893, the Swiss male population had accepted a referendum prohibiting kosher butchering. This issue, which from 1887 till 1893, had completely replaced vivisection in Swiss animal protection circles as can be seen in Figure 7.2, had also had its repercussions in Germany. The *Thier- und Menschenfreund* had supported the abolition of kosher butchering for years.[163] It interpreted the Swiss result as a victory for animal protection brought about by the mass of the population against the power and money of state and church.[164] Had not Richard Wagner himself written that he would prefer to become a socialist if the present state was unwilling to abolish vivisection, rather than be forced to live in a world in which 'no dog would wish to live any longer'?[165] Such political tactics required aggressive itinerant speakers who were sought by advertisement.[166] In addition, young doctors were repeatedly invited by the *Thier- und Menschenfreund* to participate in a competition for a prize essay on the uselessness of animal experimentation. No manuscripts came, however, so that this idea had to be dropped, despite the high prize money of up to 1,000 Marks.[167]

Second, the success of the kosher butchering referendum had stimulated the founding of an anti-vivisection society in Zurich, which in 1895 started a popular initiative to bring about the prohibition of vivisection by another referendum. The initiative harvested the number of signatures required by the constitution so that the proposal had to be discussed in parliament and submitted to general suffrage. It was defeated by a majority of two to one, but anti-vivisectionists interpreted the vote as a hopeful start, particularly if one considered that the workers had been propagandistically misled to vote against abolition.[168] Förster, who then travelled to Switzerland, was very impressed.[169]

As shown in Figures 7.1 and 7.2, in the late 1890s anti-vivisection experienced a resurgence in both Germany and Switzerland, and even in Austria, if the writings of its advocates can be taken as a measure. But there were also new organisations. In 1899, new anti-vivisection societies were founded in Munich and Vienna, and the old one in Berne resuscitated.[170] Soon parliamentary discussions took place in Berlin, Dresden, Munich, Vienna and Berne.[171] This new start went hand in hand with the emergence of a new generation of leaders. Reverend Knoche died in 1892, Alfred von Seefeld in 1893, Count Zedtwitz and Dr Nagel in 1895, Dr Lawson Tait and Espérance von Schwartz in 1899 and Ernst von Weber in 1902. The same was true for the old vivisectors. Charles-Edouard Brown-Séquard disappeared in 1894, Carl Ludwig and Louis Pasteur in

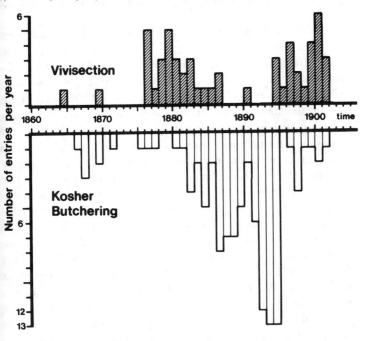

Figure 7.2: Articles on, and short references to, vivisection and kosher butchering, 1864–1901, in the periodicals of the Swiss Society for the Protection of Animals, namely the Schweizerische Thierschutzblätter *(1864–86) and its successor* Der Thierfreund *(1887–1901), adapted from Neff (see note 2)*

1895, Moritz Schiff in 1896, Rudolf Heidenhain in 1897 and Rudolf Virchow in 1902. Had their jubilee birthdays previously offered the *Thier- und Menschenfreund* opportunities for vigorous attacks against their work and their personalities, their deaths now did so for a last time.[172] With the disappearance of the old enemies a new leadership and new motives emerged. A thorough analysis of these, however, would go beyond the scope of this chapter.

Yet the late nineteenth-century issues of both kosher butchering and vivisection had an anti-semitic aspect which was not overlooked by the *Thier- und Menschenfreund*. In 1896, it reprinted passages on vivisection from an explicitly anti-semitic book which, quoting experiments by twelve Jewish authors, spoke of the 'Judaification of doctors' and the ensuing 'penetration of cynicism into medicine'.[173]

Anti-semitic utterances came also from the *Bayreuther Blätter*, continuing Wagner's thoughts on the regeneration of the true German nature.[174] Had it not given space to Paul Förster's brother Bernhard (1843–89), in 1880 the originator of an anti-semitic petition to the

Reichstag, and in 1882 the author of an anti-vivisection brochure
This combination was not surprising given the anti-Judaic world
view of Schopenhauer, particularly with respect to his belief that
Jews considered animals merely as things, which had so struck
Wagner.[175]

Towards the end of the century, the anti-vivisection movement
also received help from theosophists. They felt themselves in agreement with 'our great German composer [i.e. Wagner] and his
philosopher Schopenhauer'.[176] Hermann Stenz described vegetarians and teetotallers, the working class and the Christian churches
as being the 'natural allies' of anti-vivisection, besides a whole range
of nature-healers, the movement's traditional confederates.[177] All
this meant a further radicalisation, illustrated in 1900 by a definitive
clash at the thirteenth International Animal Protection Congress
in Paris. After stormy debates and a vote under dubious circumstances it came to a break between 'false' and 'true' animal protectionists, the latter being the radical anti-vivisectionists, who wanted
to make their cause a compulsory part of all international animal
protection meetings. Under the leadership of Paul Förster a new
international counter association was founded, the 'Weltbund zum
Schutze der Tiere und gegen die Vivisektion'.[178] Thus Förster in
the *Thier- und Menschenfreund* greeted the new century in a combative
mood, using the military style characteristic of the time: 'The movement against vivisection is a battle, a highly necessary and holy battle
against inhumanity and unreason in modern medicine and in the
natural sciences.'[179] And he looked optimistically to the future:

> Our troops increase, our movement is spreading through the
> entire population. We continue, restless, unremitting,
> unflinching as good comrades in arms . . . to press hard on
> the enemy . . . we stretch our hand to related movements,
> according to the ever victorious tactical principle 'march separ-
> ately — strike with united forces!'[180]

Summary and conclusion

In the course of the nineteenth century, concern about the torture
of animals emerged in German-speaking lands as it did elsewhere.
Notwithstanding a rather rapid and thorough institutionalisation
of experimental physiology in twenty-seven universities, the use of
animals for medical experiments seems not to have been a major
concern till the mid 1870s. Around 1878, Marie-Espérance von

Schwartz, Ernst Gryanowski, Ernst von Weber and Richard Wagner organised a campaign in Germany exclusively to fight for this particular aspect of animal protection. With dogmatic *a priori* arguments, the anti-vivisectionists advocated that any experiment using living animals was evil — as was modern medicine, in as much as it relied on the wrong and misleading knowledge derived from such experiments. Agitators did not differentiate between possible abuses and justified needs. An equally unshakeable conviction was that of the fundamental superiority of drugless and non-interventionist, but natural and painless methods of healing such as homeopathy, magnetopathy, psychotherapy, dietary, water and air cures, i.e. of the 'true medicine of the future'.[181] With their ample resources of time, money, social connections and organisational skill anti-vivisection leaders managed to produce a positive response particularly from conservative political circles.

Despite ceaseless agitation skilfully directed at the educated general public (von Weber), the young ladies (von Schwartz), the churchgoers (Knoche and Knodt), the academics (Grysanowski) and the moral leaders of the nation (Wagner), this response was ephemeral. It faded quickly after parliamentary defeats in the mid 1880s. With the death of Mrs von Schwartz in 1899 and Ernst von Weber in 1902 the first and last typical representatives of this first phase of agitation disappeared. The movement failed to attract influential members from government, from the church or from the medical profession which had just established itself in the eyes of the state largely on the grounds of representing truly scientific medicine. High-ranking aristocrats such as one of the several dukes of Oldenburg and princesses of Baden (but none of the reigning German princes or princesses) and the composer Richard Wagner were the principal public figures who supported anti-vivisection. But their influence was restricted to their own circles, which finally proved politically insufficient.

With their implacable attitude, anti-vivisectionists had manoeuvred themselves into a position of isolation from the great majority of animal protection societies in Germany and Switzerland which accepted the notion of the potential usefulness of animal experiments. Admittedly there were a minority of less than a dozen societies among some 150 animal protection groups. Yet the anti-vivisectionists had to stick to their radically *theriocentric*[182] views, because these alone distinguished them as defenders of animal rights from the still *anthropocentrically* orientated general animal protectionists.

By the turn of the century, realising the fading of interest,[183] and in order to strengthen their movement with new arguments, methods and members, anti-vivisectionists sought the help of vegetarians (kept at a distance by Grysanowski), theosophists, anti-vaccinationists, teetotallers and even pacifists and socialists (abhorred by von Weber). Such were the signs of a rejuvenation of anti-vivisection. But the main feature of this second phase of agitation was that new leaders saw the final solution in a mobilisation of the whole population, making it possible to win by force of numbers. As one of them put it: one no longer looked for 'the majesty of princes . . . but for the majesty of the people'.[184]

Acknowledgements

The authors thank Mr Michael Tröhler for his help in collecting financial data on the 'International Society . . .', Miss Sabine Mildner for her bibliographical assistance and Mrs Heide Engel and Mrs Monika Tietze for the preparation of the manuscript.

Notes

1. See above, pp. 28–36.
2. H. Bretschneider, *Der Streit um die Vivisektion im 19. Jahrhundert* (Fischer, Stuttgart, 1962), p. 12; R. Neff, *Der Streit um den wissenschaftlichen Tierversuch in der Schweiz des 19. Jahrhunderts* (Schwabe, Basel, 1989).
3. Neff, *Tierversuch*.
4. U. Hahn, *Die Entwicklung des Tierschutzgedankens in Religion und Geitstesgeschichte* (Diss. med. vet. Tierärztle. Hochschule, Hannover, 1980), p. 131.
5. Ibid. and below, p. 178.
6. See e.g. Neff, *Tierversuch*, p. 3. and below, p. 163.
7. See above, pp. 35–6.
8. Hahn, *Tierschutzgedanke*, pp. 121–3.
9. Ibid., pp. 123–4.
10. See above, pp. 16–18, 36–7.
11. A. Schopenhauer, 'Über die Grundlage der Moral' in Schopenhauer, *Sämtliche Werke*, ed. A. Hübscher, 2nd edn (7 vols, E. Brockhaus, Wiesbaden, 1948–50), vol. 4, pp. 103–275, p. 162. For Bentham and Kant see above, pp. 36–9.
12. H.-J. Störig, *Kleine Weltgeschichte der Philosophie*, 11th edn (2 vols, Frankfurt, 1975), vol. 2, pp. 171–87.
13. A. Schopenhauer, 'Parerga und Paralipomena', in Schopenhauer, *Sämtliche Werke*, vol. 6, p. 399.
14. Ibid., pp. 398, 400. This and all following quotations translated by the authors.
15. Ibid., pp. 177, 400.
16. Ibid., pp. 396–7.
17. See below, pp. 164, 177.

18. H.-H. Eulner, *Die Entwicklung der medizinischen Spezialfächer an den Universitäten des deutschen Sprachgebietes* (Enke, Stuttgart, 1970), p. 60.

19. E. Hintzsche, *Gustav Gabriel Valentin (1810–1883)* (Haupt, Bern, 1953), pp. 49–50.

20. See above, p. 22.

21. F.W. Theile, *Ueber den Nutzen physiologischer Versuche an Thieren für die Heilkunde und über die Vorurteile gegen solche Versuche* (Weingart, Bern, 1842).

22. J.J. Dreifuss, 'Moritz Schiff et la vivisection', *Gesnerus*, vol. 42 (1985), pp. 289–303; C. Borschel, 'Das Physiologische Institut in Göttingen 1840–1952' (unpublished MD thesis, Georg August Universität. Göttingen, 1987), pp. 344–52.

23. Neff, *Tierversuch*, pp. 4–5.

24. Ibid.

25. Ibid.

26. See below, p. 188.

27. In this chapter the term 'vivisection' is consistently used in its *broad* sense, as defined above, p. 14, which corresponds to current usage in late nineteenth-century debates on all kinds of animal experimentation.

28. G. Fleming, *Die Vivisection. (Zergliederung lebendiger Thierkörper). Ist sie nothwendig oder zu entschuldigen?* (Grieben, Berlin, 1870).

29. Neff, *Tierversuch*, pp. 6–7; Dreifuss, 'Moritz Schiff', p. 297.

30. Neff, *Tierversuch*, p. 7.

31. See above, pp. 105–24.

32. Dreifuss, 'Moritz Schiff', pp. 292–300.

33. Neff, *Tierversuch*, p. 7.

34. Ibid, p. 8.

35. C. Hermann, *Die Vivisectionsfrage für das grössere Publicum beleuchtet* (Vogel, Leipzig, 1877), pp. 3–4.

36. Ibid., p. 50.

37. See e.g. A. von Seefeld, *Altes und Neues über die vegetarische Lebensweise* (Schmorl und von Seefeld, Hannover, 1880), p. 36.

38. Hermann, *Vivisectionsfrage*, pp. 26–7.

39. Ibid., pp. 17–18.

40. Ibid., pp. 14–17, 59–64. Hermann had figures at hand, prepared by his colleague, the professor of agriculture at the Federal Polytechnic School in Zurich, showing that the annual number of castrations in Germany had amounted in 1873 to 65,000 horses, 650,000 cattle, 2 million sheep and 8 million pigs.

41. See above, pp. 23, 35.

42. Ibid., p. 18.

43. Ibid., pp. 17–22.

44. For an accurate short account of Vogt's publications see Bretschneider, *Vivisektion*, p. 34.

45. This was the modern Greek translation of her name and surname, literally meaning 'Hopefulness' and 'Black'. The data concerning her publications, as given in *Allgemeine Deutsche Bibliographie* (56 vols, Duncker and Humblot, Berlin, 1967–71), vol. 54, pp. 277–8, are probably correct. As to those concerning her private life, they must be compared with the entry concerning her second husband in *Gothaisches Genealogisches Taschenbuch der Briefadeligen Häuser* (34 vols, J. Perthes, Gotha, 1907–42), vol. 1, p. 711,

which has been used here.

46. An article mentioned *expressis verbis* by Mrs von Schwartz was a letter by Dr George Hoggan to the *Morning Post*, 2 February 1875. It is reprinted in extract form in R.D. French, *Antivivisection and Medical Science in Victorian Society* (Princeton University Press, Princeton and London, 1975), pp. 414–15. With reference to Britain, French states that of 'all medical testimony against vivisection, before or since, George Hoggan's letter had the greatest impact' (ibid., p. 68). It is remarkable that this holds for Germany, too.

47. E. Melena (alias Marie-Espérance von Schwartz), *Dr. E.G.F. Grisanowski. Mitteilungen aus seinem Leben und seinen Briefen* (Schmorl und von Seefeld, Hannover, 1890), p. 142.

48. Ibid., pp. 143–4.

49. Ibid., pp. 53–4.

50. Ibid., pp. 1–143.

51. Ibid., pp. 144–5.

52. E. Melena (alias Marie-Espérance von Schwartz), *Gemma oder Tugend und Laster* (Franz, München, 1877); Iatros (alias E.G.F. Grysanowski), *Die Vivisektion, ihr wissenschaftlicher Wert und ihre ethische Berechtigung* (Barth, Leipzig, 1877).

53. Iatros, *Die Vivisektion*, p. 62.

54. Ibid., p. 35.

55. Ibid., pp. 26, 43, 49–60, 79.

56. Ibid., pp. 16–17, 45.

57. Ibid., pp. 78–9.

58. Melena, *Gemma*.

59. See above pp. 17, 28, 33–4, 37; see also note 93 below.

60. See *Thier- und Menschenfreund*, vol. 9, no. 10 (1880), p. 80.

61. Melena, *Dr. Grisanowski*, pp. 174–5.

62. Ibid., p. 143 (footnote).

63. F. Bornmüller, *Biographisches Schriftstellerlexikon der Gegenwart* (Bibliograph. Institut, Leipzig, 1882), p. 757; E. von Weber, *Vier Jahre in Afrika* (2 vols, Brockhaus, Leipzig, 1878), vol. 1, pp. 1–8, 407–8, vol. 2, pp. 526, 544.

64. Von Weber, *Afrika*, vol. 2, p. 544; E. von Weber, *Die Erweiterung des deutschen Wirtschaftsgebiets und die Grundlegung zu überseeischen deutschen Staaten, ein dringendes Gebot* (Twietmeyer, Leipzig, 1878).

65. Von Weber, *Afrika*, vol. 1, pp. 387, 402–6, 425–6, vol. 2, pp. 287–8, 292.

66. See below, p. 189.

67. Von Weber, *Afrika*, vol. 2, pp. 288–92, appendix pp. 575–9.

68. E. von Weber (ed.), *Bisher ungedruckte Briefe von Richard Wagner an Ernst von Weber* (Internationaler Verein zur Bekämpfung der wissenschaftlichen Thierfolter, Dresden, 1883), p. 5; E. von Weber, *Die Folterkammern der Wissenschaft* (Voigt, Berlin and Leipzig, 1879).

69. Von Weber, *Folterkammern*, p. 4; for an accurate short account of this brochure see Bretschneider, *Vivisektion*, pp. 40–3.

70. Bretschneider, *Vivisektion*, p. 63.

71. Melena, *Dr. Grisanowski*, pp. 164–6; n.b.: Melena gave Grisanowski's letter an incorrect date.

72. Von Weber, *Briefe von Richard Wagner*, pp. 6–8; C. Wagner, *Die Tagebücher*, 2nd edn (4 vols, Piper, München and Zürich, 1982), vol. 3, pp. 402, 408–9, 411.

73. R. Wagner, *Offener Brief an Ernst von Weber, Verfasser der 'Folterkammern der Wissenschaft' ueber die Vivisection* (Voigt, Berlin and Leipzig, 1880); von Weber, *Briefe von Richard Wagner*, pp. 10–13.

74. Wagner, *Brief an Ernst von Weber*, pp. 3–8, 14.

75. For Wagner's ideological writings of the last decade of his life see M. Gregor-Dellin, *Richard Wagner* (Piper, München, 1980), pp. 760–77; R. Wagner, *Dichtungen und Schriften* (10 vols, Insel Verlag, Frankfurt am Main, 1983), vol. 10, pp. 77–180.

76. Gregor-Dellin, *Richard Wagner*, pp. 388–92.

77. Wagner, *Brief an Ernst von Weber*, p. 14.

78. Wagner, *Tagebücher*, vol. 3, pp. 423, 428.

79. See e.g. the index for the years 1877–1902, *Bayreuther Blätter*, vol. 26, appendix to no. 12 (1903), pp. 1–24, particularly p. 9; see also below, notes 106, 107, 112, 124, 127, and above, pp. 177–8.

80. Bretschneider, *Viviektion*, pp. 61–3; Melena, *Dr. Grisanowski*, p. 143 (footnote).

81. A. v. Steiger-Jeandrevin, *Die Vivisektion vom Standpunkte des sittlichen Gefühls* (Haller, Bern, 1880); Neff, *Tierversuch*, pp. 9–11, 14–18; see also below, p. 170.

82. Von Weber, *Folterkammern der Wissenschaft*, pp. 32–6.

83. Melena, *Dr. Grisanowski*, pp. 166–7 (footnote), 175.

84. Neff, *Tierversuch*, p. 10.

85. E. von Weber (ed.), *Stimmen der Presse über die "wissenschaftliche" Tätigkeit in den physiologischen Instituten* (Voigt, Leipzig, 1879).

86. See below, p. 168.

87. R. Nagel, *Der wissenschaftliche Unwerth der Vivisektionen in allen ihren Arten* (Humanitätsschriften des neuen Berliner Tierschutz-Vereins, no. 1, by the author, Berlin, 1881). It was also distributed as a supplement to the *Bayreuther Blätter*, vol. 4, nos 2–3 (1881); G. Voigt, *Zukunfts-Medizin* (2 vols, Scholtze, Leipzig, 1879).

88. *Se. Eminenz der Cardinal Manning und die Vivisection* (Culemann, Hannover, 1882); *Lord Coleridge, Lord Oberrichter von England, über Vivisection* (Schmorl und von Seefeld, Hannover, 1882); L. Tait, *Die Nutzlosigkeit der Thier-Vivisection als wissenschaftlicher Forschungs-Methode* (Verlag Int. Verein z. Bekämpfung d. wiss. thierfolter, Dresden, 1883).

89. Von Weber, *Briefe von Richard Wagner*, p. 6; see above, p. 169; see also *Thier- und Menschenfreund*, vol. 19, no. 7 (1899), p. 57, no. 8, pp. 75–6.

90. See above, p. 160.

91. *Thier- und Menschenfreund*, vol. 20, no. 2 (1900), p. 13.

92. Bretschneider, *Vivisektion*, p. 57.

93. F. Zöllner, *Über den wissenschaftlichen Missbrauch der Vivisection mit historischen Documenten über die Vivisection von Menschen* (Staackmann, Leipzig, 1880), pp. 1–62.

94. C. Ludwig, 'Die wissenschaftliche Tätigkeit in den physiologischen Instituten', *Im Neuen Reich*, vol. 9 (1879), p. 121; C. Ludwig, 'Die Vivisection vor dem Richterstuhle der Gregenwart', *Die Gartenlaube*, vol. 27, no. 25 (1879), pp. 417–19; R. Heidenhain, *Die Vivisection im Dienste der Heilkunde* (Breitkopf und Härtel, Leipzig, 1879); A.-H. Maehle, 'Der Literat Christlob Mylius und seine Verteidigung des medizinischen Tierversuchs im 18. und 19. Jahrhundert', *Medizinhistorisches Journal*, vol. 21 (1986), pp. 269–87.

95. 'Erklärung. In Sachen der freien, der menschlichen Wohlfahrt zu

Gute kommenden Forschung . . . ', Dekanatsakten der medizinischen Fakultät Göttingen, Dekanat Ebstein, Januar-Juli 1879, 19. Februar 1879 (Universitätsarchiv Göttingen), Med. 39.

96. 'Sehr verehrliche Fakultät . . . ', letter by the Medical Faculty of Leipzig to the Medical Faculty of Göttingen, trying to persuade the latter to sign the declaration of February 1879 joined in remodelled form, ibid., 8. März 1879.

97. Ibid., signed annotation in handwriting.

98. 'Hochgeehrte Herren Collegen . . . ', answer to the Leipzig Medical Faculty by their colleagues in Berlin, a printed copy of which was sent to the Göttingen Faculty, ibid., 2. März 1879.

99. 'Am 15. Februar d. J. . . . ', answer to the Leipzig Medical Faculty by their colleagues in Würzburg, a handwritten copy of which was sent also to the Göttingen Faculty, ibid., 21. März 1879.

100. Bretschneider, *Vivisektion*, p. 74.

101. See above, p. 161.

102. Bretschneider, *Vivisektion*, pp. 66–7.

103. Ibid., pp. 64–6.

104. Ibid., pp. 75, 80–1.

105. See above p. 161. The debate was printed verbatim in the *Stenographische Berichte über die Verhandlungen des Reichstages, V. Legislaturperiode, I. Session 1881/2* (Pindter, Berlin, 1882), pp. 871–85.

106. For the London Medical Congress, see below, pp. 189–94; R. Virchow, 'Ueber den Werth des pathologischen Experiments', in W. MacCormac and G.H. Makins (eds.), *Transactions of the International Medical Congress, London 1881* (4 vols, Kolckmann, London, 1881), vol. 1, pp. 22–36. Grysanowski commented angrily on this speech in 'Das ärztliche Concil in London', *Bayreuther Blätter*, vol. 4, no. 11 (1881), p. 340.

107. Bretschneider, *Vivisektion*, pp. 81–4; B. Förster, *Die Frage der Vivisektion im Deuschen Reichstage. Ein Stück Kulturkampf* (Burger, Bayreuth, 1882). This pamphlet was distributed in 2,000 offprint copies from the original paper in the *Bayreuther Blätter*, vol. 5, no. 3 (1882), p. 90.

108. Bretschneider, *Vivisektion*, pp. 74, 84–5, 98.

109. Von Weber, *Briefe von Richard Wagner*, pp. 15–16.

110. The debate occurs verbatim in the *Stenographische Berichte über die Verhandlungen der durch die Allerhöchste Verordnung vom 2. November 1882 einberufenen beiden Häuser des Landtages. Haus der Abgeordneten* (3 vols, Moeser, Berlin, 1883), vol. 3, pp. 1438–58; see also Bretschneider, *Vivisektion*, pp. 89–91.

111. Ibid., p. 92; 'Ministerium der geistlichen, Unterrichts- und Medicinal-Angelegenheiten . . . an den königlichen Universitäts-Kurator . . . zu Göttingen, Berlin, den 13. Dezember 1883', Kuratorialakten der Universität Göttingen (Universitätsarchiv Göttingen), XVI III. Ba I, II, a 8.

112. On the side of the anti-vivisectionists Paul Förster wrote 49 pages. See P. Förster, *Die Frage der Vivisektion, mit besonderer Rücksicht auf die Verhandlungen im preussischen Abgeordnetenhause am 16. April 1883* (by the author, Guben, 1883). Critical comments by Grysanowski and Lawson Tait, the notorious British anti-vivisectionist surgeon, were edited by von Weber's International Society. See L. Tait and E. Grysanowski, *Kritische Beleuchtungen der Vivisectionsdebatte im Preussischen Abgeordnetenhause* (Internat. Verein z. Bekämpfung d. wiss. Thierfolter, Dresden, 1883). Grysanowski also reported to the readers of

the *Bayreuther Blätter*, vol. 6, nos 7–9 (1883), pp. 228–49.

113. R. Heidenhain, *Die Vivisection. Auf Veranlassung des Königlich-Preussischen Ministers der geistlichen, Unterrichts- und Medicinal-Angelegenheiten* (Breitkopf und Härtel, Leipzig, 1884), p. 71 (footnote).

114. Bretschneider, *Vivisektion*, p. 100.

115. 'Auszug aus den Fakultätsberichten', Dekanatsakten der Medizinischen Fakultät Göttingen, Dekanat Henle, 1. Juli 1884–30. Juni 1885, 2. Februar 1885 (Universitätsarchiv Göttingen), Med. 50, Universitäts-Curatorium, no. 168.

116. Heidenhain, *Die Vivisektion*.

117. Ibid., pp. 70–1 (footnote).

118. 'Circular-Verfügung an die medizinischen Fakultäten', Dekanatsakten der Medizinischen Fakultät Göttingen, Dekanat Henle, 1. Juli 1884–30. Juni 1885, 2. Februar 1885 (Universitätsarchiv Göttingen), Med. 50.

119. Bretschneider, *Vivisektion*, pp. 102–3.

120. Ibid., p. 104; *Thier- und Menschenfreund*, vol. 8, no. 5 (1888), p. 35; vol. 11, no. 12 (1891), pp. 100–3; vol. 12, no. 1 (1892), pp. 5, 26.

121. Bretschneider, *Vivisektion*, p. 102.

122. See above p. 168; Weber, in 1888 wrote once again to Bismarck, see *Thier- und Menschenfreund*, vol. 8, no. 6 (1888), p. 42; for Princess Bismarck see below, pp. 170, 173.

123. Ibid., vol. 12, no. 3 (1892) p. 18.

124. Melena, *Dr. Grisanowski*, p. 193; E. Grysanowski, 'Die Vivisektion. Zur Verständigung über die Motive und Zwecke der Agitation', *Thier- und Menschenfreund*, vol. 8, nos 7–8 (1888), p. 56; see also ibid., vol. 15, no. 1 (1895), p. 1 and vol. 20, no. 2 (1900), p. 11; P. Förster, 'Ernst von Weber 7. 2. 1830–4. 1. 1902', *Bayreuther Blätter*, vol. 25, nos 4–6 (1902), pp. 169–71.

125. Neff, *Tierversuch*, pp. 16–18.

126. *Thier- und Menschenfreund*, vol. 8, nos. 7–8 (1888), p. 15.

127. 'Förster, Paul' in G. Lüdtke (ed.), *Kürschner Deutscher Gelehrten-Kalender auf das Jahr 1925* (de Gruyter, Berlin and Leipzig, 1925), p. 239; P. Förster, *Die Frage der Vivisektion*, see note 112, above; see also note 124 above, and P. Förster, 'Ernst Grysanowski', *Bayreuther Blätter*, vol. 11, nos 7–8 (1888), pp. 268–9.

128. Melena, *Dr. Grisanowski*, pp. 1–221; 'Dr. E.G.F. Grisanowski's wissenschaftliche Schriften gewürdigt von Pastor Emil Knodt', ibid., pp. 223–376; E. Grysanowski, *Gesammelte antivivisectionistische Schriften* (Basch, Münster, i.W., 1897).

129. W. von V[oigts]-R[heets], 'Die Betheiligung der Frauen an der Bewegung gegen die Vivisektion', *Thier-und Menschenfreund*, vol. 8, no. 10 (1888), pp. 78–9.

130. E. von Weber, 'Anna Kingsford', *Thier- und Menschenfreund*, vol. 8, no. 4 (1888), p. 26.

131. See above, pp. 153, 157. For reference to women and anti-vivisection in Britain and particularly to Cobbe and Kingsford see R.D. French, *Anti-vivisection*, pp. 223, 230, 239–50.

132. F.P. Cobbe, *Licht an dunkeln Stäten*, Deutsch von Agnes Gräfin Egloffstein (Schmorl und von Seefeld, Hannover, 1883).

133. A. Engel, 'Auch eine Emanzipirte', *Thier- und Menschenfreund*, vol. 8, no. 2 (1888), pp. 12–13.

134. See entry 'Zedtwitz' in *Allgemeine Deutsche Biographie*, vol. 44, pp. 753–6.

135. See entries 'Seefeld' in *Gothaisches Genealogisches Taschenbuch*, vol. 9, p. 873, and in B. Fabian (ed.), *Deutsches biographisches Archiv*, microfiche edn (Saur, München etc., 1982–5), microfiche 1168, p. 389.

136. P. Förster, 'Dem Andenken Kaiser Friedrichs III., des Friedfertigen . . . ', *Thier- und Menschenfreund*, vol. 8, nos 7–8 (1888), p. 54.

137. Grysanowski, 'Die Vivisektion', p. 56.

138. Ibid., pp. 56–8.

139. Förster, 'Kaister Friedrich [. . .] III.', p. 54.

140. Ibid., p. 54; see also *Thier- und Menschenfreund*, vol. 8, no. 11 (1888), pp. 87–8.

141. H. Stenz, 'Verborgene Greuel. Tatsachen und Vernunftgründe gegen die Vivisektion', *Thier- und Menschenfreund*, vol. 8, no. 6 (1888), pp. 42–6; A. Lill v. Lilienbach, 'Ueber das Wesen der Kuhpocke und die Folgen der Kuhpockenimpfung', ibid., pp. 46–81; A. Graf Zedtwitz, 'Die neueste Kundgebung der Impfanwälte', ibid., no. 11, pp. 88–90. For the links in British anti-vivisectionism with agitation against compulsory vaccination see French, *Antivivisection*, pp. 228–30.

142. *Thier- und Menschenfreund*, vol. 8, no. 1 (1888), p. 7; no. 4, p. 31. A petition by this Society for the abolition of compulsory smallpox vaccination was reprinted *in extenso* in vol. 14, nos 7–8 (1894), p. 57.

143. Melena, *Dr. Grisanowski*, p. 179. For vegetarianism and anti-vivisection in Britain see French, *Antivivisection*, pp. 230–1.

144. Rothschuh, in his recent volume on nineteenth-century medical reform, does not mention one single anti-vivisectionist cited in this chapter. See K.E. Rothschuh, *Naturheilbewegung, Reformbewegung, Alternativbewegung* (Hippokrates, Stuttgart, 1983).

145. V. Gützlaff, *Schopenhauer. Ueber die Thiere und den Thierschutz. Ein Beitrag zur ethischen Seite der Vivisectionsfrage* (Nauck, Berlin, 1879).

146. *Thier- und Menschenfreund*, vol. 8, no. 2 (1888), pp. 15–16, no. 4, p. 26, no. 8, pp. 65–6.

147. In 1889 there was an even more magnificent commemoration ball featuring great names in music, opera and drama among the 2,000 guests, see ibid., vol. 9, no. 4 (1889), p. 32.

148. Ibid., vol. 8, no. 2 (1888), pp. 14–15.

149. Ibid., no. 6, p. 49, nos 7–8, p. 55.

150. Ibid., no. 1, pp. 1–2, nos 7–8, pp. 53–4, no. 11, p. 85.

151. Ibid., no. 2, p. 14. Accordingly, the death some months later of Princess Eugénie stimulated von Weber to write a long obituary, see ibid., vol. 9, nos 5–6 (1889), pp. 36–7.

152. Ibid., vol. 8, no. 4 (1888), p. 32.

153. Von Weber, *Folterkammern der Wissenschaft*, p. 74.

154. See above, pp. 168–9.

155. P. Förster, 'Vivisektion und Sozialdemokratie', *Thier- und Menschenfreund*, vol. 9, no. 9 (1889), p. 72.

156. *Thier- und Menschenfreund*, vol. 10, no. 1 (1890), p. 1.

157. Ibid., vol. 19, no. 2 (1899), p. 15.

158. Ibid., vol. 16, no. 6 (1896), p. 46; Bretschneider, *Vivisektion*, p. 61 (footnote).

159. *Thier- und Menschenfreund*, vol. 15, no. 11 (1895), p. 86.

160. Ibid., vol. 21, no. 1 (1901), p. 2, no. 2, p. 22, no. 3, p. 25.

161. For Johnson see above, pp. 32–3; for nineteenth-century Britain see French, *Antivivisection*, p. 238.

162. *Thier- und Menschenfreund*, vol. 20, no. 10 (1900), p. 112, no. 11, p. 117; vol. 21, no. 12 (1901), p. 130.

163. See e.g. ibid., vol. 9, nos 2–3 (1889), pp. 21–2; vol. 12, no. 4 (1892), pp. 30–1; vol. 14, no. 1 (1894), p. 5, no. 2, pp. 14–15, no. 6, pp. 43–4; and particularly H. Stenz, 'Eine Zusammenfassung der wichtigsten Gründe gegen das Schächten', ibid., nos 7–8, pp. 52–7.

164. *Thier- und Menschenfreund*, vol. 13, nos 7–8 (1893), pp. 67–8.

165. Wagner, *Brief an Ernst von Weber*, p. 16.

166. *Thier- und Menschenfreund*, vol. 19, no. 8 (1899), p. 80.

167. Ibid., no. 1, p. 6, no. 3, p. 25, no. 7, pp. 57–8, no. 8, p. 80; vol. 20, no. 1 (1900), pp. 4–5, no. 3, p. 28.

168. Neff, *Tierversuch*, pp. 19–21; *Thier- und Menschenfreund*, vol. 15, no. 4 (1895), pp. 27–8, nos 7–8, p. 54, no. 10, pp. 75–6; no. 11, pp. 81–2; vol. 16, no. 1 (1896), pp. 2–3.

169. Neff, *Tierversuch*, pp. 37, 48.

170. *Thier- und Menschenfreund*, vol. 20, no. 5 (1900), p. 58; vol. 21, no. 1 (1901), p. 2, no. 4, p. 42, no. 6, p. 68.

171. Ibid., vol. 20, no. 5 (1900), p. 55; vol. 21, no. 12 (1901), pp. 132–3; Neff, *Tierversuch*, p. 24.

172. *Thier- und Menschenfreund*, vol. 12, no. 1 (1892), p. 5; vol. 13, no. 1 (1893), pp. 11–12; vol. 14, no. 5 (1894), pp. 35–6; vol. 15, no. 10 (1895), p. 76; vol. 16, no. 11 (1896), p. 88; vol. 21, no. 10 (1901) p. 121.

173. Ibid., vol. 16, no. 2 (1896), p. 15, no. 3, pp. 17–19.

174. H. Zelinsky, *Richard Wagner – ein deutsches Thema* (Zweitausendeins, Frankfurt, a.M., 1976), pp. 56–7, 74–81; J. Katz, *Richard Wagner, Vorbote des Antisemitismus* (Athenäum Verlag, Königstein, 1985), ch. 9.

175. Schopenhauer, 'Grundlager der Moral', pp. 773–80. For Schopenhauer's and Wagner's anti-semitic attitudes see Katz, *Richard Wagner*, pp. 23, 103, 156.

176. R. Wolf, 'Mensch, Tier und Vivisektion', in *Theosophische Schriften* (30 vols, Schwetschke und Sohn, Braunschweig, 1894–96), vol. 28, p. 16.

177. *Thier- und Menschenfreund*, vol. 15, no. 4 (1895), p. 31; H. Stenz, 'Die wissenschaftliche Unhaltbarkeit und die sittliche Verweflichkeit der Vivisektion (Schluss)', ibid., vol. 20, no. 2 (1900), pp. 15–18.

178. Ibid., vol. 20, no. 5 (1900), pp. 51–2, no. 6, pp. 63–4, no. 9, pp. 87–93.

179. Ibid., vol. 21, no. 12 (1901), inner cover.

180. P. Förster, 'Zum neuen Jahrhundert', ibid., vol. 20, no. 1 (1900), pp. 2–3, p. 3.

181. For Grysanowski see above pp. 157–8; H. Stenz, 'Drei Bundesgenossen gegen die Thierfolter', *Thier- und Menschenfreund*, vol. 12, no. 12 (1892), p. 95; Stenz, 'Die wissenschaftliche Unhaltbarkeit der Vivisektion (part 8)', ibid., vol. 19, no. 11 (1899), pp. 105–11; see also Voigt, *Zukunfts-Medizin*, see above, p. 165.

182. For explanation of the term 'theocentric' see above, pp. 46–7.

183. Stenz, 'Die wissenschaftliche Unhaltbarkeit', p. 13.

184. *Thier- und Menschenfreund*, vol. 20, no. 5 (1900), pp. 57–8.

8

Pro-vivisection in England in the Early 1880s: Arguments and Motives

Nicolaas Rupke

Science, politics and the public

The Cruelty to Animals Act of 1876 was, among other things, a traumatic development in the still informal and largely untried relationship between scientists, the government and the lay public. In the period leading up to the new Act, the scientists, in order to protect and further their professional interests, were forced to justify their aims and methods when having to account for physiological research to both parliamentarians and the general public. The anti-vivisectionist attack on the young subject of physiology, combined with the restrictions imposed on animal experimentation by the 1876 Act, awakened in many practitioners of biomedical research the need for self-protection in the form of an organisation to promote their cause.

Historians of physiology, from Sharpey-Schafer onwards,[1] have attributed the formation in 1876 of the Physiological Society of Great Britain to the contemporary anti-vivisection agitation. There can be little doubt that the anti-vivisection movement was indeed the immediate cause of its formation; in Geison's words, outside criticism created an *esprit de corps* among the small band of British physiologists.[2] But, as Paton points out,[3] the need for such a society had deeper roots. Like its older sister organisations such as, for example, the Geological or Zoological Societies, the Physiological Society grew out of the success of the subject which it represented, and it would have come into being regardless of the outside threat.

It would therefore be a mistake to see the young Physiological Society as a major side in the triangle of science, politics and public concern, occasioned by the vivisection controversy of the 1870s and 1880s. In fact, the organised self-defence by scientists to the anti-vivisection onslaught took place considerably later than 1876, and involved not only physiologists, but leaders of the entire biomedical establishment.

This chapter documents when, and on what occasion, the pro-vivisection lobby became organised; it further presents the arguments which the scientists put forward to defend animal experimentation; and lastly, it probes the deeper motives behind the biomedical community's pro-vivisection campaign.

The International Medical Congress of 1881: the origin of organised pro-vivisection

French, Ozer and other historians of the British vivisection debate understandably focus on the origin of the anti-vivisection movement and on the events surrounding the Cruelty to Animals Act of 1876.[4] But five years after the Act received its royal assent, a new wave of interest in the question swept across the pages of the periodical press, this time engendered by the activities of a new pro-vivisection lobby.

In testimony before the Royal Commission of 1875 the scientists had explained why they believed that vivisection was necessary, and some of this testimony had been printed in various scientific and medical journals.[5] Generally, however, no concerted effort had been made to put their case before the public and to counter the accusations made by the anti-vivisectionists in numerous pamphlets and articles. As the American journal *Science* commented, noting that what it called 'the anti-vivisection craze' was spreading not only across the Channel but also across the Atlantic:

> People in general do not read official blue-books: so, in spite of the fact that the royal commission appointed to investigate the matter reported, that, after prolonged and careful inquiry, it could find no evidence that English physiologists were guilty of cruelty, it has been possible for certain anti-vivisectors, by a persistent course of malignant vituperation and brazen mendacity, to produce a wide-spread belief that vivisection essentially consists in torturing an animal for the object of seeing how much it can suffer without dying . . . The physiologists kept silent, and left the field to their enemies, with disastrous result; no one, not a brute, who believed half the stories circulated, could fail to hate physiology and physiologists.[6]

But, *Science* commented, there were signs that British physiologists were at last 'coming to their senses'. And indeed, in the early 1880s, the scientists launched an organised publicity campaign in defence of animal experimentation.

Figure 8.1 gives a semi-quantitative illustration of the interest in the vivisection question during the period 1870–90. It plots the annual number of articles, news items and letters relating to the controversy over animal experimentation in a number of leading periodicals. The *British Medical Journal*, the *Lancet* and *Nature* obviously gave much space to the cause of experimental physiology. The *Fortnightly Review* published a series of articles in favour of animal experimentation, but it also accepted lengthy replies. The *Spectator*, on the other hand, showed a one-sided support for the critics of vivisectional science. The two major peaks in Figure 8.1 occur in 1875 and 1882. Significantly, the second peak does not occur on the curve of the anti-vivisectionist *Spectator*; this peak represented first and foremost the delayed reaction by the scientists to an anti-vivisection movement which was becoming increasingly extreme. In 1881, for example, the Victoria Street Society changed its moderate policy of restriction to that of total abolition.

The clarion call to organised self-defence came from the International Medical Congress (IMC), held in London in August 1881. It was arguably the largest and grandest medical congress ever held. There were 3,181 registered participants, and among these were some of the world's greatest scientific and medical names: Rudolph Virchow, Louis Pasteur, Robert Koch and others. Britain was represented by surgeons such as James Paget (elected President of the Congress), anatomists such as Richard Owen, and naturalists such as T.H. Huxley.

Much publicity was generated by the medical men's unanimous and repeated assertions that vivisection was a justifiable and much-needed means to advance medicine. Several speakers devoted full-length addresses to the issue. Foremost among these was Virchow's aggressive 'Ueber den Werth des pathologischen Experiments', delivered to the general meeting of the Congress, and received with 'repeated and warm applause'.[7] Among the sectional addresses about vivisection was John Simon's 'Experiments on Life, as Fundamental to the Science of Preventive Medicine'.

To contemporaries, in England and abroad, the vivisection issue characterized the IMC of 1881. At its conclusion a general resolution was unanimously passed stating:

That this Congress records its conviction that experiments on living animals have proved of the utmost service to medicine in the past, and are indispensable to its future progress; that, accordingly, while strongly deprecating the infliction of unnecessary pain, it is of opinion, alike in the interests of

Figure 8.1: The fluctuating intensity of the British vivisection debate from 1870 till 1890, based on the annual number of news items, letters and articles in representative examples of the medical, scientific and general periodical press; the frequencies of vivisection entries in other magazines such as the Medical Times and Gazette *or the* Nineteenth Century *show a trend similar to that of the summation columns*

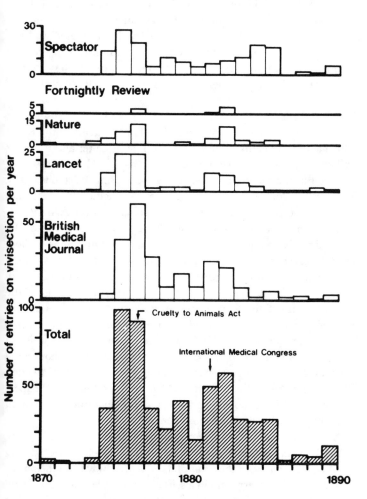

man and of animals, that it is not desirable to restrict competent persons in the performance of such experiments.[8]

Only two days after the IMC had come to an end, the annual
meeting of the British Medical Association was addressed on the
topic of 'Vivisection: what good has it done?' by its President, G.M.
Humphrey, Professor of Anatomy and Physiology at Cambridge.
On a wave of vivisection euphoria the BMA issued its own, national
resolution which declared:

> That this Association desires to express its deep sense of the
> importance of vivisection to the advancement of medical
> science, and the belief that the further prohibition of it would
> be attended with serious injury to the community, by preven-
> ting investigations which are calculated to promote the better
> knowledge and treatment of disease in animals as well as
> man.[9]

A few months later, in March 1882, the Presidents of the Royal
Colleges of Physicians and Surgeons, William Jenner and Erasmus
Wilson respectively, issued invitations to distinguished members of
the scientific and medical professions for a meeting to establish 'The
Association for the Advancement of Medicine by Research'
(AAMR). A motion was passed which stated that the AAMR was
formed 'with the view of bringing the legitimate influence of the
medical profession more effectively to bear on the promotion of those
exact researches in physiology, pathology, and therapeutics, which
are essential to sound progress in the healing art'. But it was widely
recognised that its real objective was the repeal (or at least the
modification) of the Cruelty to Animals Act. Some money was
handed out in support of medical research, but the most visible
accomplishment of the AAMR was the publication of a series of
pamphlets which were designed to defend vivisection, although the
Association's own resolution stated more generally that it intended
'to publish and distribute as widely as possible addresses and papers
explanatory of the object and methods of scientific research in
physiology, pathology, and therapeutics'.[10]

Some twelve brochures were published under the aegis of the
AAMR during the relatively short period 1882–4. But gradually
the Association turned the focus of its activities away from the public
and towards the government in a self-appointed role of advisory body
to the Home Office in the administration of the 1876 Act. This was

the outcome of another resolution adopted at the founding meeting which stated that the 1876 Act 'shall engage the watchful attention of the council, and may rightly become the ground of interposition on their part'.[11]

The role of informing the public was taken over many years later, during the Second Royal Commission, by the Research Defence Society, founded in 1908.[12]

The degree to which the IMC of 1881 had been dominated by the vivisection question may be gauged from the fact that the fairly considerable profits of £300 (receipts £9,030, expenditure £8,730) were donated to the AAMR, i.e., to the pro-vivisection lobby.[13]

The initial aim of the AAMR was to inform the public of the scientists' side in the vivisection controversy. The first and also the largest publication seeking to attain this objective was a full-scale book by Owen, entitled *Experimental Physiology: its Benefits to Mankind*. This was the enlarged version of an address he had delivered on unveiling a statue of William Harvey at Folkestone in August 1881, while the IMC was in progress in London. This event probably represented the most public and sensational act on the part of the scientific and medical establishment in support of animal experimentation. Money for the statue had been donated by the Royal Colleges of Physicians and Surgeons, and Owen was invited to unveil it. The South-Eastern Railway Company laid on a special train to transport many members of the IMC to attend the ceremony. Owen's 'Harveian Oration' was exclusively devoted to a defence of the experimental method in physiological research, and to an attack on its critics.

Much publicity was engendered too, not so much by the AAMR pamphlets, but by a number of articles in the *Nineteenth Century* and the *Fortnightly Review*. The former magazine invited Paget, Owen and Samuel Wilks (a physician at Guy's Hospital) to write about 'Vivisection: its Pains and Uses'. Their essays were published in December 1881, and were followed the next year by several further articles, both for and against.[14] The *Fortnightly Review* published rebuttals to the pro-vivisection essays, by such prominent members of the Victoria Street Society as Frances Power Cobbe and Lord Coleridge, but it also allowed the case for vivisection to be argued by, among others, Gerald Francis Yeo, physiologist at King's College, London, and known for his work on cerebral localisation in monkeys.[15]

At last, the physiologists' case was widely publicised, the anti-vivisectionists were met on public ground, pamphlet was countered with pamphlet, argument with argument, slur with slur, insult with insult, exaggerated misrepresentation with unfair hyperbole.

Arguments about the utility and morality of vivisection

The main arguments of the anti-vivisectionists were that experiments on living animals are both useless and immoral (or irreligious). In his Folkestone address, Owen countered primarily the first point, namely that of the alleged uselessness of vivisection. He did this by citing a number of historical examples of beneficial experimentation, beginning with Harvey's discovery of the circulation of the blood. This discovery had proved of immense significance to medicine, Owen argued, and Harvey would not have been able to establish his doctrine nor convince his contemporaries of its truth without the aid of experimentation on dogs. In an extraordinary *non sequitur*, Owen tried to sweep aside the accusations, saying of Harvey:

> He was a truly religious man; charitable and compassionate as such. He felt his deep responsibility for the gifts he had received from the Fountain of all Knowledge. He could not but be conscious of the rarity and value of such entrusted talent; he shrunk from the sin of 'hiding it under a bushel'. Accordingly, he laid bare the heart in a living animal; . . .[16]

Second only to Harvey's discovery, according to Owen, was John Hunter's discovery of how to treat aneurysms. This he had done by tying the diseased artery above the aneurysmal bulge, because the arterial capillaries are capable of taking over the function of arterial blood flow. Hunter had come upon this method by experimentation on a stag; he had put a ligature around the carotid artery supplying a growing antler, still covered with velvet. The pulsations of the vessels in the formative velvet ceased, but a week later they turned out to have resumed and the normal growth of the antler continued.

To these seventeenth- and eighteenth-century examples, Owen added more recent work, citing experiments by Charles Bell on the sensory-motor division of the spinal roots; by Joseph Lister on antiseptic surgery; by Claude Bernard, by Pasteur, etc.

The indebtedness to animal experimentation of Harvey's and

Hunter's discoveries, and also of Bell's work, had been a point of fierce controversy since the Royal Commission of 1875. Owen's address was widely reported, and his historical examples were hotly contested by the anti-vivisectionists, in letters, articles and such pamphlets as *Owen and the Stag*.[17]

The emotional nature of the controversy was only increased by the fact that Owen referred to the anti-vivisectionists as 'bestiarians' and to the Victoria Street Society as 'the Bestiarian Society', calling the scientists 'humanitarians'. After all, Owen argued, many bestiarians were keen huntsmen who might break a hare's or rabbit's jaw by an ill-aimed shot, thus condemning the animal to long drawn-out suffering and a slow death from starvation.

> But even these inhumanities, inseparable from sport, are scarce comparable to the agonies of the prolonged chase, when fox or stag are ultimately torn by the howling four-footed fiends hounded on by biped masters.
>
> Do bestiarians hold 'annual meetings for the protection of animals from' — tortures inflicted year by year, and by thousands of inflictors for sport only? No! Their sensibilities are solaced at the expense of the blessings to humanity due to a Harvey and a Hunter; . . .[18]

The two principal points of the controversy were, as stated above, the *utility* and the *cruelty* of animal experiments. The scientists had little difficulty in proving the utility of vivisection, in spite of assertions to the contrary, even by such rare medically-qualified anti-vivisectionists as Anna Kingsford, who contributed to the 1881–2 exchanges in the *Nineteenth Century*, or a James Macaulay, who wrote a prize essay on 'Vivisection: Is It Scientifically Useful or Morally Justifiable?'[19] Owen's historical examples were readily augmented by more contemporary instances of the importance of experimental physiology. Even if certain experiments did not have a demonstrably direct bearing on the maintaining of health and the curing of diseases, it could be argued that scientific and medical knowledge are one and indivisible, and that knowledge as such means progress.

In a pro-vivisection letter, printed shortly before the IMC of 1881, Charles Darwin cited Pasteur's work in immunology and Virchow's work in parasitology.[20] Once the Congress had been held, claims as to the utility of vivisection were made in an even more confident, almost euphoric manner. Nearly all new remedies added to the 1864 edition of the British Pharmacopoeia were owed, T. Lauder Brunton claimed, to experiments upon animals.[21] And George Fleming added: 'If mankind benefits, so do animals. A discovery which will avert disease in one will probably do so in the others: every advance of knowledge is a boon to all.'[22]

The AAMR listed no fewer than six useful purposes of animal experiments, namely, to increase the knowledge of the function of the living body, to obtain exact knowledge of the process of disease, to test remedies, to test means of inoculation, to instruct and to detect poison.[23] Yeo concluded: 'I think that the question of the utility of vivisection has been satisfactorily answered by . . . competent authorities . . ., namely the largest gathering of medical men that has ever taken place.'[24]

The anti-vivisectionists reeled under the shock of this international medical broadside, and, in the years immediately post-1881, they focused their criticism more than ever on the issue of cruelty and its implicit immorality. Is vivisection not a form of interrogating nature by torture? To torture man is not wrong because he has an immortal soul, but because he has a sensitive body. But so have all vertebrates, especially mammals. One author cited Jeremy Bentham's *dictum*: 'the question is not, Can they *reason*? nor Can they *talk*? but Can they *suffer*?' The cry 'rights of animals', so loud in today's debate, began to be heard.[25]

The scientists had more difficulty disposing of this issue. Their general line of defence was that if science is black, certain pastimes are even blacker. Paget, for example, argued that the pain inflicted on animals in laboratory experiments must be weighed against the pain caused by sport: '. . . the question is whether vivisections inflict less or more pain than do sports or any other generally encouraged pain-giving practices, on animals of the same kind.'[26] He concluded that in the ordinary practice of animal experimentation it was not possible that a vivisector in a day or a month caused nearly as much pain as would, in the same time, be caused by an active sportsman hunting game.

This line of reasoning was followed in many medical discussions of the vivisection question. More pain is inflicted on animals for sport and for material want than by scientific experimentation. Paget generalised: 'All the vivisectors in Paris will hardly be the cause of nearly so much suffering as the promotors of the scheme for preserves of lions and other carnivores, to be shot at, in Algeria.'[27] Owen went further and maintained that 'more cruelty is inflicted in one afternoon at Hurlingham than by a year's amount of physiological experiment.'[28] And Wilks went further yet, calling most vivisection 'nothing more than pricking mice with the point of a needle'.[29]

Time and again the advocates of vivisection pointed out that society allows the painful treatment of animals for human pleasure and comfort; why then forbid animal experiments which may lead to the alleviation of human suffering for millions and for countless years to come? An AAMR pamphleteer stated:

> By the common consent of mankind also, largely including 'anti-vivisectionists' themselves, tens of thousands of animals are daily mutilated and subjected to pain, for the sake of sport, pastimes, luxuries, ornaments, social enjoyments, tastes, customs, and other inferior objects of infinitely less necessity than new knowledge, and if the former are justifiable, the latter must be so.[30]

One correspondent to *Nature* turned the tables on the Victoria Street Society by noting that Cobbe had been seen in public wearing an ostrich feather ('plucked from the *living bird*'), a bird of paradise in or near her muff ('birds of paradise, which, in order to enhance their beauty and lustre, are *skinned alive*') and carrying an ivory-handled umbrella ('*cut out* of the dying elephant's jaw').[31] It was no good Cobbe replying that she had never possessed such objects in her whole life, or Anna Kingsford writing to *Nature* that she detested blood sports and was a vegetarian.[32] The utilitarian approach to the ethics of animal suffering was widely echoed through the media. The suffering caused by experimenting on laboratory animals is less than the pain it alleviates through medical progress, which would be much slower if one were to revert to traditional anatomical physiology.[33]

A somewhat more philosophically literate discussion of the issue was put forward by William Benjamin Carpenter in *The Fortnightly Review*. He argued that the morality of a pain-giving act lies not in the act itself, nor in its result, but in the motive for the act. It is torture which is unethical, not painful experimentation for a beneficial purpose. Moreover, the moral nature of animals is limited and undergoes no increase, not even by association with man.

> Thus, then, the *narrow limitation and unprogressive range* of the moral nature of animals justify a corresponding limitation of their moral rights, as compared with those of beings of *unlimited*

capacity for progressive elevation; and I hold this to be the ethical justification of those dealings with them . . .[34]

This was an improvement on the more extravagant ethics of Virchow who, in his address to the IMC in London, had produced the following justification for vivisection: killing is generally regarded as worse than torture; society accepts the daily killing of animals for food and other purposes; ergo, no one can object to the lesser act of torturing animals, especially not if this is for scientific purposes. 'Whoever acknowledges that he has the right to kill animals has no right to forbid physicians to vivisect animals for the purposes of investigation, or to subject them to painful influences of other kinds.'[35]

Carpenter declared himself utterly opposed to this line of reasoning, although he did not say why. At the same time, he maintained that the truly horrific examples of scientific torture of animals were from abroad, from Continental laboratories, not Britain. Others, such as Yeo, also used this argument. To this was added that in Britain the use of aneasthetics in animal experimentation had long been recommended.[36]

Motives for the vivisection controversy

Behind the facade of public debate, however, there existed a motive for the vivisection controversy which was far larger than all arguments taken together. This motive was rarely publicly voiced, but it related to the single-most important issue at stake. To the scientist, the anti-vivisection movement did not just threaten the progress of physiological research; far more comprehensively, it seemed to impede the progress of biomedical science and be aimed at bringing down its practitioners from the prestigious position which they were acquiring during the Victorian era.

Any impediment to the progress of science and medicine was the more sensitive as their social status was, at the time, still very tenuous. Medical men in particular had worked hard through much of the nineteenth century to raise the status of their profession, and considerable headway had been made. Most importantly, an enormous effort to make medicine more scientific seemed to be bearing fruit and raising the prestige of, for example, surgery from a lowly artisan's manual skill to a profession which required an education.[37] Obviously, progress had been made since 1832, when William

Hamilton wrote in the *Edinburgh Review* that the practice of medicine had not advanced since the time of Hippocrates.[38]

Both Huxley and Owen, adversaries in matters of Darwinism but in agreement when it came to defending animal experimentation, had stressed the importance of making medicine more scientific, in their addresses on medical education to St Mary's Hospital Medical School.[39] Owen had been very explicit when he stated that only by placing medical education on a scientific basis could any progress be made in raising public confidence in the profession as a whole:

> In fact, we see at the present day that the public confide not so much in medicine as a science as in the particular practitioner. It is characteristic also of the present phase in the growth of medicine, that the public are liable to be deluded and led astray by its shams; and not until medicine becomes a science can such simulacra be expected to vanish, and quacks and quackery become extinct.[40]

Similarly, during the IMC in London, both Huxley and Owen re-emphasised the importance of scientific medicine. Huxley concluded his address as follows:

> There can be no question then as to the nature of the value of the connection between medicine and the biological sciences. There can be no doubt that the future of Pathology and Therapeutics, and therefore that of Practical Medicine, depends upon the extent to which those who occupy themselves with these subjects are trained in the methods and impregnated with the fundamental truths of Biology.[41]

And Owen, speaking 'On the Scientific Status of Medicine', proclaimed: 'The aim of every student of medicine . . . is to raise the healing art to the status of a science.'[42]

Thus, during the Congress of 1881, the two themes of 'provivisection' and 'scientific medicine' were firmly linked. Many saw animal experimentation as the connecting link between medicine, biomedical research and true science. The experimental method gave to biomedical work its status as an exact science. Bernard and several other coryphaei of French and German physiology had been very explicit on this point.[43] The AAMR made the connection equally clearly in one of its brochures:

Indeed, it would be as unreasonable to expect the 'Institute of Medicine' (as physiology and pathology are rightly called) to advance without laboratories and experiments on animals, as to hope for progress in chemistry or physics by allowing only observations upon metals and gases and forbidding the performance of experiments.[44]

In other words, animal experimentation became a widespread practice in the course of the nineteenth century, not just because of the medical benefit which was said to flow from it, but because it helped to legitimate biomedical research as a true science and thus to confer on its practitioners the social prestige they sought. The same can be argued for the frequent use by Owen and his colleagues of the historical examples of Harvey and Hunter. The primary purpose of this was not to show the past importance of vivisectional work, but to make the Victorian vivisectors the legitimate heirs of the great scientific names of yore.

This had been done before, although in different contexts and on different occasions, for example in the annual Hunterian Orations. Jacyna argues that the way in which Hunter was portrayed by successive Hunterian Orators represented not so much an objective sketch of his accomplishments or talents, but a form of scientific iconolatry which served contemporary polemical purposes.[45] To praise Harvey or Hunter as great scientists was part of a strategy to confer new prestige on those who made them their scientific forerunners.

Thus medicine nailed its colours firmly to the mast of science, which was rapidly becoming a 'fourth estate' of cultural authority in Victorian society, detracting from such traditional ones as the aristocracy, the clergy and, to a lesser extent, the judiciary.[46] The emergence through the nineteenth century of science as a new cultural force has been the subject of a number of historical studies.[47] A dramatic illustration of the transfer of prestige from the nobility to professional scientists was provided by the presidency of the Royal Society. In the course of the early Victorian period each successive president was of a lower rank by birth, but of higher scientific merit, namely the Duke of Sussex (1830–8), the Marquis of Northampton (1838–48), the Earl of Rosse (1848–54), the Baron Wrottesley (1854–8) and afterwards commoners such as Airy who *earned* their knighthoods.[48]

French argues that at the heart of the anti-vivisection movement there was the public concern over the emergence of science and medicine as leading institutions of Victorian society.[49] Significantly, the most prominent members of the anti-vivisection lobby were not scientists, but members of those 'estates' who saw their cultural influence waning. The parliamentary spokesman for anti-vivisection was the Earl of Shaftesbury, whose prestige did much to legitimise the movement in the eyes of the public. The President of the Victoria Street Society was the Lord Chief Justice Coleridge. Among the active, campaigning anti-vivisectionists were Cardinal Manning, the Archbishop of York, and the Bishops of Carlisle and of Oxford. On the Continent too, the nobility was prominently represented in the various anti-vivisection societies. This even held true, *mutatis mutandis*, for America.[50]

This is not to say that the clergy, for example, tended to sympathise in its entirety with the anti-vivisection cause. The *Lancet* advertised a sermon by a Rev. Richard Hill on 'Scientific Experiments on Organic Life a Necessity — No Sin!', and a Mark Thornton complained bitterly in a brochure on *The Clergy and Vivisection* about the complacency of many churchmen and their lack of interest in the issue.[51] But it is true that the public front of the anti-vivisection movement was painted in aristocratic and ecclesiastical colours.

Moreover, the rhetoric of anti-vivisection societies was often explicitly anti-scientific. As one scientist commented:

That the opposition of these Societies is not only directed against physiology and physiologists, but also against science and scientific men in general, is shown by the very frequent and unnecessary use of the words science, scientific, scientists, scientific discovery, men of science, etc. in the hostile language employed.[52]

This was indeed true. One example should suffice: 'the man of science never seems more ridiculous than when wearing the mask of philanthropy, with his keen, remorseless eyes peering out of it.'[53] The anti-vivisectionist Marie Louise de la Ramée, the popular novelist Ouida, called science 'the new priesthood'; 'in our time, the superstitious awe of science has succeeded to the superstitious awe of religion, and science profits by the credulity of the multitude as religions did before it.'[54] The new estate of science was encroaching on the traditional ecclesiastical estate.

Conversely, the pro-vivisection lobby saw itself not just defending experimental physiology, but science in general, its authority and autonomy. The pro-vivisection group was virtually identical with the entire community of medical and biological scientists. This was demonstrated at the IMC of 1881, and even more so the following year when the AAMR was formed. This vivisection association had among its ex-officio members not only various professors of physiology and medicine from Oxbridge, London and the Scottish universities, but also the presidents of no fewer than twenty-three different scientific and medical societies in England, Scotland and Ireland, including those of the Royal (T.H. Huxley), Linnean (John Lubbock) and Zoological (W.H. Flower) Societies. Even the Director of Kew Gardens (Joseph Hooker) was an official member. The majority of these men had little if anything to do with animal experimentation.[55]

Such unanimity had not always existed. Earlier in the century a group of thirty-eight medical men from the Bath area had signed a circular condemning animal experiments as 'discreditable to our profession'; and the *Medico-Chirurgical Review* had more than once raised its editorial voice against vivisection. Even Owen had objected to it if used for teaching purposes.[56] The new unanimity of the 1880s showed how much during the preceding decade the practitioners of the biomedical sciences had developed a sense of professional identity, closing ranks when outsiders demanded public accountability.

Prestige of science

To the Owen of the 1880s the vivisection issue had come to symbolise the expertise and thus the authority of his profession. Such sovereignty the traditional bearers of cultural authority refused to acknowledge. Had the founders of Oxbridge geology, William Buckland and Adam Sedgwick, not been clergymen? Had the fathers of the British Association for the Advancement of Science not been 'gentlemen of science'? Had many an illustrious aristocrat not patronised societies for natural knowledge? Had Owen, moreover, not cultivated in the earlier part of his career the acquaintance of royalty, both British and foreign? Why should he now stake out a segregated estate of cultural authority?

Yet Owen frequently made thinly-veiled, sarcastic references to 'men, eminent in Divinity and Law, and ladies of high social position', to 'noble lords, church dignitaries, and learned judges' or to 'a Cardinal, a Bishop, a learned Judge, and an Earl'.[57]

'Tis true', the consistent bestiarian may say, 'I never had an "ovarian tumour" or a "Fallopian pregnancy", or am ever likely to have. Let those women with such complaints get rid of them as they can. My mission, with the help of a Lord Chief Justice of England, a Cardinal, an Archbishop, Bishops, Peers, Baronets, "Heads of Colleges", is to haul up to "Bow-street" every experimental advancer of physiological and healing sciences, as an immoral offender, an unfeeling, inhuman wretch, a displeaser of the Almighty God, a horrible torturer of His creatures.'[58]

The reason that Owen dealt with the issue of morality in such emotional and class-related terms was that it had a direct bearing on the question of the scientists' social rank. As Elston points out in this volume, the membership of both the animal protection and anti-vivisection societies was predominantly made up of middle- and upper-class women who saw their role as one of feminine philanthropy, purifying the impure and fighting licentiousness, whether in working men's clubs or in laboratories. For them animal protection had been a means of curtailing cruel working-class sports and thus of morally elevating the deprived members of society. Similarly, their anti-vivisection mission envisaged the moral reform of depraved experimental physiologists — thus lumping together lower-class manual workers and scientists into a single object of their charity.

The defence of vivisection by reference to hunting, shooting and other blood sports, mentioned above, was in fact a disguised attack on the fox-hunting and grouse-shooting aristocratic membership of the anti-vivisection societies. To Owen, these dastardly aristocrats not only chased animals but equally indulged in persecuting the weak, socially not very powerful scientific community: 'It is cowardly to clamour for legislative interference, exclusively, with the much fewer of men, weaker in social position . . .'[59]

That the authority of science was at stake in the vivisection controversy is also apparent from repeated claims by scientific authors that only they are the proper judges of the right or wrong of animal experimentation, not the lay public. To Wilks, scientists 'are alone capable of forming a judgement of the value of the experiments in question'.

On the one side there are those who alone can know the best methods of scientific research and can recount its beneficial

results, while on the other side there are those of every profession and trade, who are non-scientific, who by their speeches
show themselves transparently ignorant of the simplest laws
of nature . . .[60]

One AAMR brochure asserted that 'a venerable osteologist'
(Owen) and 'a world-famed naturalist' (Darwin or possibly Huxley)
are better judges than an average person in matters of research and
its moral aspects, 'because they possessed the additional knowledge
indispensable to form a correct judgement'.[61] Similarly, Lyon
Playfair, the parliamentary spokesman for the pro-vivisection lobby,
appealed to the House of Commons not to pass Reid's abolitionist
Bill in view of the testimony against it by famous scientists.[62]

Such bills were seen by the scientists as an unwarranted infringement on the autonomy, the freedom of science. This sentiment was
at the heart of Virchow's speech to the general meeting of the IMC
of 1881. A few years earlier, in 1877, he had devoted an entire speech,
delivered to the general meeting of the *Versammlung deutscher Natur-
forscher und Aerzte*, to 'Die Freiheit der Wissenschaft im modernen
Staat'. In London he scaremongered: if one bill is passed, soon
another may follow, even forbidding the anatomical sectioning of
dead human corpses. There is no need to fear science itself, he proclaimed to the assembled thousands.[63]

This conviction was echoed in subsequent brochures and articles.
Knowledge is the source of human progress, without it mankind
cannot advance. The government should on no account interfere
in matters scientific: 'It is a question which must admit of but one
solution — freedom of action for those who are known to be engaged
in scientific research.'[64] Owen too fulminated against legislative
interference in medical research; why should a scientist have humbly
to petition the Home Office to grant him absolution for carrying
out experiments?[65] To Owen, to Wilks and to countless other scientists, any sort of restriction or supervision represented an infringement and a slur on an honourable class of men.

Conclusion

The pro-vivisection lobby of the early 1880s produced a considerable
number of publications in which the anti-vivisectionist accusations
of uselessness and cruelty were answered. The case for the utility
of animal experimentation seemed overwhelmingly made out by

the International Medical Congress of 1881. But the charge that vivisection is cruel and immoral was inexpertly dealt with by the scientists. They stuck to a naïve utilitarianism, and although Bentham himself had advocated animal rights based on the criterion of sentience, few if any of the scientists seemed to possess the philosophical literacy to enter into a serious discussion of the moral issue.

The question arises: why should one group of people, led by prominent members of the aristocracy and clergy, select from a mixed pool of arguments for and against vivisection, only the arguments *against* it, and another group, the biomedical scientists, choose every possible argument *for* animal experimentation? The answer to this question is not to be found on a rational level, in fundamental differences of intelligence between the two groups, but in people's contrasting motives and values. The anti-vivisection societies were deeply perturbed by the cultural ascendancy of science; the scientists, on the other hand, were concerned with the legitimation of their professional and social status which the experimental method helped provide. Their concern was expressed in, among other things, the founding of the AAMR. Its tendentiously formulated propaganda material was as biased as that of any other partisan lobby.

Thus vivisection should be discussed not merely as part of science taken as a disinterested search after beneficial knowledge, but also as a social phenomenon — in particular as a profession with a self-centred concern for its practitioners and their careers.

This aspect of science as a self-serving organisation makes it fundamentally no different from such other professions as industry, and lends weight to Lord Coleridge's retort to the demand by scientists for autonomy and freedom from legal interference. Why should the average layman be a lesser authority, he asked, when the question is the legality of how knowledge is gained or what the moral consequences may be of a particular practice? This need not imply that the expertise of the scientists is disregarded; after all, when the Factory Acts and the Mining Acts were passed, Parliament did not question the doctrines of 'venerable' and 'world-famed' economists such as Adam Smith, or Mill and Ricardo, 'but it decided that mischievous things, which could be prevented, should be'.[66]

Acknowledgement

The research on which this chapter is based has been supported by a Wellcome Research Fellowship.

Notes

1. E. Sharpey-Schafer, *History of the Physiological Society during its First Fifty Years, 1876–1926* (Cambridge University Press, 1927), p. 5.

2. G.L. Geison, *Michael Foster and the Cambridge School of Physiology* (Princeton University Press, 1978), p. 19.

3. W.D.M. Paton, 'An Experiment of Claude Bernard on Curare: the Origins of the Physiological Society', *Journal of Physiology*, vol. 263 (1976), pp. 26–9.

4. R.D. French, *Antivivisection and Medical Science in Victorian Society* (Princeton University Press, 1976); M.N. Ozer, 'The British Vivisection Controversy', *Bulletin of the History of Medicine*, vol. 40 (1966), pp. 158–67.

5. For example in *Nature*, vol. 13 (1876), pp. 321–2.

6. *Science*, vol. 2 (1883), p. 551.

7. R. Virchow, 'Ueber den Werth des Pathologischen Experiments', in W. MacCormac and G.A. Makins (eds.), *Transactions of the International Medical Congress, Seventh Session, London, 1881* (4 vols, J.W. Kolckmann, London, 1881), vol. 1, pp. 22–37. An English translation was published in *Lancet* (6 August, 1881), pp. 210–16.

8. *Transactions of the Seventh International Medical Congress*, vol. 1, p. 101.

9. Quoted by Lyon Playfair, *Speech delivered in the House of Commons on the Second Reading of Mr Reid's Bill for the Total Suppression of Scientific Experiments upon Animals* (J.W. Kolckmann, London, 1883), p. 7.

10. Anon, *Facts and Considerations Showing the* raison d'être *of the Association for the Advancement of Medicine by Research* (undated pamphlet), p. 3. See also Minute Books of the AAMR (1882–92), Wellcome Institute Library, MSS. 5310–11; *BMJ*, 1882(1), pp. 465–6, 476–8; *Lancet*, 1882(1), pp. 530, 542–4; French, *Antivivisection*, pp. 204–15.

11. Anon., *Facts and Considerations*, p. 2.

12. See Lawrence, Chapter 12, this volume.

13. Reported in *Nederlandsch Tijdschrift voor Geneeskunde*, vol. 12(1) (1876), p. 526.

14. 'Vivisection: its Pains and its Uses', *Nineteenth Century*, vol. 10 (1881), pp. 920–30 (by James Paget), pp. 931–5 (by Richard Owen), pp. 936–48 (by Samuel Wilks). The 1882 volume carried contributions by R.H. Hutton, Anna Kingsford, William W. Gull, George Fleming and T. Lauder Brunton.

15. Frances Power Cobbe, 'Vivisection: Four Replies', *Fortnightly Review*, vol. 31 (NS) (1882), pp. 88–104; Lord Coleridge, 'The Nineteenth Century Defenders of Vivisection', ibid., pp. 225–36; Gerald F. Yeo, 'The Practice of Vivisection in England', ibid., pp. 352–68.

16. R. Owen, *Experimental Physiology. Its Benefits to Mankind* (Longmans, Green and Co., London, 1882), pp. 25–6.

17. Anon, *Hunter and the Stag: a Reply to Professor Owen from the Scientific Point of View* (Williams and Norgate, London, 1881). See also J.H. Bridges, 'Harvey and Vivisection', *Fortnightly Review*, vol. 20 (NS) (1876), pp. 1–17; W.B. Carpenter, 'Sir Charles Bell and Physiological Experimentation', ibid., vol. 31 (NS) (1882), pp. 468–75.

18. Owen, *Experimental Physiology*, p. 36.

19. Anna Kingsford, 'The Uselessness of Vivisection', *Nineteenth Century*,

vol. 11 (1882), pp. 171–83; J. Macaulay, 'Vivisection: Is It Scientifically Useful or Morally Justifiable?', in Anon, *Vivisection, Scientifically and Ethically Considered in Prize Essays* (R. Grant & Son, Edinburgh, 1884), pp. 1–89.

20. 'Mr. Darwin on Vivisection', *Nature*, vol. 23 (1881), p. 583.

21. T. Lauder Brunton, 'Vivisection and the Use of Remedies', *Nineteenth Century*, vol. 11 (1882), pp. 479–87.

22. G. Fleming, Vivisection and the Diseases of Animals', ibid., p. 478.

23. 'Facts and Considerations Relating to the Practice of Scientific Experiments on Living Animals, Commonly Called Vivisection', *Nature*, vol. 27 (1883), pp. 542–6.

24. Yeo, 'Practice of Vivisection', p. 364.

25. Macauley, 'Vivisection', p. 78. The quotation is from J. Bentham, *An Introduction to the Principles of Morals and Legislation* (Clarendon Press, Oxford, 1907), Chapter XVII, 4, p. 311.

26. Paget, 'Vivisection: its Pains and Uses', p. 922.

27. Ibid., p. 923.

28. Owen, 'Vivisection: its Pains and Uses', p. 935.

29. Wilks, 'Vivisection: its Pains and Uses', p. 937.

30. G. Gore, *The Utility and Morality of Vivisection* (J.W. Kolckmann, London, 1884), p. 20.

31. H.H. Johnston, 'Miss Cobbe and Vivisection', *Nature*, vol. 25 (1882), p. 459.

32. Frances Power Cobbe, 'Muffs and Vivisection', ibid., p. 483; Anna Kingsford, 'Vivisection', ibid., p. 482.

33. Gore, *Vivisection*, p. 17.

34. W.B. Carpenter, 'The Ethics of Vivisection', *Fortnightly Review*, vol. 31 (NS) (1882), p. 242.

35. Virchow, 'Value of Pathological Experiment', *Lancet* (6 August 1881), p. 215.

36. Yeo, 'Practice of Vivisection', p. 353.

37. See M. Jeanne Peterson, *The Medical Profession in Mid-Victorian London* (University of California Press, Berkeley, 1978), pp. 12–13, 65.

38. See (Ch. Creighton), 'The Progress of Medicine', *Quarterly Review*, vol. 156 (1883), p. 59.

39. Anon, *Addresses on Medical Education by the Archbishop of York, Professor Owen, Professor Huxley, Dr. Alderson, and the Right Honorable Robert Lowe* (Robert Hardwicke, London, 1868).

40. Ibid., p. 6.

41. T.H. Huxley, 'The Connection of the Biological Sciences with Medicine', in MacCormac and Makins (eds.), *Transactions*, vol. 1, p. 101.

42. R. Owen, 'On the Scientific Status of Medicine', ibid., vol. 3, p. 440.

43. See Elliott, Chapter 3, this volume.

44. *Nature*, vol. 27 (1883), p. 542.

45. L.S. Jacyna, 'Images of John Hunter in the Nineteenth Century', *History of Science*, vol. 21 (1983), pp. 85–108.

46. The three estates originally referred to the Crown, the Lords and the Commons. The term 'fourth estate' was first used for the press.

47. See for example T.W. Heyck, *The Transformation of Intellectual Life in Victorian England* (Croom Helm, London, 1982).

48. See Mary Boas Hall, *All Scientists Now. The Royal Society in the Nineteenth*

Century (Cambridge University Press, 1984).

49. French, *Antivivisection*, pp. 371–2.

50. See Guarnieri, Chapter 5; Tröhler and Maehle, Chapter 7; Bromander, Chapter 9; Lederer, Chapter 10, this volume.

51. *Lancet* (31 December 1881), p. 1147; M. Thornhill, *The Clergy and Vivisection* (Hatchards, London, 1883).

52. Gore, *Vivisection*, p. 28.

53. Ibid.

54. Ouida, 'The Future of Vivisection', *Gentleman's Magazine*, vol. 252(1) (1882), p. 412.

55. See R. Heidenhain, *Die Vivisection* (von Breitkopf and Härtel, Leipzig, 1884), pp. 97–8.

56. Macaulay, 'Vivisection', pp. 7–13.

57. Owen, 'Vivisection: its Pains and Uses', p. 931 *Experimental Physiology*, pp. 31, 33.

58. *Experimental Physiology*, p. 101. The issue of ovariotomy is discussed by Elston, this volume, pp. 278–9.

59. *Experimental Physiology*, p. 37.

60. Wilks, 'Vivisection: its Pains and Uses', p. 937.

61. Gore, *Vivisection*, p. 27.

62. Playfair, *Speech*, p. 7.

63. Virchow, 'Pathological Experiment', pp. 212, 216.

64. Wilks, 'Vivisection: its Pains and Uses', p. 936.

65. Owen, *Experimental Physiology*, pp. 80–1.

66. Coleridge, 'Nineteenth Century Defenders', p. 236.

Plate 1. Joseph Wright of Derby, 'The Picture of the Air Pump' (so called by the painter), 1768. Oil on canvas, 1.829 × 2.438 m. National Gallery, London. See pp. 29–30, 340–7.

Plate 2. *Emile-Edouard Mouchy, oil-painting on canvas, 112 × 143 cm, signed and dated 'Mouchy 1832'*

Plate 3. *Charles John Tomkins after John McLure (or McClure) Hamilton, 'Vivisection' (legend lightly engraved at foot of sheet). Engraving (mixed method), 61 × 43.5 cm, 1883, after a drawing or painting dated 1882. Wellcome Institute Library, London. See pp. 350–1.*

Plate 4. Michael Joseph Holzapfl after Gabriel Cornelius Max. 'Der Vivisector' ('Vivisector' inscribed on painting, lower right), etching. 15.4 x 26

Plate 5. Anon. after Léon Augustin Lhermitte, 'Claude Bernard dans son laboratoire' (legend at foot of image), photogravure, 18.5 × 24.2 cm, n.d., after an oil painting on canvas, dimensions unknown, 1889, currently in the Académie Nationale de Médecine, Paris. Wellcome Institute Library, London. See pp. 354–6.

9

The Vivisection Debate in Sweden in the 1880s

*Lennart Bromander**

Introduction

When, therefore, I consider this much-praised physiology
which is founded on vivisection, and hear the so-called truths
which supposedly owe their origin to research in that field,
and perceive how physiologists employ all their mental powers
to kill belief in the divine and spiritual element in the universe,
I at least am resolved for my own part to renounce all the fruits
of trust in and obedience to modern scientific research, and
when I express myself in those terms I do so in full awareness
of the implications of such a statement.[1]

Such withering evaluations of physiological research, which was
making rapid progress in the second half of the nineteenth century,
were to be heard in the course of the three debates — very heated
at times — on the vivisection question which took place in the
Swedish Riksdag during the 1880s; it also gives a clear illustration
of the problems at the bottom of this conflict. The debate was ostensibly concerned with a question of cruelty to animals, but even if
it is rarely expressed with such clarity as in Commander Carl Gustaf
Lindmark's address to the Riksdag, it is still the conflict which constantly recurs throughout the nineteenth century between idealism
and materialism, between a view of the world coloured by religion
and the progress of scientific research, which forms the historical
and ideological background to the vivisection debate.

It is chiefly this fundamental conflict which will be examined here

*Translated by Susan H. Reynolds from an edited version of the Swedish text, origin-
ally published in *Lychnos* (1969–70), pp. 249–91.

to show that the vivisection debate in Sweden in the 1880s was not an isolated question of cruelty to animals. I did not, however, want to confine myself to this angle; the conflict has not been treated before and therefore demands a more detailed presentation. The object of the following account is, in consequence, partly to attempt to trace the most important features of the whole turbulent course of this cultural debate, and partly to set it in its historical context.

Adolf Leonard Nordvall,
his ideas and their background

It is, in general, a very dubious practice to state that a trend in public opinion depends on a single person and his ideas, but in connection with the Swedish agitation against vivisection in the 1880s there are factual grounds for doing so. The movement was often criticised by its opponents for being imported and meaningless in Sweden for the simple reason that there was nothing to agitate against in that country. A charge which naturally annoyed the anti-vivisectionists, but which was quite difficult to answer.

Sweden's first chair of physiology was established at Uppsala in 1864 and occupied by Frithiof Holmgren. He had been educated in Germany by leading physiologists such as Carl Ludwig, Ernst Brücke and Emil du Bois-Reymond; unprejudiced and radical in his views, he was the first person in the world to introduce laboratory experiments for students. Holmgren's research methods were by no means particularly 'vivisectional', and the number of experiments on animals carried out at Uppsala was very small. The same is true in the case of Christian Lovén, likewise a pupil of Carl Ludwig, who in 1874 became Sweden's second professor of physiology, at the Carolinian Institute. According to Holmgren's own data, about 1,000 frogs, seventy or so rabbits and a few dogs were used at Uppsala and Stockholm in one year.[2] Of these, the frogs were used for demonstrations and were killed immediately before the experiment. The anti-vivisectionists did not succeed in discovering a single example in Sweden of experimentation on an animal which had not been anaesthetised.

It is obvious that these were hardly conditions that could be expected to arouse a storm of popular opinion. But nevertheless Sweden experienced just such a thing in the 1880s, and we must therefore look elsewhere for the causes. To attribute them solely to foreign influence is an unsatisfactory explanation. Why, then, did the movement become so very strong and gain such influence? Its actions bear to the highest degree the mark of a single person, and we must turn to him and the ideas that he represented to find an answer to the question.

Adolf Leonard Nordvall was born in 1824 in Linköping, the son of a clergyman, and became a student at Uppsala in 1843. Nordvall's doctoral thesis on Kant's deduction of the concept of pure reason was published by Sigurd Ribbing in 1851 and won the latter the Crown Prince's major prize. A brilliant academic career was prophesied for him; he was held in high esteem by Christopher Jacob Boström, the foremost Swedish philosopher of the time, but after a year as lecturer in ethics he preferred to retire to Strängnäs as a schoolmaster. In 1858 Nordvall was appointed head of the Ecclesiastical Department's newly-formed section for the organisation of education. From 1861 he held the title of Assistant Secretary, which he himself preferred to use even in later life, but in 1865 he resigned at his own wish and resumed his teaching post, which he occupied until 1890, two years before his death. He had long periods of leave from this post, however, both for academic (and anti-vivisectional) writing and for health reasons. Apart from his years in Stockholm, where, among other things, he was able, as a leading member of the society named Idun, to make the acquaintance of most of his future enemies in the medical profession, Nordvall led a very quiet secluded life, and not once during the time that the debate was at its liveliest was he willing to leave his home in Strängnäs. As a person he seems to have made a favourable impression.[3]

Nordvall's main subject was philosophy, and he served his basic apprenticeship in it in the Uppsala of the 1840s, where philosophical studies were dominated by Christopher Jacob Boström, and likewise from 1850 onwards by the latter's pupil Sigurd Ribbing. It was under Ribbing's aegis that Nordvall defended his dissertation on Kant. Both these philosophers represented a markedly idealistic view of the world in which empirical reality met with only a kind of secondary interest. This Platonic doctrine, which in many cases was combined with devout religious feeling and reactionary social views, was to be absorbed by the young Nordvall in generous measure, and was to stamp his mode of thought for the rest of his life. These philosophers did not rate the natural sciences very highly, and contempt for the practical use to which they could eventually be put was as great as contempt for scientific research as such.[4]

Medical science, which is of particular interest in connection with Nordvall, had its leading representative at this time at Uppsala in Israel Hwasser, a man who represented a point of view no less idealistic than that of his philosophical colleagues. Hwasser never failed to proclaim the high ethics and idealistic nature of the medical profession both to his pupils and to the world at large. From time to time, alarmed by the materialistic tendencies of the age, he would come out with such phrases as 'The sophistry of shallow science and the self-satisfied audacity of frank brutality.'[5] As his medical idols he worshipped Hippocrates, Galen and Sydenham.

But it may be appropriate to cite a more concrete example of the prevailing attitude to the natural sciences. Nordvall's teacher, Sigurd Ribbing, wrote:

The primary consequence of this (the rapid progress made in the natural sciences) has been that material resources and comforts have increased all at once, while progress in moral and religious education, without which there is scarcely any guarantee that they will be put to proper and truly human use, cannot indeed be said to have kept pace with it.[6]

This statement might well have served as a motto for the Swedish vivisection debate. A remarkable under-estimation of the importance of the natural sciences colours everything that Nordvall wrote about the question of vivisection. The sovereignty of philosophy over the natural sciences for which Ribbing argued was self-evident to Nordvall, making it possible for him to take quite a different approach from the ordinary protesters against cruelty to animals. But Nordvall was not alone in being influenced by this idealistic philosophy. Many of the country's philosophers educated their pupils in the spirit of Boström, and similarly a long line of other people with an humanistic education who belonged to the influential strata of Swedish society had their spiritual roots in this environment. Mention should also be made of Viktor Rydberg, perhaps the most important of Sweden's writers in the second half of the nineteenth century, whose Platonic ideas were extremely influential in the years in question. A propensity to attack the non-speculative sciences was widespread in these circles.

As far as medical science was concerned, Hwasser's view of the doctor as one called by higher powers to give support at the sickbed with all kinds of cures survived for a long time. The concept of medical science at that time was essentially different from that of the present day; the doctor was certainly held in high esteem as a professional, chiefly because of Hwasser's contributions, but the almost boundless faith in the possibilities of medicine which is so common nowadays was wholly alien to the people of the 1880s. If, then, the doctor started to make use of new experimental methods, there was every reason to adopt a sceptical attitude. For the majority of educated people, the doctor as a natural scientist was an incongruous figure, a repulsive mésalliance between the revered humanist and the crude empiricist. It is extremely important to bear this background in mind as we go on to examine some of Nordvall's most important ideas, which were to gain such influence among many people from just the ideological background that is outlined here.

What, then, did Nordvall have to say about the function of animals in the world, a central question when one wishes to attack the use of animals as objects of research? Animals are for man's use; Nordvall certainly maintained that.[7] But use is of two essentially different kinds, the first of these aiming to further merely earthly purposes, i.e. to give us food, etc. The second, on the other hand, is what improves and ennobles us, i.e. makes us morally better. Thus there is a higher and a lower use, and it is by no means the case, said Nordvall, that animals are only there for the lower one. No, they are created for both, but chiefly for the higher one. For they can teach us to be considerate towards those who do not demand consideration of us, to act rightly towards those who do not force us to do so, to show mercy to those who are wholly at the mercy of our caprices. Thus animals are here to give us 'moral ennoblement'. If a choice has to be made between the higher and the lower use, the higher must naturally take precedence.

Vivisection, on the other hand, asserts the opposite, namely that the higher use should be sacrificed to the lower which, however, is against the decrees of morality. According to Nordvall, physiologists rely on vivisection because with its help it is so easy to make new scientific discoveries, which bring those who made them the rewards of honour and fame. This, of course, must be classified as a lower use. The eventual practical use for the curing of diseases which vivisection allegedly had was strongly doubted by Nordvall, who supported his case with quotations, chiefly from the English doctors Charles Bell and Lawson Tait.

Thus Nordvall maintained in his view of animals that they are defenceless and require the protection of human beings, but he was not content with this, the commonest attitude among those who seek to protect animals; he gave the question a carefully studied moral significance which makes the torturing human more interesting than the tortured animal. Not a trace of the sentimental worship of our defenceless friends in nature's realm, so common at the time, was to be found in Nordvall. He was a scholar and a philosopher, and it was as such that this problem engaged his attention. This, naturally, did not prevent him from holding forth with vehement pathos and lengthy descriptions of the poor creatures' suffering. In addition, Nordvall also took an anthropomorphic view of animals, which has something strange about it to a modern reader. He freely attributed human feelings to them, even in the case of frogs and ants.

But what interested Nordvall most of all was not the wretched animals but the demoralisation of humanity through vivisection. In his writings he constantly returned to this theme in various ways. Vivisection is of course a flagrant breach of morality. How, then, can physiologists go about their work with so little restraint? Why, in his search for scientific truths, is the vivisector seized by an unbridled passion which blinds him to the crime he is planning to commit, and at the same time makes him more and more callous, so that he eventually emerges as a moral monster?

In support of his argument Nordvall cited various statements from, among others, Claude Bernard: 'The physiologist is no ordinary man; he is a scholar, totally and entirely absorbed by a scientific idea; he no longer hears the cry of animals, he no longer sees the blood that flows . . .'[8] Shocked by this and similar quotations, Nordvall asked: 'Can love of the truth so demoralise human beings that they can carry out experiments with cold-blooded calmness — nay, with unspeakable pleasure, and so openly mock at all justice and mercy?'[9] No, it is merely their own pleasure and satisfaction that they are seeking. If they had been seeking the truth, they would first have asked themselves whether they had the right to act in such a way. But it is that very question which passion always evades. And where, then, does he end up, this impassioned, amoral vivisector? He ends up (and here Nordvall played his trump-card) as a materialist and a denier of Christianity.

It is not, perhaps, so easy to see that experimental and particularly vivisectional methods are materialistic, but, Nordvall argued, 'there is something called the logic of object and action, . . . an inner connection which unites things which are akin to one another'. Moreover, if we bear in mind that the vivisectionists make use of the Jesuitical principle that the end justifies the means, the likeness between them and nihilists is so complete that we can fairly speak of one soul in two bodies. Nordvall found proof of this in an article in the *Nya Dagligt Allehanda* about Russian literature. Referring to Chernyshevsky's *What is to be Done?* (1863), he wrote:

> This book, banned in Russia . . . is in a certain sense the crude gospel of crude nihilism. Every nihilist has it in his possession — Nothing could be more typical than this shameless novel. In it, natural scientists are held in high esteem, and one of the book's main characters, an ordinary student, has written a dissertation on physiology, which even the great Claude Bernard has mentioned wth respect.[10]

We must remember here that this particular work of Nordvall's appeared less than a year after the assassination of Tsar Alexander II. The Swedish press showed a great interest in the Russian nihilists and their activities, and terrifying reports of their progress were to be read every day. Nordvall, therefore, tried to evoke the connection between physiologist, nihilist and regicide, which is naturally not expressed in so many words; on the other hand, Nordvall pointed out that one never knows what atrocities to expect next from these demoralised people. What he was primarily warning his audience about was, of course, that the next step would be vivisection on human beings.

Nordvall seems not to have known or in any case did not wish to declare his opinion of the views of Ludwig Büchner, the most famous popular philosopher of materialism, on animals and humans. In his *Kraft und Stoff* — a very widely-read book in the latter part of the nineteenth century and translated also into Swedish — Büchner provided, in a chapter on 'die Thierseele', allegedly incontrovertible proof that only a quite insignificant quantitative difference exists between the souls of human beings and animals. The notorious materialist's arguments and examples from the animal world were strikingly similar to Nordvall's.

We have seen now how Nordvall's principal charges were presented. Animals have a primarily moral function; they exist so that we may practise mercy. Because of this, it is a flagrant breach of morality consciously to cause an animal suffering. The most important point, though, is that the physiologist, the offender against morality, is himself hardened by doing so, and drifts into materialism and nihilism, which he also spreads among his students. Vivisection, then, is a cancer in the body of society, a danger to our culture. This was the essence of Nordvall's views. For others, naturally, the issue was above all one of animal protection, but most of those who took part in the debate saw the problem with Nordvall's eyes.

Agitation before the first Riksdag debate

Nordvall began his animal welfare activities remarkably early. Already in 1857 he published a longish article in the *Svenska Tidningen* under the title 'The Ill-treatment of Animals'.[11] The article was written in connection with a debate in the Riksdag about a law for the protection of animals, and Nordvall's exposition of the moral grounds for animal protection strongly resembled the reasoning which he was to employ twenty-five years later during the vivisection debate. Vivisection as such was not yet mentioned; at that time Sweden still did not have its first physiological laboratory. The article was conceived first and foremost as propaganda for societies for the protection of animals.

Nordvall seems to have met with no response, and nine long years were to pass before he returned to the theme in an essay in the *Pedagogisk Tidskrift* for 1866.[12] There, Nordvall presented a series of examples of ordinary cruelty to animals, which he condemned, quoting passages from the Bible. Vivisection received a brief mention in connection with, among other things, the impropriety of cutting worms in two and pulling the legs off flies. Experiments in vivisection are 'in most cases real atrocities, which vainly seek cover and justification under the cloak of science'.[13]

Nordvall, then, had opposed vivisection very early on when the anti-vivisection movement had not yet made any great progress, even in England. There were a few hints that a debate on the question might be forthcoming in Sweden in 1867. Nordvall mentioned later, at the beginning of the 1880s, that quite a vehement conflict broke out in connection with a newspaper article about the new institute of physiology at Uppsala.[14] This quarrel is also mentioned elsewhere: 'In the 1860s he (Nordvall) became involved in a spirited argument with Holmgren, a relative of his, about vivisection, but neither would admit defeat.'[15]

The debate of 1867 was probably not all that vehement, consisting mainly of protestations on the grounds of principle on Nordvall's part. It seems, indeed, to have been very difficult for him to get hold of any effective protest material. For the whole of the 1870s he let the matter drop. But Nordvall continued his animal welfare activities. In Strängnäs in 1870 he founded the first real society for the protection of animals in Sweden. There is evidence from letters dating from 1870–1 that Nordvall also urged that a society for the protection of animals be founded at a national level.[16] Such a society, the Swedish National Society for the Protection of Animals, came into being in 1875. Nordvall, however, does not appear to have been involved in this; he was not even a member.

The great debate of the 1880s was sparked off by the book *New Documents on the Vivisection Question* in 1880. This contained an introduction by Nordvall, observations on the vivisection question by the Faculty of Medicine at Zürich, *The Torture Chambers of Science* by Ernst von Weber and 'Can Vivisection be Defended?', a lecture given by Nordvall at Strängnäs on 18 December 1879. Nordvall mentioned in his introduction how vivisection experiments had increased to an extraordinary degree in the preceding ten to fifteen years, and that the credit for disclosing this to the general public had to go to Ernst von Weber because of the epoch-making lecture delivered in 1878.

The statement from the Faculty of Medicine at Zürich which followed seemed out of place in a collection of writings against vivisection; it was, in fact, a well-balanced and lucid *defence* of vivisection. On this very document, however, Nordvall chiefly concentrated his fire in his closing essay. That the statement was published in its entirety in Swedish is evidence of Nordvall's readiness to provide a fair balance of documentation.

The most important book opposing vivisection apart from those in English was, as has been said, Ernst von Weber's *Die Folterkammern der Wissenschaft*. It was an extraordinary action on Nordvall's part to launch the campaign in Sweden by presenting this masterly polemic. The outstanding feature of the work, which emerged as a remarkably successful piece of propaganda, was its grasp of the subject; von Weber presented his readers with quotations from physiological publications. He claimed that through these 'the scientists accuse themselves', and in this way he made the accusations seem well-founded. Nordvall's writings contained many long quotations, often taken from von Weber's work, but not infrequently dug out of contemporary physiological literature by Nordvall himself. Von Weber called attention to the scientist's moral turpitude, and stressed that the question was primarily one of morality. But he did not make such a fuss about the matter as Nordvall, and he did not use the question as a pretext for an attack on materialism. Nordvall's analyses of the function of animals and the pattern of the degeneration of the scientists seem to have been his own contribution to the debate. Apart from these most of his remaining arguments were already to be found in von Weber's work.

In the lecture which followed, 'Can Vivisection be Defended?', Nordvall made an attack on the Zurich doctors' pronouncement. There is no need to examine his arguments in detail; they were visibly weak in construction. It is a pity, however, that we have no testimony of Nordvall's powers of oratory; there is no doubt that a skilful speaker could have made a great feature of this lecture, which was very effectively formulated. Nordvall concluded: 'Let us hope that the people of Sweden will be the first to show by an absolute ban on vivisection that they will not let themselves be deceived by the false promises of self-interest when the great cause of saving science from dishonour and mankind from barbarism is at stake.'

The scientists were later criticised for maintaining complete silence for so long and not replying immediately to the charges. It is true that the Swedish physiologists did not express an opinion on the subject until they were forced to do so after the first Riksdag debate, but as far back as 1880 we find a defence of vivisection in the May issue of *Eira*.[17] The article was called 'The Use of Vivisection for Therapeutic and Hygienic Purposes', and was written by Charles Richet, and taken from the English medical journal the *Lancet*.[18] Richet did not attack the anti-vivisectionists; he simply demonstrated by means of a series of examples the great impact of vivisection on the practice of medicine.

The Riksdag debate of 1881

In January 1881 Robert Arfwedson put forward a proposal in the Riksdag for a law to restrict vivisection. In his first contribution to the debate he pointed out that it was the reading of *New Documents* that made him resolve to propose this motion. Arfwedson was not one of the most prominent members of the Second Chamber of the Riksdag, where he represented Sörmland from 1867 to 1869 and from 1879 to 1881. He was a landowner, the son of the famous chemist J.A. Arfwedson, the discoverer of the element lithium; politically, he belonged to the intelligentsia. Arfwedson's motion was a fairly lengthy document, and contained little that was original.[19] He described animal experiments in other countries (mostly reported by von Weber), maintained the uselessness of vivisection and its moral dangers, etc.

Arfwedson was conscious, however, of the weakness of his position in only being able to adduce examples from abroad for a new law in Sweden, but he could only argue that 'because of the mystery with which vivisection everywhere tries to surround itself, it is probable that no one can say what has been done in this line in Sweden and what is still being done'. He pointed out in addition that laws are not made for what has been done but for what may be done in future, an argument which was to be put forward time and time again in the succeeding debates. The proposals which Arfwedson finally submitted were wholly modelled on the English Cruelty to Animals Act of 1876.

The motion was dealt with by the Law Committee, whose findings were discussed on 2 April in both the First and Second Chambers. But a few days previously a brochure had been distributed among the members of both chambers which was to be of great importance to the outcome of the debate. It was *On the Vivisection Question: Criticism and Information relating to Motion 100 in the Second Chamber*, by Gustaf von Düben, professor of anatomy at the Carolinian Institute.[20] It was above all *New Documents* that von Düben set out to pulverise. True, it only touched on examples from abroad, 'but now that the rubbish is beginning to ferment and to spread mephitic vapours in the form of the recently proposed motion and other "sighs of living creatures", it is time to think about disinfection'.[21]

Throughout his paper von Düben used a spiteful and withering tone towards his opponents. First of all he attacked von Weber's choice of quotations in the case of the brain operations performed by the Strassburg physiologist Friedrich Leopold Goltz, in which von Weber took a close interest. He drew attention to some tendentious turns of phrase, and pointed out von Weber's failure to mention that the animal was under chloroform. In addition, von Düben examined Darwin's part in the matter, to which we shall return. He was also sarcastic about Arfwedson's proposed bill. In particular he made fun of the control measures which Arfwedson suggested, and pictured how the police would first have to search for willing witnesses, and when these eventually turned up 'it may not infrequently happen that the professor, or frog, or rat, is prevented from appearing'.[22] He reproached his opponents with inconsistency: they should not eat oysters, for example, 'since they are, as is well known, served up vivisected, and usually receive an anaesthetic only when it is swallowed after them'.[23]

But von Düben was by no means hostile to those who sought to protect animals in general. He was a member of the Society for the Protection of Animals, and its auditor until 1881. After that

his name disappeared from the list of members. We can imagine the scene when the temperamental von Düben left the Society after seeing that the majority of its members had chosen to support the anti-vivisectionists. His colleague Christian Lovén was also a member until 1881, and seems to have left the Society at the same time as von Düben.

Three newspapers took an interest in the vivisection question, the *Stockholms Dagblad*, *Aftonbladet* and *Nya Dagliga Allehanda*. The first two supported the scientists, while the *Nya Dagliga Allehanda* was the organ of the anti-vivisectionists. On 30 March both the *Aftonbladet*'s and *Stockholms Dagblad*'s leaders dealt with the vivisection question. The tone of both articles was similar and distinctly caustic; the arguments were taken from von Düben, who was also apostrophised by name. Both papers took it for granted that the fate of this highly inappropriate bill was a foregone conclusion.

The *Nya Dagliga Allehanda*'s favourable attitude to the anti-vivisectionists was not yet so marked during this first Riksdag debate. In a short leader of 2 April a diplomatic point of view was expressed, and it is hard to make out what the writer actually thought. But in conjunction with this leader, an article against vivisection appeared, based on religious and moral grounds, by E.v.Q., a signature which would appear to have concealed the well-known journalist and agitator for Finnish independence, Emil von Quanten. Later on, the *Nya Dagliga Allehanda* came under the editorship of Carl Adam Lindström, and became the only daily paper in which the anti-vivisectionists could get their articles published.

Such was the general situation before the Riksdag took up the matter, with no definite tendency in either direction. The Law Committee rejected Arfwedson's motion, giving as one of its reasons that no abuse in Sweden had been established.[24] One of the committee's members abstained. The debate in the Second Chamber was introduced by Arfwedson.[25] In a long defence of his motion he took a very different tone from von Düben's harsh one in replying to the latter's charges. He readily admitted that there were questionable points both in *New Documents* and in his own motion. He then used the opportunity to give further examples (from abroad) of vivisectionists' barbarity.

There was much in Arfwedson's speech which must have appeared obsessive even to a critical listener in 1881, but the very fact that it was delivered orally, giving the impression of spontaneous and apparently righteous indignation, made a positive impression on his hearers. Above all, his balanced discourse contrasted favourably with von Düben's rancour. This was actually stated by the next speaker, Captain Alarik Fredenberg, who 'harbours the greatest sympathy for Mr Arfwedson's motion, a particularly commendable one from a Christian, moral and humane point of view'. What a contrast, Fredenberg maintained, to von Düben's words, which 'in a markedly detrimental fashion' bore witness to 'the scientist's lack of fairness and common sense'. He then protested forcefully against 'this appalling science'.

Of interest also was the next contribution, which came from one of the more prominent members of Parliament, Carl Edward Casparsson.[26] He was not conversant with the matter in question, but shocked, not so much by the charges as by von Düben's defence. Casparsson demanded that the bill should be sent back for further consideration so that the government could investigate the matter in greater depth. No fewer than twenty members supported this recommendation. Both these contributions, especially Casparsson's, which was presumably delivered with all the eloquence for which he was famous, show how much von Düben's work had succeeded in supplying the anti-vivisectionists with concrete material in default of examples of abuse in Sweden. Casparsson elegantly insinuated that there might be something after all in the accusations against the scientists of moral dereliction. Both speakers emphasised the importance of the members of the Chamber working for mercy and justice, something which the scientists did not do.

The next to ascend the rostrum was the liberal Göteborg doctor Charles Dickson, who was the only medical man in the Chamber.[27] His defence of the Law Committee's rejection of the motion did not command the same interest as Casparsson's contribution; only one member seconded it. Dickson tried to demonstrate the importance of vivisection to research and education, but he did not seem to have been well prepared, and had no concrete examples with which to support his defence. Instead he trivialised the accusations by showing that much more suffering was caused to animals by hunting, fishing, slaughter for food, etc., an argument which recurred frequently. After Dickson's weak speech in defence of science, the matter was already settled, and the remaining speeches mostly supplemented earlier charges.

The result of the debate was that the Chamber proposed to let the King consider whether vivisection should be banned or restricted by law. It is worth noting that the presenter of this strongly-worded proposal was the well-known journalist and politician Sven Adolf Hedin. It was naturally supported by Riksdag members with a strongly moral, religious and also conservative outlook on life. Hedin, however, was an exception to this rule; he was almost what might be called a liberal left-winger. His anti-vivisectionism was not primarily moral; the motives for his attack on science were liberal. As he saw it, the scientists' demand that they should settle the question for themselves revealed an authoritarian attitude. Every individual in society, not just the specialist, should have the right to make up their mind on the matter.[28]

Hedin was in close contact with Nordvall as well as with Holmgren. In a letter of 10 April 1890, Nordvall expressed his thanks for the interest that Hedin had shown in the matter and declared that he felt strengthened by the support of so famous a politician.[29] In another letter of 1 March 1881 Hedin was subjected to pressure from the opposition.[30] It was Holmgren, his political ally and close friend, who expressed his dismay at the rumours he had heard that Hedin was joining the opponents of science. Holmgren's interpretation of the vivisection question, based on the same liberal grounds, was very different from Hedin's: it is a very serious matter to 'want to place hitherto free scientific research under police surveillance'. Is Hedin really, on the basis of a 'scandal-sheet', going to regard his old friend as one of 'the greatest criminals that ever lived?' He suggested that they should meet and discuss the matter. This they did, but without Holmgren's managing to change Hedin's mind. The latter stated that he had not let himself be convinced by the writings on the subject 'which one of my friends among the physiological gentlemen pressed into my hand'. They remained friends, however, and there is a letter dating from 1893 in which Holmgren heartily thanks Hedin for supporting a bid for increased financial aid to the Physiological Institute at Uppsala.[31]

To sum up the content of this Riksdag debate, there is no doubt that von Düben's unfortunately-worded polemic achieved an entirely different result from what he had intended. His acrid and flippant jargon was ill-suited to the serious atmosphere of the Chambers of the Riksdag, and when, in addition, no solid medical authority could be found to back him up, the result was sealed. Obviously there was no fixed opinion to corroborate Arfwedson's motion, but the accusations were so serious and passions ran so high that even the sceptical members of the Riksdag called for an inquiry to clarify the matter.

Protests from 1881 to 1884. Founding of the Scandinavian Association

Nordvall lost no time in publishing a reply to von Düben, which appeared a few months after the Riksdag debate.[32] There was no difficulty in finding points on which to attack von Düben, and here Nordvall produced possibly his most successful polemic ever. He avoided his opponent's spiteful tone; instead he was calm and objective. In the introduction he discussed the barbarous and useless nature of Goltz's brain experiments, but revealed his inadequate grasp of the subject by his dismissal of an experiment which showed that removing the left hemisphere of the brain reduced feeling in the right-hand side of the body as 'innocent diversion'.[33]

Nordvall scored a point, however, in the matter of Darwin's attitude to the question. In von Weber's *The Torture Chambers of Science* Darwin was alleged to have expressed his views on vivisection in the following words: 'It deserves abhorrence and should be deprecated in the strongest terms.' Von Düben was indignant at this misleading quotation from the report by the English commission. He placed the sentence in its context, and it became clear from this that what Darwin meant was not vivisection in general but unnecessary and painful experiments. But Nordvall continued the quotation from the original text and was able to show that Darwin expressly supported a proposal aimed at the restriction of vivisection by law.[34] Von Düben must have known the full text, and therefore presented a misleading quotation in the very way that he accused his opponents of doing.

However, a small storm blew up in Nordvall's victory cup with the letter from Darwin to Holmgren which was published in the *Aftonbladet* and *Stockholms Dagblad* on 22 and 24 April of the same year.[35] This was because Holmgren had asked a number of eminent scientists about their views on the vivisection queston. Darwin replied immediately, and also published his answer in *The Times* of 18 April. This time he expressed dissatisfaction with the English Act, which had taken a form of which he could not approve. He cited the examples of Virchow's and Pasteur's brilliant results to demonstrate the necessity of vivisection. At the same time he admitted that because of his great love of animals he had previously worked for some kind of legal assurance against experiments which were not absolutely necessary. This explicit statement by Darwin provoked Nordvall to comment sourly that 'Darwin had moved somewhat closer to the "terrorists" of physiology'.

By December of the same year Nordvall was ready with the next paper, which was first presented before the Strängnäs Society for the Protection of Animals at its annual meeting.[36] For the first time Nordvall came up with a constructive suggestion. To reduce the great number of experiments on animals that were being carried out in laboratories all over Europe, a single 'vivisection institute' should be set up, an international physiological laboratory. Thus a number of animals' lives could be spared, and researchers could more readily exchange the results of their experiments. To a modern reader this idea seems the most sensible that Nordvall contributed to the debate.[37]

But at about the same time as Nordvall published this paper, his opponents began to gather for their first great onslaught, occasioned by the inquiry that had been carried out at the request of the Riksdag. Various authorities expressed their view on the matter, but the statements which carried most weight naturally came from the parties directly affected, the Faculty of Medicine at Uppsala and the College of Preceptors of the Carolinian Institute (of the other statements, I have only been able to examine that by the Academy of Sciences). These two speeches were circulated in print and distributed among the members of the Riksdag.

Holmgren was the author of the first.[38] It was a long and detailed general discussion of the question. Holmgren emphasised the same thing as in his letter to Hedin: there must be complete freedom, otherwise the result will be the decline of physiological and therefore also of medical research. He based the main part of his argument on the difference between what he called 'scientific' and 'popular' vivisection. The animals used in scientific vivisection in Sweden were insignificant in number. On the other hand, hundreds of thousands of animals were involved in 'popular' vivisection in Sweden and he concluded that it was altogether absurd to blame physiologists for the death of a few hundred frogs when such a great number of acts of cruelty to animals were committed openly and without punishment. It was a familiar and powerful argument. But it is of course a dubious defence merely to assert that there are others who commit worse crimes. The anti-vivisectionists were not slow to attack Holmgren along these very lines.

The Carolinian Institute's statement was composed by Christian Lovén and Axel Key.[39] They had learned from von Düben's mistake and employed considerably better tactics in phrasing their speech. In their introduction they declared respect for the fine feelings which are the basis of the anti-vivisectionists' protest. They tried to calm the wave of disquiet which the question had roused. They also picked up the gauntlet and asked themselves whether vivisection really is consistent with the decrees of morality. Their answer was, of course, an unqualified yes. According to the custom which prevails in society, man has unlimited power over animals, but humans must always consider the purpose when they make use of animals. In this case the end is so important and necessary for both animals and humans that the experiments which are performed on animals must be regarded as consistent with prevailing moral standards.

Lovén and Key then maintained that it is only through experimental and not speculative research that science has advanced and has contributed to medicine. They also gave concrete examples of important results achieved by means of vivisection. The remaining charges, such as the moral degradation of the researcher, were thoroughly demolished. After pointing out that not a single example of abuse of vivisection in Sweden had been produced, they ended by rejecting the proposed legislation as unnecessary and detrimental to research. Loven and Key had clearly put a great deal of care and hard work into the composition of their speech, and their opponents had great difficulty in finding weak points.

In the spring of 1883, Nordvall published a *Review* of this statement which, with its 122 pages, is the longest contribution to the debate.

On 7 October 1882, in the Royal Palace at Stockholm, the Scandinavian Association for the Prevention of Cruelty to Animals in Science was founded, a society which still exists. The event took place in the Stockholm Palace because of the interest Princess Eugénie displayed in the matter. No minutes of this meeting have been preserved, but four days later nineteen members met at the Hotel Rydberg to elect a committee.[40] It is no longer possible to find out how preparations for the founding of the society progressed, but after the Riksdag debate it cannot have been difficult to arouse people's interest in the matter. It appears from an article in the *Aftonbladet* of 26 April 1881 that there was much to discuss 'over tea-cups or toddy-glasses'. Since the society was Scandinavian, the leading Danish anti-vivisectionist Lembcke, who was present at its foundation, may have taken some initiative as well. This, however, is of minor interest; there were no problems about choosing a president: Nordvall was chairman *ex officio*. Vice-chairman was Georg von Rosen, the director of the Academy of Art, a well-known painter of historical subjects, and extremely conservative and aristocratic in disposition.

The aim of the Association was, according to its statutes, to work for the gratest possible restriction of vivisection as a scientific method of research, together with the abolition of cruel experiments on living animals in general. The Society sought to achieve these aims by supporting legislation in that area, by spreading information about cruelty to animals in science, and by awarding prizes for discoveries and essays intended to further the Association's activities. Establishing such a competition was one of the first steps taken by the committee. An award of 300 kronor was to be made for the best and 100 kroner for the next best essay demonstrating 'the irreconcilability of vivisection with true science and its harmful influence on morality'. But only one entry was submitted; it was given the consideration it deserved, but after the manuscript had been sent back and forth among the members of the jury in the various Scandinavian countries it was decided that it did not deserve a prize.

On 8 and 9 January 1883 the *Nya Dagliga Allehanda* and *Stockholms Dagblad* published an advertisement by the Association. After explaining its purpose the Association declared the greatest respect for scientists who worked in accordance with the decrees of morality and by humane means. At the same time, however, it felt compelled to oppose with every means at its disposal the unfortunately all too common view that science was the highest good of all, and that its practitioners had the right to consider almost any method justifiable.

Since Nordvall was living in Strängnäs, von Rosen almost always acted as chairman of the Association, but there is no evidence that he took a more active part in its work. On 30 October 1883 the first annual meeting was held, at which Nordvall delivered a much-praised lecture on the public discussion of the vivisection question.[41] After one year the Association had 546 members, of whom 226 were in Sweden. From the list of members we find that nearly all had their roots in the nobility and the upper middle class, chiefly in Stockholm. Of the 226 members 78, i.e. almost 35 per cent, bore noble names. Von Düben had already drawn attention to this social bias in the movement in England, where anti-vivisectional ideas were 'supported by a priesthood hostile to accurate scientific research and by wealthy and ostensibly good-hearted but idle and scandal-hungry members of the middle and upper classes of society.'[42]

Through Nordvall's ideas, which naturally enough found an echo particularly among conservative members of the Riksdag, and the link with the *Nya Dagliga Allehanda*, the Society came to recruit its members largely from conservative circles, in spite of the fact that Hedin was in the front line. That the nobility showed so much interest was naturally connected with Princess Eugénie's and Georg von Rosen's involvement in the movement. This particular foothold in influential Stockholm circles was responsible for the Association's early influence. This is illustrated, for example, by the bazaar held by the Association's ladies' committee under Adele Rudenschöld, a maid of honour at Court. It raised 12,000 kronor, of which 7,483 kronor and 39 öre went to the Association, an impressive sum in 1883.

When replies from the scientific institutes reached the government, it decided that no further action should be taken in the matter. But as early as the spring of 1884, a new anti-vivisection motion was introduced to the Riksdag by Carl Magnus Björnstjerna, who was a member of the Association. Surprisingly, the motion did not have the Association's fore-knowledge. This time the trend of opinion in the Riksdag was different. Medical science had a new, well-informed and eloquent spokesman in the Second Chamber, namely Axel Key, professor at the Carolinian Institute. The anti-vivisectionists, on the other hand, were ill-prepared for a new battle. Under these circumstances Björnstjerna's motion was bound to fail, and it was even more of a disaster for the anti-vivisection movement in Sweden in that this defeat of 1884 precluded any further bill, unless conditions altered radically in some way. Yet in 1888 a fresh anti-vivisection motion was debated in the Riksdag. However, we shall not enter into that here, since no new conditions had arisen and no new arguments were heard.

Postscript

After 1888 there was no longer much public interest in the anti-vivisection movement. The number of members fell, but the movement's writings continued to be circulated. In 1892 Nordvall died, and the Association felt that his place could not be filled, so that the office of chairman remained vacant. In this the committee was undeniably right. In spite of the fact that Nordvall himself could not participate in any of the debates that went on in the Riksdag, the Swedish anti-vivisection movement depended on his contribution. It was thanks to his extensive writings, which in many respects were independent of his predecessors in other countries, that all Swedish anti-vivisectionists saw the matter through Nordvall's eyes. The specific character of a conflict between idealism and materialism which the Swedish debate gained derived from Nordvall's firm roots in the idealist philosophy which he absorbed during his years of study at Uppsala. That his protest aroused such a response shows the extent of resistance to the natural sciences at that time.

Acknowledgement

Valuable help in preparing the references was given by Urban Jonsson, Office for History of Science, Uppsala University.

Notes

1. *Riksdagens Protokoll 1888, Andra Kammaren*, vol. 2, no. 26, p. 7.
2. *Utlåtande, Medicinska fakultetens i Uppsala, om vivisektionen* (Läkareföreningen, Uppsala, 1882), p. 12. Statement by the Faculty of Medicine at Uppsala on the vivisection question.
3. Fritiof Nordberg (ed.), *Magistrar och pojkar* (Fritiof Nordberg *et al.*, Strängnäs, 1921), p. 25.
4. See Sten Lindroth, 'Svensk naturforskning kring 1800-talets mitt', *Lychnos* (1953), pp. 162ff. English summary on pp. 180–1.
5. Israel Hwasser, *Program och tal vid medicine doctors-promotionen i Uppsala d. 14 juni 1841* (W. Hörlin, Uppsala, 1841), p. 62.
6. Sigurd Ribbing, *Om fysikens förhållande till den filosofiska spekulationen* (Uppsala Universitet, Uppsala, 1858), pp. 6 and 16.
7. Nordvall went on to develop these ideas in his pamphlet *Om vivisektionens förhållande till moralen* (Looström & K., Stockholm, 1884), i.e. 'On Vivisection's Relation to Morality', and in the lecture 'Animal Protection and Vivisection', which was later published in the Scandinavian Association's year-book for 1885, 'Djurskydd och vivisektion', *Nordiska samfundet till bekämpande av det vetenskapliga djurplågeriets årsberättelse* (1885), pp. 13–34.
8. Quoted after Adolf Leonard Nordvall, *Ytterligare belysning af vivisektionsfrågan* (Looström & K., Stockholm, 1882), p. 29.
9. Ibid.
10. Ibid., p. 38.
11. Published as a series of articles in the newspaper *Svenska Tidningen* on 25, 28 and 30 September and on 7, 12 and 16 October 1857.
12. Adolf Leonard Nordvall, 'Hvad återstår att göra till förekommande af misshandling mot djuren?', *Pedagogisk Tidskrift*, vol. 2 (1866), pp. 341–59.
13. Ibid., p. 349.
14. Adolf Leonard Nordvall, *Granskning af de yttranden som afgifvits rörande vivisektionen* (P.A. Huldbergs bokförlagsaktiebolag, Stockholm, 1883), p. 4.
15. K.G. Odén, *Östgöta minne* (K.G, Odén, Stockholm, 1902), p. 492.
16. Royal Library, Stockholm, Ep. S, 3:5. Letter from Nordvall to N.F. Sander.
17. Charles Richet, 'Vivisektionens nytta i terapeutiskt och hygieniskt

afseende', *Eira, tidskrift för helso- och sjukvård*, no. 9 (1880), pp. 264–72.

18. Charles Richet (1850–1935), a pupil of Bernard's and an eminent physiologist. His important discoveries in serum therapy won him the Nobel Prize for medicine in 1913.

19. *Bihang til Riksdagens Protokoll 1881*, 1:a saml., 2:a avd., 2:a vol., motion no. 100 i andra kammaren. Motion no. 100 in the second chamber of the Swedish parliament, the Riksdag, 1881.

20. Gustaf von Düben, *I vivisektionsfrågan* (Samson & Wallin, Stockholm, 1881). Gustaf von Düben (1882–92), professor at the Carolinian Institute from 1858 to 1860 of pathological anatomy, from 1860 to 1874 of physiology and anatomy and from 1874 to 1887 of pure anatomy. He is also famous as an explorer of Lapland and the Lapps.

21. Ibid., p. 6.

22. Ibid., p. 27.

23. Ibid., p. 30.

24. *Bihang till Riksdagens Protokoll 1881*, 7:e saml., Lagutskottets utlåtande no. 33.

25. *Riksdagens Protokoll 1881, Andra Kammaren*, vol. 3, no. 35, pp. 18–45. Proceedings of the second chamber.

26. Carl Edward Casparsson (1827–99), superior officer and landowner from Uppland. Member of the Riksdag from 1867 to 1899. One of the leaders of the conservative opposition to the farmers' party. Famous as a great orator, he devoted himself in particular to questions of agriculture and defence.

27. Charles Dickson (1814–1902) practised as a doctor in Göteborg, where he made a considerable contribution to social welfare, sanitary reforms, poor relief, etc. As a Liberal he sat in the Riksdag from 1867 to 1895.

28. His views on the question are best expressed in the subsequent Riksdag debate *Riksdagens Protokoll 1884, Andra Kammaren*, vol. 4, no. 42, pp. 30–2.

29. Royal Library, Stockholm, Ep.H, 7:2. Letter from Nordvall to S.A. Hedin.

30. Royal Library, Stockholm, Ep.H, 7:2. Letter from F. Holmgren to S.A. Hedin.

31. Ibid.

32. Adolf Leonard Nordvall, *Svar på friherre von Dübens skrift: 'Kritik och upplysningar med anledning af motionen om en lag till vivisektionens inskränkning'*, (Looström & K., Stockholm, 1881).

33. Ibid., p. 13.

34. Ibid., pp. 21ff.

35. Francis Darwin (ed.), *The Life and Letters of Charles Darwin Including an Autobiographical Chapter* (3 vols, John Murray, London, 1888), vol. 3, p. 205.

36. Nordvall, *Ytterligare belysning af vivisektionsfrågan*.

37. Ibid.

38. *Utlåtande, Medicinska fakultetens i Upsala, om vivisektionen.*

39. Vivisektionsfrågan. *Utlåtande af Karolinska institutets lärarekollegium* (Samson & Wallin, Stockholm, 1882).

40. Record of the Nordiska samfundet till bekämpande av plågsamma djurförsök, Bromma. Here and in the account which follows I have been able to make use of the minutes of the Association, which are still to

be found in its possession.

41. *Nordiska samfundet etc., årsberättelse*, 1883. First annual report of the Scandinavian Association.

42. Von Düben, *I vivisektionsfrågan*, pp. 31f.

10

The Controversy over Animal Experimentation in America, 1880–1914

Susan E. Lederer

In 1895 the American Humane Association conducted a census of opinions on vivisection in America.[1] Using the term vivisection as synonymous with scientific experimentation on animals, the special committee solicited the opinions of physicians, educators, clergymen and literary men (defined as authors and editors) in order to determine the range of opinions about regulation or restriction on the practice of animal experimentation in the United States. Their survey focused largely on the metropolitan areas of the north-eastern states and revealed a striking 84.1 per cent of those polled as opposed to the practice of vivisection without restrictions.

The American Humane Association's special committee on vivisection, like many committees, found what they had expected to uncover, or, at least, what their inquiry was intended to elicit. For example, in the case of physicians, the committee polled only those practitioners whose practice extended over at least fifteen years, so as to obtain mature medical opinions. This had the perhaps unexpected effect of eliminating younger physicians whose medical education had been completed in the context of newer physiological techniques and demonstrations. The study, while not valuable as an unbiased look at attitudes towards the practice of animal experimentation, none the less revealed that the mainstream animal protection movement favoured restrictions, governing the species and type of pain involved, on the practice of vivisection. Those wholly opposed to the practice of vivisection were always visible in both animal protection and anti-vivisection societies, but the thrust of the mainstream movement was the regulation of animal experimentation in medical schools and laboratories and the abolition of vivisectional demonstrations in front of young children in the public schools.

Animal protection and anti-vivisection

Animal protection in the United States first emerged publicly through the efforts of Henry Bergh, the scion of a wealthy New York ship-building family.[2] Bergh's personal fortune allowed him to travel extensively in Europe, where he was reportedly shocked by the mistreatment of animals. His familiarity with the Continent and his desire for a congenial career led him to secure a diplomatic appointment as Secretary of the American Legation in St Petersburg. When ill-health led him to resign, Bergh travelled to England where in the spring of 1865 he attended the annual meeting of the Royal Society for the Prevention of Cruelty to Animals and met Lord Harrowby, the president of the Society.[3] Upon his return to the United States, Bergh resolved to organise an American association for animal protection. In 1866, with the aid of New York's financial and social elites, Bergh obtained an act of incorporation for the American Society for the Protection of Cruelty to Animals.[4]

Bergh's attention soon turned to the use of live animals in experimental medicine. The actual vivisection of animals in American hospitals and medical schools was extremely rare. The first use of vivisectional demonstration in the teaching of physiology apparently occurred in 1854, when John Call Dalton, an American physician who had studied experimental physiology with Claude Bernard, produced under experimental conditions a gastric fistula in a dog to illustrate William Beaumont's classic experiments on a living human being.[5] Dalton's use of vivisectional demonstrations soon spread to other medical schools, but it was not until the 1870s that medical students could take an active part in the physiology laboratory. In fact, physiology was not even a required course in the medical curriculum until the turn of the century.[6] Despite the rarity of vivisection, Bergh accused the medical profession of New York of cruelty to animals. After a vituperative public exchange with Dalton, Bergh attempted to gather information about hospital practices and vivisection through ASPCA spies. In 1867, under the cover of an anti-cruelty to animals bill, he attached a clause abolishing the practice of vivisection. Dalton and the New York Medical Society were able to forestall Bergh's attempts and the New York press chastised him for attempting to obtain legislation under false pretences.[7] In 1874 Bergh instituted an educational programme against vivisection under the auspices of the ASPCA. Six years later, in 1880, he introduced a bill into the New York legislature that made the practice of vivisection a misdemeanour.

This bill, the first American anti-vivisection bill, received adverse reports not only from New York medical societies, but from medical organisations throughout the nation. Like Bergh's other attempts against vivisection, it too proved unsuccessful.[8]

The ASPCA devoted the lion's share of its attention to the protection of animals, including the transportation and sale of livestock. Not until 1883 was an organisation formed for the specific purpose of opposing animal experimentation. Like Henry Bergh, Caroline Earle White laid the foundation for her anti-vivisection activities in mainstream animal protection. White enjoyed a childhood of wealth and privilege; her father, Thomas Earle, was a wealthy Quaker attorney and prominent abolitionist. An active clubwoman, in 1866 White sought out Bergh and armed with his counsel, instituted a campaign to enlist wealthy Philadelphians in the cause of animal protection. In 1867 the Pennsylvania Society for the Prevention of Cruelty to Animals was formed. Although White had been instrumental in organising the society, her colleagues deemed it unseemly for a woman to appear on the board of managers and selected her husband as her representative on the board. In 1869 the PSPCA formed a Women's Branch, whose membership selected White as president, a post she held for nearly fifty years.[9]

Like Henry Bergh, Caroline Earle White greatly admired the British lead in the work for animal protection. Influenced not only by the example of the British success in securing the Cruelty to Animals Act of 1876, White fell under the personal spell of the doyenne of the British anti-vivisection movement, Frances Power Cobbe. At Cobbe's suggestion, White organised in 1883 the first society in the United States focusing entirely on the issue of animal experimentation, the American Anti-Vivisection Society.[10] During the first four years of the society's existence, the name was changed to the American Society for the Restriction of Vivisection and then in 1887, back to its original name, reflecting White's own extreme views on animal experimentation. Although membership of the society remained small compared to the much larger animal protection associations, it commanded attention through the publication of the *Journal of Zoophily*, edited by White and published under the joint auspices of the PSPCA and the American Anti-Vivisection Society. Perhaps more significant, Caroline White's assistant editor, Mary Frances Lovell, also served as the superintendent for the Department of Mercy for the Women's Christian Temperance Union, the largest women's group in the United States, which effectively spread the gospel of anti-vivisection to women's clubs throughout the nation.[11]

The formation of the American Anti-Vivisection Society was followed by the organisation of a number of like-minded societies, including the New England Anti-Vivisection Society (1895), the Anti-Vivisection Society of Maryland (1898), the Vivisection Reform Society (1903), the Society for the Prevention of Abuse in Animal Experimentation (1907), the New York Anti-Vivisection Society (1908), the California Anti-Vivisection Society (1908), and the Vivisection Investigation League (1912).[12] In addition to such unifocal societies, the American Humane Association, organised in 1877, allowed a national focus for the work of local humane societies. Although the AHA never adopted an anti-vivisectionist stance, the society took an active role in soliciting the regulation of animal experimentation. Information about membership in anti-vivisectionist societies is difficult to obtain. As Richard French observes in the case of the British anti-vivisection movement, information about rank-and-file membership often consisted of little more than lists of names and pseudonyms of contributors. One generalisation can safely be made, however. Although men were visible on the boards of directors of such societies, particularly in the lists of honorary vice-presidents, the bulk of the membership was female; an observation that did not escape contemporary critics of the movement.[13]

The District of Columbia hearings of 1896 and 1900

In the last decade of the nineteenth century, animal protectionists and anti-vivisectionists devised a new strategy in the battle against vivisection. Focusing on the nation's capital, these groups, together with the influential Women's Christian Temperance Union and the support of several US Senators, sponsored legislation restricting the practice of vivisection in the District of Columbia.[14] In 1896 and 1900 two bills regulating vivisection were presented to the Senate Committee of the District of Columbia. Public hearings on the proposed legislation provided a national forum for the ethical issues of animal experimentation.[15]

In the three decades since Bergh founded the ASPCA, American medical research had grown significantly. Whereas in the 1860s only a handful of investigators engaged in animal experimentation, in the 1890s several medical schools, notably Harvard, the University of Pennsylvania and Johns Hopkins, provided quality physiological instruction to medical students and actively encouraged physiological research.[16] Several cities sponsored bacteriological laboratories for the diagnosis of such contagious diseases as diphtheria and tuberculosis, and pioneered techniques involving the use of anti-toxin and sera.[17] The District of Columbia was the centre of several federal research installations, including the laboratories of the Bureau of Animal Industry, the US Hygienic Laboratory and the Army Medical Museum.[18] Restrictions on animal experimentation in the district would not only compromise scientific work there, but opponents of anti-vivisection feared that such legislation would be the 'opening wedge' for similar restrictions on the practice at the state and local levels.[19]

As part of their campaign to gain national attention for vivisection restriction, the Washington Humane Society arranged for Albert Tracy Leffingwell to speak on behalf of the bill in 1900. With his first article on vivisection in 1880, Leffingwell emerged as the most visible spokesman for the restriction of vivisection in the United States.[20] As a physician and a moderate on the subject of animal experimentation, his articles on vivisection commanded respect. Leffingwell's appearance at the Washington hearings on vivisection testified to the importance the movement accorded the legislation for the campaign against unrestricted animal experimentation.

Leffingwell received his medical degree in 1874 and taught physiology for a brief period at the Polytechnic Institute of Brooklyn.[21] His postgraduate medical education in Europe led him to examine the ethics of animal experimentation:

> Having witnessed experiments by some of the most distinguished European physiologists, such as Claude Bernard (the successor of Magendie), Milne-Edwards and Brown-Sequard; and still better (or worse, as the reader may think), having performed some experiments in this direction for purposes of investigation and for the instruction of others, the present writer believes himself justified in holding a pronounced opinion on this subject, even if it be to some extent opposed to the one prevailing in the profession.[22]

Leffingwell advocated a cautious approach to vivisection. He believed that abuses of laboratory animals occurred, but that careful restrictions would diminish the possibilities for abuse. Regulation of the practice of vivisection would also sponsor a more humane and compassionate medical profession than was found in the rest of Europe: 'nowhere in Great Britain would be tolerated for an hour, the bruality and indifference toward suffering humanity, manifested in certain hospitals of Germany, France and Austria, where vivisection is absolutely without restraint.'[23] Leffingwell's moderate stance on vivisection separated him from the stridency of Caroline Earle White; his cautious approach and his status as a physician made the medical profession more wary of him than of other anti-vivisectionists.

Leaders of the American medical profession regarded the proposed legislation for the restriction of animal experimentation in Washington as a serious threat to medical research.[24] Led by William Henry Welch, professor of pathology at Johns Hopkins University School of Medicine, defenders of unrestricted animal experimentation marshalled an impressive array of medical testimony from prominent medical men and women about the utility of vivisection for medical progress and the threat that any infringement of medical research posed to the health of human beings. Although the bill in 1896 might have been passed through a combination of political machinations and apathy on the part of policymakers, the interval of the Spanish-American War allowed medical researchers to gather their collective forces for the hearing in 1900. Bolstered by a considerable number of petitions from scientific and medical societies against the proposed restrictions, American opponents of the bill added the epistolary testimony from such leading British medical researchers as Lord Lister, T. Lauder Brunton and Michael Foster to their opposition to any vivisection regulation.[25] In contrast, the supporters of the bill made a poor showing. They offered virtually no evidence of existing abuses of animal experimentation, preferring to rely on older and often foreign examples of cruel and unnecessary animal experiments. No legislation regulating vivisection resulted.

Anti-toxins and the utility of vivisection

Arguments about the uselessness of vivisection represented a pragmatic response to the medical defence of vivisection. Medical defenders of unrestricted animal experimentation almost exclusively devoted their discussion to appeals to the clinical benefits accruing from vivisection. Arguing that the differences between animals and human beings, sometimes termed species error, invalidated much of this research, animal protectionists suggested that clinical research on human patients, or even the vivisection of an occasional human being, would be of greater value than experimentation on dogs or cats.[26] Other observers claimed that medical defenders of vivisection greatly exaggerated the utility of animal experimentation for modern medical practice. Whereas medical writers ascribed declines in mortality rates from infectious diseases to specific gains in bacteriology or immunology, anti-vivisectionists countered that these declines resulted from the implementation of public health measures. Anti-vivisectionists not surprisingly focused on several spectacular failures of scientific medicine, most notably Robert Koch's claim of a cure for tuberculosis in 1891 and Charles-Edouard Brown-Séquard's elixir of life (an extract compounded of animal glands that purportedly rejuvenated men).[27]

The scepticism concerning the utility of vivisection for progress in medicine deserves some consideration. Lloyd Stevenson has described the resistance of some English sanitarians to the germ theory of diseases and their adherence to an earlier model of disease causation grounded in filth and malignant environmental influences.[28] Many Americans shared such beliefs and objected to inoculations. Many American anti-vivisectionists rejected not only the utility of injecting foreign animal matter for disease prevention or treatment, but objected on moral grounds to the pollution of human bodies with diseased animal matter. There was a considerable overlap between those opposed to compulsory vaccination and anti-vivisectionists.[29] However, anti-vivisectionist scepticism towards bacteriological claims was shared by many American physicians.[30]

James Turner claims that the announcement of the discovery of diphtheria anti-toxin in 1894 doomed American anti-vivisection. Yet it was neither 'simple' nor 'disappointingly anticlimactic'.[31] Like antiseptic surgery, rabies vaccine and virtually all bacteriological claims in this period, the introduction of anti-toxin was muddied by initial scepticism and disillusionment. In the case of diphtheria, the complex aetiology of the disease process and the disappointment just three years earlier of Koch's tuberculin cure hindered the acceptance of the anti-toxin by the medical profession.[32]

Although the diphtheria bacillus had been isolated in 1883 through the efforts of Edwin Klebs and Friedrich Loeffler, the disease process remained obscure until the end of the decade. Emile Roux and Alexandre Yersin, associates of the Pasteur Institute, discovered the role of the toxin produced by the bacillus in the disease process. Diphtheria was a frightening disease; a killer of children, it was difficult to diagnose because it was so often confused with other diseases. The prospect of bacteriological diagnosis seemed promising to many physicians for this reason. However, bacteriological diagnosis also introduced confusion because of the conflicting results of bacteriological and clinical diagnoses. The discovery of a similarly-shaped bacillus in the throats of healthy individuals (pseudo-bacillus), as well as that of pseudo-diphtheria (a streptococcal infection) also created difficulties for clinicians.[33]

In 1890 Emil Behring and Shibasaburo Kitasato, two of Koch's associates, discovered that animals inoculated with doses of diphtheria toxin built up an immunity to the disease through the production of a substance in the blood which they named anti-toxin. Not only would the inoculation of this substance protect animals and human beings from contracting the disease, anti-toxin was also of use in treatment of diphtheria. In 1894, Roux, Yersin and Louis Martin advocated the use of horse serum in the large-scale production of anti-toxin.[34]

In the United States the medical profession responded with considerable interest, if little genuine enthusiasm. In 1891 Robert Koch, at the insistence of the Prussian government, had announced a cure for tuberculosis, tuberculin. As a cure for tuberculosis, tuberculin proved disappointing. Not only was tuberculin ineffective in many cases, in some cases it aggravated the symptoms and made patients worse. The hysteria that greeted Koch's announcement and the subsequent disillusionment made American physicians sceptical of European announcements of cures for specific diseases.[35]

One method of convincing American physicians of the utility of diphtheria anti-toxin was the use of clinical statistics. Introduced by Hermann Biggs and William Hallock Park of the New York City Department of Health, clinical statistics of diphtheria led critics of the anti-toxin to introduce their own conflicting statistics, which undermined reports of the anti-toxin's utility by questioning bacteriological diagnoses of the disease. The picture was further blurred by the fluctuating annual incidence of diphtheria.[36] Anti-vivisectionists, for example, pointed out that after the introduction of the anti-toxin, mortality from the disease had actually increased.[37]

This is not to suggest that diphtheria anti-toxin did not have dramatic results in many cases. The success of the anti-toxin did ultimately convince many Americans of the utility of animal experimentation for medical advance. However, this process occurred over a period of several years. Anti-vivisectionists capitalised on the conflicting reports of the anti-toxin's utility and the hesitancy of many

American physicians in accepting the treatment, and they consolidated their rejection of the anti-toxin after 1901 when several children died as a result of inoculation with diphtheria anti-toxin contaminated with live tetanus bacilli.[38]

Animal suffering in the laboratory

The immorality of using sentient creatures for the purposes of scientific knowledge troubled anti-vivisectionists. As David Cochran, a former president of the Polytechnic Institute of Brooklyn observed at the Senate hearing on the restriction of vivisection: 'the endowment of sensibility is the endowment of rights. Without sensibility there is no right. A being without sensibility can suffer no wrong.'[39] No progress in medicine, many anti-vivisectionists argued, was worth the pain inflicted in laboratories on helpless animals. Moreover, the very practice of vivisection demoralised practitioners and their students. Of particular concern was the effect of vivisection on young and impressionable minds; with the support of the humane societies anti-vivisectionists scored their only legislative successes in this period with laws banning vivisection in elementary and secondary schools.[40] Not content with the protection of schoolchildren, anti-vivisectionists sought to limit the use of vivisectional demonstrations in medical schools. They quoted Henry Jacob Bigelow, a professor of medicine at Harvard (whose death in 1871 did not prevent anti-vivisectionists from quoting him in the ensuing four decades): 'Watch the students at a vivisection. It is the blood and suffering, not the science, that rivets their breathless attention. If hospital service makes young students less tender of suffering, vivisection deadens their humanity and begets indifference to it.'[41]

One of the most serious areas of dispute between anti-vivisectionists and physiologists and physicians was the issue of pain in the laboratory. In Britain, the Cruelty to Animals Act (1876) included a provision that experiments performed without anaesthesia or procedures that allowed the animal to recover from anaesthesia (thus introducing the possibility of post-operative pain) were permitted only when certified as necessary by a professor of medicine and by the president of one of the eleven medical or scientific bodies in England.[42] A consistent feature of American attempts to obtain legislative restrictions on animal experimentation was a similar provision for pain alleviation, particularly in mammalian species.

Pain is a complex phenomenon. *Stedman's Medical Dictionary* defines pain as 'an unpleasant sensory and emotional experience associated with, or described in terms of, actual or potential tissue damage'.[43] The problem in terms of laboratory animals is determining pain thresholds. In spite of the long history of legislation that requires the amelioration of pain in experimental animals, there has been relatively little progress in developing methods of reducing animal pain.[44] The subjective nature of pain assessment in animals was already an issue in the nineteenth-century debate over vivisection. There was a consistent tension in the American debate between anti-vivisectionists, who attempted to identify themselves completely with animals undergoing experimentation, and medical researchers, who attempted to distance themselves from subjective judgements of animal distress.

American anti-vivisectionists were obsessed with the issue of pain. Descriptions of animals strapped to tables, legs outstretched, mouths gagged, appeared ubiquitously in anti-vivisectionist pamphlets and circulars. Perhaps more compelling were illustrations and photographs of animals in vivisectional apparatus. Most of the anti-vivisectionist propaganda was pitched on a visual level. Medical supporters of unrestricted vivisection tried to counter such images with pictures of children saved by researches involving animal subjects.

The determination of animal pain was problematic. The author of *Physiological Cruelty*, for example, observed that human beings, through centuries of experience and based on a common nature, had developed an average standard of human sensibility, which guided daily activity and allowed assessments of deviation from this common scale.[45] But species difference, the gap between human beings and animals, invalidated such a standard; 'When we have to do with animals, we lose ourselves at once . . . We have nothing left to guide us except an analogy with ourselves which we know must be misleading, and "signs of pain," which are of all indications the vaguest.'[46] Henry Pickering Bowditch, a professor of physiology at Harvard Medical School, concurred with this description. He insisted that the cries, movements and other external manifestations of stimulation in animal experiments could mislead human observers. Examples from human beings undergoing anaesthesia further complicated the understanding of pain. Bowditch cited hospital patients suffering from lower spinal cord injuries, who were not conscious of the violent reflex motions of their own limbs, and surgical patients, undergoing anaesthesia, who were seen to scream and struggle during an operation but who subsequently declared they had suffered no pain.[47]

245

If animals could not experience pain to the same degree as human beings, physiologists objected to the premise that the pain associated with laboratory experiments was worse than the pain suffered by animals in other human activities, including hunting, sport and butchering. Moreover, they resisted the imputation that physiology required special restrictions. Surgeon-General George M. Sternberg, at an 1896 hearing before a Senate committee, observed: 'It is an unjust reflection upon those engaged in scientific research work to suppose that they are less humane than other members of the community, and that special legislation is necessary to cause them to administer anaesthetics to animals subjected to painful experiments.'[48] Other defenders of unrestricted vivisection employed a less high-minded approach, which involved the ridicule of women who attended anti-vivisectionist meetings clothed in the plumage of birds and the skins of exotic mammals.

Critics of attempts to regulate animal experimentation endeavoured to defuse anti-vivisectionist criticism by pointing out that even if investigators were so callous as to attempt painful procedures without anaesthesia, science demanded that animals be anaesthetised so as to protect the integrity of the experimental outcome. William Williams Keen, a prominent American surgeon active in the fight against anti-vivisection, observed:

> In almost all experiments not only can an anesthetic be used, but in all involving difficult and delicate operations it is essential to do so; for it is impossible to do such an operation on an animal struggling from pain. Not only, therefore does sentiment lead the vivisectionist to spare the animal all suffering that is possible, but scientific accuracy points in the same direction.[49]

Keen insisted that most animal experiments involved little or no pain for animal subjects. Citing bacteriological researches (which were termed vivisections), Keen observed that at most an animal might feel a pin-prick, although it might subsequently suffer from a disease.

Anti-vivisectionists were not appeased by such explanations. Believing that experimenters desired only the immobility of animals, anti-vivisectionists questioned the degree of anaesthesia administered during vivisections, particularly in conjunction with the drug curare. Ignorance and uncertainty over the number of anaesthetics available for different animal species compounded anti-vivisectionist distrust of physicians.[50] Despite the protestations of defenders of unrestricted vivisection that pain amelioration received primary consideration, anti-vivisectionists realised that not all animal workers shared their concern over animal pain. In American veterinary circles, for example, it was readily admitted that pain avoidance was not a principal object. In 1906 L.A. Merillat, the author of a textbook on veterinary surgery observed: 'Anaesthesia in veterinary surgery today is a means of restraint and not an expedient to relieve pain. So long as an operation can be performed by forcible restraint . . . the thought of anaesthesia does not enter into the proposition.' Merillat believed, however, that this climate of opinion was changing and that soon the veterinary profession would take advantage of the progress in surgical anaesthesia.[51]

Anti-vivisectionists were not the only Americans preoccupied with pain. The discovery of anaesthesia, which greatly advanced the use of vivisectional techniques by minimising the variable of animal distress, by the end of the nineteenth century, made procedures without its use seem more horrible. In part, this explains the abuse accorded to François Magendie, whose experiments were largely performed before anaesthesia was available. The increased concern about physical pain did not escape contemporary observers. William James, the Harvard philosopher, in 1902 noted that the shift in attitude towards pain constituted a watershed in human sensibility:

> We no longer think that we are called upon to face physical pain with equanimity. It is not expected of a man that he should either endure it or inflict much of it, and to listen to the recitals of cases of it makes our flesh creep morally as well as physically.[52]

Physicians and physiologists were not unaffected by the new sensitivity to pain. The process by which medical students are trained for 'detached concern' has been the object of study by medical sociologists, who have observed that humour is a common means for relieving tensions associated with the dissection of cadavers and experimentation on live animals, particularly dogs.[53] Coral Lansbury describes the use of comedy and sporting humour by late nineteenth- and early twentieth-century vivisectionists to distance themselves from animal distress.[54] Examples of medical school pranks or practical jokes appeared in anti-vivisectionist literature. Such examples, however, anti-vivisectionists interpreted as further evidence of the demoralisation that vivisection necessarily entailed, rather than a means to alleviate anxiety.[55]

The Rockefeller Institute and the CDMR

Undaunted by the failure to obtain restrictive legislation in Washington, D.C., anti-vivisectionists continued in the first decade of the twentieth century to pursue legislation regulating animal experimentation. They were spurred by a new development in American medical research, the opening of the Rockefeller Institute for Medical Research.[56] Prior to the opening of the Institute in 1904, the United States possessed no research centres to compare with those of Robert Koch or Louis Pasteur on the Continent. When John D. Rockefeller endowed the Institute, he and his advisers hoped to establish a research laboratory with adequate facilities for the scientific study of medicine. Almost from the initial announcements of the Institute, anti-vivisectionists warned of the dangers inherent in a laboratory wholly devoted to vivisectional experiment.[57]

Two New York-based anti-vivisection societies maintained a careful watch on the Institute's activities and publications. The New York Anti-Vivisection Society, for example, operated a small booth on a nearby street where they encouraged owners of lost pets to seek their animals in the Rockefeller animal houses. In 1907, when the Institute announced the purchase of a New Jersey farm for the production of laboratory animals, a New York newspaper, sympathetic to anti-vivisection, sent a reporter to investigate charges of cruelty to animals on the farm. These articles, as well as numerous others appearing in the pages of the *Herald*, sparked protests.[58] In February 1908, the New York Anti-Vivisection Society, led by Mrs Diana Belais, held a mass meeting in which those assembled called on John D. Rockefeller personally to reconsider his support of the medical centre. Belais's meeting attracted considerable public attention; in addition to two popular actresses, Clara Morris and Minnie Maddern Fiske, she had invited the celebrated opera singer Emma Eames to speak on the programme against vivisection.[59]

Anti-vivisection agitation was not confined to public meetings. In December 1909 the New York *Herald* published the affidavit of an employee at the Rockefeller Institute animal house alleging numerous cruelties to animals within the Institute. Anti-vivisectionists again tried to influence Rockefeller by applying personal pressure through members of the Rockefeller's Bible class at a New York church. Simon Flexner, the scientific director of the Institute, took other steps to refute the charges in the *Herald*. He swore to an affidavit charging the employee with attempts to bribe a fellow-worker to testify against the Institute and, more damaging, of attempting to sell dogs and cats for experimental use.[60]

The vitriolic attack on the Rockefeller enterprise spurred defenders of vivisection to create new responses to the anti-vivisectionist challenge. Previous responses to anti-vivisectionist legislation had generally been handled on an *ad hoc* basis. Although the New York Medical Society as early as 1880 had appointed a standing committee on the defence of experimental medicine, the committee did not take an active role. In 1899 the American Medical Association appointed a Committee on National Legislation, intended in part to combat anti-vivisection legislation.[61] As a result of administrative and budgetary constraints, William Keen and William Henry Welch bypassed the committee and organised the medical defence of vivisection for the 1900 hearing. In addition to anti-vivisection, the committee had other responsibilities, including legislation calling for the creation of a national department of health.

In 1907 and 1908, the American Medical Association established the Council for the Defense of Medical Research. In addition to the attacks on the Rockefeller Institute, leaders of American medical research were disturbed by reports that physicians were lending support to laws restricting vivisection. In 1907 over 700 physicians signed a petition supporting a bill regulating vivisection in the New York state legislature.[62] The *New York Medical Journal* published an editorial favourable to the bill, although one week later it carried a retraction of that support.[63] Concerned by the apparent ignorance of general practitioners about the utility of vivisection for medical practice, Walter Bradford Cannon, Bowditch's successor to the chair of physiology at Harvard Medical School, chaired the Council for the Defense of Medical Research. In addition to Cannon, the committee included representatives from major centres of research where anti-vivisection sentiment was strong. Members included Simon Flexner, William Williams Keen, Harvey Cushing, a professor of surgery at Johns Hopkins University Medical School, and Reid Hunt, a pharmacologist associated with the United States Public Health Service in Washington, D.C.[64]

Cannon directed the activities of the Council for eighteen years. During his tenure, he maintained a careful watch over anti-vivisectionist publications, attempting to correct mis-statements and challenging anti-vivisectionists to account for discrepancies between published accounts of experiments and reports in anti-vivisectionist literature. Cannon organised a survey of medical school practices concerning experimental animals, including such questions as the number of animals used and precautions for ameliorating animal pain. In the wake of the survey, Cannon formulated a code of regulations governing laboratory procedures involving animals. He took personal responsibility for circulating the rules regarding animals among the deans of seventy-nine medical schools.[65] Not only did such guidelines protect animals; they served to disarm anti-vivisectionist criticism of laboratory procedures and to convince the public that medical researchers were taking an active role in self-regulation. The guidelines included significant protection for pets; dogs and cats were to be held for a period equal to or greater than that of the city pound and, if claimed, they were to be returned to their owners.

Under the auspices of the Council for Medical Research, Cannon organised a pamphlet series aimed at informing general practitioners of the utility of animal experimentation for medical practice. The Defense of Research Series was intended not only to instruct physicians, but also to accumulate a body of facts establishing the benefits of animal experimentation with which practitioners could authoritatively respond to the questions or complaints of their patients on the subject of vivisection. As Cannon observed in 1909, laboratory workers were hampered in the fight against anti-vivisection because their motives and objectivity were called into question:

> The only persons who are in a strong strategic position to defend research and preserve to it that freedom which is necessary for the unrestricted advance of our knowledge of disease and its control, are you, the practising physicians and surgeons . . . you meet in the course of your duties persons whose feelings have been harrowed by the tales of torture that the antivivisectionists put forth.[66]

Authored by recognised leaders in such fields as pediatrics, surgery, obstetrics, tuberculosis, cancer and syphilis, the articles appeared first in the *Journal of the American Medical Association*, available to nearly three-quarters of the American medical profession, and later in pamphlet form for dissemination.[67] In all, the series produced twenty-eight articles, written between 1909 and 1915; almost twenty appeared before 1910.

American anti-vivisectionists, like their British counterparts, drew heavily on published accounts of medical experimentation for material against vivisection. Typically, anti-vivisectionists pointed to the conspicuous absence of anaesthesia for pain relief and to a lack of regard for experimental subjects. Realising the importance of such accounts, Cannon circulated a letter among editors of medical journals requesting that considerable care be exercised in the publication of research involving animals and human beings. 'The omission or vague statement of the facts that an anesthetic was used in experimentation upon animals is seized upon and only too often serves as a text or basis of a diatribe against scientific research', wrote Cannon in 1914.[68] Although Cannon deplored the fact that anti-vivisectionists assumed that anaesthesia would not be given to animals, he recognised the public relations value of forestalling anti-vivisectionist criticism.

As chairman of the Committee for the Protection of Medical Research, Cannon engaged in numerous battles with anti-vivisectionists over the veracity of their reports of medical experimentation. In 1909 he charged a fellow Harvard professor with misstatements about the efforts of the American medical profession to take steps to protect animal well-being and the progress of American medicine.

Contemporary assessments of the controversy

In 1909 the Vivisection Reform Society invited William James, professor of philosophy at Harvard University, to serve as an honorary vice-president. James declined the invitation; his letter of explanation was published by the New York *Evening Post*.[69] James's name on the letterhead of the society would have been a considerable coup. He was a distinguished psychologist, who had once taught physiology as an assistant professor at Harvard. Moreover, his son, Henry James Jr, who served as business manager for the Rockefeller Institute, played a large role in combating anti-vivisectionist criticism of the New York medical research institute. James's letter, cited by both anti-vivisectionists and defenders of unrestricted animal experimentation, assessed the outcome of the nineteenth-century debate over animal experimentation.

James credited the anti-vivisectionists with the development of a heightened sense of responsibility towards animals on the part of medical researchers:

> There are, perhaps, fewer lecture-room repetitions of ancient vivisections, supposed to help out the professor's dullness with their brilliance, and to 'demonstrate' what not six of the students are near enough to see, and what had all better take, as in the end they have to, upon trust. The waste of animal life is very likely lessened, the thought for animal pain less shamefaced in the laboratories than it was.[70]

James observed that the anti-vivisectionist agitation, 'with all its expensiveness, idiocy, bad temper, untruth, and vexatiousness', continued because the medical profession as an organised body refused to recognise the legitimacy of the concern for animals and failed to act responsibly by establishing a code of ethics, enforcing the rules and condemning those practitioners who transgressed.

Cannon wrote to James about his mistaken views concerning American physiologists, citing the regulations regarding animals.[71] Although James admitted his unfamiliarity with the new guidelines, he allowed the Vivisection Reform Society to issue his letter as a circular, thereby incurring the wrath of William W. Keen. Throughout his professional medical career, Keen had devoted himself to the fight against anti-vivisection. Spurred by James's letter, Keen wrote letters to several anti-vivisectionist publications challenging the veracity of James's assertions and continued in his own articles and books to dispute James's reading of the corporate responsibilities of American physicians and physiologists.

James's analysis of the American agitation over vivisection merits consideration. The nineteenth-century debate over animal experimentation was characterised by extreme defences and criticism of the practice of using live animals in laboratories. Anti-vivisectionists confronted physicians not only in print but in practice. Agitation for legislation restricting the practice of vivisection required physiologists to defend publicly their research practices. Moreover, criticism of laboratory practices and control of municipal pounds required medical researchers to make alternative arrangements for acquiring animals for experimental purposes. In 1913 William Pepper, Dean of the University of Pennsylvania Medical School, explained the difficulties encountered by the medical school in obtaining sufficient dogs for research. In a letter to Henry James Jr, Pepper acknowledged that the school purchased 'dogs from practically anyone who brings us a dog'.[72] With the aid of the Society for the Prevention of Cruelty to Animals, municipal policemen began a policy of arresting disreputable men bringing dogs to the medical school. This led to higher prices for animals and a temporary shortage. The policy of the medical school required that animals be maintained for two weeks before experimental use and that owners of lost pets be allowed to look in the kennels. On several occasions, Pepper noted, individuals had located lost dogs and cats in the kennels. Difficulty over obtaining sufficient animals led the medical school to obtain the names of animal dealers and to champion the passage of legislation allowing the purchase of pound animals for laboratory use.

Just five months after Pepper wrote of the difficulties in obtaining animals, the medical school encountered other problems. In August 1913 the District Attorney's Office indicted five members of the physiology department of the medical school for cruelty to animals.[73] The trial of the five physiologists received daily newspaper coverage in Philadelphia and New York. The jury in the case was unable to reach a verdict and the charges were eventually dropped. None the less, the public controversy revealed the divisive nature of the conflict between animal rights and medical interests.

Postscript

America's entry into the First World War crystallised the divisions between animal protectionists and the more extreme anti-vivisectionist societies. At the turn of the century, most animal protection groups advocated restrictions on the practice of animal experimentation, often supporting anti-vivisectionists in their attempts at legislation. By 1914, animal protectionists commiserated with medical researchers about anti-vivisectionist excesses.[74] Anti-vivisectionists contributed to the decline of popular support for anti-vivisection through their continued support of outmoded medical therapies, alliances with discredited sectarians, and their shrill denunciations of the progress in medical understanding of bacteriology, immunology and replacement therapies.[75]

In the face of the decline of anti-vivisection, American medical researchers continued to pursue broad public support for biomedical research. In 1923 the American Association for Medical Progress, an organisation of interested lay people, was established to further the advancement of unrestricted animal experimentation.[76] Cannon had long campaigned for such an association, believing that it would expedite the channelling of information about medical research to the public. Three years later he resigned from the Council for the Protection of Medical Research, assured that anti-vivisection no longer threatened laboratory freedom.[77]

Notes

1. *Report of the American Humane Association on Vivisection in America* (American Humane Association, Chicago, 1896).

2. Sydney H. Coleman, *Humane Society Leaders in America* (American Humane Association, Albany, New York, 1924), pp. 33–64.

3. James Turner, *Reckoning with the Beast: Animals, Pain and Humanity in the Victorian Mind* (Johns Hopkins University Press, Baltimore, 1980), pp. 46–8.

4. William J. Shultz, *The Humane Movement in the United States, 1910–1922* (AMA Press, New York, 1924), pp. 141–5.

5. John Harley Warner, 'Physiology', in Ronald L. Numbers (ed.), *The Education of American Physicians* (University of California Press, Berkeley, 1980), p. 58.

6. Gerald L. Geison, 'Divided We Stand: Physiologists and Clinicians in the American Context', in Morris J. Vogel and Charles E. Rosenberg (eds.), *The Therapeutic Revolution: Essays in the Social History of American Medicine* (University of Pennsylvania Press, Philadelphia, 1979), p. 72.

7. Zulma Steele, *Angel in Top Hat* (Harper & Brothers Publishers, New York, 1942), pp. 272–3. Steele's biography is a book-length treatment of Henry Bergh and his works.

8. Shultz, *Humane Movement*, pp. 141–2.

9. Coleman, *Humane Society Leaders*, pp. 178–86; see also Turner, *Reckoning with the Beast*, pp. 48–9 and 50–2.

10. Caroline Earle White, 'The History of the Anti-Vivisection Movement', in *Proceedings of the International Anti-Vivisection and Animal Protection Congress* (Tudor Press, New York, 1914), pp. 25–35.

11. Coleman, *Humane Society Leaders*, pp. 186–7.

12. Shultz, *Humane Movement*, pp. 146–9.

13. Richard D. French, *Antivivisection and Medical Science in Victorian Society* (Princeton University Press, Princeton, New Jersey, 1975), pp. 221–2, 236, 239–46. See also French, 'Animal Experimentation: Historical Aspects', in Warren T. Reich (ed.), *Encyclopedia of Bioethics* (Free Press, New York, 1978), I, pp. 75–6.

14. The legislation was Senate bill 1552 (1896) and Senate bill 34 (1900). See Senate Report no. 1049, 54th Congress, 1st Session, May 26, 1896, Serial no. 3366, and *Vivisection. Hearing before the Senate Committee on the District of Columbia* (Government Printing Office, Washington, 1900).

15. Any American medical journal in the years 1896–1900 carried news of the impending legislation and lists of scientific and medical bodies opposed to it. For examples, see 'The Antivivisection Bill', *Journal of the American*

Medical Association, 34 (1900), p. 51; C.W. Eliot, 'Legislation against Medical Discovery', *Popular Science Monthly*, 57 (1900), p. 436; and 'Antivivisection in the District of Columbia', *Boston Medical and Surgical Journal*, 84 (1896), p. 626.

16. See Henry K. Beecher and Mark D. Altschule, *Medicine at Harvard: The First Three Hundred Years* (University Press of New England, Hanover, N.H., 1977); George W. Corner, *Two Centuries of Medicine: A History of the School of Medicine of the University of Pennsylvania* (J.B. Lippincott Co., Philadelphia, 1965); and Simon Flexner and James T. Flexner, *William Henry Welch and the Heroic Age of Modern Medicine* (Viking Press, New York, 1941)

17. David Anthony Blancher, 'Workshops of the Bacteriological Revolution: A History of the Laboratories of the New York City Department of Health, 1892–1912', unpublished PhD thesis, City University of New York, 1979.

18. These developments are discussed in P.P. Gossel, 'William Henry Welch and the Antivivisection Legislation in the District of Columbia, 1896–1900', *Journal of the History of Medicine*, 40 (1985), pp. 404–7.

19. C.F. Hodge, 'The Vivisection Question', *Popular Science Monthly*, 49 (1896), pp. 614–24, 771–86.

20. Albert T. Leffingwell's writings on vivisection were collected in *The Vivisection Question* (Vivisection Reform Society, Chicago, 1907) and *An Ethical Problem or Sidelights upon Scientific Experimentation on Man and Animals*, second ed. revised, C.P. Farrell (New York, 1916).

21. See entry on Leffingwell in Irving A. Watson (ed.), *Physicians and Surgeons of the United States* (Republican Press, Concord, N.H., 1896), pp. 56–7.

22. Leffingwell, *Vivisection Question*, p. 3.

23. Leffingwell, 'State Supervision of Vivisection', in Senate Report 1049.

24. Donald Fleming, *William H. Welch and the Rise of Modern Medicine* (Little, Brown and Co., Boston, 1954), pp. 146–51; Flexner and Flexner, *William Henry Welch*, pp. 254–62; Gossel, 'Welch and Antivivisection', pp. 411–19.

25. *Vivisection*, pp. 96–100.

26. See Senator Henry Blair to Philip Peabody, 29 March 1890, in Frances Power Cobbe and Benjamin Bryan, *Vivisection in America* (Swan, Sonnerschein and Company, London, 1890), p. 15; see also William W. Keen, *The Influence of Antivivisection on Character* (American Medical Association, Chicago, 1912).

27. For tuberculin, see R.Y. Keers, *Pulmonary Tuberculosis: A Journey Down the Centuries* (Baillière Tindall, London, 1978), pp. 79–89. For Brown-Séquard, see Merriley Borell, 'Brown-Séquard's Organotherapy and Its Appearance in America at the End of the Nineteenth Century', *Bulletin of the History of Medicine*, 50 (1976), pp. 309–20.

28. Lloyd Stevenson, 'Science Down the Drain: On the Hostility of Certain Sanitarians to Animal Experimentation, Bacteriology, and Immunology', *Bulletin of the History of Medicine*, 29 (1955), pp. 1–26.

29. Martin Kaufman, 'The American Anti-Vaccinationists and Their Arguments', *Bulletin of the History of Medicine*, 41 (1967), pp. 463–79.

30. This scepticism is discussed in Russell C. Maulitz, '"Physician versus Bacteriologist": The Ideology of Science in Clinical Medicine', in Vogel and Rosenberg, *Therapeutic Revolution*, pp. 91–107.

31. Turner, *Reckoning with the Beast*, p. 115.

32. See Paul Starr, *The Social Transformation of American Medicine* (Basic Books, New York, 1982), p. 138.

33. See F. Loeffler, 'The Bacteriology of Diphtheria', *American Journal of Medical Science*, n.s., 57 (1894), pp. 1–52.

34. Harry F. Dowling, *Fighting Infection: Conquests of the Twentieth Century* (Harvard University Press, Cambridge, 1977), pp. 36–7.

35 See Nicholas Senn, 'Away with Koch's Lymph', *Medical News*, 58 (1891), p. 625; and T.J. Happel, 'Quo Vadis?', *Journal of the American Medical Association*, 32 (1899), p. 271.

36. William G. Rothstein, *American Physicians in the Nineteenth Century* (Johns Hopkins University Press, Baltimore, 1972), pp. 272–8.

37. Senator Jacob H. Gallinger introduced the following article in the record of the Senate hearing in 1900 as evidence — J. Edward Herman, 'The Failure of Antitoxin in the Treatment of Diphtheria', reprint from the New York *Medical Record*, 27 May 1899, in *Vivisection*, pp. 43–54.

38. Dowling, *Fighting Infection*, p. 38.

39. 'Statement of Dr. David H. Cochran,' in *Vivisection*, p. 17.

40. In 1894 Massachusetts enacted a law disallowing vivisectional demonstrations in public schools; see 'Anti-vivisection for Children', *Medical News*, 67 (1895), p. 181.

41. Quoted in Leffingwell, *Vivisection Question*, p. 48.

42. French, *Antivivisection*, p. 143.

43. *Stedman's Medical Dictionary*, 24th edn (Williams & Wilkins, Baltimore, 1982), p. 1015.

44. P.A. Flecknell, 'The Relief of Pain in Laboratory Animals', *Laboratory Animals*, 18 (1984), pp. 147–61.

45. Philanthropos, *Physiological Cruelty: Or, Fact v. Fancy* (John Wiley and Sons, New York, 1883).

46. Philanthropos, ibid., p. 5.

47. Henry P. Bowditch, 'Vivisection Justifiable', *Sanitarian*, 38 (1896), pp. 230–1.

48. George M. Sternberg in a speech delivered 17 April 1896, quoted in *Vivisection*, pp. 140–1.

49. William W. Keen, *Animal Experimentation and Medical Progress* (Houghton Mifflin Company, Boston, 1914), p. 108.

50. For discussion for the 'anesthetic delusion', see E. Westacott, *A Century of Vivisection and Anti-vivisection* (C.W. Daniel Co., Ltd, 1949), pp. 479–90.

51. L.A. Merillat, *Principles of Veterinary Surgery* (Alexander Eger, Chicago, 1906), p. 223; see J.F. Smithcors, 'History of Veterinary Anesthesia', in Lawrence R. Soma (ed.). *Textbook of Veterinary Anesthesia* (Williams & Wilkins Company, Baltimore, 1971), pp. 1–23.

52. William James, *The Varieties of Religious Experience* (Collier Books, New York, 1961), p. 239. See T.J. Jackson Lears, *No Place of Grace: Antimodernism and the Transformation of American Culture 1880–1920* (Pantheon Books, New York, 1981), pp. 45–6.

53. Harold Lief and Renee Fox, 'Training for "Detached Concern" in Medical Students', in Harold Lief, Victor Lief and Nina Lief (eds.), *The Psychological Basis of Medical Practice* (Harper and Row, New York, 1963), pp. 21–2; and A. Gregg, *For Future Doctors* (University of Chicago Press, Chicago, 1957), pp. 25–6.

54. Coral Lansbury, *The Old Brown Dog: Women, Workers and Vivisection in Edwardian England* (University of Wisconsin Press, Madison, 1985), p. 178.

55. For an example involving medical students sewing together two puppies; see 'Vivisection Legislation', New York *Herald*, 18 April 1908. See also *Some Recent Expressions in Favor of Restricting Vivisection* (Vivisection Reform Society, 1909).

56. George W. Corner, *A History of the Rockefeller Institute* (Rockefeller Institute Press, New York, 1964).

57. See 'Rockefeller Institute for Medical Research', reprint of letter to New York *Tribune*, 13 May 1906, pamphlet in Rockefeller University Archives, 600–1.

58. See 'The Antivivisection Agitation in N.Y.', *Journal of the American Medical Association*, 54 (1910), 1062–3; 'Origin of the New York Herald's Anti-vivisection Propaganda', typescript by Fred W. Eastman to Frederic Schiller Lee, 19 June 1911, Rockefeller University Archives, Anti-vivisection Files. See New York *Herald*, 20 October 1907 and 27 November 1909, for details of the fire.

59. *Collier's Weekly*, 4 April 1908.

60. Corner, *Rockefeller Institute*, pp. 86–7.

61. Jonathan Dine Wirtschafter, 'The Genesis and Impact of the Medical Lobby: 1898–1906', *Journal of the History of Medicine*, 13 (1958), pp. 15–49.

62. See *Annual Report* (Vivisection Reform Society, Chicago, 1908), pp. 4–5.

63. 'Vivisection in the State of New York', *New York Medical Journal*, 87 (4 January 1908), pp. 29–30 and 87 (11 January 1908), p. 73.

64. Saul Benison, 'In Defense of Medical Research', *Harvard Medical Alumni Bulletin*, 44 (1970), pp. 16–23.

65. Walter B. Cannon, *Medical Control of Vivisection* (American Medical Association, Chicago, 1910).

66. Walter B. Cannon, 'The Responsibility of the General Practitioner for Freedom of Medical Research', *Boston Medical and Surgical Journal*, 161 (1909), p. 432.

67. See Rosemary Stevens, *American Medicine and the Public Interest* (Yale University Press, New Haven, 1971), p. 73; see also James G. Burrow, *Organized Medicine in the Progressive Era* (Johns Hopkins University Press, Baltimore, 1977).

68. 'Report of the Committee on the Protection of Medical Research', *Journal of the American Medical Association*, 63 (1914), p. 94; 'Protecting Medical Research', *Chicago Medical Recorder*, 36 (1914), p. 360.

69. *Concerning Vivisection* (Vivisection Reform Society, Chicago, 1909); Letter in New York *Evening Post*, 22 May 1909. The text of the letter appears in Roswell C. McCrea, *The Humane Movement: A Descriptive Survey* (Columbia University Press, New York, 1910), pp. 274–5.

70. McCrea, *Humane Movement*, p. 275.

71. William Gary Roberts, 'Man Before Beast: The Response of Organized Medicine to the American Antivivisection Movement', unpublished senior thesis, Harvard University, 1979, pp. 38–9; Benison, 'In Defense of Medical Research', pp. 18–19.

72. Letter of William Pepper to Henry James Jr, 18 March 1913, Rockefeller University Archives, Anti-vivisection files.

73. See 'Recent Antivivisection Activity', *Journal of the American Medical Association*, 61 (1913), pp. 282–3; 'University of Pennsylvania Professor

Defends Vivisection', *Public Ledger* (Phila.), 21 December 1913, p. 6; and 'The Atrocious Charges of Cruelty Against Dr. Joshua A. Sweet', *American Medicine*, 20 (1914), p. 325.

74. Richard Mills Pearce to W.B. Cannon, 26 October 1914, and Anna Harris Smith to W.B. Cannon, 25 April 1912, in Cannon Papers, Harvard Medical School Archives.

75. For alliance with sectarians, see Manfred Waserman, 'The Quest for a National Health Department in the Progressive Era', *Bulletin of the History of Medicine*, 49 (1975), pp. 353–80. For an example, see attitudes towards rabies treatment in Harriet Ritvo, 'Plus Ca Change: Antivivisection Then and Now', *Bioscience*, 34 (1984), pp. 628–30.

76. Flexner and Flexner, *Welch*, pp. 261–2.

77. W.B. Cannon to W.W. Keen, 8 February 1926, Keen-Cannon Correspondence, American Philosophical Society Library. See also Andrew N. Rowan and Bernard E. Rollin, 'Animal Research — For and Against: A Philosophical, Social, and Historical Perspective', *Perspectives in Biology and Medicine*, 27 (1983), pp. 5–7.

11

Women and Anti-vivisection in Victorian England, 1870–1900

Mary Ann Elston

Somnia Medici
Wailings of silly women led astray,
By full-fed ignorance, or sentiment
Fostered by falsehood. Not that these invent
Their tales of horror. Meaner spawn than they,
Hired agitators, scent their meal, and bray
Persistent. O'er their work of love downbent
The foemen of disease are discontent
With the disturbing clamours, and their way
Beset with gadflies; but they will endure
Whilst truths increase, and blatant falsehoods die;
Whilst nature yields her hidden gifts of cure,
While human sorrows for compassion cry,
Time will disperse with certain hand and sure
This swarm of buzzing idlers, whose obscure
Humanitarians foul humanity.[1]

Sentiment versus science: women versus men

These two dichotomies have co-existed throughout the vivisection controversy. Over the past century, anti-vivisection has often been dismissed as the ill-informed sentimentality of 'old women', albeit of both sexes.[2] Many anti-vivisectionists have shared this image of their movement as a women's movement, though without the denigratory implications. Avowedly sentimental, caring women have been exhorted to ally themselves with the animals to oppose the militaristic, inhumane science of men, as in this example from the 1980s.

Modern women, when left alone to devise a recall of ancient survival, know that they can heal, regenerate, live in tune with the seasons . . . Women know and understand, more easily than men do, the workings of animal communities . . . The direct fact is this: how men treat the domesticated and indigenous animals is exactly how they will treat the women who surround them . . . Woman is appalled when she awakes to her inner sense of natural healing, that men could conceive to inoculate the tiny arms of children with the pus of a farm animal to 'protect' them from ill-health . . . that man could know her better by ripping open her female animal counterpart with the zeal of a shaman.[3]

Though the increase in direct and violent action, since the beginning of the 1980s, may have rendered the anti-vivisection movement's image rather less sentimental, connections like this between the cause of animals and the cause of women are often made today. Those who campaign for animal rights, for animal *liberation*, not just animal welfare, are explicitly claiming parallels with the women's, gays' or black liberation movements. Intrinsic links between anti-vivisection and feminism are often claimed, but on two quite different grounds. The first is that they are similar moral enterprises, concerned with extending the moral rights of oppressed groups, and eliminating 'discrimination based on an arbitrary characteristic like race or sex' or species. This is the argument set out in Singer's enormously influential *Animal Liberation*. The second is that women and animals are linked by women's 'natural' closeness to animals and a common oppression by patriarchal power.[4]

Singer begins his book with an historical example of the alleged connection between feminism and animal rights. He reminds us that when Mary Wollstonecraft's *Vindication of the Rights of Woman* was published, in 1792, it was soon followed by an anonymous pamphlet, *Vindication of the Rights of Brutes*, known to have been written by the Cambridge philosopher Thomas Taylor.[5] The significance, for Singer, lies in the fact that connections were made. He does not analyse the background to that connection, the complex symbolic association between women, sentiment and nature that was so significant in late eighteenth- and nineteenth-century thought.[6] Wollstonecraft had attacked those who claimed that women were solely made for men's delight or that they were more governed by their passions than men, and, therefore, closer to nature. She explicitly extended Jacobin arguments to women. If reason was what distinguished man (species) from brutes, women had it no less than men. Women, therefore, were distinct from 'brutes', they had moral autonomy and moral rights. What women lacked was education to develop reasoning ability rather than vanity, sentimentality and frivolousness. Taylor attempted a *reductio ad absurdum*, reasserting the association between women and nature, as signifying women's unreason. If those as close to nature as women had reason, then those who were part of nature, animals, must also have reason, and, hence, rights. For Taylor, the manifest absurdity of this conclusion entailed the falsity of the first premiss.

For Singer the *reductio* fails. Animals do have moral rights. But this is because he rejects the premiss shared by Wollstonecraft and Taylor: that moral rights stem from the possession of reason. Singer rejects the premiss on which Wollstonecraft had based her claim for women's rights. For him, moral rights, having interests which deserve equal consideration, are to be attributed on a different basis. Quoting Bentham, Singer suggests that the correct question to ask in determining who has moral rights is not 'Can they *reason*? Nor Can they *talk*? but, Can they *suffer*?'[7] In his utilitarian ethical philosophy, anything with the capacity to suffer pain deserves equal consideration. If 'the sexist violates the principle of equality by favouring the interests of his own sex . . . the speciesist allows interests of his own species to override the greater interests of members of other species'. 'Speciesism' is as immoral and irrational a prejudice as sexism or racism.[8]

In human movements, the term 'liberation' connotes rejection of the paternalism of experts or the powerful to speak for the oppressed. For Singer, 'animal liberation' is a special case. Precisely what is denied in the wholly human situation is essential here. As non-human animals cannot speak for themselves, people have to do it for them.[9] Some are more specific. 'A true feminist would uphold the rights of those who cannot speak for themselves — those who trust and depend on us — as *children do*.'[10] Or, 'It is fitting that feminists, aliens as animals are, in a male-dominated world, should not only raise their voices for non-humans but live a life which shows by example their contempt for patriarchal attitudes towards animals.'[11]

Here we have a move to the second putative connection between feminism and animal rights. In this view, the man who exercises power over nature is clearly *vir* not *homo*. He dominates and exploits women and animals alike. Both are treated as tools to be manipulated, objects to be penetrated. This view stems from a form

261

of radical feminism that accepts the identification of women with nature/man with culture as universal, and as the starting point for a critique of almost all of male culture. Women's closeness to nature is to be celebrated and acted on. For one radical feminist, animals have an advantage over women: they are not constrained by male-dominated language.[12]

Elements of this view underlie some parts of the women's peace movement and 'eco-feminism' and some, but not all, of the feminist critiques of 'masculinist' science and medicine as permeated with patriarchal assumptions, systematically denigrating and excluding women's natural healing skills and knowledge, while controlling women's lives.[13] For some feminists, women and animals alike are victims of 'scientific' medicine.

Not all of those concerned about both animal suffering and women's rights today hold either of these positions. They are controversial within both movements. Singer's argument for speciesism, and his conception of animal rights, are contested by some philosophers who emphasise that rejecting Singer's arguments does not entail that it is morally right to ill-treat animals.[14] Many feminists are uncomfortable with a depiction of women as having an essentially sentimental nature, or with a portrayal that sometimes appears tautologically to identify all evil with maleness and all good with femaleness.[15] But allusions to these two ideas are frequent in modern anti-vivisection literature.

Further discussion of possible logical links between feminism and 'animal rights' is beyond the scope of this brief history. My concern is with the historical connections that are frequently appealed to, in support of the case for intrinsic links. I have said enough to indicate that the historical precedent of Taylor's riposte to Wollstonecraft does not support the logic of either the patriarchy case or Singer's argument. But both appeal to other historical connections. They claim the precedent of women who were prominent in both the women's movement and anti-vivisection in the late nineteenth century in Britain and the United States. Singer suggests that the overlap of leaders of these two movements, and the anti-slavery campaign, was 'so extensive as to provide an unexpected confirmation of the parallel between racism, sexism and speciesism'.[16] The rest of this chapter is concerned with the historical links between the women's movement and anti-vivisection in Victorian Britain.

An organised movement against vivisection began in the last quarter of the nineteenth century. It was a more powerful movement hen than at any time since, until the mid-1970s. This course is paralleled by the rise of 'first- ' and 'second-wave' feminism, though neither movement disappeared in the interim. What was women's role in the first phase of organised anti-vivisection? Was it a movement as dominated by women as both sides suggest? If so, why? And what connections exist between it and the many, sometimes conflicting, activities that make up the late nineteenth-century women's movement? Feminism then was not a single movement or set of beliefs, any more than it is now.[17]

Women's involvement in anti-vivisection, 1870–1900

The most cursory glance at the movement's history reveals the presence of women such as Anna Kingsford and Frances Hoggan, and later Louise Lind-af-Hageby and Anna Louisa Woodward, among the best-known advocates. Above all, there was Frances Power Cobbe (1822–1904), co-founder of the Victoria Street Society for the Protection of Animals liable to Vivisection (VSS) in 1875. Resigning in 1898, when this society decided to campaign for restriction not abolition of vivisection, she then founded the British Union for the Abolition of Vivisection (BUAV). She, more than anyone else, articulated the role for women in the movement. Queen Victoria and the immensely wealthy Angela Baroness Burdett Coutts, strongly opposed to most aspects of the contemporary women's movement, shared their anti-vivisectionism with pioneer doctor Elizabeth Blackwell, suffragette and Irish Republican Charlotte Despard, and Annie Besant, sometime socialist and birth control campaigner, after her conversion to theosophy.[18]

Anti-vivisection was, however, never exclusively a woman's cause. Nor have I identified any women-only anti-vivisection societies analogous to the Ladies' National Association for the Repeal of the Contagious Diseases Acts.[19] Among male anti-vivisectionists were such supporters of women's causes as James Stansfield MP and such opponents as R.H. Hutton, editor of *The Spectator*, and the positivist Frederic Harrison. The Hon. Stephen Coleridge, Honorary Secretary of the National Anti-Vivisection Society for many years from 1897, concluded his memoirs, in 1913, with a diatribe against emancipated women.[20] Conversely, we find some women prominent in the feminist movement opposed to anti-vivisectionists' activity, such as Elizabeth Garrett Anderson and Eleanor Sidgwick.[21] Among the vivisectors and their supporters we find both the archenemies of women medical students, toxicologist Robert Christison and Lyon Playfair MP, and supporters of women's higher education, such as Huxley, Darwin, Edward Sharpey-Schafer and Victor Horsley.[22] These names alone should warn against assuming strong links between anti-vivisectionism and feminism in the nineteenth century.

French suggests that, 'if contemporary testimony is to be trusted, levels of female participation in the anti-vivisection movement would seem to have been among the very highest for movements without overtly feminist objectives'.[23] Throughout the period, press reports of anti-vivisectionist meetings usually described audiences as composed mostly of ladies. Occasionally, the presence of large numbers of young men was reported, indicating that hostile medical students had packed the meetings, further evidence to anti-vivisectionists of the degrading effects of their contaminated education.[24] Some, but not all, of the contemporary women's papers gave space to the controversy.[25]

This image of female dominance was occasionally confirmed by denial. Anti-vivisectionist Lord Chief Justice Coleridge claimed, 'we have great men, and those surely not weak or effeminate, on ours . . . It is not true that fools and women are on one side, and wise men on the other.'[26] But this was rare. More often, anti-vivisectionist men and women affirmed their cause as a *woman's cause*. One image recurred: that those who mock the movement for being one of ladies, would do well to remember, 'so were they who stood beside the Cross; and that always, in every age, women have invariably been the earliest and most numerous adherents to all movements of good and benevolence'.[27]

Cobbe recognised that such a movement was liable to be dismissed as based on ill-informed sentimentality. She cautioned women supporters against excessive displays of emotion, calling instead for vigorous denunciations of injustice, based on women's moral superiority, not their womanly 'privileges'.[28] As Lord Coleridge's comment implies, male anti-vivisectionists, especially clergymen, had their masculinity impugned by critics. They too were sentimental, ignorant, easily led, falsely claiming moral superiority.[29] One anecdote revealed this and the qualities which made Cobbe such a controversial figure. Huxley was reportedly delighted by 'the most beautiful double-barrelled score', when Darwin said of the anti-vivisectionist, R.H. Hutton, 'he seems to be a kind of *female Miss Cobbe*'.[30]

Attacks on women anti-vivisectionists, as being either too

womanly or too unwomanly, were frequent. Allegations of anti-vivisectionist hypocrisy in eating flesh, wearing animal products or supporting blood sports oblivious to the cruelty these entailed, took on special force when directed at 'foolish women' with their 'murderous millinery' and furs. No doubt this charge was justified against some of the elegant women who attended VSS meetings, but it was taken to absurd lengths. Cobbe was repeatedly accused of possessing a fabulous muff made from bird of paradise feathers, though she was notorious for her plain and unfashionable clothes.[31] Attacks on individual women often became attacks on the whole movement and the whole sex. In 1892, Lord Aberdare, President of the RSPCA, stung by an accusation of inertia from Cobbe, told his society's Annual Meeting,

> And I grieve to say that these attacks [on the RSPCA's alleged indifference to vivisection] come chiefly from ladies. Although I am addressing an audience composed chiefly of ladies, and although I have an excellent opinion of womankind, I may be permitted to repeat the statement of an old bachelor friend of mine, who said they had one great fault: 'What is that?' I asked. 'They are absolutely without sense of justice' was his reply; and I hardly ever tell the story without ladies shaking their heads and saying, 'Alas, too true'.

Cobbe responded characteristically, asking how, if they lacked a sense of justice, was it possible that women were campaigning for justice for brutes? And, she added, if the charge were to be proven, would this be so surprising, given the example that men had set in their dealings with women?[32]

Direct attacks on women anti-vivisectionists from experimentalists themselves, rather than from their supporters, were rare in the 1880s.[33] The Continental physiologist Elie de Cyon accused his British peers of pusillanimity towards a movement of despised old maids. 'Let my adversaries contradict me, if they can show among the leaders of the agitation one young girl, rich, beautiful and beloved, or one young wife who has found in her home the full satisfaction of her affections.' De Cyon claimed that the movement flourished only in Protestant countries, as in Catholic countries 'old maids' had their energies absorbed in religous orders.[34] An anonymous reponse retorted that English old maids were neither despised nor frustrated, but,

. . . we are quite ready to accept our share of the charge. It may be sentimental to side with the weak . . . to deal blows with a parasol rather than applaud a skilfully conducted experiment, to prefer humanity to science . . . But the fact remains. The English public is largely composed of men and women with warm hearts and tender consciences, and both, and particularly of late, the women are beginning to think and act, and form their own judgements on matters they hitherto took for granted.[35]

For vivisectors to attack ladies would have given support to the charge that they were ungentlemanly. Yet when women such as Cobbe claimed the right to act for 'themselves', they were undermining the grounds for being treated with special 'courtesy'. How, then, should they be treated in public life? The implications of Cobbe's claims for women's right to speak in the public sphere were dramatically demonstrated in 1892. Victor Horsley, outspoken and ebullient surgeon and vivisector, delivered a swingeing attack on the morality of anti-vivisectionists at the Church Congress at Folkestone.

He cited, as an example of the 'rankest imposture', *The Nine Circles*, a book describing a large number of experiments as 'tortures'. Cobbe had stated in the preface that all the descriptions were 'verbatim extracts with reference to the actual reports of the vivisectors themselves'. Horsley declared that reference to the use of anaesthesia had been deliberately omitted for twenty of the experiments described.[36] Cobbe's initial response was denial and counter-attack. Horsley's conduct showed that 'the conscience even of eminent vivisectors are like their victims' nerves, imperfectly under the influence of the scientific anaesthetic'. Horsley reiterated his charge in even blunter 'Anglo-Saxon': Cobbe was a liar. If, as she had so often claimed, ladies had a superior moral sense, then Cobbe was no lady. In the ensuing public exchanges, the question of the truth about Horsley's allegations was lost beneath controversy over the propriety of Horsley's behaviour. The dominant issues became, first, his claim that Cobbe's conduct deprived her of the consideration normally accorded ladies and, secondly, her short-lived attempt at a dignified withdrawal claiming the privileges of womanhood.[37]

Horsley was one of the most hated animal experimenters, and, after 1892, anti-vivisectionists described him as a stigmatiser of women.[38] But his attack on Cobbe cannot be dismissed immediately as prejudice against women in public life. He was an equally outspoken advocate of women's suffrage as of vivisection. Later, he was a leader of the medical opposition to force-feeding of imprisoned suffragettes.[39] In interpreting the exchanges between anti-vivisectionists and their critics, we should not forget that we are examining propaganda on both sides.

Women and anti-vivisection societies

Was this image of a woman-dominated movement, shared by both sides, a justified one? Evidence of the membership of anti-vivisection societies sheds some light on this, but needs to be treated with caution. As for most contemporary social questions, societies against vivisection proliferated in this period, often attacking each other as vehemently as vivisection itself. But disquiet about vivisection was clearly not confined to those who joined societies. Societies' membership was mainly middle and upper class. French suggests that societies' efforts to arouse working-class sympathies, couched 'mostly in tones of righteous and fiery oratory or outright condescension', fell on deaf ears in the 1870s and 1880s. Lansbury has recently suggested that there was substantial male working-class support in Battersea in the 1900s, and this needs further investigation.[40]

Not all middle- and upper-class opponents of vivisection joined societies enthusiastically. (Indeed, Cobbe herself established a specifically anti-vivisection society with reluctance in 1875. She knew it meant giving up, at the age of fifty-three, her life of independent philanthropy and crusading journalism.) Some might have disagreed with the tactics or the abolitionist position of most societies between 1876 and the 1890s.[41] But the majority of those who joined the major societies were women. Women were about 70 per cent of members of the Victoria Street Society, and of the International Association for the Total Suppression of Vivisection (merged with the VSS in 1883) throughout the period.[42] The much older RSPCA also had a majority of women members, rising from 50 per cent in 1850 to 69 per cent (of a larger total) in 1900.[43] Towards the end of the nineteenth century the majority of members of most major philanthropic societies were women. But women's subscriptions did not necessarily carry the same weight as men's, or entitle them to leadership positions.[44]

Leadership of such societies lay with three groups. Paid officials were formally subordinate to the other two groups: titular leaders — presidents, patrons and vice-patrons — whose eminent names

lent respectability and prestige to the cause, and executive committee members who managed the day-to-day work of societies. In anti-
vivisection societies, paid workers in the period were few and almost
all male. French states that 40 to 60 per cent of the titular and
executive leadership of anti-vivisection societies was female. He con-
trasts this with the RSPCA where, he says, women were denied an
active role, being excluded from the RSPCA General Council until
1896.[45] But closer inspection suggests a more complex picture.

Though, in practice, symbolic leaders might be active, and some
executive committee members passive, their formal functions were
different. And so, often, was the sex composition. Cobbe revealed
the importance of titular leaders when she wrote, 'Lord Shaftesbury
[President] never joined the Victoria Street Society, it was around
him, and attracted in great part by his name that the whole body
eventually gathered.'[46] In the 1870s, outside the Royal Family and
the aristocracy, there were few women whose names would give lustre
to the anti-vivisectionist cause. And some royal women and peeresses
might have been unable or reluctant to lend their names publicly
to such a controversial cause, even though they privately supported
it.[47]

When the Victoria Street Society was founded, the president and
all the vice-presidents were male. By 1890, only three of the thirty-
three were women, all peeresses.[48] In the 1870s and 1880s, it was
controversial for women to serve on the executive committees of
societies dedicated to 'the masculine form of philanthropy — large
and comprehensive measures, organizations and systems planned
by men and sanctioned by parliament'.[49] Yet the first executive
committee of the Victoria Street Society, in 1876, had five women
and eight men, and a woman (Cobbe) as an Honorary Secretary.
It is one of only twelve major philanthropic societies with mixed
management identified by Prochaska in the period.[50] Thereafter,
until 1900, the sex balance was approximately even, or women were
the majority. Women were in the majority on the executive committee of the BUAV at its foundation in 1898.[51] But approval of
women committee members was not universal.

In 1881, an advertisement for the International Association for
the Total Suppression of Vivisection listed only male executive committee members, though adding that supporters included 'many
ladies of distinction'.[52] The theosophist Edward Maitland described
the Association's committee at the time, as carrying 'the traditional
antagonism of the priest to the woman to the extreme extent of refusing to allow one of that sex to appear in public as a teacher

on any subject whatever', let alone join the committee. An exception was made for Anna Kingsford, MD. Having studied medicine in Paris to aid her crusade against vivisection and meat-eating, Kingsford 'though a woman by her sex, . . . was a man by her mind and her profession . . . I [Maitland] hailed [the exception] as a sign of the times . . . at last the "woman" was in very deed to "crush the head of the serpent" of the corrupt orthodoxy hitherto in possession.'[53] Maitland celebrated by publishing a pamphlet, *The Woman and the Age*, under the name of the International Association. In theosophical language, he argued that vivisection represented the renunciation by scientists and society of the female side of human nature for the rational, calculative side. Women, as symbols and representatives of the moral and spiritual side of human nature, should be, and were, active in suppressing this evil. Only this offered hope for moral evolution. The pamphlet was disowned by the Association's committee, and Maitland and Kingsford resigned.[54]

Though barred from election to the General Council until 1896, women did have an active place in, or association with, the RSPCA before then. They were more prominent as titular leaders than in anti-vivisection societies. At least one-third of patrons were women from 1850 onwards. Chief among these were Queen Victoria, patron of the Society from 1835 until her death, and Angela Burdett Coutts, supporter of many human and animal causes.[55] The RSPCA encouraged its less prudent members to work outside the main society, by forming rescue homes and species-specific missions. Many of these were started by women, perhaps seeking an executive role denied them within the RSPCA. Best known of these was the Home for Lost and Starving Dogs started in 1860, which moved to Battersea in 1871.[56] In RSPCA tradition, it was run throughout the period by a committee composed mainly of aristocrats and scientific experts, but including some women. The scientists' presence, and fear that rescued dogs would be used for vivisection, meant that annual meetings were often the scene of bitter argument. In 1882, Cobbe, her friend Miss Lloyd and Lord Shaftesbury resigned from the Dogs' Home committee when a known supporter of vivisection was permitted to be a candidate.[57]

Of all the RSPCA's activities, one, educating the public (especially children) against cruelty, was considered pre-eminently suitable for women. In 1869, this was formalised through the Ladies Humane-Education Committee (LHEC) with Burdett Coutts as president. The editor of *Animal World*, the RSPCA journal, reassured his readers:

As we stated before, and cannot repeat too often, 'it is not proposed to identify ladies with agencies for the prosecution of offenders, which functions would probably alarm as they would perplex and annoy them. Their vocation is peculiarly to influence the children, youth and adults of all classes with whom they associate, or whom they meet during their eleemosynary visits. Far more effectually than men, they can awaken minds and soften hearts — indeed it is to their influence we must look for the humane education of the people.'[58]

Though, initially, the LHEC was represented in public by men and its meetings chaired by the president of the General Council or his deputy, the LHEC's president attended General Council meetings *ex officio*. Coutts may have had some influence on the council and on RSPCA policy, not least because of her huge wealth. In 1875, *Animal World* published a leading article denying it was solely an organ for Coutts's views.[59] Coutts had opposed the 1876 bill, because it did not go far enough in limiting vivisection. But she was outvoted in RSPCA discussions and the RSPCA gave the bill qualified support. She was one of the first to call publicly for the withdrawal of subscriptions from hospitals where vivisection was practised. Coutts and Queen Victoria are alleged to have withheld donations to Edinburgh University, because satisfactory assurances of the absence of vivisection were not given.[60] While Longford exaggerates in suggesting that without Queen Victoria's pressure the 1876 Act would 'not have seen the light of day', it was one factor that led Disraeli to set up the 1875 Royal Commission. She expressed a horror of animal experiments *and* of dissection and the study of anatomy, especially by women, in her correspondence.[61]

Queen Victoria and Coutts symbolised and shaped the role of women in the RSPCA. Without their pressure, the RSPCA's policy on vivisection might have been even more cautious. If their role was hidden from public gaze compared with the parts played by Cobbe and Kingsford, this was in accord with their interpretation of what women's role in public life should be. The different views about women's leadership of anti-vivisection societies that I have identified reflected contemporary controversies about women's place. Any movement in which women sought to play an active and public part in the 1870s and 1880s was inescapably entangled with 'the woman question' — because 'the woman question' was mainly about the place and role of women in public life. In this sense, to claim an association between women's activity in organised anti-vivisection and the women's movement in late nineteenth-century feminism is tautologous. But this does not explain why women, in particular middle- and upper-class women, were so concerned about vivisection and animal welfare.

Why anti-vivisection was a woman's cause

Establishing the motivation for individual women's anti-vivisectionist commitment is a difficult task, but it is possible to analyse why the cause might have appealed more to women, and to examine the reasons that anti-vivisectionists themselves gave for its being a woman's cause. These reasons were mostly put forward to inspire others, and should be read accordingly, but they were clearly believed by many. In the poem at the beginning of the chapter two reasons for women's involvement were implied: women's ignorance of science and their sentimentality. These may have played a part, but do not entirely explain women's involvement.

Most nineteenth-century women were ignorant of science and scientific method, but so were most men. Many anti-vivisectionist women were no more ignorant of science than many of the experimentalists' supporters. Some had medical degrees. More generally, to put ignorance forward as a reason for anti-vivisectionist beliefs implies that scientific knowledge in itself leads to approval of animal experimentation. To attribute women's anti-vivisectionism to their greater sentimentality towards animals presupposes that women actually were more sentimental than men, and that sentimentality was a key motivating factor in anti-vivisection. But as French has shown, nineteenth-century anti-vivisectionism was far more than a movement of animal lovers or scientific ignoramuses.[62]

The implied association between women and sentimentality brings us back to nineteenth-century ideology about women's nature, to the association of women with feelings not reason, and with nature not culture. This ideological association was more complex and less rigid than has sometimes been implied. If women were governed by emotions then this was held to be reason for both their superstitiousness and their guardianship of emotional matters. It was the grounds of both their scientific backwardness and their responsibility for tradition and the maintenance of moral standards. Women were part of nature and had a fundamental civilising role. Describing these ideas as ideologies does not imply they were the

271

direct reflection of material conditions or that they uniformly determined women's lives. Rather, they provided the images and the terms in which controversy over woman's nature and woman's place might be argued. Whether or not women actually were more sentimental cannot be disentangled from this.[63]

In the aftermath of the Industrial Revolution, with its physical separation of home and work, this ideology was elaborated in the idea of men's and women's separate sphere of influence. The public sphere of politics and industry was men's sphere, the private, domestic sphere women's. Women's work, their mission, was to safeguard the home. For middle- and upper-class women, this work was, in time, extended into a mission to those who were less fortunate than themselves, into the homes of the working class, even to the whole of society, on a strictly personal basis. This was feminine philanthropy: not just charity, but moral reform. 'The pure woman was enabled by the very possession of her purity to understand and to help the impure far better than the most sympathetic man.'[64] Animal welfare was, for some, part of this civilising role. Those who maltreated beasts were themselves 'beasts'. Anti-vivisection could be represented as part of moral reform, part of woman's duty to help the helpless and purify the impure. This vision of women's mission was compatible both with an alliance of all women and with taking responsibility, analogous to motherhood, for those who could not help themselves — children, fallen women and animals.

Far from rigidly determining women's roles, these ideas were to prove malleable tools. Initially, women's mission implied only the 'eleemosynary' influence typified by the RSPCA's LHEC. But, for women like Josephine Butler and Cobbe, it was the grounds for extending women's influence to the public sphere. This was, they claimed, not at odds with women's guardianship of the domestic sphere, but the means by which this could be guaranteed. If pure women had no influence on public life through their 'wise maternity', immoral laws would continue, condoning (male) injustice, vice and cruelty, degrading women and, hence, society.[65] Thus, philanthropy was an important base for that strand of nineteenth-century feminism which shared much of its vision of women's role with opponents of women's active participation in the public sphere.[66]

Links between anti-vivisection, philanthropy and the women's movement were spelt out in Cobbe's prolific writing. Her Theism and her intuitionist moral philosophy, based on Kant and Bishop Butler, provided an unbroken thread throughout her essays.[67] From Kant, and like Wollstonecraft, she asserted that women, like men, were free moral agents. How else, she demanded, could one speak of women's moral duties? These were primarily to their families and to themselves, but also to society. Duties could be fulfilled in the active campaigning way Cobbe herself preferred, or through personal influence, by shunning vivisectors and the unchaste. She campaigned for the franchise, reform of marriage laws, higher education and many other reforms for women, in order that they should better pursue their duty. Women would become more, not less virtuous, and, as a result, so would men. Moral reform meant abolition of double standards of morality for men and women, raising each sex to the highest standard. Women's courage should be fostered so that it could be judged by the same standards as men's. Far more fundamentally, men must be subject to the same standards of chastity as women. If emancipation were to result in women adopting typically male vices, unchastity, intemperance and cruelty, then it was better never obtained.[68]

Cruelty, for Cobbe, was the most evil of vices. One of her earliest campaigns had been for the legal protection of women subjected to 'wife-torture'.[69] To her, it was an intuitive moral truth, akin to a mathematical law, that cruelty was wrong. Arguments from utility, that pain for a few might benefit many, were, for her, irrelevant. What was morally wrong could not be justified by its consequences. Humans, she argued, had moral duties towards all creatures with the capacity to suffer, a view she explicitly attributed to Bishop Butler, not Bentham. She went beyond Kant's view, that the evils of animal cruelty lay *solely* in its degrading effects on its exponents. But she spoke only of the moral 'claims' of animals, not of rights, because animals had no duties. Animals were not autonomous agents. Initially she placed the claims of animals below the claims of humans, whose duty was to avoid unnecessary pain.[70] Later, she was to 'raise considerably the "claims" . . . of brutes', convinced that animal suffering could not be prevented by anaesthesia. Cruelty *deliberately* inflicted on a helpless animal was the worst possible form. The *knowing* cruelty of scientists, was more evil than blood sports (which she opposed) and farming (she was not vegetarian).[71]

Abolition of double standards, rejection of arguments based on utility, and vindication of individuals' autonomy, were themes shared with many contemporary moral reform campaigns and with the earlier anti-slavery movement, repeatedly held up by anti-vivisectionists as a paradigm.[72] Anti-vivisection had especially strong affinities with campaigns against compulsory smallpox vaccination and the Contagious Diseases (CD) Acts and the associated campaign for sexual purity. Organised opposition to compulsory vaccination began in 1871, as the mandatory appointment of vaccination officers in all localities heralded implementation of the previously unenforced 1853 Vaccination Act. The CD Acts, passed in 1864, 1866 and 1869, established state regulation of prostitution in garrison towns. Women suspected of prostitution were subject to compulsory medical inspection, and, if found to have venereal disease, to compulsory detention in 'lock' hospitals. Action against them began in 1869 and continued until their suspension in 1883 and repeal in 1886. The controversial campaign of the Ladies' National Association against the Contagious Diseases Acts, inspired by Josephine Butler, pioneered women's involvement in 'masculine philanthropy'.[73]

Though more research is needed to establish the extent of overlapping involvement, a few individuals were certainly involved in all three. In Parliament, Duncan McLaren, William Cowper-Temple, W.E. Forster, James Stansfield, P.A. Taylor, A.J. Mundella and other 'metropolitan radicals', together with Russell Gurney, lent varying degrees of support to all three campaigns, just as Lyon Playfair and Lord Harcourt opposed them. William Shaen, chairman of the National Anti-Contagious Diseases Acts Association, was a 'great friend' of the anti-vivisectionist cause.[74] At least three of the thirty-three members of the executive board of the Ladies National Association were members of the Victoria Street Society.[75]

Whatever the actual overlap of support, from the mid-1880s anti-vivisectionists increasingly claimed links with the other two movements. Their successes were used to boost flagging anti-vivisection morale. As French points out, all three movements appealed to 'the same kinds of fears of, and hostilities toward, science and medicine.'[76] All three were campaigns against the increasing claims of science and medicine to the right to dictate morality and personal behaviour. When Josephine Butler attacked 'those terrible aristocratic doctors' who defended the vice of licentious gentlemen, and Frances Power Cobbe deplored the parvenu origins and attitudes of the new breed of self-seeking scientific doctors, they were making a similar point. The novelist Ouida captured this in her savage attack on *The New Priesthood*.[77] Concern was not just about the growing power and prestige of doctors, but about the very basis of practitioners' claims to authority, about what was becoming the basis of medical education, materialist science.

The CD Acts and vivisection alike ruptured the causal connections between sin and disease in ways which many Victorians found profoundly disturbing. The CD Acts allowed men to go unpunished for the consequences of sin, while the speculum symbolised the moral degradation medicine was imposing on women. Vivisection was the weapon by which the new materialist medical science was eliminating both vitalist concepts from physiology, and the links between physical health and moral order that were the foundation of sanitarian beliefs.[78] The discoveries of those 'scientific devils', Pasteur and Koch, reduced disease to a matter of chance encounters with germs. Far from relieving suffering, this led to obsessive concern with disease. Health, not virtue, was becoming the *summum bonum*, disease the greatest of evils, prevention or treatment justifying any vice. Cobbe termed this obsession with health 'Hygeiolatry'. The error and danger in materialism's rejection of the influence of mind over body was, for Cobbe, dramatically demonstrated by Pasteur's so-called cure for rabies. Far from curing this disease, Pasteur's claims engendered panic. This, not germs, was producing the symptoms in those who flocked to be killed by his methods.[79]

Attacks on materialist medicine took on a new dimension in the sector of the anti-vivisection movement that connected with the Fellowship of the New Life, spiritualism and, especially, Theosophy. Here again, women were prominent, and possibly predominant. The founder of the Theosophical Society in 1875, Madame Blavatsky, 'launched a spirited attack on the "twin tyrannies" of contemporary institutionalised religion and materialistic science, lambasting the Pope and T.H. Huxley with equal fervour'.[80] Annie Besant had once been a cautious defender of vivisection, resisting the attempts of Anna Kingsford to convince her of the evils of the practice. But when her growing dissatisfacton with materialist philosophy coincided with receiving *The Secret Doctrine* to review in 1889, she turned away from Western science's aggressive interrogation of nature to Eastern science 'which uses as its scientific instruments the penetrating faculties of the mind alone'.[81]

Burfield suggests that Theosophy appealed especially to women because of the opportunities it offered for leadership and self-expression. Central to theosophical doctrine is the idea that the body is only a temporary vessel for the immortal soul on its evolutionary journey from mineral to spiritual form. Reincarnation can successively take male or female forms, human or animal. Each soul has within itself both male and female natures. Hence, Theosophy provided grounds for women's claim to equality with men, on the grounds of complementarity, two halves of a single soul. It was also compatible with a militant feminism that identified male nature with materialism, carnality and evil, and female with moral superiority and spiritual love, as in the writing of Frances Swiney.[82] And, for some, it was the basis of a vehement opposition to feminism as promoting the male qualities of women at the expense of their female ones, as in the writing of Arabella Kenealy, qualified doctor, novelist, anti-vivisectionist and eugenicist.[83] Theosophist women holding all three positions were involved in anti-vivisection, for experiment on live animals was torture of past and future souls.

Anna Kingsford (1846–88) is probably the best known of the anti-vivisectionist Theosophists. She had been an active suffrage campaigner in the early 1870s when editor of *The Ladies Own Paper*. Later, according to her companion and biographer, Edward Maitland, she withdrew active support, though still sympathising. For her, women's emancipation was to be gained through their demonstrating their capacity for serious work rather than clamouring for freedom and castigating men. But, for Kingsford, any reform that failed to campaign for the abolition of meat-eating was doomed, for it could never bring peace and harmony.[84] As a medical student in Paris from 1874 to 1880, she had set out secretly to prove that it was possible to qualify without witnessing a vivisectional experiment. She succeeded, not without difficulty, gaining her MD in 1880 with a controversial thesis on the merits of vegetarianism. Her anger at the injustice and inhumanity of the Paris vivisectionists led to her offering herself as a human subject for vivisection, and to launching spiritual maledictions against the worst offenders. She claimed responsibility for the deaths of Claude Bernard and Paul Bert as a result of these curses. Accounts of her dreams about animals' suffering in laboratories are suffused with theosophical imagery of the soul trapped in the suffering body.[85] After qualifying she was active in the anti-vivisection campaign, until her death in 1888, writing and lecturing all over Europe despite ill-health.[86] According to Maitland, she was subjected to personal vilification by Cobbe because she shared a house with him, not her husband, and because of Cobbe's jealousy of Kingsford's beauty, scientific knowledge and spiritual powers.[87] Cobbe was implacably hostile to spiritualism, to fads and asceticism, and she was a meat-eater.[88] But Cobbe and Kingsford shared an abhorrence of the arrogance of materialist medicine.

Women, vivisection and vice

Women had special reason to be concerned about changes in medicine. As wives and mothers, they were the guardians of family health. As women, they were especially vulnerable to doctors. The CD Acts were the most extreme manifestation of this. Women alone suffered the degradation of internal inspection, and loss of liberty. Male vice was explicitly condoned by the very existence of the Acts. How, Cobbe wondered, could one expect medical students, brutalised by their exposure to vivisection, to metamorphose overnight into respectable, courteous and caring doctors? She accused the medical profession of betraying the trust that ladies put in them. Far from improving ladies' health, as they claimed, doctors had failed to prevent their being trapped into a condition of *petite santé*, permanent valetudinarianism, a lucrative source of income for doctors.[89] But, because doctors needed them as patients, ladies had leverage, in anti-vivisectionist eyes. They could boycott vivisecting doctors.[90]

Anti-vivisectionist criticism of doctors' treatment of poor women was even sharper. Hospitals, especially teaching hospitals, were depicted as giant laboratories in which patients' interests were subordinated to doctors' research interests. After all, experiments on patients would avoid species error, so this was a logical step for the vivisectors. And, anti-vivisectionists claimed, it was already happening. Women and children, it was stressed, were especially at risk, thus appealing simultaneously to women as women and as mothers, and to male paternalism. The callous attitude of hospital doctors was produced by any contact with materialist medicine, not confined to vivisectors.

Frances Hoggan, MD, a member of the first executive committee of the Victoria Street Society, had studied in Zurich in the early 1870s. There students were exposed to the evil practice though they did not themselves vivisect. Hoggan described how hospital patients were evaluated as a 'greater or lesser quantity of material . . . If the feeling that prompts considerate treatment is conventional not genuine, the poor, and especially women of the poorer classes are sure to be the greatest sufferers.' Ten years later her descriptions were alluded to as ones 'you would quarrel with me for defiling my lips with', by a woman speaker at a national anti-vivisection conference.[91]

Disagreement among doctors was evidence to anti-vivisectionists of the hollowness of medical claims to scientific knowledge.

277

Gynaecology was one of the most controversial fields in medicine in the late nineteenth century. The difficult and dangerous operation of ovariotomy divided doctors as much as lay commentators in the 1870s and 1880s. And, in this controversy, the conflicts over materialist, experimental medicine and the values associated with it were clearly revealed. The death rates from ovariotomy were initially so high as to warrant the charge from within the profession, as well as from outside, that it was an experiment for the benefit of the surgeon not the woman. Moreover, ovariotomists were in public disagreement over the value of animal experiments in furthering safer techniques. But controversy did not diminish as mortality declined. The operation, and controversy over it, cannot be seen as a straightforward example of medical misogyny and feminist protest. Some women sought the operation and some benefited (eventually). Mosciucci suggests gynaecologists and wealthy patients may have sometimes colluded in abortion under the guise of therapeutic surgery.[92] Medical women were as divided as medical men. Frances Hoggan had resigned from the New Hospital for Women over Elizabeth Garrett Anderson's decision to undertake one in 1872. Elizabeth Blackwell, the first woman on the British Medical Register, active moral reformer, sanitarian and anti-vivisectionist, was a remorseless critic of the *prurigo secandi* (itch to cut) in gynaecology, criticising male and female doctors alike.[93]

Anti-vivisectionists were also divided over ovariotomy. On the one hand, they condemned the experimental attitude that led to over-zealous operating, and the use of rabbits in preparatory experimental work by surgeons such as Spencer Wells. On the other hand, they claimed as a supporter the flamboyant Birmingham surgeon, Robert Lawson Tait, one of Spencer Wells's greatest rivals and critics as an ovariotomist, and a man whose surgical career was ended by an accusation that he had performed an abortion on one of his nurses. Tait himself was often accused of over-operating by other doctors. Mary Putnam Jacobi, an American doctor well known for her experimental work with animals, condemned his disregard for the well-being of women. She, in turn, was attacked by the editor of the BUAV journal: 'Her standpoint may be readily understood from her statement that Lawson Tait "while objecting to experiments on frogs and rabbits devoted his life to the vivisection of women." This, of course, is the lady vivisectionist's way of alluding to the great number of suffering women cured by his skill as an ovariotomist.'[94]

In 1894, public attention was drawn to the high mortality rates at the Chelsea Hospital for Women, where Spencer Wells was a senior surgeon. This coincided with the construction of a new 'temple to materialism' in Chelsea, the Institute for Preventive Medicine. Many anti-vivisectionist public meetings and demonstrations were held in the district. The resignation of staff at the Chelsea Hospital, including Spencer Wells, was claimed as a victory for the cause. The twenty-nine women who had died were mourned as martyrs, though the official enquiry emphasised defective drains, not excessive surgery, as the main cause of the deaths.[95]

Underlying the controversy over ovariotomy in the 1870s and 1880s was not just technical success but the values that the operation symbolised, and threatened. The key question was whether it *unsexed* women. Destroying women's essence was, to critics, the ultimate example of Bernard's analogy between vivisection and surgery, the investigative attitude taken to its logical extremes, reducing the living patient to animal or even inanimate status. The operation was described as 'spaying' or even as 'vivisection' by doctors, as well as by its lay critics.[96] The language of the controversy over ovariotomy reveals the sexual imagery which permeated contemporary medical and anti-vivisectionist writings. Male scientists strip and penetrate female nature.[97] It is clear in Cobbe's writings.

> Nature has veiled between her beautiful covering of skin her secret workings . . . and other still more wonderful and sacred mysteries of these fleshly tabernacles wherein human spirits sojourn on their way to the eternal world. Not rudely and irreverently can those mysteries be explored without injury to the finer susceptibilities and modesties of humanity, least of all the young.[98]

The metaphor of medical science, and medical practice on women, as rape, became a dominant theme in anti-vivisection literature, especially that written by women, from the 1880s onwards. Women were explicitly invited to identify themselves with the animals, as potential victims of sexual assault by materialist medical men. This sexual imagery was a key link between anti-vivisectionist claims and a much wider public debate about sexual morality in the late nineteenth and early twentieth century. Anti-vivisectionism drew on and became an outlet for this concern. In the early 1870s, the campaign against the CD Acts was controversial. But by the 1880s it had gained respectability and become part of a wider campaign around sexual purity and the 'double standard'.[99] This was the movement with which anti-vivisectionists claimed alliance. Cobbe had originally thought the CD Acts regrettable necessities. Her disillusionment with doctors over vivisection brought about a radical change of mind. In the words of one obituarist, from the end of the 1870s she strove unceasingly to 'establish the solidarity of the two great vices, of cruelty and sensuality'.[100]

From the mid-1880s, 'White Slavery', the age of consent, venereal disease and chastity for both sexes all became subjects for public debate, arousing concern among men and women, feminists and anti-feminists. Ellice Hopkins's White Cross Army built on the alliances forged between middle-class women and working-class men in the CD Acts campaign, fighting for male chastity and continence. Feminists involved with the Social Purity Union argued for women's right to control access to their own bodies in and outside of marriage, for celibacy as a normal way of living, free of male control, and, in some cases, for 'psychic love' as superior to mere carnality. This militant feminist critique of male sexuality was to be dramatically expressed at the height of the suffrage campaign in the militant Women's Social and Political Union's slogan 'Votes for Women, Chastity for Men' and in Christabel Pankhurst's pamphlet *The Great Scourge and How to End It*, which claimed that 75 per cent of men had venereal disease.[101]

These concerns were echoed in contemporary fiction, especially in the 'New Woman' novels of the 1880s and 1890s, in which calls for women's emancipation were combined with the 'revolting' topics of divorce, marital violence and venereal disease. The term 'New Woman' is attributed to 'Madame' Sarah Grand, didactic novelist, anti-vivisectionist and sexual purity campaigner. In her best-selling, loosely autobiographical *The Beth Book*, first published in 1897, the heroine has put up with her medical husband's jealousy, his coarseness about his female patients, and even the revelation of the degradation of womanhood in the Lock Hospital where he worked. But when she discovers he has vivisected a dog in his study, 'from that time forward everything he did was an offence to Beth'. She confronts her husband, contrasting the nobility of traditional doctors with the callousness of vivisectors, obsessed with 'zymotic diseases' like measles or smallpox, 'nature's way of ensuring the survival of the fittest, often leaving no permanent mark on the human constitution', while conniving at 'the spread of the worst disease to which we are liable'. Beth condemns the double standard under which no official action is taken against men with venereal disease. Women, however, are subjected to public humiliation, degrading and brutal physical examinations and deprived of their liberty, to 'make vice safe for men'.[102]

This was the context in which women and animals alike were portrayed as the victims of the sexually depraved monster, the vivisector. Physiologists' enthusiastic accounts of their work were seized on as evidence of barbarism. This 'Sadeism', as it was explicitly termed by 1901, was not confined to the laboratory.[103]

> Besides these horrors [in laboratories] do we not see every-day no less disgusting experiments practised on the lunatics and hysterical patients in the Salpetrière? The nurses drag these unfortunate women, not withstanding their cries and resistance, before men who make them fall into catalepsy. They play on these organisms . . . on which experiment strains the nervous system and aggravates the morbid conditions, as if it were an instrument . . . One of my friends told me that she . . . had seen a doctor of great reputation make one unhappy patient pass, without transition from a celestial beatitude to a condition of infamous sensualment. And this before a company of literary men and men of the world.[104]

The horrendous series of murders of women in Whitechapel in 1888, the work of 'Jack the Ripper', occasioned widespread concern about the dangers of unrestrained male sexuality in which doctors, especially vivisectors, figured strongly. Cobbe suggested that female detectives' 'mother wit' might be quicker than conventional male police methods in finding the murderer. She also commended a proposal to use bloodhounds: 'Should it so fall out that the demon of Whitechapel prove really to be . . . a physiologist delirious with cruelty, and should the hounds be the means of his capture, poetic justice will be complete.'[105]

The lady vivisector

If vivisecting indicated depravity in a man, in a woman it would be even more horrendous. As women entered new fields and took up activities hitherto confined to men, some anti-vivisectionists became preoccupied with the consequences. After the 1880s, the anti-vivisectionists' cause was linked not only to calls for reform of men's sexual morality and the demands of women for justice but also to fears about the changing place of women. And these fears were expressed by women as well as men. In the animal welfare movement as a whole, there was much concern at the increasingly frequent public spectacle of women attending the pigeon *battues* at Hurlingham, riding to hounds, wearing spurs and controlling their horses with harsh bits. This concern was as much about women's enjoying such activities as about animal suffering. And, many asserted, women, once aroused, would be far crueller than men.[106]

Women contaminated by the evil practice became a target for anti-vivisectionist criticism. Those whose contact was enforced and acknowledged as repulsive were represented as victims of their fiendish masters. Madame Bernard, known to have been unhappily married, was a potent symbol.[107] Wives who did not dissociate themselves from their husbands' work were castigated. When George Eliot endowed a physiology scholarship as a memorial to G.H. Lewes, she was condemned as a woman who had 'never shrunk from the frightful experiments of the man she called her husband . . . Naturally enough it is those who, like George Eliot, have lost faith in the existence of a higher life than this, who are most prone to fall down and worship the modern Moloch and offer it holocausts of harmless victims.'[108]

For Cobbe, if improved education for girls meant teaching of the new physiology, 'then should we mourn that that education had ever been heard of . . . '[109] From the 1880s onwards the anti-vivisection journals carry scores of items about regrettable lectures at women's colleges.[110] Oxford and Cambridge, where the influence of physiologists such as Burdon Sanderson and Foster might be felt, were particularly closely scrutinised. In 1881, Mrs Burdon Sanderson was proposed for election to the council of Somerville Hall, Oxford. Cobbe protested that this was an insult to the memory of her friend, the late Mary Somerville, who had signed the memorial against Schiff in Florence in 1863. Association with the name of Burdon Sanderson would 'prejudice not only Somerville Hall, but in a measure the whole movement for the advancement of female education, . . . for which I have personally pleaded publicly and privately, through a long life-time.' Subsequent correspondence revealed further insult. The women students of Somerville were attending Burdon Sanderson's lectures.[111] In 1891, a rumour that women students were actually doing vivisection in Cambridge was denied by Mrs Sidgwick, who disapproved of Cobbe's anti-vivisectionist literature as itself hardening and demoralising to women.[112]

If women's contact with vivisection was corrupting, what then of women doctors? Many anti-vivisectionists had been active supporters of women's access to medical education in the 1860s and 1870s. Cobbe had clearly hoped that medical women would be a bulwark against male, materialist medicine.[113] But, in 1881, she warned: 'The entrance [of women] into the medical profession is a danger. It is *possible* that there may arise such a monster as a woman vivisector, a female Schiff or Bernard, though, thank God, as yet there are no signs of such ignominy.'[114] Initially, Cobbe's hopes may have been fulfilled. At least nine of the fifty-five British women known to have had formal medical qualifications by 1885 took part in some public anti-vivisectionist activity. These included Elizabeth Blackwell, Anna Kingsford, Frances Hoggan and Arabella Kenealy.[115] Kingsford began medical studies to further the anti-vivisectionist cause. In Blackwell's case, anti-vivisection was part of her vision of medicine as moral reform, and her opposition to all forms of materialism. For her, medicine should be the exercise of 'spiritual maternity'. It was medical women's task to ensure this was so.[116] Views like hers, based on the ideology of women's mission to women, that women doctors would enable women to have medical treatment while preserving their modesty and delicacy, had been a central argument in the public campaign for women to gain access to medical education in the 1860s and 1870s.[117]

But Cobbe's fears were soon proved to be justified, first of all overseas. In July 1881, anti-vivisectionist Edward Berdoe reported Mary Putnam's 'cruel system' in New York. 'Think of that, you who have daughters at Girton College.'[118] A *Vivisectors' Directory* for 1884 included one woman, Hope Bridges Adams. She was on the British Medical Register, but working in Germany.[119] In Britain, after the 1880s, active opposition to vivisection was confined to a tiny minority among women doctors, though no woman held a Home Office licence until 1898. Because of the sensitivity of the issue, the main women's medical school, the London School of Medicine for Women (LSMW), did not register with the Home Office for live animal experiments until after the Royal Commission on Vivisection's Final Report in 1912, in favour of vivisection subject to legal control.[120]

One factor behind the decline of active anti-vivisection among medical women, as their number slowly grew, was their increasing socialisation into the values of experimental medicine. As curricula changed under the auspices of the General Medical Council's education committee, women medical students, as well as men, had to study experimental physiology to obtain a registerable qualification.[121] And they were taught, as anti-vivisectionists became

aware, by some of the leading physiologists in London and Edinburgh, in lectures in their own schools and through attending lectures and demonstrations in men's schools. This did not go
uncontested. Anti-vivisectionists regularly sought, and, until 1912,
received, reassurance that vivisection was not actually carried out
in the LSMW. Some, such as Elizabeth Blackwell and her friend,
Mrs Woolcott Browne, were members of the LSMW's Executive
Council or Governors, and tried to limit the physiologists' influence.
But they were remote from the day-to-day teaching organised by
such men as Sharpey-Schafer, lecturer at the LSMW from 1877 to
1883, and chairman of the school's curriculum subcommittee from
1892 to 1897, or Halliburton, lecturer from 1886 to 1897.[122]

Moreover, with the possible exception of the midwifery teacher,
Annie McCall MD, the women teachers were not actively opposed
to the 'new physiology'. The surgeon, Mary Scharlieb, described
Burdon Sanderson as 'a saint' and she and her children shared a
house with the Schafers for many years. The first woman Dean of
the school, Elizabeth Garrett Anderson, stressed the need for women
to get as good a scientific training as men, publicly criticising the
activity of anti-vivisectionists, though recognising the sensitivity of
the issue, and the undesirability of unnecessary experiments or
hardening of students.[123] Most of the women teachers did not fully
embrace Blackwell's vision of women's special spiritual mission in
medicine. They and, increasingly, their younger students, sought
equality within the profession, rather than a special place. This tension between equality and a special role for women seeking a place
within the medical profession was hinted at as early as 1875. At an
anti-vivisection meeting a woman medical student declared, 'she
did not object to women performing experiments, but on the contrary she contended that whatever a man might do, a woman had
a right to do if she so desired', a very different view of feminism,
and of women's role in medicine, from Cobbe's or Blackwell's.[124]

The fact that women medical students were learning the 'new
physiology' was to give two women anti-vivisectionists, Liesa von
Schartau and Louisa Lind-af-Hageby, an opportunity to extend their
scientific knowledge and supply fresh ammunition for the cause.
They enrolled for physiology classes at the LSMW in 1902, and
gained permission to attend physiology lectures in other institutions
in the University of London. On 2 February 1903, they attended
their first lecture at which 'real vivisection' (by which they meant
a cutting operation) took place, the third in a series of ten given

by W.M. Bayliss on 'The Mechanism of the Secretory Process' at University College. What they claimed to have seen there, an unanaesthetised 'brown dog of the terrier type' struggling in agony, set in train a series of events whose ramifications are still part of the vivisection controversy in Britain in the 1980s.[125]

Their claims, publicised by Stephen Coleridge, Honorary Secretary of the NAVS, led Bayliss to sue Coleridge for libel. At the sensational trial, in November 1903, Bayliss obtained a verdict against Coleridge and damages of £2,000. Lind-af-Hageby and von Schartau withdrew *The Shambles of Science*, the published diary of their experiences as physiology students, for revision.[126] The libel trial, and the evidence on physiologists' practices revealed there, was one factor behind the establishment of the Second Royal Commission on Vivisection in 1906. A statue commemorating the Brown Dog was erected, in 1906, in Battersea. This, in turn, became the focus of attacks by riotous medical students, further legal actions and furious political argument within Battersea Council before being removed and destroyed in 1910. In 1985, a new 'Brown Dog' statue was erected in Battersea and it is, again, a tangible symbol of anti-vivisectionist ire.

The trial, and the events surrounding and succeeding it, exposed the tension between anti-vivisectionism, feminism and medicine. On the one hand, after 1903, male medical students disrupted suffrage meetings and anti-vivisectionist meetings alike with cries of 'Down with the Brown Dog'.[127] On the other hand, women medical students testified for Bayliss at the trial, denying the dog was unanaesthetised. This was surely a deliberate strategy on the part of Bayliss's counsel to defuse the sexual antagonism implicit in Lind-af-Hageby and von Schartau's charges. But it was further public demonstration that the 'woman vivisector' had arrived in spirit, if not in deed, in England. The 'ignominy' Cobbe feared had come about, and the fury and sense of betrayal among some anti-vivisectionists was intense. The authors of *The Shambles of Science* condemned this bitterly. 'It is degrading for a man to spend a life in acts of cruelty. In a woman the pernicious effects of such deeds is even more manifest.'[128] In this they echoed the words of Ouida when she warned her readers against the dangers of the *New Priesthood*. If medical men were bad, there was one even worse:

Woman, also, when once she is cruel, is tenfold more cruel than men, and when she is pitiless is a hundred-fold more pitiless than he, is now in the laboratory, causing and watching the agonies of tortured animals with all the thirst and avidity of the neophyte for the unknown. As the inquisitor had his female witch-searcher who drove the pins into the breast of his accused sorceresses, so the male physiologist has his female pupil, who may be trusted to outrun his teachings in ingenious cruelty and patient torture . . .[129]

The degrading effects of exposure to vivisection on male medical students had long been condemned by anti-vivisectionists. From the 1890s, and especially after the Brown Dog trial, reference to the doubly degrading and desexing effects of such exposure on women recurs in anti-vivisectionist writing.[130]

Conclusion

We seem to have come full circle. A movement that began by claiming women's special tenderness and kindness was, twenty years later, warning against women's capacity for evil and cruelty. Both claims had their roots in the ideological association of women with nature, with sentiment and emotional instability. Women were both more caring and more dangerous if their emotions became misdirected. Appealing to women's mission of moral reform could unite women and men, with very different views as to how that mission might be fulfilled, around vivisection. But it was an appeal that emphasised essential and 'natural' differences between women and men, and their associated spheres of life or interests. By the late nineteenth century, this emphasis co-existed uneasily with an alternative basis for feminism, the view that women had equal capacity and equal rights to compete with men in the public sphere, including in professional and scientific life. Within organisations established with the specific aims of furthering women's emancipation, women's clubs, suffrage societies and the like, vivisection, or opposition to it, was a controversial not a settled issue.[131]

Nineteenth-century anti-vivisection was undoubtedly a movement dominated numerically, and in its public image, by women. This meant the issue was inextricably caught up in contemporary controversy over women's role in public life. But the historical connections between organised anti-vivisection and the women's movement in the late nineteenth century were a great deal more complex than some modern commentators have suggested.

Acknowledgements

This chapter presents material from my unpublished MA thesis, 'Gender, Medicine and Morality in the late Nineteenth Century: A Study of the Anti-vivisection Movement 1870–1904', University of Essex, 1984, and from my forthcoming PhD thesis on the work of women in medicine. I am grateful to Nicolaas Rupke for advice on earlier drafts of this paper, and to Sandy Persaud for preparing the final typescript.

Notes

1. Quoted in *Zoophilist*, vol. v (1 May 1885), p. 1.
2. L. Rogers, *The Truth about Vivisection* (Churchill, London, 1937), p. 97.
3. C. Salamone, 'The Prevalence of the Natural Law Within Women: Women and Animal Rights,', in P. McAllister (ed.), *Reweaving the Web of Life* (New Society, Baltimore, 1982), pp. 365–8.
4. On the first, see P. Singer, *Animal Liberation: Towards an End to Man's Inhumanity to Animals* (Jonathan Cape, London, 1976: references to paperback edition, Thorsons Publishers, Northampton, 1980), p. x. On the second, see, for example, N. Benney, 'All of One Flesh: The Rights of Animals', in L. Caldecott and S. Leland (eds.), *Women Reclaim the Earth* (Women's Press, London, 1983), pp. 141–51; I. Newkirk, 'Animal Rights and the Feminist Connection', *Liberator* (March/April 1983), p. 11.
5. Singer, *Animal Liberation*, p. 1; M. Wollstonecraft, *Vindication of the Rights of Woman* (reprinted Everyman, London, 1929 and 1974); Anonymous [T. Taylor], *Vindication of the Rights of Brutes* (London, 1792).
6. On the dichotomy nature/culture in Enlightenment thought see J.B. Elshtain, *Public Man, Private Woman: Women in Social and Political Thought* (Princeton University Press, Princeton; Martin Robertson, Oxford, 1981), esp. pp. 147–70; S. Tomaselli, 'The Enlightenment Debate on Women', *History Workshop*, vol. 20 (Autumn 1985), pp. 101–24; L.J. Jordanova, 'Natural Facts: a Historical Perspective on Science and Sexuality', in C.P. MacCormack and M. Strathern (eds.), *Nature, Culture and Gender* (Cambridge University Press, Cambridge, 1980), pp. 42–69. On Wollstonecraft, see J. Rendell, *The Origins of Modern Feminism: Women in Britain, France and the United States* (Macmillan, London, 1985), pp. 55–66.
7. Singer, *Animal Liberation*, p. 8; quotation from J. Bentham, *Introduction to the Principles of Morals and Legislation* (1789), ch. 17–4.
8. Singer, *Animal Liberation*, p. 9.
9. Ibid., p. xii.
10. Newkirk, 'Animal Rights and the Feminist Connection', p. 11. Emphasis added. The 'us' are clearly women.
11. Benney, 'All of One Flesh', p. 144.
12. M. Daly, *Gyn/Ecology: The Metaethics of Radical Feminism* (Beacon Press, Boston, 1979), p. 414. Feminist arguments for the universality of the association include S.B. Ortner, 'Is Female to Male as Nature is to Culture?' in

M.Z. Rosaldo and L. Lamphere (eds.), *Women, Culture and Society* (Stanford University Press, Stanford, 1974), pp. 67–88 and S. Griffin, *Woman and Nature: The Roaring Inside* (Harper and Row, New York, 1978).

13. E.g. C. Merchant, *The Death of Nature: Women, Ecology and the Scientific Revolution* (Wildwood House, London, 1980); B. Easlea, *Science and Sexual Oppression: Patriarchy's Confrontation with Woman and Nature* (Weidenfeld and Nicolson, London, 1981). For criticisms see references in note 6 above and L. Birke, '"They're worse than animals": Animals and Biological Research' in L. Birke and J. Silvertown (eds.), *More than the Parts, Biology and Politics* (Pluto Press, London, 1984), pp. 219–35; L. Birke, *Women, Feminism and Biology* (Harvester, Brighton, 1986), pp. 107–25.

14. M. Midgley, *Animals and Why They Matter* (Penguin, London, 1983); J. Harris, *The Value of Life* (Routledge & Kegan Paul, London, 1985), esp. pp. 218–19. More hostile to Singer are B. Williams, *Ethics and the Limits of Philosophy* (Fontana, London, 1985), pp. 117–19, and R.G. Frey, *Rights, Killing and Suffering: Moral Vegetarianism and Applied Ethics* (Blackwell, Oxford, 1983), esp. pp. 103–17.

15. E.g. J. Radcliffe Richards, *The Sceptical Feminist* (Routledge & Kegan Paul, London, 1980); J.B. Elshtain, *Public Man, Private Woman*, esp. pp. 201–27; Tomaselli, 'The Enlightenment Debate on Women'.

16. Singer, *Animal Liberation*, p. 246.

17. On nineteenth-century feminisms, see O. Banks, *Faces of Feminism* (Martin Robertson, London, 1981).

18. Elston, 'Gender, Medicine and Morality'. On Cobbe, see ibid., pp. 64–94; F.P. Cobbe, *Life of Frances Power Cobbe told by herself*, with additions by the author and Introduction by Blanche Atkinson (Swann Sonnenschein, London, 1904); French, *Antivivisection and Medical Science in Victorian Society* (Princeton University Press, Princeton, 1975), pp. 241–5. The Victoria Street Society was renamed the National Anti-Vivisection Society (NAVS) at the time of the split. Both the BUAV and the NAVS are active in the 1980s.

19. J. Walkowitz, *Prostitution and Victorian Society* (Cambridge University Press, Cambridge, 1980).

20. Elston, 'Gender, Medicine and Morality', pp. 36–63; S. Coleridge, *Memories* (John Lane, The Bodley Head, London, 1913).

21. E. Garrett Anderson, 'The Ethics of Vivisection', *Edinburgh Review* (July 1899), pp. 147–69; Letter Mrs Sidgwick to Mrs Henry Fawcett (circa Spring 1891), Fawcett Library Autograph Letter Collection; *Zoophilist*, vol. xix (May 1899), p. 77.

22. Elston, 'Gender, Medicine and Morality', pp. 95–123.

23. French, *Antivivisection*, pp. 239–40.

24. E.g. *Zoophilist*, vol. i (1882), p. 240; vol. xvii (1897), p. 87.

25. French, *Antivivisection*, p. 248. Two editors of the feminist *Englishwoman's Review*, Jessie Boucherett and Caroline Ashurst Biggs, supported the cause. See *Englishwoman's Review* (1875), pp. 81–2, 180–1, 274–5; (1876), pp. 173–5, 259–62, 319–20; (1877), pp. 135–7, 219–23. *Shafts*, a feminist periodical of the 1890s, also gave support.

26. Lord Coleridge, 'The Nineteenth Century Defenders of Vivisection', *Nineteenth Century*, vol. 11 (1882) (reprinted as VSS pamphlet, London, *c.* 1882).

27. M. Thornhill, *The Clergy and Vivisection*, 1884, quoted in *Zoophilist*, vol. iii (1 Feb. 1884), p. 250. Stevenson has drawn attention to the frequency

of crucifixion metaphors in anti-vivisectionist writings. L.G. Stevenson, 'Religious Elements in the Background of the British Anti-Vivisection Movement', *Yale Journal of Biology and Medicine*, vol. xxix (1956), pp. 125–57.

28. F.P. Cobbe, *A Charity and a Controversy* (VSS pamphlet, London, 1889); idem, *Duties of Women* (Swann Sonnenschein, London, 1881).

29. E.g. E. Hart, 'Women, Clergymen and Doctors', *New Review*, vol. 7 (1892), pp. 708–18.

30. *British Medical Journal*, vol. ii (28 May 1904), p. 1266 (emphasis in original).

31. E.g. *Zoophilist*, vol. i (2 May 1882), p. 13; vol. vi (1886), p. 63.

32. *Zoophilist*, vol. xi (1 July 1892), p. 70.

33. See Rupke's chapter in this volume for a full discussion of the scientists' response.

34. E. de Cyon, 'The Anti-Vivisectionist Agitation', *Contemporary Review*, vol. 43 (1883), p. 506.

35 Anonymous, 'Hysterical Old Maids', *Englishwoman's Review* (15 June 1883), pp. 249–50. The style is clearly Cobbe's.

36. *The Times*, 7 Oct 1892; F.P. Cobbe, 'Preface' to G.M. Rhodes (ed.), *The Nine Circles of the Hell of the Innocent described from the Reports of the Presiding Spirits* (Swann Sonnenschein, London, 1892), p. vii (emphasis in original). The title and the structure of the book are based on Dante's *Inferno*.

37. *The Times*, 11 to 28 Oct, 1 to 3 Nov 1892, 5 Oct 1899; *Zoophilist*, vol. xii (1 Dec 1892), pp. 213–15; Hart, 'Women, Clergymen and Doctors'; B. Wilberforce, 'Reply', *New Review*, vol. 8 (1893), pp. 84–95; Garrett Anderson, 'The Ethics of Vivisection'; French, *Antivivisection*, pp. 249–50.

38. E.g. *Zoophilist*, vol. xvi (1 July 1896), p. 20.

39. J.B. Lyons, *The Citizen Surgeon: A Biography of Sir Victor Horsley, FRS, FRCS* (Dawnay, London, 1966), pp. 130–49, 220–7.

40. On moral reform societies, see B. Harrison, 'Philanthropy and the Victorians', in *Peaceable Kingdom* (Oxford University Press, Oxford, 1982), pp. 217–59 and idem, State Intervention and Moral Reform in Nineteenth Century England', in P. Hollis (ed.), *Pressure from Without* (Edward Arnold, London, 1974), pp. 288–322. French, *Antivivisection*, esp. pp. 159–287, discusses the range and size of societies in detail. On working-class support see French, *Antivivisection*, p. 238; C. Lansbury, *The Old Brown Dog: Women, Workers and Vivisection in Edwardian England* (University of Wisconsin Press, Madison, 1985), pp. 26–62.

41. Cobbe, *Life*, vol. ii, p. 568. For example, suffragists and anti-vice campaigners, Millicent Fawcett and Josephine Butler, were sufficiently concerned to sign petitions against developments such as the British Institute for Preventive Medicine in 1891, but appear never to have joined societies, *Zoophilist*, vol. xi (2 Nov 1891), p. 147. On these issues, Fawcett disagreed with her doctor sister, Elizabeth Garrett Anderson, R. Strachey, *Millicent Garrett Fawcett* (J. Murray, London, 1931), pp. 110–11.

42. In 1882 the VSS had 213 female (72 per cent) and 81 male identifiable subscribers; in 1885 315 women (75 per cent) and 105 men, and in 1890 240 women (73 per cent) and 89 men (*Zoophilist*, 1882–1900). In 1883, the year it merged with the VSS, the International Society had 69 per cent female members (55 women and 24 men). *Zoophilist*, ii (1 March 1883), p. 102.

43. F. Prochaska, *Women and Philanthropy in 19th Century England* (Oxford University Press, Oxford, 1980), pp. 233 and 251. On the RSPCA see French, *Antivivisection*; J. Turner, *Reckoning with the Beast: Animals, Pain and Humanity in the Victorian Mind* (Johns Hopkins Press, Baltimore, 1980); B. Harrison, 'Animals and the State in Nineteenth Century England', in *Peaceable Kingdom*, pp. 82–122.

44. Prochaska, *Women and Philanthropy*, esp. pp. 4–6.

45. French, *Antivivisection*, pp. 83 and 239.

46. *Zoophilist*, vol. v (1 Nov. 1885), p. 114.

47. Queen Victoria was described by anti-vivisectionists as prevented by constitutional propriety from giving public support to the cause. Her honouring and entertaining vivisectionists was similarly explained. *Zoophilist*, vol. viii (1888), p. 113; vol. ix (1888), p. 71; *A Guest for Queen Victoria* (VSS Pamphlet, London, n.d.).

48. The BUAV, when founded by Cobbe in 1898, had ten female vice-presidents and nine male. Figures are derived from advertisements in *Zoophilist* and *Abolitionist* for the relevant years.

49. J. Butler, 'Introduction' to J. Butler (ed.), *Women's Work and Women's Culture* (Macmillan, London, 1869), p. xxxvii.

50. Prochaska, *Women and Philanthropy*, pp. 242–3.

51. From advertisements in *Zoophilist* and *Abolitionist*.

52. *Animal World*, vol. xii (Dec. 1881).

53. E. Maitland, *Anna Kingsford: Her Life, Letters, Diary and Work* (2 vols, Watkins, London, 1896), 3rd edition, 1913, pp. 7–8.

54. *Zoophilist*, vol. i (1881), pp. 58 and 71.

55. E. Healey, *Lady Unknown: The Life of Angela Burdett Coutts* (Sidgwick & Jackson, London, 1978); J. L'Esperance, 'Women's Mission to Women: Explorations in the Double Standard and Female Sexuality in Nineteenth Century England', *Social History — Histoire Sociale*, vol. 12 (1979), pp. 316–88.

56. Turner, *Reckoning with the Beast*; A.W. Moss, *Valiant Crusade: The History of the RSPCA* (Cassell, London, 1961); G. Cottesloe, *Lost, Stolen or Strayed: The Story of the Battersea Dog's Home* (Arthur Barker, London, 1971).

57. *Animal World*, vol. xviii (1 April 1882), pp. 49–50, 54–9; *Zoophilist*, vol. ii (1882), p. 240.

58. *Animal World*, vol. ii (1 Aug 1870), p. 200. Cobbe objected strongly to this exclusion of women from the political and legal work of the RSPCA. F.P. Cobbe, 'Remonstrance', *Animal World* (1 Sept 1870), p. 220.

59. *Animal World*, vol. vi (1875), p. 162.

60. *Animal World*, vol. xviii (1 April 1882), pp. 49–50, 54–9; *Zoophilist*, vol. ii (1882), p. 240; 'Letter' to *Daily News* (1876), reprinted as VSS pamphlet c. 1887; *Zoophilist*, vol. i (1882), p. 159. L'Esperance, 'Women's Mission to Women'.

61. E. Longford, *Victoria R.I.* (Weidenfeld & Nicolson, London, 1964), p. 406. French, *Antivivisection*, pp. 54–7, 123–8, 145–6; Queen Victoria to Gladstone, 6 April 1881, quoted in J. Vyvyan, *In Pity and in Anger* (Michael Joseph, London, 1969), pp. 137 and 162. M.R. Rogers, 'The Vivisection Controversy in Victorian Britain', unpublished MPhil thesis, University of London, 1979, discusses Queen Victoria's role in detail.

62. French, *Antivivisection*, pp. 5–15.

63. Jordanova, 'Natural Facts', pp. 63–7; Tomaselli, 'The Enlighten-

ment Debate on Women', pp. 101–24.

64. C. Hall, 'The Early Formation of Victorian Domestic Ideology', and A. Summers, 'A Home from Home — Women's Philanthropic Work in the Nineteenth Century', in S. Burman (ed.), *Fit Work for Women* (Croom Helm, London, 1979), pp. 15–32, 33–63; L'Esperance, 'Woman's Mission to Women', p. 317.

65. The phrase is Josephine Butler's; see L'Esperance, 'Woman's Mission to Women', p. 330.

66. B. Harrison, *Separate Spheres: The Opposition to Women's Suffrage in Britain* (Croom Helm, London, 1981).

67. Cobbe, *A Life*, vol, i. pp. 83, 89, 98, 116; idem, *Essay on the Theory of Intuitive Morals* (Macmillan, London, 1855). Elston, 'Gender, Medicine and Morality', pp. 64–94.

68. E.g. F.P. Cobbe, *Essays on the Pursuits of Women* (reprinted from *Fraser's Magazine* and *MacMillan's Magazine*, 1863); idem, *The Duties of Women* (Swan Sonnenschein, London, 1881).

69. F.P. Cobbe, 'Wife Torture in England', *Contemporary Review*, 32 (1878), pp. 55–87.

70. F.P. Cobbe, 'The Rights of Man and the Claims of Brutes', *Fraser's Magazine*, vol. 68 (1863), pp. 586–602. On Kant and animals, M. Midgley, *Animals and Why They Matter*, pp. 52–64.

71. Cobbe, *A Life*, vol. ii, p. 248; idem, *The Modern Rack: Papers on Vivisection* (Swann Sonnenschein, London, 1889).

72. French, *Antivivisection*, pp. 229–33.

73. A. Beck, 'Issues in the Anti-Vaccination Movement in England', *Medical History*, vol. 4 (1960), pp. 310–21; R.M. MacLeod, 'Law, Medicine and Public Opinion: The Resistance to Compulsory Health Legislation, 1870–1907', *Public Law* (1967), pp. 107–28, 189–211. On the CD Acts see Walkowitz, *Prostitution and Victorian Society*; P. McHugh, *Prostitution and Victorian Social Reform* (Croom Helm, London, 1980).

74. French, *Antivivisection*, p. 229; Cobbe, *A Life*, ii, pp. 273–4; McHugh, *Prostitution and Victorian Social Reform*.

75. From the list given in Walkowitz, *Prostitution and Victorian Society*, pp. 126–7.

76. French, *Antivivisection*, p. 229. 'Appealed' is deliberately ambiguous here. Certainly anti-vivisectionist rhetoric made reference to these other campaigns in seeking support. How far such arguments were, in fact, influential in motivating individuals' support is much harder to establish.

77. J. Butler to J. Edmundsen (28 April 1872) quoted in Walkowitz, *Prostitution and Society*, p. 108; F.P. Cobbe, 'The Medical Profession and Its Morality', *Modern Review*, vol. 2 (1881), pp. 296–326; L. de la Ramée [Ouida], *The New Priesthood: A Protest Against Vivisection* (Allen, London, 1893).

78. L. Stevenson, 'Religious Elements'; idem, 'Science Down the Drain', *Bulletin of the History of Medicine*, vol. 29 (Jan–Feb 1955), pp. 1–26.

79. F.P. Cobbe, *The Scientific Spirit of the Age* (Smith Elder & Co., London, 1888), p. 12; idem, 'Hygeiolatry' and 'Sacrificial Medicine', in *Peak of Darien* (Williams and Norgate, London, 1882); idem, 'Faith Healing and Fear Killing', *Contemporary Review*, vol. 51 (1887), pp. 794–813.

80. D. Burfield, 'Theosophy and Feminism: Some Explorations in Nineteenth Century Biography', in P. Holden (ed.), *Women's Religious Experience*

(Croom Helm, London, 1983), p. 32.

81. A.H. Nethercott, *The First Five Lives of Annie Besant* (1961), p. 187, records that Besant, Aveling and Drysdale wrote an article, in 1883, in *The Reformer*, attacking a bill to prohibit vivisection before parliament. On her conversion see A. Besant, *An Autobiography* (1893), p. 346.

82. Burfield, 'Theosophy and Feminism', pp. 35–6. F.R. Swiney, *Women and Natural Law* (League of Isis, London, 1912). Swiney's views were criticised, from a different theosophical perspective, by fellow anti-vivisectionist and militant suffragette, Charlotte Despard, in *Theosophy and the Woman's Movement* (London, 1913).

83. A. Kenealy, 'Women as Athlete', *Nineteenth Century*, vol. 45 (1899), pp. 636–45. For a critical reply by another woman writer, social purity campaigner and anti-vivisectionist see L. Ormiston Chant, 'Women as Athlete: A Reply to Dr Arabella Kenealy', *Nineteenth Century*, vol. 45 (1899), pp. 745–54.

84. Maitland, *Anna Kingsford*, vol. i, pp. 17–20.

85. Ibid., pp. 75, 138, 258; vol. ii, p. 290.

86. W.T. Stead, 'Mr Maitland's Life of Anna Kingsford: Apostle and Avenger', *Review of Reviews* (1896), pp. 74–5.

87. Maitland, *Anna Kingsford*, vol. i, pp. 425–7, vol. ii, pp. 27, 44–5, 57, 232.

88. F.P. Cobbe, *Health and Holiness: A Criticism and an Address* (Fisher Unwin, London, 1894).

89. F.P. Cobbe, 'The Little Health of Ladies', *Contemporary Review*, vol. 31 (Jan 1878), pp. 276–96; idem, 'The Medical Profession and its Morality', *Modern Review*, vol. 2 (1881), pp. 296–326. (The latter was published anonymously.)

90. E.g. *Zoophilist*, vol. iv (1884), p. 116; vol. x (1890), pp. 28–9, 49.

91. F. Hoggan, *The Scientist at the Bedside* (VSS pamphlet, reprinted from *Zoophilist* (12 April 1882), London), pp. 3–4; *Zoophilist*, vol. viii (1 Dec 1893).

92. O. Mosciucci, 'The Science of Women; British Gynaecology, 1849–1890', Unpublished DPhil thesis, University of Oxford, 1984; T.S. Wells, 'Vivisection and Ovariotomy', *British Medical Journal*, vol. ii (1879), p. 794; R. Lawson Tait, *The Uselessness of Vivisection* (VSS pamphlet, London, 1882).

93. J. Manton, *Elizabeth Garrett Anderson* (Methuen, London, 1965), pp. 228–9; E. Blackwell, 'Scientific Method in Biology' in *Essays in Medical Sociology* (Bell, London, 1902), vol. ii, pp. 119–22; Elston, 'Gender, Medicine and Morality', p. 113.

94. *Abolitionist*, vol. ii (15 Jan 1901); see also R.M. Morantz, 'Feminism, Professionalism and Germs: The Thought of Mary Putnam Jacobi and Elizabeth Blackwell', *American Quarterly*, vol. 34 (Winter 1982), pp. 459–78; M. Elston, 'Aping the Monstrous Males? Women Doctors and Vivisection, 1870–1904' (unpublished paper, 1985).

95. *The Times*, 21 July 1894: *Zoophilist*, vol. xiv (1 Oct 1894), p. 81; vol. xv (1 Aug 1895), pp. 192, 211. French records this incident but does not comment on the significance of its being a women's hospital, *Antivivisection*, p. 325.

96. Mosciucci, 'Science of Women', esp. pp. 227–52.

97. Jordanova, 'Natural Facts', pp. 54–9.

98. F.P. Cobbe, *The Study of Physiology as a Branch of Education* (VSS Pamphlet, London, reprinted from *Zoophilist* (15 July 1893), p. 2).

99. Walkowitz, *Prostitution and Victorian Society*; McHugh, *Prostitution and Victorian Social Reform*.

100. *Zoophilist*, vol. v (20 April 1904), pp. 1–3. In 1897, Cobbe attributed her initial view to 'misdirection' by Elizabeth Garrett Anderson who shared the dominant medical view on the Acts as a necessary preventive measure. F.P. Cobbe to Mrs. H. Fawcett, Autograph Letter Collection, Fawcett Library.

101. D. Gorham. ' "The Maiden Tribute of Modern Babylon" Re-examined: Child Prostitution and the Idea of Childhood in Late-Victorian England', *Victorian Studies*, vol. 21 (Spring 1978), pp. 142–73; S. Jeffreys, *The Spinster and Her Enemies: Feminism and Sexuality, 1880–1930* (Pandora Press, London, 1985); L. Gordon and E. Dubois, 'Seeking Ecstasy on the Battlefield: Danger and Pleasure in Nineteenth Century Feminist Thought', *Feminist Review*, 13 (Spring 1983), pp. 42–54.

102. S. Grand, *The Beth Book* (reprinted Virago, London, 1980), pp. 442–4; G. Kersley, *Darling Madame: Sarah Grand and Devoted Friend* (London, Virago, 1983), pp. 9–15, 90–4. Lansbury (*Brown Dog*, pp. 144–9) refers to this and similar incidents in other anti-vivisectionist novels but does not set them in the context of the sexual purity movement or the explicit imagery of contemporary anti-vivisectionist literature.

103. F.P. Cobbe, *The Higher Expediency* (VSS Pamphlet, London, 1882, pp. 19–20); *Abolitionist*, vol. i (15 Feb 1901), pp. 271–2.

104. *Zoophilist*, vol. vii (1 Nov 1887), p. 110.

105. *The Times* (11 Oct 1888); J. Walkowitz, 'Jack the Ripper', *Feminist Studies*, vol. 7 (1982), pp. 543–74.

106. E.g. *Animal World*, vol. ix (1878), pp. 91–3, 127, 141–2; vol. xxix (Feb 1898), pp. 19–20.

107. E.g. *Zoophilist*, vol. iv (1 Aug 1884), pp. 85, 111; Vyvyan, *In Pity*, pp. 42–3.

108. *Zoophilist*, vol. iii (1 March 1884), pp. 267–8.

109. Cobbe, *Study of Physiology as a Branch of Education*; Anonymous, *Lady Students of Vivisection* (VSS pamphlet, London, c. 1881), quoted in *Zoophilist*, vol. iii (2 April 1883), pp. 55–6.

110. E.g. *Zoophilist*, vol. v (1 Jan 1886), p. 158; vol. v (1 March 1886), pp. 226–7; vol. viii (1 Jan 1889), p. 154; *Abolitionist*, vol. i (15 Sept 1899), p. 65; vol. ii (15 Jan 1900), p. 70.

111. 'Somerville Hall — A Misnomer', *Zoophilist*, vol. x (1 Jan 1891), pp. 172–3, 192.

112. Mrs H Sidgwick to Mrs H. Fawcett, c. March 1891. Fawcett Library Autograph Letter Collection.

113. Elston, 'Gender, Medicine and Morality', pp. 100–4.

114. Cobbe, *Duties of Women*, p. 24 (emphasis in original).

115. Elston, 'Aping the Monstrous Males?'

116. E. Blackwell, 'The Influence of Women on the Profession of Medicine', in *Essays in Medical Sociology* (2 vols, Bell, London, 1902), vol. ii, pp. 8–10.

117. M. Elston, 'Gout is in My Field, but Gentlemen are not', paper presented to British Sociological Association Medical Sociology Conference,

Sheffield, 1984.

118. *Zoophilist*, vol. i (1 July 1881), p. 56.

119. B. Bryan (ed.), *The Vivisectors' Directory* (VSS pamphlet, London, 1884).

120. Annual returns to Home Office published annually in *Parliamentary Papers*; Elston, 'Aping the Monstrous Males?'; *Royal Commission on Vivisection, 1906–1912, Final Report*, Parl. Papers, 1912/13, Cd. 6114, xlviii, p. 401.

121. S.V. Butler, 'Science and the Education of Doctors in the Nineteenth Century: A Study of British Medical Schools with Special Reference to the Development and Uses of Physiology', unpublished PhD thesis, University of Manchester, 1981.

122. Elston, 'Aping the Monstrous Males?'; M. Scharlieb, *Reminiscences* (Williams and Norgate, London, 1924), p. 65; Garrett Anderson, 'The Ethics of Vivisection', pp. 147–69.

123. Elston, 'Aping the Monstrous Males?' discusses this in detail.

124. *Animal World*, vol. vii (1 June 1875), p. 99.

125. *Zoophilist*, vol. xxiii (1 Feb, 1 March 1904), pp. 200–72; L.E. Bayliss, 'The "Brown Dog" Affair', *The Potential: Journal of the Physiology Society*, no. 2 (Spring 1957), pp. 11–22; on subsequent events, J.H. Baron, 'The Brown Dog of University College', *British Medical Journal*, vol. ii (1 Sept 1956), pp. 547–8; E.K. Ford, *The Brown Dog and His Memorial* (St Clement's Press, London, 1908); Lansbury, *Brown Dog*, pp. 3–26. See also Lawrence, this volume, p. 296.

126. The first edition was L. Lind-af-Hageby and L. Schartau, *Eye-Witnesses* (Bell, London, 1903). After the trial a chapter entitled 'Fun', depicting students' amusement at vivisection demonstrations, was withdrawn and the book republished as *The Shambles of Science: Extracts from the Diary of Two Students of Physiology* (Animal Defence and Anti-Vivisection Society, London, 5th edition, 1913).

127. Lansbury, *Brown Dog*, p. 16; Harrison, *Separate Spheres*, p. 68.

128. Lind-af-Hageby and von Schartau, *Shambles of Science*, p. 192.

129. De la Ramée, *New Priesthood*, pp. 17–18.

130. Elston, 'Gender, Medicine and Morality', pp. 117–23.

131. For example, the Women's Liberal Federation passed a resolution at its 1894 annual meeting calling for prohibition of vivisection, in the face of strong opposition. *Zoophilist*, vol. xiv (1 May 1894), p. 28. Two years later, to anti-vivisectionist horror, Horsley addressed the WLF's general council on temperance, *Zoophilist*, vol. xvi (1 May 1896), p. 51.

12

Cinema Vérité?: The Image of William Harvey's Experiments in 1928

Christopher Lawrence

Anti-vivisection in the 1920s

If the physician Thomas Lewis and the physiologist Henry Dale had been privy to William Harvey's thoughts as to when he should publish his work, *De Motu Cordis*, they might well have suggested to him that, had he an eye to posterity, 1628 was the least helpful of dates to have chosen. Some 300 years later, in 1928, Harvey's announcement of the discovery of the circulation of the blood was being celebrated by the Royal College of Physicians of London, and Lewis and Dale had engaged to produce a film of Harvey's investigations. This cinematographic re-enactment, however, coincided with an intensification of anti-vivisectionist agitation. The making of the film, which includes a number of scenes containing experiments on animals, illustrates various aspects of the anti-vivisection controversy in the 1920s, not least the difficulties of interpreting an Act which had been passed fifty years earlier and which, therefore, made no provision for representations of experiments on film. In addition, material in the Lewis and Dale archives documents the arguments of senior medical men and basic scientists in favour of animal experimentation, and demonstrates their relations and delicate negotiations with a Home Office sympathetic to medical research but sensitive to public opinion.

One of the striking features of the disagreements between the supporters of animal experiment and the anti-vivisectionists is the absolute incommensurability of the language of the two parties. Anti-vivisectionists talked in anthropomorphic terms of the feelings and intelligence of animals, and consistently used the term vivisection to mean torture. Medical men, on the other hand, deplored the use of the term vivisection to describe their work, preferring the term animal experimentation. In addition, they situated themselves by reference to history, identifying their work with scientific progress, and themselves as the party of humanity. To do this they used an empirical philosophy, in which facts gathered by experiment were designated as the only true and useful form of knowledge. In this respect cinematography proved to be a powerful new vehicle for underwriting their progressivist epistemology. To understand their language, it is necessary to recognise that the active medical campaigners for animal experimentation were relatively few in number and spoke with the voice of a beleagured minority. They were to a large extent the London-based, leading members of the profession. As they saw it, it was they who had inherited the mantle of historical responsibility for the extirpation of suffering. Conversely, they stigmatised the anti-vivisectionists as misguided or devious and, at best, politically irresponsible or, at worst, the enemies of mankind.

In the years following the passage of the 1876 Cruelty to Animals Act, experiments using animals had increased greatly in Britain. This followed from the expansion of older professional disciplines, for instance experimental physiology, the creation of new subjects, for instance immunology, and the increase in size and number of medical schools, which meant, therefore, a corresponding increase in numbers of students being instructed. The 1876 Act had done little to disperse opposition to animal experimentation. Indeed in the first half of the twentieth century, the issue of vivisection remained an important one, capable of mobilising powerful establishment figures or groups to pronounce on it, and periodically erupting across the front pages of the newspapers.

Not surprisingly, because of their distinguished experimental tradition, University College and its hospital were continuously involved in wrangles with anti-vivisectionists. The most notorious of these encounters was the widely publicised 'brown dog' case that finished up in court, and which centred on the physiologist William Maddox Bayliss and, peripherally, his colleagues Ernest Starling and Henry Dale.[1] Another University College figure who frequently crossed swords with the anti-vivisectionists before the First World War was one of Thomas Lewis's teachers, Victor Horsley. Both makers of the Harvey film, Henry Dale and Thomas Lewis, were closely associated with University College.[2] Henry Dale (1875–1968) was a Cambridge trained physiologist, a student of Michael Foster and W.H. Gaskell who, from 1902 to 1904, continued his education under Starling and Bayliss at University College. Although medically qualified, Dale's enthusiasm was for experimental physiology and, in 1904, he accepted a position at the newly established Wellcome Physiological Research Laboratories in London. In 1914 he left this post to become a member of the scientific staff of the Medical Research Committee (Council after 1920). A brilliant physiologist, Dale was also a politician amongst the intellectual aristocracy of science, figuring frequently on scientific committees and so forth. His voice in medical politics, like that of his co-author Thomas Lewis (1881–1945), was an important one.[3] Lewis studied medicine at University College Hospital Medical School, but, from his earliest days, fell under the spell of experimental physiology. Lewis's perceptions of physiology, however, were always far more clinically orientated than those of Dale and, throughout his working life, he remained a clinician, primarily a heart specialist. At the same time, however, he endeavoured to develop clinical research in tandem with laboratory experiment. Lewis, who made his mark before the First World War with the newly invented electrocardiograph, was also actively involved with the Medical Research Committee and, symbiotically, they used each other to create the new subject, 'clinical science'. In the 1920s Lewis was at the height of his power, he had been knighted, was an FRS and his words were listened to in British, and especially London, medicine.[4]

Although anti-vivisectionism has been the subject of a small amount of serious scholarship, this has concentrated on the years surrounding the passage of the 1876 Act and the post-Second World War.[5] The interwar years still await exploration. The 1920s, however, saw no loss of intensity of anti-vivisectionist activity, although, by this time, the framework within which the debates occurred had changed somewhat. By the 1920s the medical profession in general supported, albeit not actively, its leadership's stance on animal experimentation. The anti-vivisection party, on the other hand, was coloured with the shade of crankiness with which medical opinion had been able to stain it in the late Victorian and Edwardian period. The alliance of the anti-vivisectionists with other causes such as homeopathy and anti-vaccination had given medical men the opportunity to stigmatise them in the public eye as anti-science, anti-progress, anti-modernity, not a position which would find much public approval in the days of scientific optimism which characterise *The Long Weekend*.[6] Thus any confrontation between medicine and the anti-vivisectionists in these years was likely to be resolved in the former's favour, especially when the government was the referee. This, however, did not mean doctors felt they could be cavalier about anti-vivisectionists; quite the reverse, they felt constantly under attack from without and feared professional apathy within. There was one area too where doctors had to be extremely careful not to upset public sentiment — the question of experiments on dogs.

Much of the anti-vivisectionist controversy in the 1920s was specifically associated with attempts to pass a Bill through parliament prohibiting experimentation on dogs. Crucial to the understanding of the debate is the fact that medical men had great difficulty in acquiring dogs and that, by law, stray dogs were prohibited for use in research. Dogs were a subject of particular concern to many anti-vivisectionists and, because dogs were widely kept as pets, the movement could readily mobilise public opinion. Understandably, therefore, anti-vivisectionists sought and made an ally in the National Canine Defence League. Both parties had a tireless champion in Lord Banbury, much of whose political career was devoted to getting a Protection of Dogs Bill through Parliament. In 1919, Westacott reports, he almost succeeded in having the Bill made law until the Ministry of Health stepped in to ensure that a government 'three-line whip' defeated it. It was Banbury's opinion that had not Christopher Addison intervened the bill would have passed unapproved.[7] Addison was a qualified medical practitioner and a former practising anatomist, who had been made the first Minister of Health in June 1919. He was more than a friend of the profession in government, he symbolised the degree to which medical orthodoxy had become embodied in the running of the modern state.

Controversy over the use of dogs in research boiled over periodically in the national and medical press. On 20 November 1926, a man was convicted for stealing two Irish terriers, after being arrested while taking them to the Physiology Department at University College.[8] A few days later Charles Lovatt Evans, Jodrell Professor of Physiology, stated that the college had purchased dogs from the man under the impression he was their legal owner. Although the college was not implicated it is notable that, according to the research lobby, 'the Magistrate gave vent to an expression of opinion which savoured of anti-vivisectionist sentiment'.[9] The *British Medical Journal* addressed the question and, in an interesting turn of phrase, put responsibility on the state for initiating experimentation on dogs, noting that 'Parliament and the Government *require* various researches to be carried out which call for the employment of dogs.'[10] This research, it noted, was done by way of grants to the Medical Research Council and was concerned with the prevention and cure of tropical diseases. The journal said nothing about experimental physiology. Six days after this conviction the distinguished, former University College physiologist, A.V. Hill, wrote to *The Times* arguing that the 50,000 stray dogs destroyed each year should be made available for experimental purposes.[11] By this action, it was argued, the lives of 1,000 dogs per year could be saved.[12]

As a consequence of these events the Science Committee of the BMA prepared a memorandum setting out reasons why dogs were essential to certain classes of experiment. The reasons were practical (healthy monkeys in large quantities were unavailable) and physiological: 'The diet and metabolism of the dog are almost unique in their similarity to man.'[13] The Committee pointed to a number of areas, beginning with the discovery of insulin and including work on the parathyroid, rickets and gall bladder surgery, where dogs had been central to the research. The Committee concluded with a strongly worded historical argument, aligning itself with a long tradition of experiment and progress in Europe and anti-vivisectionism with the stagnancy of the Middle East.

> Medical science cannot remain stationary; unless it advances it will cease to attract the best brains and will retrogress; freedom for research is essential. It is an impossible position if a scientist arrives at a point where the next step involves research on dogs and then has to stop. Restriction will as surely kill research as the forbidding of dissection on human bodies in Mohammedan countries killed Arabic medical science, which — as a result of the knowledge obtained from Greek science as advanced by experiment in Alexandria — was in the early Middle Ages far in advance of European medical science of the time.[14]

Anti-vivisectionists of course were not likely to be convinced, and in December 1927 they brought an unsuccessful case against E.B. Verney, Professor of Pharmacology at University College.[15]

Thomas Lewis and experimental medicine

The year 1927 saw no easing up of anti-vivisectionist activity, and the controversy simmered in the medical and national press. Early in the year a new Dogs Protection Bill was to be presented to Parliament and medical men were alarmed, not least since the RSPCA had also decided to petition the House in support of the Bill.[16] The Bill was framed to stop all experiments on dogs. The first recorded involvement of Thomas Lewis in the debate was in January 1927. Lewis, who had used dogs in his electrocardiographic work, signalled his alarm to Dawson Williams, editor of the *British Medical Journal*, 'You must be very aware of the trouble that is brewing in regard to vivisection.' Lewis was worried about 'the large amount of hearsay that has fallen into the lap of the enemy'. He urged a strong statement of medical opinion backed by the whole profession and suggested that the BMA organise a 'massive' petition 'to the effect that the vivisection of dogs is necessary to the progress of medicine'. To further medical progress, Lewis urged that the petition should state that stray dogs should be made available for experimentation. He added that Knutsford knew of his 'writing to you in this sense'.[17] Viscount Knutsford was Chairman of the London Hospital and, more important in this connection, of the Research Defence Society, an organisation founded in 1908 by Stephen Paget to promote the cause of animal experimentation. In the same month that Lewis wrote this letter, the Research Defence Society increased its campaign for the use of dogs in research, and published in its journal, *The Fight against Disease*, an article on the importance of dogs in medicine, and a piece deploring the support the RSPCA was giving to the forthcoming Bill. The *Daily Telegraph* reported this on 2 February.[18] On 4 February, W.E. Dixon, Reader in Pharmacology at Cambridge, wrote to Lewis, saying he had seen Lewis's letter to Williams and that, after consulting with Starling at a Physiological Society meeting, he, Dixon, would do what he could 'regarding the BMA in the way of a preliminary article and leader'.[19] Ten days later, on 14 February, Robert Gower presented a Bill to prohibit the vivisection of dogs. It was put down for a second reading on 29 April.[20]

Pressure on the government to pass the Bill was by no means trivial. Besides the lobbying of the RSPCA, the National Canine Defence League presented to Parliament a petition, with a million signatures, opposing the use of dogs in research.[21] Lewis possessed a copy of this petition, and he used it to set out his argument for the importance of dogs in medical research. The petition referred to dogs as 'exceptionally intelligent and peculiarly sensitive to suffering and to terror' and as 'docile and obedient under torture', for which reason, the petition stated, they were invaluable to the experimental scientist. In his copy of the petition Lewis underlined another sentence which accused medical men of performing experiments on dogs before students, when the experiments were merely demonstrations 'of a prolonged and agonising nature'. Underneath Lewis noted: '(1) Part played by experiments on living animals is building present day knowledge. (2) Importance of dogs for this purpose. (3) Aspects of urgent anticampaign with particular reference to conditions under which experiments are performed and the character of the work.'[22]

Lewis possibly used these notes to draft a lengthy defence of animal experimentation, especially experimentation on dogs, which he later delivered at a BMA conference. His argument was fundamentally historical, situating the modern medical profession as the inheritors of a responsibility for maintaining progress which was to be achieved through experimental science. Without experimentation, he noted, medicine 'would have failed to emerge from the status it held in the dark ages'. The case for animal experimentation however, he continued, was a complex one and not to be supported simply by referring to 'an array of brilliant discoveries'. The argument for experimentation should be more 'deeply founded' on an understanding of what medical knowledge would be without such a method. To illustrate this he went on: '*I start with Harvey*, the *pioneer* of this method . . . *Harvey's great work* conducted in large part upon dogs.' Lewis developed an argument for the importance of *routine* experimentation, especially on dogs, for revealing 'the fundamentals of human physiology'. The term 'vivisection' he noted, was inaccurate and stigmatising, implying 'barbarous' treatment of conscious animals. Lewis next defended University College, identifying it as the premier centre of medical research which, because of cardiovascular work carried out there, had to use the 'most suitable' animal: the dog. Lewis vehemently repudiated the accusation that experiments performed at University College were done on conscious animals or performed secretly. He then turned, with equal venom, on the National Canine Defence League's petition and its claim that dogs were used in agonising demonstrations performed before students. Such a claim, he noted, simply displayed the credulity of a large number of people and he added that the signatories to the petition were 'unfitted to influence the decisions of Parliament'. Their misapprehension was the consequence of a 'mischievous campaign directed against a chief method of assuring the progress of medical science'. The anti-vivisectionists, he noted, were a 'curious group' led by unscrupulous men who 'pervert the meaning of plain words'.[23] As the Research Defence Society put it, experimenters were having to deal with 'serious annoyance by crank societies'.[24]

On 26 February the *BMJ* ran a leader on the subject of experiments on dogs. The similarity to Lewis's argument is striking. Lewis, of course, may have had a hand in the piece, although possibly the journal was simply marshalling the commonest arguments for animal experimentation. The journal took a strongly historical line, condemning the 'mystical and subjective speculations in past centuries [which] have left us little or nothing for the good of humanity'. It lamented the 'misguided' support the RSPCA was giving to the dogs Bill, adding: 'We yield to none in our affection for the dog.' It singled out for special attention the National Canine Defence League's petition and its claim that medical men performed demonstrations of an agonising nature, noting 'no person acquainted with the facts' could support the accusation.[25] The appeal to facts was another feature of the medical argument. By analogy with the language of experimental science, the facts were, once established, incontrovertible. As *The Fight Against Disease* put it: 'We are dealing with *facts* not theories or feelings on this subject.'[26]

By the first week in March things were looking up for the doctors, the *BMJ* reporting that the RSPCA had withdrawn its support for the Bill.[27] A week later the journal announced that the BMA was convening a major conference on 4 April to discuss the whole question.[28] During the following week, in mid March, the parliamentary Medical Committee met a deputation from the BMA. On 28 March Knutsford wrote to Lewis, urging him that, when he attended the 4 April meeting, he should insist that leading medical men and societies should be unanimous in their condemnation of the Bill. Knutsford regretted that the Research Defence Society was supported only 'by a small number of the medical profession' who were really the only people who could 'answer the lies about dogs being tortured'.[29] Lewis, or someone, did manage to mobilise support for the BMA conference since it attracted the leading figures in British medicine including Lord Dawson, the King's physician. Lewis presented his historical paper.[30] Medical lobbying did the trick: on 29 April the Bill, according to the *BMJ*, was talked out 'by its supporters' or, according to an anti-vivisectionist historian, lost through time-wasting by its opponents.[31] Later, a memorandum by the MRC on the Dogs Protection Bill was issued as a White Paper.[32] The White Paper used the familiar arguments about the dog's unique physiology, it defended the profession's practice and repudiated accusations of torture and recommended that stray dogs be made available for experimentation.

The temporary demise of the Dogs Bill did not, of course, dissipate anti-vivisectionist activity, the remainder of the year witnessing continued agitation over the question, including a lengthy correspondence in *The Times*.[33]

Filming William Harvey

1928, the year following this heated debate, was the tercentenary of the publication of *De Motu Cordis*. The Royal College of Physicians, not surprisingly, intended to commemorate the occasion. In late 1927 Thomas Lewis and the President of the College, John Bradford, were discussing how best to celebrate the event. On 2 November, Lewis wrote to Bradford suggesting, as part of the festivities, 'demonstrations at University College'. These would include the exhibition of anatomical specimens, the making of polygraphic and electrocardiographic tracings and demonstrations by T.R. Elliot of the action of adrenaline on blood vessels. In addition Lewis suggested that Henry Dale repeat Harvey's experiments, show Starling's heart-lung preparation and include 'Anything else he fancies'. Lewis proposed that he would demonstrate heart-block experimentally, although he did not say on what animal.[34] The demonstrations, it should be noted, had a strong *historical* dimension, identifying a continuous thread of discovery in clinical medicine and science following Harvey's work. Clearly, to Lewis the use of experimental animals to celebrate Harvey's discovery and to identify this line of historical progress did not seem improper; the demonstrations were educational. In January 1928, Bradford was writing formally to Lewis of 'the desire of the College that a series of demonstrations on the physiology of the circulation should form a part of the celebration'. He also reminded Lewis of his 'willingness to prepare with Dr. Dale a cinematographic film of some of Harvey's fundamental experiments'.[35]

Knowing of Lewis's admiration for Harvey, and his fervent defence of animal experimentation, his 'willingness' no doubt can be interpreted as enthusiasm. The College offered to make £200 available for the making of the film. By March the project was well advanced.[36] About this time it was also agreed that the film would become the long-term property of the College of Physicians, Lewis himself having to ask the College's permission to obtain a copy for University College.[37] The film was probably made early in April, against a background hum of anti-vivisectionist activity.[38] On 13

February, a Dogs Protection Bill had achieved a first reading and on 20 April Sir Robert Gower moved the Bill be read a second time; the hour of adjournment, however, intervened.[39] Although dogs were a sensitive political issue, there is no doubt that on the matter of animal experimentation in general, governments stood beside the medical profession, sharing its ideology. If there had been an increase in the use of animals 'it was due principally to the development of medical science' as W. Joynson-Hicks put it for the government at question time in March 1928.[40]

To coincide with the showing of the film, Lewis and Dale produced a prospectus. In it they declared that the reasons for making the film were the difficulties associated with repeated live demonstrations of Harvey's experiments, a practice which did not ensure that the same result was always achieved in public. It was Lewis, the prospectus said, who had taken the responsibility for the general scheme while 'we have shared the performance of the experiments'.[41] It seems that on the advisability of making such a film the Home Office had been consulted.[42] The Harvey celebrations occurred between 14 and 18 May and the demonstrations, much in the form Lewis had originally planned them, took place at University College on the mornings of 15 and 16 May. The film was shown at these meetings. It was, the *BMJ* reported, a 'brilliant conception' and a 'quiet rebuke to guesswork without experimentation'.[43] The film contained a number of scenes showing the hearts of live fish, frogs and dogs in the hands of an unidentifiable demonstrator.[44] The animals were anaesthetised. The film began with a diagram identified as Galen's view of the body, followed by a number of pellucid animal experiments identified with those of Harvey which, in the context of the film, refute point by point the Galenic account and establish the doctrine of the circulation.[45]

Cinematography proved to be a wonderful device for conveying Lewis's sense of medicine's historical situation. By skilful concentration on a number of experiments, it was used to represent Harvey as an experimental scientist, performing manipulations identical to those familiar to twentieth-century researchers. The visual establishment of continuity between past and present could hardly have been more striking. The audience *knew* the experiments were performed by modern hands, yet, in context, were encouraged to identify them as Harvey's. Film could also do something else. It solved the problem of the replicability of classic experiments. By showing the film, experiments which had been raised to crucial historical status were replicated without the necessity of having to repeat them. Before sympathetic audiences, persuaded of the unique historical nature of the experimental method and the cumulative nature of medical knowledge, the film is a moving document. As the *BMJ* put it: 'Something of the thrill which Harvey must have felt as he slowly and cautiously traced the steps which led to his epoch-making discovery was conveyed to those who, three centuries later, have watched the graphic unfolding of the argument by the art of film'.[46] Film, however, did have its disadvantages. It offered a visual experience of experimental practice in a form which was not so easily policed as a university laboratory. Moreover, film was not associated with the sombre domain of science but with the world of entertainment.

The ethics of cinematography in medicine

At the beginning of June 1928 Lewis wrote to J.A. Giles, Under-Secretary at the Home Office, notifying him that he and Dale were about to transfer the copyright of the film to the College of Physicians. Lewis added that the film had 'met with more than expected success' and was in 'considerable demand' from medical schools. It was for reasons associated with this success that Lewis was writing. He reminded Giles that, when the film was made, the Home Office had expressed the desire that it should not be shown to lay audiences. Lewis pointed out that, once it was out of his hands, he had no control over the use of the film; in which case, he suggested, the President of the College should be asked to give a similar commitment to the Home Office.[47] Giles discussed the matter with Eagleston the Assistant Secretary in charge of 'vivisection affairs', and both agreed that the College should be requested to write to the Home Office 'informally to the effect that the film is not intended to be used for exhibition to lay audiences'.[48] On 6 June Bradford wrote to Lewis saying the required letter had been sent.[49] The next day Lewis and Dale transferred copyright to the College.[50] A day later, on 8 June, however, Dale wrote a letter which Lewis would not have been so pleased to receive.

The contents of the letter refer to the sections of the 1876 Act under which the experiments shown on the film were made. The Act empowered holders of a licence to experiment on animals in a named place, the animal to be killed after the experiment. Licence-holders could apply for additional certificates to perform special experiments. Certificate A, for example, permitted experiments without anaesthesia, and Certificate B permitted experiments to be carried out in which the animal was allowed to recover. There were a number of other categories, of which the one of relevance here is Certificate C, which permitted experiments to be carried out for the purposes of demonstration. When experiments were performed by more than one person, only one person was required to return, dual returns being illegal. In his letter of 8 June, Dale reported that Giles had been to see him and Dale relayed the gist of Giles's visit: 'One of the anti-vivisection journals has published the usual sort of paragraph criticising our action in producing this film, asking what gain to scientific knowledge could thereby be obtained.' Although Dale thought such a position 'ridiculous' he reported that Giles was concerned whether some question might be asked in the House.

> Strictly speaking there is nothing in the Act which provides for such a method of demonstration, but Giles agrees that even the lawyers might be expected to take the view that application of the cinematograph to such demonstrations carries out the spirit and intention of the Act, although the letter of the law could not provide for what did not exist when it was passed.

There was, however, a further problem. The Home Office had advised Dale that, technically, the making of those parts of the film which involved experiments under the Act would probably be regarded as 'experiments under Certificate C, at University College . . . the exhibition of the film being on the same footing as the publication of records of such a demonstration'. The hitch, however, was that Lewis did not seem to have possessed any such certificate. Dale 'fortunately' had obtained such a certificate in 1903 when he was Starling's demonstrator. Thus Dale proposed: 'If any question arises, therefore, the experiments under the Act, performed in the course of the making of the film, would have to be recorded as made by me with your assistance.' Dale said he would record the experiments in his return for the year under Certificate C, and 'you must understand that this is the legal position in the event of an official enquiry'. The Home Office, at the same time, was preparing itself for any embarrassing questions. Giles wished to see the film, possibly with John Anderson, Permanent Under-Secretary. Eagleston was drawing up a memorandum for use in the House. This memorandum, Dale suggested, might be read by him and

Lewis. Giles also thought this useful.[51]

The following day, 9 June, Giles at the Home Office sent Lewis application forms for Certificate C suggesting that he should fill them in and indicate that he wanted the certificate in order to perform 'experiments to illustrate the fundamental facts and important discoveries of medicine and physiology' before medical students and learned societies. Giles assured Lewis 'I shall see they are put through safely.' On the general issue of whether the Act put any difficulties in the way of making films Giles said 'Mr. Eagleston is going into the question' but none was anticipated.[52] Possibly a bit puzzled Lewis had obviously written back to Giles asking him if the C Certificates were to be used in retrospect 'in any circumstances'. Giles said no, and Lewis told Dale that he had made it clear that he could not support such a course of action.[53] He added that in the event of trouble he was not going to be represented as Dale's assistant in the making of a film which, as Dale admitted, 'Lewis was chiefly, and I myself to a minor extent, responsible'.[54] Lewis wrote to Dale:

> In your letter of June 8th, you say, referring to your own certificate C, 'you must understand that this is the legal position in the event of an official enquiry.' I cannot accept this; from my standpoint an official enquiry would mean a precise statement of how the experiments were performed; nothing else would be possible. My intention is to enter the experiments with others done by me under Licence for the year.[55]

Given the powerful medium that cinema had proved to be, it is not surprising that the film turned out to have a more long-standing use than the few days of the Harvey jamboree, the College receiving 'numerous requests' for it.[56] The College was happy to lend it to medical bodies, but all applications had to carry with them an undertaking that the film would not be shown to 'lay audiences'.[57] Requests for the film came from Cape Town, Mexico, New York and Romania. In Belgium the Queen expressed her 'desire that the opportunity should be taken for a show of the Harvey Film at the Royal Palace in Brussels'.[58]

The College remained vigilant in its custody of the film, not surprisingly, since these years saw continued agitation over the use of dogs in experiments. In 1930, however, someone seems to have slipped up. At the beginning of June, Dale received a short note from A. Landsborough Thomson of the MRC: 'The enclosed extract from Hansard is for your information.'[59] The extract was dated 29 May 1930:

VIVISECTION (FILM)
27. *Mr. Freeman* asked the Secretary of State for the Home Department whether his attention has been called to a film shown publicly at the Professional Nursing, Midwifery, and Public Health Exhibition, Horticultural Hall, Westminster, on 6th March 1930, illustrating vivisection experiments on certain animals, including a dog, performed by Dr. H.H. Dale; and, in view of the provisions of the Cruelty to Animals Act, namely, that an experiment must be performed with a view to the advancement of new discovery of physiological knowledge or of knowledge which will be useful for saving or prolonging life or alleviating suffering, what action he proposes to take in the matter?

It is notable that the experiments in the film were attributed to Dale, not Lewis. The question was interesting in another way too, for it nearly touched a crucial issue: the film's use as a celebratory device. The questioner, however, was preoccupied with asking about the film's research value. This enabled the Secretary of State for the Home Department, Mr Clynes, to refer to the educational passages in the 1876 Act. Presumably armed with Eagleston's memorandum, Mr Clynes referred the Member to a proviso:

If the hon. Member will refer to Section 3 of the Act, he will see that the words which he quotes are qualified by a proviso which expressly lays down that experiments may be made for the purpose of illustrating lectures in medical schools, hospitals, colleges, or elsewhere, with a view to instruction in physiological knowledge or knowledge which will be useful in saving life or alleviating suffering, on the appropriate certificate (C) being given by the scientific authorities mentioned in the Act.

He added: 'The experiments referred to in the question were performed under the authority of such a certificate, and no action on my part is necessary or possible.' The Member however was not quite satisfied, wondering whether a film which could be shown to the public (which effectively had been the case) could really be regarded as being covered by the proviso. Clynes replied: 'I have referred to the terms of the Act. The proviso in question is highly technical and scientific, and, if my hon. Friend wishes to press any other point, I should require notice of it.'[60] Here the matter rested. Dale washed his hands of it, telling Thomson it was now a matter for the College, adding, however: 'I am frankly puzzled by their allowing it to be put on show at the Horticultural Hall.'[61] Whether Lewis ever knew that, in the House, the film was designated as Dale's and the Home Office declared it was covered by all proper certificates is not recorded.

Conclusion

For the historian, and perhaps especially the historian of science, historical films have a far wider significance than any local difficulties associated with their making. For example, in the case of the Harvey film, its value to the exponents of experimental medicine was that it made it possible, at any time, to show perfect replications of experiments identified with Harvey, but avoiding all the local difficulties surrounding actual replication. Not only this, since the film combined a number of experiments presented in a specific context, the *meaning* the viewer was asked to impute to the sequence was highly constrained. It is crucial to note, however, that although the film was held to be a reproduction of Harvey's work, the makers of the film could not recreate the perceptions which Harvey or his contemporaries had of these experiments. These are, in many ways, beyond recovery, let alone filmable. Perceptions are highly informed accounts of the world, and our perceptions of the replicated experiments are informed by our account of their meaning. One of the reasons why we can be sure we have only limited knowledge of what Harvey's experiments would have 'looked like' to contemporaries, is that, however clear they seem to us, we know that they did not, initially, demonstrate to others what Harvey said they did. Even in the case of Harvey, although their meaning was that the blood circulated, this was a limited part of a wider framework of interpretation which was, broadly, a confirmation of Aristotelian cosmology. In other words, we perceive in the replicated experiments only certain aspects of Harvey's work, since these were the ones which were, *historically*, made into crucial features. What makes possible the identification of seventeenth-century perceptions with modern ones is the theory of scientific knowledge. Within positivist conceptions of science, knowledge accumulates through observation and experiment. Within this account the experimental method may require skill and imaginative hypothesising, but it ultimately relies on observation of what are conceived of as unproblematic natural phenomena. Indeed, positivist historiography creates tradition by the use of the concept of the possibility of repeated observation of the same natural phenomenon.

Films can be used to reinforce this historical conception, but in doing so add a further layer of epistemological complexity. Film is a highly complicated representational system, which conventionally, like the photograph, from which it has been derived, is variously designated as recording, copying or looking like reality. That a well-made film can 'look like' Harvey's experiments relies on a viewer who understands the experiments' twentieth-century meaning, and can read the representational language of the cinema. Film is thus a very powerful medium for reinforcing positivist historiography and its implicit assumptions about nature. What we see when we view a film of Harvey's experiments, however, is a series of twentieth-century perceptions of physiological knowledge encoded in a twentieth-century representational system. Lewis's and Dale's historical account of seventeenth-century medicine 'looked like' Harvey's work but, to the historian, the film is a document containing the perceptions of twentieth-century experimental scientists represented in a contemporary medium.

Acknowledgements

For permission to quote from unpublished material I should like to thank: Viscount Knutsford, Lady Lewis, Lady Todd, the Harveian Librarian of the Royal College of Physicians, the Medical Research Council, the Librarian of the Wellcome Institute for the History of Medicine, the Home Office and The Royal Society. For reading and commenting on this chapter I should like to thank: Bill Bynum, John Henry, Nicolaas Rupke, Simon Schaffer and Tilli Tansy.

Abbreviations

CMAC	Contemporary Medical Archives Collection, Wellcome Institute for the History of Medicine, London
RCP	Royal College of Physicians, London
RS	The Royal Society

Notes

1. See Coral Lansbury, *The Old Brown Dog* (The University of Wisconsin Press, 1985). See also Elston, this volume, pp. 259–94.

2. Stephen Paget, *Sir Victor Horsley* (London, Constable and Company Ltd, 1919).

3. There is no full-length biography of Dale, but see *Biographical Memoirs of Fellows of the Royal Society*, vol. 16 (1970), pp. 77–173.

4. Likewise, there is no full-length biography of Lewis, but see A.N. Drury and R.T. Grant, *Obituary Notices of Fellows of the Royal Society of London*, vol. 5 (1945), pp. 179–202. On Lewis's modern experimental outlook see Christopher Lawrence, 'Moderns and Ancients: the "New Cardiology" in Britain 1880–1930'. In W.F. Bynum, C. Lawrence and V. Nutton (eds.), *The Emergence of Modern Cardiology* (London, Wellcome Institute for the History of Medicine, 1985), pp. 1–33.

5. See Richard D. French, *Antivivisection and Medical Science in Victorian Society* (Princeton, Princeton University Press, 1975) and Judith E. Hampson, 'Animal Experimentation 1876–1976: Historical and Contemporary Perspectives', unpublished PhD thesis, University of Leicester, 1975. This work concentrates on the late Victorian period and the years after the Second World War, skipping the intervening period.

6. The title of the work, by Robert Graves and Alan Hodge, subtitled *A Social History of Great Britain* (London, Faber and Faber, 1940), which nicely conjures up the heady faith in science and progress of these years.

7. E. Westacott, *A Century of Vivisection and Anti-Vivisection* (Ashingdon, The C.W. Daniel Company Ltd, 1949), pp. 530–1. This work, by an anti-vivisectionist, is an invaluable guide to the debates of the period.

8. *British Medical Journal (BMJ)*, no. 2 (1926), p. 1028.

9. *The Fight Against Disease*, no. 15, vol. 1 (1927), p. 3.

10. *BMJ*, no. 2 (1926), p. 1028. Emphasis mine.

11. Westacott, *Vivisection*, p. 532.

12. *The Fight Against Disease*, no. 15, vol. 1 (1927), p. 15.

13. *BMJ*, no. 2 (1926), p. 1073.

14. Ibid.

15. *The Fight Against Disease*, no. 15, vol. 1 (1927), pp. 4–11.

16. Westacott, *Vivisection*, p. 533, and *BMJ*, no. 1 (1927), p. 394.

17. [?January 1927], Thomas Lewis to Dawson Williams, CMAC D1/4.

18. *The Fight Against Disease*, no. 15, vol. 1 (1927); Westacott, *Vivisection*, p. 533 and *BMJ*, no. 1 (1927), p. 394.

19. Cambridge, Pharmacological laboratory, 4 February 1927, W.E. Dixon to Thomas Lewis, CMAC D1/5.

20. *BMJ*, no. 1 (1927), p. 359.

21. Westacott, *Vivisection*, p. 534.

22. National Canine Defence League, Petition, CMAC D1/5.

23. Untitled typescript, CMAC D1/5.

24. *The Fight Against Disease*, no. 15, vol. 1 (1927), p. 11.

25. *BMJ*, no. 1 (1927), p. 390.

26. *The Fight Against Disease*, no. 15, vol. 1 (1927), p. 13. Emphasis in original.

27. *BMJ*, no. 1 (1927), p. 440.

28. *BMJ*, no. 1 (1927), p. 485.

29. London, 28 March 1927, Viscount Knutsford to Thomas Lewis, CMAC D1/5.

30. *The Fight Against Disease*, no. 15, vol. 2 (1927), pp. 15–19. Curiously, this journal states that its account is reprinted from the *BMJ*, 9 April. Yet the whole number of that volume is taken up with the Lister centenary celebrations.

31. *BMJ*, no. 1 (1927), p. 858 and Westacott, *Vivisection*, p. 535.

32. *BMJ*, no. 1 (1927), p. 1066.

33. *The Fight Against Disease*, no. 16, vol. 1 (1928), pp. 1–22.

34. London, 2 November 1927, Sir Thomas Lewis to John Bradford, Copy CMAC B2/1.

35. London, 16 January 1928, Sir John Bradford to Sir Thomas Lewis, CMAC B2/3.

36. London, 25 March 1928, Sir Thomas Lewis to Sir John Bradford, RCP 1024/263. Lewis wrote 'The Harvey film which Dale and I have been making . . . '

37. Ibid., and Raymond Crawfurd to Thomas Lewis, London, 30 March 1928, RCP 1024/264.

38. On 30 March 1928 Raymond Crawfurd, College Registrar, wrote from the RCP to Lewis 'A few minutes after I had left you today, it came to my mind that Edinburgh University Library has a copy of the original Christianismi Restitutio of Servetus: no doubt you could get a photo, if it seemed suitable for your film.' CMAC B2/5.

39. *BMJ*, no. 1 (1928), p. 289 and p. 740. The journal reported 'members from almost every constituency had assured correspondents that they would vote for the second reading this year.'

40. *BMJ*, no. 1 (1928), p. 474.

41. H.H. Dale and Thomas Lewis, *William Harvey and the Circulation of the Blood* [N.D.], copies at CMAC and RCP. This was presumably printed in April 1928. On 29 March 1928 Crawfurd had written to Lewis 'I have your MS and will have 500 copies suitably printed out and sent to you', CMAC B2/4.

42. London, 1 June 1928, Thomas Lewis to J.A. Giles [Under-Secretary at the Home Office] 'You may remember that, when we discussed the question of experiment on living animals for the Harvey film . . . ' CMAC B2/7.

43. *BMJ*, no. 1 (1928), pp. 819 and 870.

44. London, 4 June 1928, Thomas Lewis to Dr Philips. Lewis incurred expenses to the total of £2 14s 2d for 'live fish, frogs and material specially used in making up the film'; he added 'I think that Dr. Dale has a small account against you for snakes.' There is no indication of where and how the dogs were obtained. CMAC B2/16.

45. Douglass Taylor has pointed out to me that the diagrams incorrectly represent Galen's account of the blood's motion.

46. *BMJ*, no. 1 (1928), p. 870. This was no by means the first film to depict animal experiments. A number of films were made in the mid-1920s, when the profession first seems to have started using the medium for educational purposes. In 1926 the Massachusetts Institute of Technology produced a 17-minute film on the circulation of the blood, using animals. (A

copy exists in the British Medical Association Film Archive.) The Harvey film, so far as I am aware, is the first *historical* medical film to include shots of animal experiments.

47. London, 1 June 1928, Sir Thomas Lewis to J.A. Giles, CMAC B2/7.

48. London, 2 June 1928, J.A. Giles to Sir Thomas Lewis, CMAC B2/8.

49. London, 6 June 1928, Sir John Rose Bradford to Sir Thomas Lewis, RCP 1024/265.

50. London, 7 June 1928, H.H. Dale and Sir Thomas Lewis to Sir John Bradford, RCP 1024/266.

51. London, 8 June 1928, H.H. Dale to Sir Thomas Lewis, CMAC B2/12.

52. London, 9 June 1928, J.A. Giles to Sir Thomas Lewis, CMAC B2/14.

53. London, 13 June 1928, Sir Thomas Lewis to Henry Dale, CMAC B2/15.

54. London, 15 August 1928, Henry Dale to Dr W. Darrach, RS 2.15.13.

55. London, 13 June 1928, Sir Thomas Lewis to Henry Dale, CMAC B2/15. Lewis therefore intended to return the experiments under his general licence. I have been unable to ascertain whether he did this, and whether in fact dual returns were made for the experiments.

56. London, 25 June 1929, H.M. Barlow to Henry Dale, RS 2.15.5.

57. London, 8 August 1928, Circular from Raymond Crawfurd, Registrar at the RCP, RS 2.15.12.

58. London, 4 March 1930, Henry Dale to Professor J.P. Bonkaert, RS 2.15.24.

59. London, 31 May 1930, A. Landsborough Thomson to Henry Dale, RS 2.15.27.

60. Extract from *Hansard*, vol. 239, columns 1460–1461. Also in RS 2.15.28.

61. London, 3 June 1930, Henry Dale to A. Landsborough Thomson, RS 2.15.29.

13

Legislation: A Practical Solution to the Vivisection Dilemma?

Judith Hampson

History of UK legislation

The United Kingdom has recently begun to phase out its 1876 Cruelty to Animals Act,[1] the oldest piece of legislation on any statute book designed to regulate animal experimentation. Its replacement in May 1986 by the Animals (Scientific Procedures) Act[2] was an historic event, not only because it represented the culmination of 110 years of effort by animal welfarists to reform a law which had remained unamended for over a century, but because the new law represents a radical departure from the one that it replaces. It is an enabling piece of legislation, proscribing almost nothing but attempting to control and regulate almost everything. Both its weaknesses and its strengths lie in its very flexibility.

The passage of this Act far from being hailed as a success by the animal welfare movement as a whole, has again opened up bitter divisions which have dogged the anti-vivisection movement for over a century. There are interesting parallels to be drawn between this situation and that which resulted from the passage of the 1876 Act.[3]

The founders of the British anti-vivisection movement in the mid-1800s, notably the philanthropist Frances Power Cobbe and her influential ally, Lord Shaftesbury, were initially reformers. While they deplored the practice of vivisection and did not subscribe to the philosophy that the ends can justify the means, they nevertheless believed that it could be controlled by proper legislation so that animals would not be made to suffer, and scientists would be made accountable to the public for their actions. With this aim in mind it was they, and their supporters, who had drafted proposals which formed the basis for the Bill of 1875.

Had this Bill become law both biomedical science and anti-vivisectionism in the twentieth century might have been very different. However, at the 'eleventh hour', when the Bill had almost completed its passage through Parliament, a small core of experimental physiologists succeeded in mobilising almost the entire medical profession against it. While Lord Carnarvon, in whose hands the Bill lay, was called away from London by the illness and subsequent death of his mother, a deputation of over 300 medical men descending upon the Home Office resulted in amendments to the Bill which were so substantial as to change its fundamental nature. The objectives of the research and medical communities were to render the Bill 'innocuous' so that it might serve the purpose of soothing the agitated public while imposing no real restrictions on fundamental or medical research.

The anti-vivisectionists, while deeply disappointed, were urged by Lord Shaftesbury to accept the weakened Bill at least as a framework upon which subsequent amendments could be built. But Shaftesbury's hopes were never to be realised. In 110 years the 1876 Act was never amended, though a second Royal Commission (1906–12) and a Departmental Enquiry (1965) did result in substantial changes to the administration of the law.

Deeply disillusioned, the Victorian anti-vivisectionists who had campaigned so hard for a law which they now regarded as a 'vivisector's charter' became convinced that the practice of animal experimentation could not be controlled by law, that neither the scientists nor governments could be trusted and that the only way forward was to convince the public of the immorality of vivisection. Their hope was that a massive public outcry would result in the practice being prohibited. They had become abolitionists.

A clear polarisation of attitudes had taken place. In 1875 anti-vivisectionists had sought controls over animal experiments which the scientists had seemed willing to accept. Within a few years of the Act's passage, that potential common ground had been lost and never again would the two sides come so close to meeting. The abolitionists who argued that experiments were simply immoral, and the utilitarian scientists who argued that they were none the less necessary, were hardly using a common language; there could be no meeting of minds.[4]

Over a century of bitter controversy has served only to polarise the situation still further. The lurid propaganda of the late 1800s was countermanded by the setting up, by the surgeon Stephen Paget in 1908, of the Research Defence Society, whose main objective was to inform the public about the necessity of medical research. But presentations from either extreme camp have not contributed much to the public understanding of the ethical issues or of research methodology, nor have they led to a very constructive debate about how best to protect laboratory animals without impeding the essential progress of medicine and basic science. Today, as in the 1800s, the popular media are more interested in keeping the focus on the controversial aspects of the subject than on debating the real issues.

The modern anti-vivisection debate in the United Kingdom gained impetus as a result of the Departmental Enquiry chaired by Sidney Littlewood in 1963–5.[5] The failure of the government to implement the eighty-three legislative and administrative changes recommended by this Committee led to a spate of private members' bills in both Houses of Parliament throughout the late 1960s and early 19670s. This was also the time of most constructive dialogue, when it seemed that some common ground was beginning to be gained between the anti-vivisectionists and the scientific community.

The development which facilitated this communication was the promotion of 'alternatives' to the use of animals in research. Anti-vivisectionists, perhaps over-optimistically, saw alternatives as a golden hope, promising, in the long term, the replacement of all animals in research. One charity, FRAME (Fund for the Replacement of Animals in Medical Research) was founded specifically to help the research community find alternatives and to disseminate information about them. During the same period several anti-vivisection societies set up charitable research trusts to provide grants for scientists looking for alternatives to the use of animals. These included the Lawson Tait Medical and Scientific Trust, the Humane Research Trust, the Dr Walter Hadwen Trust for Humane Research and the Air Chief Marshall The Lord Dowding Trust for Humane Research.

One very positive result of this activity in the late 1960s and early 1970s was that it provided a kind of neutral platform where anti-vivisectionists and scientists could share a common goal without having to debate the issues for and against the use of animals in research. Throughout this period they were to be found on the same platforms at scientific symposia, often organised by anti-vivisectional trusts.

But in 1975 the debate once again entered the arena of public controversy. Three events were crucial in this: the publication and widespread public acclaim of the book *Victims of Science*[6] by Richard Ryder, then Chairman of the RSPCA, the story of ICI's smoking beagles in the popular newspaper, the *Sunday People*, and the conviction and sentencing to imprisonment of the two ringleaders of the newly-formed Animal Liberation Front, Ronnie Lee and Clifford Goodman. Each received three-year sentences for damage inflicted to an animal breeding unit and to sealing boats and other property.

Since this time, the topic of animal experimentation has hardly been out of the public eye. During the same period a campaign was launched, spearheaded by Lord Houghton, to 'put animals into politics'. This campaign, which followed the Animal Welfare Year of 1976, succeeded in obtaining animal welfare commitments in the 1979 election manifestos of all three major UK political parties. The Conservative Party which was elected to government had pledged to replace the 1876 Cruelty to Animals Act with a piece of modern legislation to control animal experimentation. It was this promise which resulted in the Animals (Scientific Procedures) Act which received its Royal Assent on 20 May 1986.

As in 1876, the passage of legislation on this controversial topic has led to a polarisation of attitudes. Once the government indicated its clear intention to legislate, animal protectionists faced a clear challenge, whether to accept the compromises which a government bill would inevitably contain or whether to remain true to their stronger policies to the extent of opposing new legislation for which the movement had campaigned for so long.

The first White Paper of 1983[7] was outrightly condemned by most groups. The RSPCA criticised it on the grounds that it failed adequately to meet any of its central priorities: promotion of 'alternatives', elimination of pain and suffering, elimination of 'trivial' research, and public accountability. The main anti-vivisection groups went further; they formed a coalition calling itself 'Mobilisation Against the Government White Paper'. Finding themselves unable to compromise, particularly on the issue of pain which they felt could not be regulated by the law, these anti-vivisectionists chose to focus their campaign on gaining public support for the prohibition of certain kinds of experimentation. These included the LD50 and Draize tests, weapons research, tests on cosmetics and most behavioural research.

To many who had campaigned long and hard for new legislation over the years, this strategy seemed to be missing the point. The RSPCA pointed out that pain was the central issue and could not be avoided simply by ignoring it, now that new legislation was becoming a reality. Moreover, the areas of research targeted by Mobilisation, even if it were possible to attain prohibition of them (which seemed hardly practical), accounted for only about 11 per cent of the total number of animals used. Was the animal protection movement now to turn its back on the other 89 per cent in order to feel it had kept its hands clean of compromise? Almost despairingly, Lord Houghton, who had worked for so long to get laboratory animals into the political arena, found himself accusing his erstwhile supporters of being afraid now to go through the open door on which they had been knocking for so long.

The Committee for Reform of Animal Experimentation (CRAE) of which he was Chairman continued to take the pragmatic line of pushing for attainable reform. Knowing it would need to enlist allies for this task, it formed a tripartite alliance with the British Veterinary Association (BVA) and FRAME. During the debates on the framework for new legislation this alliance submitted written proposals to the government and had regular meetings both with the Home Office and the minister responsible for the Bill, David Mellor. These efforts produced many of the changes to the government proposals which appeared in the second White Paper of 1985.[8]

One such change of major significance was that the government was persuaded to move from its position of leaving controls over pain and distress unchanged from those under the 1876 Act and now proposed a radical departure in an entirely novel system of control. This system involves grading experiments according to their severity, linking that severity to the purpose of the experiment, and applying an upper limit or 'Termination Condition', which compels the immediate destruction of any animal found to be in severe pain. (Under the old Pain Condition, an animal in severe pain did not have to be destroyed if that pain was not thought likely to endure.)

No doubt the receipt by the Home Secretary of a 300-page report from the RSPCA on pain and suffering in recent British experiments,[9] forwarded by Patrick Wall, editor of the international journal, *Pain*, also played a part in changing government thinking on this issue during these deliberations. Furthermore, the Minister received a delegation from the RSPCA which included Wall as one of the RSPCA's scientific advisers, and which focused on suffering, and refinement of experiments to remove it, as the main issue for debate.

Notwithstanding these achievements, and though the RSPCA has a continuing input into the CRAE Committee and has, as one of its own central aims, reform of the law, the Society found itself in an ambivalent position when the Bill itself appeared. The RSPCA did not wish to alienate its supporters by welcoming a Bill which, inevitably, did not go as far as its own policies on laboratory animal protection. But nor did it wish to condemn the Bill outright, thus precluding itself from working for amendments. It chose to reserve its position in the hope that the Bill could be substantially strengthened by amendment as it passed through both Houses of Parliament.

Thus it fell to none of the leading animal welfare societies to become official advisers to the government on the Bill's passage. This role was adopted by the alliance between CRAE, the BVA and FRAME. Throughout the parliamentary deliberations, this group had regular meetings with the minister. As a result of these deliberations, and of the lobbying efforts of the RSPCA, the bill received amendments during its passage through both Houses of Parliament.

Current legislative initiatives

The United Kingdom

The new British law represents perhaps the most pragmatic attempt yet enacted in any legislation to deal with the very real ethical dilemmas and practical difficulties raised by animal experimentation. As stated above, it is an enabling piece of legislation which proscribes practically nothing but seeks to control everything through a dual licensing system operated by a strong administrative machinery.

The system requires two licences to cover every scientific procedure. The personal licence testifies to the competence of the licensee, who accepts responsibility for the animals (s)he uses and for implementing the conditions attached to the licence. The project licence, which might be held by an individual researcher working alone or by a project leader in charge of a large programme of research, specifies the project in detail, including the species and number of animals to be used, the techniques to be applied and the permitted level of severity under this project licence.

The system enables the administrative authority (which in the UK is the Home Office) for the first time to have real control over what is done in a specific piece of scientific work. The project will be scrutinised by the Home Office Inspectorate before a licence is granted. They must assure themselves that there is no alternative means available of carrying out the work, and that the degree of severity likely to be attained is fully justified in terms of the aims and objectives of the research. The Home Secretary has finally accepted responsibility for *justifying* what is licensed, a responsibility which, for many years, he has been loath to accept but one for which moderate reformers have continued to press. This means that scientific work, for the first time, becomes truly publicly accountable through the parliamentary process.

Severity has been linked to purpose by the provision of three permitted severity bandings: mild, moderate and substantial. The permitted level of severity will be linked to an assessment of the objectives and purpose of the work. For example, substantial suffering might be allowed for the potency testing of a vaccine or for a piece of essential basic reseach while only mild severity would be allowed for the safety testing of a cosmetic product. It is thought that the majority of projects will fall into the first two bandings though up to 1,000 projects each year might be likely to entail substantial suffering. Before a project licence is granted the Home Secretary must be satisfied that the work could not be done using less severe procedures and that no valid non-sentient alternatives would serve the purpose.

In making these difficult judgements, the Home Office Inspectorate, which will be expanded and become more specialised, will be assisted by a panel of independent expert assessors established by the Home Office for consultation as considered necessary. Especially difficult projects will be referred to the Animal Procedures Committee (formerly the Home Office Advisory Committee), which now becomes a statutory body with powers of initiative for research and investigation. This Committee will make administration of the new law more publicly accountable. It will play an essential role in monitoring the operation of the new controls and the Home Secretary would have to make public the reasons for choosing to ignore its advice. In appointing the Committee, the Home Secretary must have regard to providing adequate representation of both user and animal welfare interests.

The Committee of twelve is currently under a Chairman who is a professor of law. At least two-thirds of the members must be doctors, veterinarians or biological scientists. Not more than half the members shall be licensees. Three professional animal welfarists and two lay persons currently serve. The Committee's duties include advising the Secretary of State on matters of policy, trends in experimental research, alternatives to the use of animals and proposals for revisions in administrative practice of the law. It will also give advice on project licences which raise special difficulties or are for work giving rise to particular public concern, such as the testing of cosmetics, research into the effects of tobacco and its products, and experiments carried out for the acquisition of manual skill in the field of microsurgery (this purpose was prohibited under the 1876 Act). It will review retrospectively all the project licences granted in the category of substantial severity, and offer advice on possible refinement of certain techniques in future projects.

In practice, the assessment of severity is a difficult business. Licensees are expected to familiarise themselves with signs of pain, discomfort or distress in the species they are using and to consult experts for advice where necessary. In order to help researchers come to terms with this, guidelines have been drawn up by the Association of Veterinary Teachers and Research Workers.[10] These are recommended by the Home Office Inspectorate and may eventually find their way into a Code of Practice which will be issued by the Home Office. Guidelines on the Care and Use of Laboratory Animals, which may be incorporated into this Code, have been drawn up by the Royal Society in collaboration with the Universities Federation for Animal Welfare. These are currently under consideration by the Home Office Advisory Committee.

In order to understand how the machinery of the new legislation will work in practice it is necessary to read the new Act in conjunction with the lengthy Guidance Note on the Operation of the New Legislation, issued by the Home Office. This document reflects the government's recognition that no law, however good in practice, will work unless a well-thought-out system is put in place to implement it.

As part of this system the law charges three people with statutory responsibility for day-to-day care of the animals. One of these persons is the holder of the registration certificate for the premises, one is a senior animal technician or curator who is in charge of the animals on a daily basis, and the other is a veterinarian, either employed by the laboratory or available to be called in whenever the need arises.

Both the veterinarian and the animal technician are authorised to apply the Termination Condition, if the licensee is unavailable. This is a condition referred to in the statute, which states that any animal found to be in severe pain which cannot be alleviated must immediately be humanely killed. It is the licensee's duty to implement this Condition if the need to do so is brought to his/her attention.

The new Termination Condition has more force than the old one applied by the Home Office under the 1876 Act which required an assessment of whether or not the severe pain was likely to endure. Moreover, the specification of the Condition in the statute itself and the nomination of persons with statutory responsibility for day-to-day care of laboratory animals, materially adds to the implementation of the controls.

It will take two to three years to switch over from the old licensing system to the new one of project licensing. Only when project licences have been issued for some time will it be possible to assess how well the new law is administered by the Home Office and the good will of those required to carry out their work and obligations under it.

Continental Europe

On 31 May 1985 the Council of Europe, which comprises twenty-one member countries, adopted a Convention for the Protection of Vertebrate Animals Used for Scientific and Other Purposes.[11] Each country which ratifies this will be required to pass legislation adopting its provisions as a basic minimum.

Weak as it is in terms of animal protection, adoption of the Convention should improve conditions for laboratory animals in those countries which have little or no national legislation. It contains reasonable minimum standards for laboratory animal husbandry and general care. Each institution must name both a veterinarian and a person responsible for day-to-day care. In addition to user establishments, breeding and supplying facilities must also be registered and there are provisions for animal marking and record-keeping which should go some way towards eliminating the trade in stolen pets, a substantial problem in some European countries. The use of stray cats and dogs is prohibited.

Severe and enduring pain (illegal under the old UK 1876 Act), is not prohibited, but requires special authorisation. The use of anaesthetics and analgesics is encouraged, but can be dispensed with if not compatible with the objectives of the procedure. Provision is made for the collection of annual statistics. This information is to be published annually by the Secretary General of the Council of Europe. At present only a few countries produce such data, including the United Kingdom, The Netherlands, Switzerland and the Scandinavian countries.

Following considerable debate in the *ad hoc* Committee of Experts which drew up the Convention and during public hearings held in Strasbourg to discuss its provisions and the subject generally, a new clause was added (Article 30) which makes provision for multilateral consultations to take place every five years so that contracting parties can examine the Convention's application and the advisability of revising or extending it. This amendment goes some way towards meeting the recommendations of the Rapporteur to the parliamentary Public Hearings in Strasbourg in 1982, that the Convention should be seen as an 'Accord évolutif', to be updated or amended whenever this was thought to be necessary by member states.

Perhaps of greater significance is the recent initiative taken by the Commission of the European Parliament to draw up a Directive covering laboratory animal protection in the twelve member countries of the European Economic Community. This document has now been considered by the Economic and Social Committee, by the Committee of the Environment, Consumer Protection and Public Health and by the Parliament. All three suggested substantial amendments. A modified text has now been produced by the Council of Ministers, though it by no means incorporates all the changes voted by the Parliament. The Directive, while applying to fewer countries, is a much stronger document than the European Convention. It does, for example, contain meaningful provisions for controlling the degree of pain and suffering allowed in scientific procedures. When passed, it will be binding upon all member states, which must ensure that their national laws are in accord with its provisions. Like the Convention, it does not preclude a member country from passing legislation containing stricter measures.

In addition to these purely European proposals, International Guiding Principles for Biomedical Research Involving Animals have been drawn up by the Council for International Organisation of Medical Sciences (CIOMS), a body established under the auspices of the World Health Organisation (WHO) and the United Nations Educational, Scientific and Cultural Organisation (UNESCO).[12] These are designed to set up a framework within which specific legislative or regulatory systems could be built in any country, including the Third World. In drawing up the principles, CIOMS had regard to vastly different legal systems and cultural backgrounds existing throughout the world with regard not only to attitudes towards animals, but also to medical science, safety testing and training of personnel.

Within the twenty-one countries of the Council of Europe, legislation relating to animal experimentation is widely variable. Some countries have little or no legislation while others have detailed laws, some with complex administrative machinery. Many countries are currently reviewing their legislation. Table 13.1 provides a brief guide to laws in force at the time of writing.

Table 13.1: Legislation controlling animal experimentation in Western Europe

Country	Legislation	Administrative authority	Main provisions
Austria	Federal Law on Animal Experimentation (1974).	*Universities:* Federal Minister for Science & Research *Trade & Industry:* Ministry of Trade Commerce & Industry *Public health, food & veterinary science:* Ministry of Health & Environmental Protection.	Permits granted to heads of institutions specifying type of experiment allowed; inspection by persons from relevant authority; adequate anaesthesia required unless it frustrates object of experiment; surgery on vertebrates restricted to suitably qualified scientists; records detailing purpose, number and origin of animals must be kept for 2 years.
Cyprus	No legislation — experiments carried out in line with UK 1876 Act.	Formal permission of Director of Department of Veterinary Sciences required.	Permission issued only to those with technical qualifications; covers mainly vaccine testing and control; other work is rare.
Belgium	Animal Protection Act (1975).	Ministry of Justice and Ministry of Agriculture.	Licence from Office of Veterinary Medical Inspection to directors of laboratories; inspection by State Veterinary Inspectors; anaesthesia required unless it frustrates object of experiment; 1981 decree requires biological, medical and veterinary students to be trained in 'alternative' methods; new legislation under discussion.

324

Country	Legislation	Administrative authority	Main provisions
Denmark	Animal Experiments (No. 220/1977).	Ministry of Justice. A board appointed by the Ministry is responsible for administration; represents all interest groups including animal welfare.	Individual licence to qualified persons for experiments likely to cause pain and suffering; anaesthesia required for all experiments likely to cause pain, but can be dispensed with; licences not required for procedures causing no more than minor and momentary suffering; 'lower' animals to be used if possible; only vertebrates covered; animals must not be used where 'alternatives' have equal relevance; records of numbers, species and purposes to be kept and presented annually to controlling board; method of euthanasia for dogs, cats and non-human primates must be declared. Order amendment to bring into line with Swedish system. New law (1986) will include strict provisions on animal supply and local ethical committee.
Eire	Legal basis as for UK Act of 1876.	Ministry of Health.	Licences, conditions and inspection by Ministry of Health; basis of control as for UK.
Federal Republic of Germany	Animal Protection Law (1972) parts 5 and 6.	Ministry of Food, Agriculture and Forestry	Licences issued by local authorities to heads of institutions only; orders issued by central Ministry are effected by local authorities; all painful/injurious procedures subject to licensing; Ministry team of veterinary inspectors;

Country	Legislation	Administrative authority	Main provisions
			anaesthesia required for all surgical procedures, but can be dispensed with if it frustrates object of experiment; surgery restricted to suitably qualified persons; 'alternatives' to be used where feasible. Legislation under review.
France	1968 Order under Decree for Animal Experiments (1963), No. 68-139. Constitutes articles R24-31 of the article 454 of the Penal Code.	Ministry of Agriculture and other ministries (has advisory inter-ministerial commission).	Individual authorisation from relevant government department; inspection by Ministry of Agriculture veterinarians or Ministry of Public Health pharmacists; anaesthesia or equivalent analgesia required unless it frustrates object of experiment; experiments without anaesthesia restricted to one only. Surveys underway to find a consensus for possible legislation.
Greece	Law 1197, concerning the Protection of Animals (1981) article 4.	Ministry of Agriculture (aided by Consultative Committee with the Veterinary Service of the Ministry).	Licence required for experiments causing pain or suffering; anaesthesia required for surgical experiments; administered by veterinary surgeon; surgical experiments restricted to graduates in medical, veterinary or biological sciences; no inspection.
Iceland	St j.tíò B. nr 77/1973.	Chief Veterinary Officer, Ministry of Culture and Education.	Experiments only allowed by special permit, granted only to persons with medical or veterinary training, or persons working in institutes with personnel with such training; untrained persons must delegate to trained persons; specific

Country	Legislation	Administrative authority	Main provisions
			instructions attached to permits, including proper provision for anaesthesia and humane euthanasia at end of experiment; all procedures must be conducted at approved institutes; records must be kept. Legislation currently under revision.
Italy	Animal Protection Law (1931), amended 1941.	Ministries for Health and Culture.	Experiments performed only by named, suitably qualified individuals in authorised institutes; director holds responsibility; inspection by medical and veterinary officers of provincial health authorities; adequate anaesthesia required unless it frustrates object of experiment; only warmblooded vertebrates covered; annual report required by pertinent authority. Services undermanned, no prospected change.
Grand Duchy of Luxembourg	Law for the Protection and Welfare of Animals (1983).	Ministry of Agriculture.	Licences issued by Ministry of Health; inspection by Ministry of Agriculture veterinarians. Same provisions as for German and Swiss laws.
Lichtenstein	Animal Welfare Act (1936), article 3 prohibits vivisection		New Law in draft will allow governmental use of animals in exceptional circumstances
Malta	No information available		
The Netherlands	Law for Animal Experiments (1977)	Ministry of Public Health: Veterinary Public Health's	Retrospective licences to institution (no project assessment); compulsory for

327

Country	Legislation	Administrative authority	Main provisions
		Department of Animal Experimentation.	all painful experiments; animals in pain must be euthanised once the experiment is satisfied; anaesthesia can be dispensed with if it frustrates object of experiment, but required for all surgery; 'alternatives' must be used where available and 'lower' vertebrates in place of 'higher' ones where possible; no cats, dogs, equines or primates used if other species will suffice; source of dogs and cats recorded; strict rules on supply but exemptions allowed; inspection and supervision by two State Veterinary Inspectors and team of 35 regional inspectors; Inspectorate requires annual returns including numbers, purpose, species and estimate of degree of discomfort; detailed statistics produced; central advisory committee to Minister for Public Health includes animal welfare member (members appointed by Royal Academy of Sciences); annual report produced.
	Order in Council (1980) provisions in process of implementation.		New controls being phased in; currently project leaders will be required (by 1986) to undergo training in laboratory animal science; detailed provisions on husbandry and care under consideration; a named person responsible for animal care in each institution (Art. 14), several now appointed; these are veterinarians, doctors and biologists who undergo training under

Country	Legislation	Administrative authority	Main provisions
			the Chair of Laboratory Animal Science at Utrecht; neither they nor Inspectors can stop experiments, but can impose restrictions; is likely that institutional ethical committees will be recommended.
Norway	Welfare of Animals Act (1974); Regulations concerning Biological Experiments on Animals (1977).	Experimental Animals Board (EAB) appointed by Ministry of Agriculture.	Licences granted to approved institute with qualified directors who accept responsibilty for all personnel; this person must supply written consent to EAB for all experiments allowed to the institute; final decision rests with the Board; premises must comply with standards set by EAB individual licences issued (exceptionally) to suitably qualified persons; licences refused if valid alternative available; inspection by police, members of EAB or persons it authorises, e.g. county, district or state veterinarians, police, members of municipal animal welfare boards; explicit requirements for anaesthesia, analgesia and euthanasia; special exemptions needed for painful experiments without anaesthesia; all vertebrates and decapoda (crustaceans covered) experiments unlikely to cause suffering exempted; special permission required for use of dogs, cats and non-human primates; annual return to EAB must be made by Departmental Head.

Country	Legislation	Administrative authority	Main provisions
Portugal	Legislation in line with Council of Europe Convention in preparation.		
Spain	No legislation.		
Sweden	Protection of Animals Act (1944) articles 12 & 13, amended 1979 and 1982.	National Board of Agriculture (under Ministry of Agriculture); (regional ethical boards and National Board for Laboratory Animals responsible to this body).	Individual licences subject to qualifications, purpose of experiment etc. purpose-bred animals must be used (exemptions can be granted); ethical review at local level; suffering not to exceed what is 'necessary'; euthanasia required if suffering continues; anaesthesia specified; pain relief required where anaesthesia not used; inspection by local veterinary officers under direction of Municipal Health Boards; 'higher' and 'lower' vertebrates to be used in teaching where other methods available; detailed records required of origin, purpose and numbers of dogs, cats, horses, ungulates, and non-human primates. Legislation under revision.
Switzerland	Animal Protection Law (1978) and Animal Protection Ordinance (1981) part 7.	Competent authority of each Canton (Cantonal committee of specialists to advise Veterinary Administration). Supervision by Federal Commission on Animal Experiments (a committee of experts including animal welfarists).	Authorisation required for each experiment or series of experiments; experiments under direction of trained scientist; special permits required only for experiments causing pain, distress or disturbance of general condition; held by director of laboratory; inspection annually by permitting authority or by Cantonal Commission; anaesthesia required but exemptions

Country	Legislation	Administrative authority	Main provisions
			allowed; detailed requirements on care and husbandry; some ethical assessment required where alternatives to animals not available; 'lower' species to be used where possible; only vertebrates covered; annual records required, kept for 2 years.
Turkey	No information available.		
United Kingdom	Cruelty to Animals Act (1876) superseded by Animals (Scientific Procedures) Act (1986)	Home Office.	See text.

The United States of America

The situation in the United States is extremely volatile. Over the last five years, exposés by animal rights activists, resulting from meticulous underground investigations and illegal break-ins, have highlighted glaring inadequacies in the current system of control. These dramatic examples have been impossible to ignore by regulatory and funding agencies. The result has been recent amendments to the law itself and an overhaul of the controls exercised by granting bodies.

The main legislation relating to animal experimentation is the Animal Welfare Act, originally the Laboratory Animal Welfare Act, passed in 1966 and amended in 1970, 1976 and 1985.[13] The existence of this law is largely the result of a case involving a stolen dog which was taken across state lines for sale to a laboratory. This history has meant that the legislation relates primarily to supply, husbandry and transport of animals. Until recently it has exerted very little control over their actual use in experimental procedures. Moreover, rats, mice and birds, species making up more than 80 per cent of animals used in the USA, are excluded from its provisions because of inadequate resources for enforcement of the law. The general feeling in America has been that there should be as little as possible bureaucratic interference with free scientific enquiry.

American researchers have, on the whole, tended to regard the system of control applied in the United Kingdom as draconian.

The Act is administered by the US Department of Agriculture (USDA) which registers premises and requires reports from them. Facilities are inspected by the Department's Animal and Plant Health Inspection Service (APHIS) which has neither the trained staff nor the budget to secure compliance even with the limited provisions of a law relating to the use of somewhere between 25 and 60 million animals per year (no reliable statistics are yet available for the USA; official sources support the lower figure while animal rights campaigners maintain that the higher estimate is more accurate).[14]

The legislation specifically states that nothing in its provisions shall be construed as authorising the Secretary of Agriculture to promulgate rules, regulations or orders with regard to design and performance of actual research. Though the 1970 amendment required the appropriate use of anaesthetic, analgesic or tranquillising drugs, these provisions were neither defined nor enforced and so failed to meet Congress's objective of exerting some meaningful control over pain and suffering in American experiments.

The trial in 1981 of Edward Taub of the Institute for Behavioural Research in Silver Spring, Maryland[15] dramatically brought to the public's attention the appalling conditions which could exist in an American laboratory. Though the conviction for cruelty to primates was overturned at appeal on a technicality, the case was a landmark in the struggle for legislative reform in the USA. At Congressional Hearings pictorial evidence and veterinary statements were produced testifying to grossly filthy conditions and neglected animals. It had to be generally admitted that both the USDA enforcement system and the system operated by the National Institute of Health (NIH) for monitoring research carried out in federally funded institutes had failed. While authorities maintained that Taub's laboratory was an isolated case, activists, who had originally infiltrated the laboratory and brought the abuses to light, claimed that they were just the tip of the iceberg.

The year 1984 witnessed excerpts of videotapes, stolen by the Animal Liberation Front from the head injury clinic at the University of Pennsylvania, networked across America on national news. They depicted researchers making fun of brain-damaged baboons, smoking whilst operating with dirty scalpels which had been dropped on the floor, failing to maintain adequate anaesthesia during surgery and unjamming a helmet, after supposed infliction of precise injury with special equipment, with a hammer and chisel. The tapes shocked responsible researchers not only in the USA but throughout the world. NIH, which had supported the research to the tune of twelve million tax dollars for thirteen years, was forced to withdraw funding after a sit-in of protesters at their headquarters in Bethesda. Following an investigation, USDA fined the university $4000 for failure to comply with the Animal Welfare Act. The research is now indefinitely suspended.

Withdrawal of NIH funding and fining by the USDA also followed investigations into conditions at the City of Hope Medical Center in Southern California and the University of Columbia. Both had been raided by the ALF, the first in 1984, the second, very recently in 1986. Documents stolen during these raids testify to filthy conditions and animals suffering lingering deaths, having received no adequate post-operative care.

A recent publication by the Animal Welfare Institute, a respected animal protection organisation in Washington D.C., has documented massive and widespread non-compliance with the Animal Welfare Act. The incontrovertible evidence comes from the USDA's own inspection reports, available for scrutiny through the Freedom of Information Act.[16]

Under the accumulating weight of evidence that the system was failing to exert even a minimum acceptable standard of control, Congress took action. In December 1985, the Farm Bill was passed[17] which contained improved standards for the laboratory animals under the Animal Welfare Act. These included the setting up, in each registered facility, of an animal committee, including at least one non-institutional representative, which is to carry out semi-annual inspections. Painful procedures are to be avoided wherever possible and appropriate pain relief given, unless it interferes with the objectives of the experiment. Provision must be made for the exercising of dogs, and non-human primates are to be provided with a physical environment adequate to promote their psychological well-being, though these provisions have yet to be defined. The inspectorate role of the USDA is expanded, each facility to be visited at least once per year and the budget and specialist training of inspectors will need to be increased accordingly.

These legislative changes apply to all registered premises, and once they are implemented through detailed regulations yet to be written by USDA, they should bring about some uniformity of laboratory conditions in the USA. Since 1963, institutions receiving federal funding have also been subjected to a largely voluntary code under the NIH *Guide for the Care and Use of Laboratory*

Animals. Though site visits are carried out by NIH, it is clear from recent evidence that compliance is often far from assured.

However, through recent amendments to Public Health Service Policy, the Guide was amended in 1985. The new Guide, which applies to all registered facilities, contains more detailed recommendations on care and treatment of animals, including provision for veterinary care, anaesthesia, analgesia, post-operative nursing, humane euthanasia and factors affecting environmental health. Multiple survival surgery is discouraged. Institutions are to designate clear lines of authority and responsibility, naming two officials, one with overall responsibility for research programmes, the other to be a veterinarian. Institutional care and use committees are to be involved with all aspects of the research programme, including review of applications for funding and approval of those sections relating to animal care and use. Funding will be dependent upon this documentation. Detailed information on each research programme is to be filed with the NIH Office for Protection from Research Risks.

Animal protection groups continue to complain that the changes offer too little and come too late. They are likely to continue to press for tougher legislative changes. To date, NIH has not relished the idea of being cast in a policing role, but it is clear from recent events that site visits will be more frequent and more thorough, that Institutional Committees will have a real role to play and will not merely exist on paper, and that penalties exacted for continued non-compliance with the regulations are likely to be severe. This at least offers some hope of control in a country with a huge research effort, fraught with administrative problems.

Conclusion: ethical dilemmas and practical realities

As the Littlewood Committee concluded in 1965, vivisection is a moral and social problem of the first order of magnitude and one which does not exclusively concern the expert.[18] Certainly the rights and wrongs of using animals in research, and the practical realities of what constraints must be placed upon the activity, are societal issues. They cannot be the sole province of the scientific community. Almost every activity in which modern society indulges, from exploring the depths of the oceans and the vastness of space, to the development of new industrial products and cosmetics, or the search for a cure for AIDS, is dependent to a greater or lesser degree on the use of laboratory animals. These animals are a shield with which we defend ourselves. Whether this is regarded as a matter of considerable moral significance, or merely a regrettable necessity, depends upon whether one considers animals to be worthy objects of our moral concern, or merely tools for our use and manipulation.

While few scientists today would openly declare that science should be pursued unhindered by any moral or legal restraints, the research community still maintains that the pursuit of knowledge is paramount. Obligations to treat animals as humanely as possible are generally recognised, but the extent to which those obligations are acted upon is variable, and very few indeed are the researchers who address the question of whether they have a right to use animals at all, or even to make them suffer. There exists a significant difference in degree of sensitivity between researchers who expect to carry out their practices unhindered (e.g. in the US) and those who have become accustomed over many years to a fairly elaborate system of constraints (e.g. in the UK).

In this can be seen the beginnings of a practical solution to the ethical dilemma. While legislative or voluntary control systems do not address themselves to the fundamental question of whether or not it is morally justifiable to experiment on animals, they do change the moral climate. Moreover, they can provide a forum in which some of the essential questions, including moral ones, can be asked by researchers themselves.

This is now happening with new control systems throughout the Western world. In the United Kingdom, the new legislation sets up 'a chain of accountability' from the Home Secretary down through all those with statutory responsibility: the licence sponsors, Inspectorate, independent assessors, Animal Procedures Committee, named veterinarian and person responsible for day-to-day care, to the licensee. Ultimately, the entire chain is responsible to the public through Parliament, because the Home Secretary now has a statutory obligation to justify what is licensed.

After years of debate over how best to control and scrutinise the purposes for which research is carried out, and how to reduce animal suffering, it was concluded by those who had thought long and hard about these issues, notably Lord Houghton, that such an administrative system was the only way to achieve the desired ends. Houghton has emphasised that such subjective issues as 'justifiable' purposes and 'permissible' levels of suffering could not be tied down in the statute law, but must be subjected to the judgement of reasonable men and women.

The weak point in the new British system may well be that a

wide range of expertise is required to foster refinement of research projects. It may well be that a statistician might know how to reduce the number of animals used in a project when the licensee does not, or that the opinion of a pain expert is needed on the best method of analgesia to use or other refinement to reduce the severity of the procedure, or that a computer expert could advise on how to replace the use of animals altogether for part of the project.[19] But nowhere in the British system is there an automatic input of varied expertise at the level of project licence assessment. Only if the Inspectorate is concerned will an application be referred to an independent project assessor or the Animal Procedures Committee, and even then a sufficient range of expertise might not be brought to bear. Refinement of procedures is a highly technical business, and the Inspectorate, which will be responsible for assessing the bulk of project licences, cannot possibly be expected to possess the range of expertise needed to suggest refinements in the very many cases where these may well be possible.

Other countries have attempted to address this problem by the establishment of ethics committees or animal care and use committees. In Canada, there is a voluntary system of control in which institutional committees play a central part. These committees are small and consist primarily of animal users and technicians, though most include a non-user veterinarian and a lay member, sometimes from outside the institution. The committees are given very specific terms of reference relating to care, husbandry and humane procedure, in comprehensive guidelines drawn up by the Canadian Council for Animal Care. Compliance with these guidelines is a prerequisite for funding from all the major granting agencies.

In Sweden, regional ethics committees have been incorporated into recent legislative controls. The committees are large and are made up of one third researchers, one third animal technicians and one third lay members. The whole committee seldom meets; instead small groups of three, one representative from each group, meet to review proposed protocols and may approve them, after suggesting refinements if necessary. They may consult additional experts, but only especially difficult cases are referred to the whole committee, the intention being to avoid bureaucratic delays.

As we have seen, the USA is now adopting institutional animal care and use committees on the Canadian model. Such committees are intended to ensure that animals are cared for adequately and treated humanely. They can also address issues such as the justification of research and whether its severity can be reduced by refinement of the experimental techniques. They also offer the possibility of bringing in the required variety of expertise to fulfil this task.

Where they work well the committees can also foster dialogue between researchers and laypersons, thus opening up the issues for rational debate and for pragmatic solution in a spirit of co-operation. However, these systems have not been without severe problems. The scheme in Sweden has been rendered almost ineffective by the adoption in many regions of radical anti-vivisectionists among the lay members. Since these persons are opposed to all animal experimentation, they are less interested in refining protocols than in impeding research by holding it up. This has led to a generally poor attendance at full committee meetings and loss of faith by scientists in the system. Thus, rather than contributing directly to a system which could improve the lot of laboratory animals, the radical anti-vivisectionists have brought that system into disfavour and threatened its continuance. In Canada, it is becoming clear that institutional commitees need some legislative back-up in order to be consistently effective. There has been wide variation between institutions, some committees existing only on paper.

While none of the control systems is without problems, we at least witness in all of them some serious attempts to get to grips with practical problems, and for animal protectionists and scientists to work together in a joint effort to tackle them. Perhaps in a decade from now the experience of the different systems will have been pooled and the best elements of all of them incorporated into systems which effectively serve the needs of individual countries. There is no doubt that a strong licensing system, such as that operated in the UK, prevents the most objectionable practices from occurring. By the same token, the British system lacks the flexibility and opportunity for peer review offered by institutional or regional review committees. While the types of committees operated in other countries would not be ideally suited to operating alongside the British licensing system, there is no doubt that committees of some kind would play an essential role in assisting the Inspectorate to discharge its duties of weighing severity against utility of purpose under the new legislation, and would assist project refinement.

The essence of any effective system is dialogue between all concerned parties. This is amply illustrated in The Netherlands where a new system of control based on co-operation between veterinarians in laboratories, institutional committees and a small central inspectorate seems to be working well. The Netherlands is perhaps the most advanced country in terms of addressing the moral issue of animal experimentation. It is now compulsory in this country for all new licensees to undergo a course of ethical training at the University of Utrecht, while a new chair has been established at Leiden University specifically to study the moral, social and practical problems around the animal experimentation issue.

In Holland the dialogue between animal rights advocates, government officials and the scientific community has been generally good. In other countries, polarisation continues to increase, with little or no dialogue. There is no doubt that the new debate on animal rights, spearheaded as it is by a number of highly articulate and deeply thoughtful philosophers,[20] will be as important in determining the course of animal experimentation activity and its regulation over the next 100 years as was the anti-vivisection movement in Victorian Britain.

Notes

1. *Cruelty to Animals Act* (15 August 1876), 39 & 40 Victoria, ch. 77.

2. *Animals (Scientific Procedures) Act* (20 May 1986), Elizabeth II, ch. 14.

3. See J.E. Hampson, 'Animal Experimentation 1876–1976: Historical and Contemporary Perspectives', unpublished PhD thesis, University of Leicester, 1978; R.D. French, *Antivivisection and Medical Science in Victorian Society* (Princeton University Press, Princeton, 1975).

4. J.E. Hampson, 'Animal Welfare: A Century of Conflict', *New Scientist*, 25 October 1978, pp. 280–2.

5. Home Office, *Report of the Departmental Committee of Experiments on Animals*, Cmnd. 2641 (HMSO, London, 1965).

6. R.D. Ryder, *Victims of Science* (Davis-Poynter, London, 1975).

7. Home Office, *Scientific Procedures on Living Animals*, Cmnd. 8883 (HMSO, London, 1983).

8. Home Office, *Scientific Procedures on Living Animals*, Cmnd. 9521 (HMSO, London, 1985).

9. RSPCA, *Pain and Suffering in Experimental Animals in the United Kingdom* (RSPCA, Horsham, West Sussex, 1983; 1985).

10. D.B. Morton and P.H.M. Griffiths, 'Guidelines on the Recognition of Pain, Distress and Discomfort in Experimental Animals and an Hypothesis for Assessment', *Veterinary Record*, vol. 116 (1985), pp. 431–6. Association of Veterinary Teachers and Research Workers, 'Guidelines for the Recognition and Assessment of Pain in Animals', ibid., vol. 118 (1986), pp. 334–8.

11. *European Convention for the Protection of Vertebrate Animals Used for Experimental and Scientific Purposes* (Council of Europe, Strasbourg, 1985).

12. *International Guiding Principles for Biomedical Research Involving Animals* (CIOMS, Geneva, 1985).

13. See J.E. Hampson, *Laboratory Animal Protection Laws in Europe and North America* (RSPCA, Horsham, West Sussex, 1985).

14. Ibid., p. 3.

15. See N. Heneson, 'Cruelty to Animals: the State versus the Scientist', *New Scientist*, vol. 92 (1981), pp. 672–4.

16. *Beyond the Laboratory Door* (Animal Welfare Institute, Washington D.C., 1986).

17. US Congress, public law 99–198, Title XVII, Subtitle F — commonly known as 'the Improved Standards for Laboratory Animals Act'.

18. Note 5 above, para. 543 (1).

19. Note 9 above.

20. See for example P. Singer, *Animal Liberation* (Random House, New York, 1975); T. Regan and P. Singer (eds.), *Animal Rights and Human Obligations* (Prentice Hall, Englewood Cliffs, New Jersey, 1976); S.R.L. Clark, *The Moral Status of Animals* (Oxford University Press, Oxford, 1977); *The Nature of the Beast* (Oxford University Press, Oxford, 1984); D. Paterson and R.D. Ryder (eds.), *Animals' Rights — a Symposium* (Centaur Press, Fontwell, Sussex, 1979); B.E. Rollin, *Animal Rights and Human Morality* (Prometheus, Buffalo, N.Y., 1981); T. Regan, *All that Dwell Therein* (University of California Press, Berkeley, 1982); *The Case for Animal Rights* (Routledge & Kegan Paul, London, 1984).

14

A Select Iconography of Animal Experiment

William Schupbach

The iconography of animal experiment consists of two principal types of picture. The first type is made up of woodcuts and engravings which have been made to illustrate books for anatomists and physiologists, from editions of Galen and Vesalius in the sixteenth century to the notorious textbooks of the 1870s.[1] These are generally small, repetitive, limited to showing the situation of the experimental animal and aimed at a restricted audience. They have a place in the documentary history of our subject, particularly those which anti-vivisectionists republished in their own literature or projected on to large screens to impress on the hearts of the public the agonies which experimental animals suffered.[2]

However, the present essay is limited to a review of five examples of the second type: ambitious works of fine art which show the experimenters as well as the experiment and depict them deliberately for public exhibition. Of the five which have been chosen, some are totally unknown to previous writers on the subject, while others, though well known, have not been fully discussed and deserve a place in this volume.

1. Joseph Wright of Derby (1734–97), 'The Picture of the Air Pump' (so called by the painter), 1768. Oil on canvas, 1.829 × 2.438 m. Reproduced by courtesy of the Trustees, National Gallery, London.[3] *See Plate 1, p. 209, above.*

A bird has been removed from the cage in which it normally lives (above right) and has been placed in a glass receiver (above centre). Air is evacuated from the receiver by means of an air-pump (on the table, left) in order to show to the assembled company the effects of deprivation of air on the bird. The demonstrator holds his left hand on the stop-cock which, if turned, would restore air to the inside of the receiver and thus save the life of the bird. The question, whether we are to suppose he will turn it in time to save the bird, is further discussed towards the end of this commentary, but first we shall examine the nature of the experiment.

In the eighteenth century the air-pump was a common item in cabinets which included instruments of experimental philosophy.[4] It was used mainly for experiments in pneumatic physics, to demonstrate the weight, pressure and elasticity of air. It was first used for animal experiments in 1659, by Robert Boyle and Robert Hooke, whose attempts to identify the physical properties of air also seemed to promise answers to certain fundamental questions in cardio-respiratory physiology which William Harvey had left to his followers on his death in 1657.[5] First Boyle and Hooke placed a lark in a receiver and pumped out the air: when the lark suffered convulsions, the stop-cock was turned to let in the air but the air came too late and the lark died. In a second experiment they placed a sparrow in a receiver and again pumped out the air: the sparrow appeared to have died, but after air had been let back into the receiver it revived. When the air was again pumped out the sparrow really did die. Thirdly, the second experiment was repeated with a mouse instead of a bird, with the same result. Two other experiments with mice ended with the death of one mouse and the survival of the other. In each case the duration of survival was noted, the dead animals were dissected after the experiment and other pertinent details were recorded.[6] A further series of similar experiments was performed by Boyle around 1662, using vipers, ducks, frogs, shellfish, kittens, birds, etc., in order to identify variations in the reactions of different kinds of animal to want of air, want of fresh air, drowning and other forms of impeded respiration.[7]

In eighteenth-century England — and perhaps elsewhere too — the repetition of these experiments of Boyle's, albeit with many variations, became a standard part of the routine of public (itinerant or established) lecturers on natural and experimental philosophy, such as John Theophilus Desaguliers (1683–1744),[8] Benjamin Worster (*fl.* 1719–30),[9] Benjamin Martin (1704/5–82),[10] James Ferguson (1710–76)[11] and Adam Walker (1731?–1821).[12] Some of the variations were intended to spare the pain of the animal: the use of a bladder or 'lungs-glass' could replace the experiment with the living animal, since, in James Ferguson's words, the latter experiment 'is too shocking to every spectator who has the least degree of humanity'.[13]

Benjamin Martin remarked that the bladder-experiment 'may suffice, to the *tender-hearted*, to convey the intended Ideas, *without torturing the Animal for Amusement*',[14] but as we shall see, it was Martin's view that, for conveying the intended ideas to the *stout-hearted*, torture was better. Other variations had a scientific purpose: for example, the animal could be exposed to charcoal fumes or expired air instead of, or in addition to, a vacuum. The experimental animal also varied: Benjamin Martin provided an engraving of a rabbit and fish in receivers; Desaguliers and Ferguson mention cats; Ferguson and Walker birds.[15] Using a bird as his experimental animal, Joseph Wright of Derby's lecturer presents his audience with a repetition of the original form of Boyle's experiment: evacuation of air. In any form the experience must have been unpleasant for the animal even if the amount of purely physical pain suffered would have been limited by loss of consciousness fairly early on in the experiment.

It is Benjamin Martin who, unwittingly, provides us with the most articulate and lively commentary on Wright's painting, in the dialogue which he published in 1755 as *The young gentleman and lady's philosophy*. The speakers here are not a professional lecturer and his customers, as in Wright's painting, but Cleonicus, a young English gentleman on vacation from the university, and his younger sister Euphrosyne. Despite the differences between the dialogue and the painting, the former serves in so many passages as a verbal illustration of the latter that the relevant sections of Martin's text are reprinted here without further comment.

> *Euphrosyne.* I hope your explosive Experiments are now at an End; for though I take Pleasure in learning the Nature and Properties of the Air by them; yet they have so much of the Terrible in them, that I can scarcely conceit I am safe while you show them.
>
> *Cleonicus.* Our Passions are given us to a very good Purpose; they are a Kind of Armour to the Mind, and defend and fortify us against disastrous Events: Others operate upon us in a different Manner, moving Pity and Compassion towards every Object we see in distressful Circumstances; and this I am sure will be your Case in the next Experiment.
>
> *Euphrosyne.* I am jealous of some baneful Experiment to follow. It gives me Pain to hear you prelude to it thus. — I thought the Life of some Animal was in the Case. — See here comes *John*, with a lovely, young Rabbit. — I hope that tender

Creature is not to be sacrificed for my Sake. —

Cleonicus. You are like all the Rest of your Sex. — You think it Cruelty to attempt the Life of a large Animal, but are quite regardless of the Destruction of those which expire under your Feet in every Walk of Pleasure you take. — We know not but the Life of one Animal is equal to that of another: Little depends on the Bulk or Size of the Creature: If any thing, it is an Argument against you, to say it is small; since all our Observations convince us, that whatever relates to animal Life, Sensation and Motion, is always more exquisite in those Creatures, in Proportion as they are smaller.[16] — The Million of Mites in Cheese, of Eels in Vinegar, which are daily sacrificed for your Appetite's Sake, do not move your Commiseration so much, as this one single Rabbit, that can hardly be said to be more than half alive, and sensible, as being so young: — But to mitigate your Concern, I shall only show, in this Experiment, that the poor Creature does really depend upon the Air for Life; and after that, I shall put it into your Hands, as well as you see it now. — Here, *John*, put the Rabbit under the Glass. — And now my *Euphrosyne*, have a good Heart, and look on; for turning away your Face will boot the Animal nothing. — See, upon exhausting [the receiver], how uneasy it appears. — As the Air is more rarified, the Animal is rendered more thoughtful of his unlucky Situation, and seeks in vain to extricate himself. — He leaps and jumps about. — A Vertigo seizes his Brain. — He falls, and is just upon expiring. — But I turn the Ventpiece, and let in the Air by Degrees. — You see him begin to heave, and pant. — At length he rouzes up, opens his Eyes, and wildly stares about him. — I take off the Receiver, and shall now deliver it as recovered from the Dead.

Euphrosyne. Poor, innocent Creature! I am grieved to think thou hast suffered so much on my Account; but be assured, my Care shall be proportionally increased for thy future Safety and Welfare. Thou shalt always be my darling Rabbit; as by thee, I have been obliged to learn how necessary the Air is for animal Life, and Respiration.[17]

Cleonicus then proceeds to perform the same experiment on three fishes placed in the receiver in a vessel of water.

Cleonicus. — See the Experiment. As soon as I turn the Winch, they find the Difference of the Air. — You see the Bubble of Air ascend from their Mouths and Gills. — They appear uneasy, and their Bodies are expanded. — They continue to rise, at the same Time, they shew an Endeavour to descend. — You see two out of the three floating on the Top, and though not in the Agonies of Death, yet they seem greatly distressed, and lie with their Backs downward, as it were, in an expiring Posture, the Third is almost perpendicular, endeavouring to reach the Bottom, but cannot. —

Euphrosyne. It is very disagreeable to see those poor Creatures in so miserable a Plight, when probably their Condition may be worse than that of Death. I have often observed the Air-bladder in Fishes; and I presume, it is owing to the Expansion of Air in those Bladders, that they are thus obliged to swim. — Pray, release them from their Misery, by letting in the Air.

Cleonicus. I will do as you require. — On turning the Ventscrew, you observe, their Bodies, as it were, contract, and by becoming less, they are rendered heavier, and by that Means able to sink, which they do with great Precipitation. — By this Experiment, you see how necessary the Air is, even for Animals that live in the Water, though they can shift with so small a Degree of finer Air, that it is not easy to kill them in the greatest *Vacuum* that can be made with the Pump; so far from it, that I remember Mr *Hawksbee* tells us, he let two Fishes stand a whole Week in *Vacuo*, and they seemed to be brisker and better at last than at first, when the Air was drawn from them.

Euphrosyne. The Usefulness of this Machine seems unlimited. What a prodigious Variety of Experiments are shown thereby to explain the Nature of Things, and the important Properties of Air![18]

For the sake of completeness, Martin's account of a third animal experiment is also reprinted, though it involves electrocution rather than suffocation.

Cleonicus. What would you say, if you were to see your favourite Linnet struck dead with the [electric] Shock?

Euphrosyne. I would not see it, nor suffer it for the World.

This Electricity, I'm afraid, will prove a terrible Affair
to my poor little Dog and Birds. Why should you take
Delight in such cruel Experiments?

Cleonicus. Were it not for them, Mankind would not be informed how far the Power of Nature could operate, and consequently, in many Cases, what could, or could not be done.
Nay, the Life of a Bird, or a Mouse, might probably save
that of a Man, and therefore the Experiments tend rather
to a good, than a bad End; tho' in Appearance they seem
incompatible with our Reason, and more delicate Passions.
Accordingly, therefore, I have prepared this little Titmose
to be a substitute Victim for your Linnet, and you must
not flinch to see it sacrificed on this Altar by electrical
Fire. — I shall call my Servant in to be the Executioner.
— Here, *John*, take this Bird, with a Chain about its Leg,
and when I speak, bring its Head within ¼ of an Inch
of the Barrel.

John. — Yes, Sir, I am ready to obey your Commands.

Cleonicus. Gently now bring its Head to the Barrel. —

John. The Bird's dead, by my Soul! —

Euphrosyne. Poor Creature! It is dead indeed! How sudden a
Death is this! What a violent Stroke it must be on the
Head of that Little Creature to deprive it of Life in an
Instant! But these Scenes are so affecting, I could wish
to have them chang'd for Experiments of another Sort.[19]

Martin's dialogue is of course didactic and cannot compare in
artistry with Wright's painting, but its shallow, even clarity makes
it a nice complement to the sublime chiaroscuro of the picture. Putting the two together, and assuming that the painter intended us
to read his picture as a unified, historically rational scene, we can
still interpret Wright's chosen moment of narrative in more than
one way.

1. The scene takes place at the house of the lecturer. The other figures
are gentlefolk or tradespeople who have come to hear his lecture.
The boy on the right is the lecturer's servant. The bird-cage hangs
where it does because the lecturer keeps the bird there for the purpose of repeating this experiment, which the bird has always hitherto
survived. We deduce that the lecturer knows how long the bird can
survive without air and will therefore not allow it to die on this
occasion. The distress of the little girls is therefore unwarranted:

or 2. The scene takes place at the house of the family or one of the families in the audience. The members of the audience are attending the performance of an itinerant lecturer. The bird is the pet of one of the little girls shown in the picture. The boy handling the bird-cage would then surely be the family's servant, not the lecturer's. The bird has not endured this experiment before, and we have no reason to suppose that it will survive this one.

Wright may have intended us to assume one of these interpretations, but, if so, it is not now clear which is correct. However, there are some hitherto neglected details which may help to clarify his attitude to the circumstances of the experiment. In the first place, the boy on the right is usually said to be lowering the cage in order to return the bird to it at the end of the experiment. But the position of his left hand and the angle of his right arm are more suitable for pulling the rope to raise the cage, not for letting the rope run in order to lower it. If so, his action suggests that he thinks the cage is no longer needed because the bird seems likely to die.[20]

Secondly, of all the experimental equipment on the table, the most conspicuous is the central feature, a large glass jar containing a liquid, a refracted rod and an unidentified object which appears to be a carious human skull. Unlike some of the other objects on the table (e.g. the air-pump and the Guericke hemispheres), this item is not mentioned in the published lectures of experimental philosophers. Presumably Wright invented the motif himself. Why?

The answer must surely have to do with the traditional use — in paintings, not in lectures — of the skull as a symbol of death. The theme of mortality is echoed in the painting by the unexpected reflection of the candle snaking up the left side of the flask containing the skull. Skull and candle are traditional companions in iconography, the candle demonstrating the consuming passage of time, the skull its effect. The philosopher seems to point with his right index-finger down to this combined reminder of mortality. The function of the rod which stands in the flask is, at a formal level, to guide the viewer's eye from the philosopher's finger to the skull.

This interpretation would make Joseph Wright's painting, in part, a *vanitas* picture employing emblems of mortality which are also found in other paintings by Wright.[21] A *vanitas* picture reminds us that death is inevitable and its moment unpredictable. The implication for the depicted bird is that it will die to remind us that our daily life is a fragile thing depending on (*inter alia*) supplies of fresh air in inexhaustible quantity.

Yet would not the scene become a tragi-comedy of manners if

we were to suppose that the itinerant lecturer will accidentally kill his customer's pet bird, or — even more farcical — one of his own props? To avoid such ineptitude, we should have to invoke the device of dramatic irony: the viewers of the *experiment* are led to believe that the bird will be killed, but the viewers of the *painting* can suspect that Wright has only weighted the internal story against the bird in order to heighten the joy of the outcome, the skill of the philosopher in choosing the critical moment, and the goodness of God in supplying us with air.

This interpretation seems to be confirmed by the species of the bird chosen for the experiment, if it is agreed that the bird in the picture appears to be a white cockatoo, *Cacatua sulphurea* (Gmelin) or *Cacatua alba* (P.L.S. Müller). In 1768 (the date of the picture) a live white cockatoo would have been a *rara avis* in the English midlands: a native of the Celebes and Philippine islands, it was not described until 1760 and then only from a museum specimen.[22] A live bird of that species would have had considerable financial value and would probably not have been risked in an experiment normally performed on sparrows and larks. In his preliminary sketch for the picture, Wright showed just such a common song-bird and not a cockatoo. One can only surmise that he had seen the cheaper kind of bird subjected to this experiment, but in the finished version of his picture (Plate 1) he substituted the white cockatoo in order to emphasise the demonstrator's confidence in his ability to retrieve the precious bird from the very threshold of extinction. We cannot even be sure that Wright ever saw a living white cockatoo, for he could have used as his source a museum specimen such as the stuffed 'Indian paroquet' in the Lichfield museum of the surgeon Richard Greene, whose collection was supported and used by many of the curiosi in Wright's circle.[23] If this is so, the picture is as much to be admired for art that conceals art as for its more obvious virtues.

2. Oil-painting on canvas by Emile-Edouard Mouchy (1802–*c*.1870?), 112 × 143 cm, signed 'Mouchy' and dated '1832'. Wellcome Institute Library, London. *See Plate 2, p. 210 above.*

In a garret a young demonstrator dissects a living dog which has been tied down on a table fitted with metal rings for that purpose. Of the twelve students in attendance, some watch the dissection, others discuss it, one makes notes in a book and one seems to refer to something outside the room. In the left foreground a second dog barks at the sight of the vivisection of its companion. A shelf on the back wall holds skeletons and chemical apparatus.

In view of the size and the unusual subject of this painting, it is surprising that its provenance is at present unknown. The only known fact of its history is that it was exhibited in 1913 in the opening exhibition of the Wellcome Historical Medical Museum, which was a precursor of the present Wellcome Institute Library.[24] For the details of the picture's commission — if it was commissioned — and for its subsequent history, the writer can at present only invite information.

The painter, Emile-Edouard Mouchy, is at least documented. He was born in 1802, entered the École des Beaux-Arts in 1816, and is described as a pupil — one of many — of Pierre-Narcisse Guérin. A list of the pictures which Mouchy exhibited in the Salon between 1822 and 1851 includes paintings of sacred subjects, history pictures and domestic scenes.[25] He does not seem to have been particularly successful and is unknown to many authors of books on French painting of his time.[26] Today it is difficult to find any of his pictures: a painting of 'Les Forgerons' (blacksmiths) is said to be in the Musée d'Art et d'Archéologie at Toulon,[27] and two enormous paintings by him, both of sacred subjects, were sold at Christie's, London, in 1981.[28]

The present painting, signed and dated 1832, appears not to have been exhibited at the Salon; if not because of its subject, possibly because the Salon for 1832 was cancelled owing to the cholera epidemic of that year.[29] In the Salon of 1833 Mouchy exhibited an 'Étude des chiens' which might or might not be connected with the dogs in our picture.[30] Reviewing the five pictures which Mouchy exhibited on that occasion, Auguste Jal found almost nothing to praise: Mouchy was an imitator, now of Jeanron, now of Delacroix, now of Géricault, now of all three. Apart from criticising Mouchy's poor drawing and his extreme use of the light-on-dark method of Decamps, Jal also stated, 'Je ne blâme point l'uniformité cadavéreuse du ton des têtes, mais celle des types; toutes les têtes se ressemblent.'[31] This observation has a bearing on our painting: without positive evidence of intention, we cannot say that it is a portrait, nor of whom it might be a portrait, since all the faces are Mouchy types, not individual portrayals. Moreover, all the figures appear to be of about the same age as Mouchy when the picture was painted (thirty years). Consequently, the obvious temptation to identify the demonstrator with the physiologist François Magendie (aged forty-nine in 1832) must, alas, be resisted. It would not seem impossible that the subject of the painting should have been derived from a particular, hypothetical group of students of experimental physiology, of whom there were many in the 1820s and still some in the next decade.[32]

Magendie, however, would appear to have been the indirect creator of Mouchy's subject. By 1830 he had become the leading champion of experimental physiology in Paris, but despite the honours he had received from foreign academies, he still had no official teaching post.[33] His physiology lectures were given in private amphitheatres.[34] His course for the year 1828 repeated a wide range of physiological experiments which he had first performed in the course of research, many of them starting with an incision in the abdomen of a dog, as shown in the painting by Mouchy.[35] These experiments had presumably been originally carried out in Magendie's own residence, if we accept the implications of the following memoir by Claude Bernard, written in the 1870s. Bernard also comments that Magendie's facilities scarcely improved when he was appointed to a chair at the Collège de France (1831):

> Formerly, and I am speaking only of thirty or so years ago, when one had an idea for an experiment, one often had to wait a long time before it could be performed: we had neither the premises, nor the instruments, nor the animals at our disposal. One needed good luck and great determination in order to be able to bring together the necessary conditions for an experiment. One experimented in one's rooms, on an animal overcome by surprise, without assistance and virtually without instruments. When, in 1830 [actually 1831], Magendie was appointed to the Collège de France, he was given for doing his vivisections only a tiny room, or rather a kind of little closet, which could hardly hold the two of us. Yet it was there, by dint of patient efforts, that his most immortal research was carried out, for it was only ten years later, in 1840, that he obtained a true laboratory, the laboratory in which we are today.[36]

In view of Bernard's remarks it would be wrong to interpret the cramped premises shown by Mouchy as an attempt to conceal the act of vivisection behind closed doors — not that there was no criticism of it at the time.[37] Nor does one find in the reactions of the students any other feature which would imply unambiguous disapproval of vivisection — and had the painter intended to include any, he would surely not have left it ambiguous. On the contrary, their elegant, thoughtful poses, composed in the tradition of Raphael's 'School of Athens' (*c.* 1509) and Rembrandt's 'Anatomy of Dr Tulp' (1632), imply his appreciation of their intellectual enterprise.

Some of the details of the dissected dog are implausible and may have been done from memory or imagination. The rope around its neck would not stop the dog biting but *would* tend to throttle it: a first step might have been to tie the muzzle and then pass a loop around the lower jaw to hold back the head. The absence of blood — contrast the painting of Bernard, Plate 5 — suggests that the painter might have seen Magendie open up a dead dog, and then have depicted the same details in the different circumstances of vivisection. Undoubtedly much more could be said about this exceptional painting which is here reproduced for the first time.[38]

3. Charles John Tomkins (b. 1847, worked *c.* 1876–*c.* 1894), after John McLure (or McClure) Hamilton (1853–1936), 'Vivisection' (legend lightly engraved at foot of sheet), engraving (mixed method), 61 × 43.5 cm, 1883, after a painting or drawing, 1882. The date of the original work and the artist's signature are reproduced in the bottom right corner. Impression in the Wellcome Institute Library, London. *See Plate 3, p. 211 above.*

John McLure (or McClure) Hamilton was born in Philadelphia, and studied in his birthplace, in Antwerp and in Paris (under Gérome).[39] He became extremely successful as a portraitist, having among his sitters Gladstone, Lord Leighton and, among scientists, John Tyndall and Silas Weir Mitchell. Towards the end of his life he published an account of his sittings with eminent subjects, but the present work, an early and provocative piece, was of course not mentioned.[40] In fact no contemporary reference to it has yet been found, but there may be some comment on it in newspapers, since it was exhibited as a fine engraving at the Royal Academy in 1884, the first item exhibited there by this engraver, C.J. Tomkins.[41] The original painting or drawing by McLure Hamilton was exhibited in London in the autumn of 1885, bearing the title 'Vivisection — the last appeal'.[42]

The bottle which the vivisector holds behind his back is presumably supposed to contain an anaesthetic: if so, the charge against his conscience is the fact that he experiments on animals at all, not that he inflicts pain on them. The object on the table in the lower left corner is a dissected gull. The figure of the dog begging for mercy may have been inspired by a letter to the press from the influential anti-vivisectionist George Hoggan, first published in 1875: dogs brought up from the cellar to Claude Bernard's laboratory

> seemed seized with horror as soon as they smelt the air of the place, divining, apparently, their approaching fate. They would make friendly advances to each of the three or four persons present, and as far as eyes, ears and tail could make a mute appeal for mercy eloquent, they tried it in vain.[43]

The print is a document of the strong propaganda campaign against vivisection which flourished in the 1880s.[44]

4. Michael Joseph Holzapfl (1860–1914) after Gabriel Cornelius Max (1840–1915), 'Der Vivisector' ('Vivisector' inscribed on painting, lower right), etching, 15.4 × 26 cm (gravure), 1886, after an oil painting on canvas, 100 × 166 cm, 1883 (present whereabouts of the painting unknown).[45] British Library. *See Plate 4, p. 212 above.*

The painting by Gabriel Max which is reproduced in this engraving was painted in 1883 and exhibited at the painter's one-man show in Munich in that year.[46] In 1884 it went on tour to Dresden, Hamburg, Düsseldorf and Vienna, provoking public discussion of the vivisection question at each venue.[47] In the first half of 1885 it was exhibited in London (French Gallery, 120 Pall Mall), where, however, its fame had run before it, for the anti-vivisection pressure group the Victoria Street Society had already sold many mounted photographs of the picture at 2s 6d each, adorned with explanatory verses by Elliott Preston of Boston, Mass., an honorary member of the Society. At the French Gallery the picture, previously called 'Der Vivisector', was entitled 'The genius of pity staying the vivisector's hand'.[48] In December 1885 it was auctioned in Vienna and in 1889 it was exhibited in Berlin.[49] Its present location is unknown, but in view of its partisan treatment of vivisection one must allow for the possibility that it may have been destroyed by supporters of an opinion opposed to the artist's.

The painting shows, on the left, an elderly grey-bearded physiologist who embodies the foreigner's notion of a German professor of the 1880s. He sits, with scalpel poised, at a well-constructed vivisection table equipped with bolts, bars and rings. The table is probably copied from an illustration in some anti-vivisection tract which had lifted it in turn from a physiological textbook. Behind him stands a female figure dressed in red and white robes: her vaguely Early Christan appearance proclaims her an allegory or personification of virtue — pity, humanity, conscience, etc. She holds a bleeding puppy which she has rescued from a physiological experiment and with her left hand holds up a balance in which one pan, inscribed 'Kain' (Cain), contains an indistinct object which turns out to be a human brain crowned with golden bay-leaves. It is outweighed by the other pan which contains a golden heart smouldering with the fire of love. The fire emits a sulphur-coloured vapour which floats in the atmosphere around the virtuous woman.[50] A writer who described the picture while Max was still painting it stated, presumably on information from the painter, that the balance illustrated a saying attributed to Kant, that a good heart was worth more than a good brain.[51]

Gabriel Max was a learned painter with a sympathy for Schopenhauer's philosophy and a dabbler's interest in the natural sciences.[52] The entire first floor of his house in Munich was filled with prehistoric antiquities, ethnographic objects and material of anthropological interest, while the top of the house contained an observatory for astronomical studies. After spending the morning in his studio or his library, the painter, we are told, would sit in his museum amidst skeletons, skulls and bones, and make anatomical dissections of dead animals.[53] Although Max was best known for his markedly mystical religious pictures, he also painted such sympathetic paintings of living animals that it would be obvious even without further evidence that he spent much time in their company, especially the company of apes. His painting of monkey critics (Munich, Neue Pinakothek) and another monkey picture in the Stedelijk Museum, Amsterdam, are among the few accessible works of his in this line, but he also painted several more unusual *singeries*: his Salome is a dancing ape eyeing the cut-off head of a simian Baptist; 'Comparative Anatomy' shows an ape seated in his study, examining a prepared simian skeleton, with a library in the background; and an extraordinary painting of a battle of animals shows an elephant wrestling with a hippopotamus while a crowd of monkeys and giraffes looks on.[54] These facts allow us to specify Max's painting 'Der Vivisector' as the protest of an anatomist against physiologists and of an animal-lover against animal experiment.

At least one early critic was not impressed by the effect of Max's intellectual interests on his art. While allowing that the 'Vivisector' was an eloquent and tenderly painted piece, he added:

The simplicity of the original sentiment always [in Max's works] becomes clouded by reflection, by morbid brooding over all kinds of conundrums and supernatural arcana, so that the artist's pictures rarely make a harmonious impression. His art has a pathological strain which makes him try to reach further than lies within his power. He wants to be a healer of the soul and to cure mankind of all moral and social maladies . . . That a talent which travels the tortuous paths of mystical speculation should now and then take a wrong turning is quite understandable. When Gabriel Max wants to bring to an appropriate form of expression an idea which fills his soul with enthusiasm, he is not deterred by fear of oddity or tastelessness.[55]

This is certainly true of Max's 'Vivisector' painting, which offers technical illustration (the table), a contemporary genre figure (the old man), a vaguely historical personification (the woman), sentimental animal painting (the dog pawing at its wound), emblematics, religious imagery and biological illustration (the contents of the balance), all thrown together in the service of propagandist aims.

Another contemporary critic faulted the expressions of the figures: not considering whether the painter might have left them vague in order to stimulate the beholder to recreate them in his own mind, the reviewer complained that the woman's expression showed so little anger or distress that she might be a young wife turning away from the oven to ask her husband if he thought she had put too much butter in the pastry, while the torturer himself looked so far from contrite, indeed so wise and reasonable, that the non-partisan viewer, drawing a lesson opposite to that intended, could almost hear him saying 'My dear lady, don't be so frightfully one-sided and subjective, and please don't take away the physiological preparation which I had just arranged so nicely.'[56]

However, Max's painting was addressed to the hearts of the masses, not to the brains of art critics. Despite being a jumble, the painting did succeed in stimulating discussion of vivisection in Germany: it was attacked in print by at least one supporter of animal experiment,[57] and it became, in reproduction, one of the favourite pictures of the American anti-vivisection campaigner George

Angell (b. 1823).[58]

5. Anon. after Léon Augustin Lhermitte, 'Claude Bernard dans son laboratoire' (legend at foot of image), photogravure, 18.5 × 24.2 cm, n.d., after an oil painting on canvas, dimensions unknown (but very large),[59] 1889, in the Académie Nationale de Médecine, Paris. Wellcome Institute Library, London. *See Plate 5, p. 213 above.*

The death of Claude Bernard in 1878 was marked by many memorials, which provided his posthumous cult with an iconography worthy of a Church Father.[60] In the year of his death, subscriptions were invited towards commissioning a statue of the sage which would be placed before the Collège de France. The sculpture, by Jean-Baptiste Guillaume, was presented to members of the organising committee in 1884 and approved by them but execrated by anti-vivisectionists, for it showed Bernard standing by a vivisection table on which a dog was tied down.[61] The committee had taken for granted, as one would expect, that vivisection was an admirable method of research which could be presented to the public without need of apology. The statue was cast in bronze and placed outside the Collège de France where it stood until it was melted down for re-use of the metal in the Second World War. It was subsequently replaced in stone.[62]

The same assumption as to the reasonableness of vivisection was paraded before the public even more ingenuously in a painting by Léon Lhermitte which was exhibited at the Salon in 1889: it is included here (Plate 5) as a counterweight to the easy sentiment of the two previous pictures (Plates 3–4). With respect to the statue, the painting has proved a *monumentum aere perennius*, for after many years in the Sorbonne it now hangs in the Académie Nationale de Médecine and has been reproduced innumerable times (though seldom from the original canvas). Strangely, the story behind the picture seems never to have been told in detail, and the present writer can add little to what has already been said by others.

The painter was commissioned by the state to portray Bernard with some of his close colleagues: they are identified, from left to right, as Nestor Gréhant (1838–1910), Amédée Dumontpallier (1827–99), (seated) Louis-Charles Malassez (1842–1909), (with arms crossed) Paul Bert (1833–86), Jacques-Arsène d'Arsonval (1851–1940), a laboratory assistant on each side of Bernard, and Albert Dastre (1844–1917).[63] The room is Bernard's laboratory at the Collège de France, which is today marked by a plaque on the wall facing the street.[64] In 1888, when Lhermitte made studies for the picture, it was already two years since Paul Bert had died in Indo-China, and Bernard himself had been dead for a decade. These facts, and the mutually inconsistent ages of the sitters, would be enough to rule out the possibility that the picture might record an actual scene, but the fact that the picture is symbolic rather than literal only adds interest to questions about the commission. Who selected the persons portrayed? What sources did the painter use to portray them as they would have appeared twenty years before? Who chose the experiment and set up the apparatus?

The person responsible, whoever he was, seems to have chosen the experiment with particular care. Bernard is shown with an electric probe in his hand for the purpose of faradising an exposed nerve in a live rabbit. The painting appears to allude to an important programme of experiments carried out by Bernard on the cervical portion of the sympathetic nervous system of the rabbit, though any incision in the neck is obscured in the painting.[65] From 1842 to 1850, Bernard had frequently cut the sympathetic nerve of animals to demonstrate the effect of this act on the pupil of the eye, an effect described first by François Pourfour du Petit in 1727 and repeated experimentally by many others in the interval. Around 1850 Bernard took a different approach to this well-known finding by cross-fertilising it with the research on animal heat which he had started with Magendie in 1844. Old anatomical observations and vague *idées reçues* now led him to hypothesise that the sympathetic nervous system was responsible for causing combustion in the blood and thus maintaining body temperature: the hypothesis, he supposed, would be confirmed by a drop in body temperature on one side of the body following sympathectomy on that side only.

In 1851–3 he tested this hypothesis, choosing as his experimental animal the rabbit, which, unlike the dog used by his rivals Budge and Waller, had a sympathetic trunk anatomically distinct from other nerves. To his surprise, the body temperature, instead of falling, rose markedly following the traditional incision, nor was this result due merely to an increased supply of blood to the parts affected, for when the arteries were ligated the increase in temperature was maintained. Faradising the upper end of the cut nerve, as in the painting by Lhermitte, temporarily reversed the effect of the paralysis, restoring the animal to its normal temperature in the affected parts. Further experiments showed that when the animal was subjected to the agony of a slow death by poisoning, the parts of the body warmed by the effect of cutting the sympathetic trunk were the last to succumb.[66]

In his *Introduction à la médecine expérimentale* (1865) Bernard used these experiments to support several cardinal points in his doctrine. They demonstrate the importance, for the experimenter, of choosing the right animal for vivisection. They illustrate the importance of the initial hypothesis: what the experiment reveals depends on what the experimenter is looking for. Many people, including Bernard himself, had performed the same experiment, but had not noticed any effect on body temperature, because they were not looking for it. When the possibility of such an effect came to mind, it was therefore necessary to repeat the experiment yet again. Finally, the unexpected result of the experiment was in some respects even more valuable than a confirmation of the hypothesis would have been.[67] The fact that Bernard himself cherished this experiment for its methodological virtues would have recommended it as the subject of an official memorial.

Notes

1. Galenus, *Omnia opera* (11 vols, L.A. Giunta, Venice, 1541–2), historiated border on title-pages; Andreas Vesalius, *De humani corporis fabrica* (J. Oporinus, Basel, 1543), p. 661, woodcut of a pig on a vivisection table, republished in Claude Bernard's *Leçons de physiologie opératoire* (J.-B. Baillière, Paris, 1879), p. 114; other illustrations after Bernard in E. Klein *et al.*, *Handbook for the Physiological Laboratory* edited by J. Burdon-Sanderson (2 vols, J. and A. Churchill, London, 1873).

2. E. Westacott, *A Century of Vivisection and Anti-vivisection* (C.W. Daniel, Ashingdon, Essex, 1949), p. 132.

3. Benedict Nicolson, *Joseph Wright of Derby. Painter of Light* (2 vols, Paul Mellon Foundation for British Art, London, 1968), vol. 1, pp. 112–14, 235.

4. Three examples, less obvious than some, of cabinets having air-pumps are the cabinet of the ducal academy at Hildburghausen, Thuringia (founded 1714), according to Friedrich Paulsen, *Geschichte des gelehrten Unterrichts auf den deutschen Schulen und Universitäten*, 3rd edn (2 vols, von Veit, Leipzig, 1919–21), vol. 1, pp. 521–2; a private Parisian cabinet *c.* 1740 (C.R. Hill, 'The cabinet of Bonnier de la Mosson 1702–1744', *Annals of Science*, vol. 43 (1986), pp. 147–61); and the cabinet of the pharmacist Christoph de Pauli in Vienna as recorded in a commemorative book of watercolours by Salomon Kleiner, 1751, sold at Sotheby's, London, 18 June 1986, *Fine Instruments of Science and Technology*, lot 86.

5. James Bryan Conant, 'Robert Boyle's Experiments in Pneumatics', in J.B. Conant and L.K. Nash (eds.), *Harvard Case Histories in Experimental Science* (2 vols, Harvard University Press, Cambridge, Mass., 1957), vol. 1, pp. 1–63; Robert G. Frank Jr, *Harvey and the Oxford Physiologists. A Study of*

Scientific Ideas (University of California Press, Berkeley, 1980), pp. 140–63; Steven Shapin and Simon Schaffer, *Leviathan and the Air-pump. Hobbes, Boyle, and the Experimental Life* (Princeton University Press, Princeton, 1985).

6. Robert Boyle, *New Experiments Physico-mechanicall, touching the Spring of the Air* (H. Hall for T. Robinson, Oxford, 1660), pp. 328–34.

7. Robert Boyle, 'New Pneumatical Experiments about Respiration', *Philosophical Transactions of the Royal Society*, vol. 5, nos 62–3 (1670), pp. 2011–31, 2035–56.

8. J.T. Desaguliers, *A System of Experimental Philosophy as Shown at the Publick Lectures in a Course of Mechanical and Experimental Philosophy* (B. Creake, London, 1719), p. 131; J.T. Desaguliers, *A Course of Experimental Philosophy* (2 vols, W. Innys, London, 1744–5), vol. 2, pp. 380–1.

9. Benjamin Worster, *A Compendious and Methodical Account of the Principles of Natural Philosophy*, 2nd edn (S. Austen, London, 1730), pp. 152, 266–7.

10. Benjamin Martin, *The Description and Use of a New, Portable, Table Air-pump* (the author, London, 1766), pp. 28–9. On the author and his bibliography see John R. Millburn, *Benjamin Martin: Author, Instrument-maker and 'Country Showman'* (Noordhoff International, Leiden, 1976) and *Retailer of the Sciences* (Vade-Mecum Press, London, 1986).

11. James Ferguson, *Lectures on Select Subjects* (A. Miller, London, 1760), p. 200.

12. Adam Walker, *Analysis of a Course of Lectures on Natural and Experimental Philosophy*, 6th edn (for the author, no place, no date), p. 37; Adam Walker, *A System of Familiar Philosophy in Twelve Lectures* (the author, London, 1799), p. 224.

13. Ferguson, *Lectures*, p. 200, also quoted by Nicolson, *Joseph Wright*, vol. 1, p. 114.

14. Martin, *Description and Use*, p. 29.

15. (Charcoal) Ferguson, *Lectures*, p. 206; (expired air) Walker, *System*, p. 224; Martin, *Description and Use*, facing p. 38 and *The Young Gentleman and Lady's Philosophy* (2 vols, W. Owen, London, 1755), vol. 1, plate XXXI facing p. 389; Ferguson, *Lectures*, p. 200 (cat) and p. 206 (bird); Walker, *System*, p. 224 (bird).

16. Martin here follows a passage from Shakespeare's *Measure for Measure*, as did later writers on vivisection: see W. Schupbach, 'Iconography of Dr William Kitchiner (1775?–1827)', *Medical History*, vol. 28 (1984), pp. 202–9 (pp. 206–8).

17. B. Martin, *Young Gentleman*, vol. 1, pp. 398–9.

18. Ibid., pp. 399–400.

19. Ibid., pp. 311–12.

20. Ruthven Todd, *Tracks in the Snow* (Grey Walls Press, London, 1946), p. 11.

21. Pictures of a boy and girl blowing bubbles, 1772, referring to the *homo bulla* theme (Nicolson, *Joseph Wright*, vol. 2, plate 93); the old man and death, 1773 (ibid., vol. 2, plate 123); Miravan opening the tomb of his ancestors, 1774 (ibid., vol. 2, plate 107); and perhaps some of the pictures with an inflated bladder such as the one of two boys fighting over a bladder, *c.* 1767–70 (ibid., vol. 2, plate 76).

22. Joseph M. Forshaw, *Parrots of the World*, illustrated by William T. Cooper, revised edn (David and Charles, Newton Abbot, 1981), pp. 127–9

and 133–4; James Lee Peters, *Check-list of Birds of the World* (15 vols, Harvard University Press, Cambridge, Mass., 1931–68), vol. 3, p. 175. Mrs Joyce Pope (British Museum, Natural History) and Dr Nicolaas Rupke kindly offered this information, though at first both thought the bird was a dove, as does Dillian Gordon, *The National Gallery Schools of Painting: British paintings* (National Gallery, London, 1986), p. 44.

For the 1760 description of a white cockatoo see Mathurin-Jacques Brisson, *Ornithologia . . . ornithologie* (6 vols, J.B. Bauche, Paris, 1760), vol. 4, pp. 212–14 and plate XXII.

23. Nicolson, *Joseph Wright*, vol. 2, plate 59; Allan Braham, *Wright of Derby: Mr & Mrs Coltman* (National Gallery, London, 1986), pp. 10–11 reproduce the preliminary sketch.

H.S. Torrens, 'Geological collections and curators of note. 1. Lichfield museums (pre-1850)', *GCG. Newsletter of the Geological Curator's Group*, no. 1 (1974), pp. 5–10; [Richard Greene], *A Descriptive Catalogue of the rarities in Mr Greene's Museum at Lichfield* (Mr Morgan, [Lichfield], 1773), p. 4. In the 3rd edn. of Greene's catalogue, *A Particular and Descriptive Catalogue of the Curiosities, Natural and Artificial, in the Lichfield Museum. Collected (in the Space of Forty-six Years;) by Richard Greene* (J. Jackson, Lichfield, 1786), what is presumably the same stuffed bird is described as 'An *African* Paroquet' (p. 27). In the sale catalogue of the museum issued when it formed part of the estate of the surgeon Richard Wright of Lichfield (who was not identical with the surgeon Richard Wright of Derby, Joseph Wright's brother), the 'paroquet' is not mentioned: see *Catalogue of the Valuable and Extensive Collection of Paintings, Natural and Artificial Curiosities . . . collected by the Late Dr Wright, of Lichfield . . . Which Will be Sold by Auction, by Mr Harris . . . in the Guildhall of the City of Lichfield* (Longman, London [1821]), of which a copy is in the library of the Royal College of Surgeons, London. Wright's museum did, however, have a number of diseased bones in bell-glasses (sale catalogue pp. 16–17), perhaps like the one in Joseph Wright's picture, though the vessel depicted there is not a bell-glass. (I thank Drs H. Torrens and R. Porter for pertinent information.)

24. *Handbook of the Wellcome Historical Medical Museum* (WHMM, London, 1913), p. 78.

25. Emile Bellier de la Chavignerie and Louis Auvray, *Dictionnaire général des artistes de l'école française* (3 vols, Renouard, Paris, 1868–87), vol. 2, p. 134.

26. Mouchy is not mentioned in the journal *L'artiste*, vols 1–8 (1831–4); in Charles Lenormant, *Les artistes contemporains*) 2 vols, Alexandre Mesnier, Paris, 1833); Jean-Baptiste-Gustave Planche, *Études sur l'école française (1831–1852), peinture et sculpture* (2 vols, M. Lévy, Paris, 1855); Jules Clarétie, *Peintres et sculpteurs contemporains* (2 vols, Librairie des bibliophiles, Paris, 1882–4); Léon Rosenthal, *Du romantisme au réalisme. Essai sur l'évolution de la peinture en France de 1830 à 1848* (Renouard, Paris, 1914); Joseph C. Sloane, *French Painting between the Past and the Present* (Princeton University Press, Princeton, 1951); Geraldine Pelles, *Art, Artists and Society. Origins of a Modern Dilemma* (Prentice-Hall, Englewood Cliffs, N.J., 1963); Gerald Schur, *Les petits maîtres de la peinture, 1820–1920* (6 vols, Editions de la Gazette, Paris, 1969–85?); Albert Boime, *The Academy and French Painting in the Nineteenth Century* (Phaidon, London, 1971).

27. E. Bénézit, *Dictionnaire critique et documentaire des peintres* (10 vols, Librairie Gründ, Paris, 1976), vol. 7, p. 573.

28. Christie, Manson and Woods, *Fine Continental Pictures*, London, 2 October 1981, lot 102 (the death of St Francis, signed and dated 1840?, oil on canvas 3.225 × 2.337 m) and lot 103 (the martyrdom of St John the Baptist, signed and dated 1845, oil on canvas 2.246 × 1.995 m).

29. Rosenthal, *Du romantisme au réalisme*, p. 36.

30. Bellier de la Chavignerie and Auvray, *Dictionnaire général*, p. 134.

31. A. Jal, *Salon de 1833. Les causeries du Louvre* (Charles Gosselin, Paris, 1833), pp. 372–3.

32. Niklaus Egli, *Der 'Prix Montyon de Physiologie expérimentale' im 19. Jahrhundert* (Juris-Verlag, Zürich, 1970); J.V. Pickstone, 'Locating Dutrochet', *British Journal for the History of Science*, vol. 11 (1978), pp. 49–64.

33. John E. Lesch, *Science and Medicine in France. The Emergence of Experimental Physiology, 1790–1855* (Harvard University Press, Cambridge, Mass., 1984), pp. 161, 174.

34. J.M.D. Olmsted, *François Magendie* (Schuman's, New York, 1944), pp. 49, 81.

35. Anon., 'A course of lectures on experimental physiology by M. Magendie', *London Medical Gazette*, vol. 1 (1828), pp. 237–9, 268–9, 397, etc.

36. Claude Bernard, *Leçons de physiologie opératoire* (J.-B. Baillière, Paris, 1879), pp. 63–4 translated.

37. François Leuret and Jean-Louis Lassaigne, *Recherches physiologiques et chimiques pour servir à l'histoire de la digestion* (Mme Huzard, Paris, 1825), pp. 5–6; Joseph Schiller, *Claude Bernard et les problèmes scientifiques de son temps* (Éditions du Cèdre, Paris, 1967), pp. 33–5, 228–30.

38. I thank Mr P. Nicolas Sainte-Fare-Garnot, Professor Lorenz Eitner, Professor M.D. Grmek, Professor Sir William Paton and Dr Nicolaas Rupke for their observations and answers to questions about this painting.

39. J.D. Champlin and C.C. Perkins, *Cyclopedia of Painters and Paintings* (2 vols, Empire State Book Co., New York, 1927), p. 205.

40. John McClure Hamilton, *Men I have Painted* (T. Fisher Unwin, London, 1921).

41. Algernon Graves, *The Royal Academy of Arts: a Complete Dictionary of Contributors . . . 1769 to 1904* (8 vols, Henry Graves, London, 1905–6), vol. 8, p. 3.

42. *Zoophilist*, vol. 5 (1885–6), p. 102 (1 October 1885), 'The pathetic picture by Mr J. McLure Hamilton . . . is now included in the gallery of paintings at the new Albert Palace . . .' The picture may have been a pastel, as Hamilton produced several works in this medium (e.g. exhibited at Carnegie Institute, Pittsburgh, 1916; Pennsylvania Academy of the Fine Arts, 1901; Westmoreland County Museum of Art, Greenburg, Pa., 1959).

43. Richard D. French, *Antivivisection and Medical Science in Victorian Society* (Princeton University Press, Princeton, 1975), pp. 68, 414–15.

44. N. A. Rupke, this volume, Chapter 8, *passim*.

45. Engraving published in Agathon Klemt, 'Gabriel Max und seine Werke', *Die graphischen Künste*, vol. 9 (1886–7), pp. 1–12, 25–36, engraving between pp. 32 and 33. The size of the original canvas is given by Friedrich von Boetticher, *Malerwerke des neunzehnten Jahrhunderts* (2 vols, F. von Boetticher, Dresden, 1895–1901), vol. 1, p. 955, no. 106.

46. Boetticher, *Malerwerke*, vol. 1, p. 955, no. 106.

47. *Zoophilist*, vol. 3 (1883–4), p. 262 (1 March 1884).

48. *Zoophilist*, vol. 5 (1885–6), p. 20 (1 June 1885).

49. Boetticher, *Malerwerke*, vol. 1, p. 955, no. 106.

50. *National-Zeitung* (Berlin), 29 April 1884, no. 259, 3rd edn, p. 1.

51. Adolf Rohut, 'Gabriel Max', *Westermanns Illustrierte Deutsche Monatshefte*, vol. 54 (1883), pp. 173–86.

52. Ibid.

53. Nicolaus Mann, *Gabriel Max. Eine kunsthistorische Skizze*, 2nd edn (J.J. Weber, Leipzig, 1890), pp. 24–30.

54. Reproductions are in the Witt Library, Courtauld Institute, University of London. The battle painting was sold by Weinmüller, Munich, 21 September 1972, lot 1532 (illus. no. 296).

55. Carl Adolf Rosenberg, *Die Münchener Malerschule in ihrer Entwickelung seit 1871* (E.A. Seemann, Leipzig, 1887), pp. 16–18.

56. *National-Zeitung*.

57. Wilhelm Ebstein, *Der medizinische Versuch mit besonderer Berücksichtigung der 'Vivisektion'* (J.F. Bergmann, Wiesbaden, 1907), pp. 38–9, 53 ('das schwülstige Bild von Gabriel Max'); cited by Hubert Bretschneider, *Der Streit um die Vivisektion im 19. Jahrhundert* (Fischer, Stuttgart, 1962), pp. 32, 138.

58. James Turner, *Reckoning with the Beast* (Johns Hopkins University Press, Baltimore, 1980), p. 102.

59. A good impression of the size of the canvas is given by the photograph in *Histoire des sciences médicales*, vol. 13 (1979), p. 17.

60. On Bernard as a cult figure: Pierre Mauriac, *Claude Bernard* (Grasset, Paris, 1941), p. 154; Ludmilla Jordanova, 'The Historiography of the Claude Bernard Industry', *History of Science*, vol. 16 (1978), pp. 214–21.

61. *The Times*, 20 March 1878, p. 5; *Zoophilist*, vol. 4 (1884–5), pp. 145–6.

62. Jacqueline Sonolet, *Musée Claude Bernard* (Fondation Marcel Mérieux, Saint Julien en Beaujolais, 1978), p. 4.

63. The names of the sitters and other information are found in Helen T. Konjias, 'Medical Portraits of the Nineteenth Century', *Ciba Symposia*, vol. 6 (1944), pp. 1772–7; Charles Singer and E. Ashworth Underwood, *A Short History of Medicine*, 2nd edn (Clarendon Press, Oxford, 1962), plate XX facing p. 552; Franz Halberg, 'Claude Bernard and the "Extreme Variability of the Internal Milieu" ', in Francisco Grande and Maurice B. Visscher (eds.), *Claude Bernard and Experimental Medicine* (Schenkman, Cambridge, Mass., 1967), pp. 193–210; Pierre Huard, 'L'oeuvre scientifique de Paul Bert', *Histoire des sciences médicales*, vol. 13 (1979), pp. 159–69. Portraits of the individual sitters are found in Spyros G. Marketos, *Claude Bernard* (Kedros, Athens, 1980).

64. Halberg, 'Claude Bernard', p. 196; Sonolet, *Musée Claude Bernard*, reproduces Lhermitte's sketches, pp. 17, 24.

65. Halberg, 'Claude Bernard', p. 195.

66. Hebbel H. Hoff and Roger Guillermin, 'Claude Bernard and the Vasomotor System', in Grande and Visscher (eds.), *Claude Bernard and Experimental Medicine*, pp. 75–104; Claude Bernard, *Leçons sur la physiologie et la pathologie du système nerveux* (2 vols, J.-B. Baillière, Paris, 1858), vol. 2, pp. 469–544.

67. Claude Bernard, *Introduction à la médecine expérimentale* (J.-B. Baillière, Paris, 1865), pp. 295–9.

15

Epilogue

Sir William Paton

'There are no votes in vivisection'; so remarked a British Member of Parliament to me at a hearing by the Council of Europe Parliamentary Assembly on animal experiment. As one reads the record of the debates in various countries over the years, one can readily agree. Issues are raised which for any save the most insensitive mind are bound to conflict: the need for freedom of human enquiry and for biological understanding; the practical demands of experiment for advancing medical and veterinary science; the duty of care for animals, whether regarded as much loved companions, as God's creations, as creatures sentient like ourselves, as creatures dependent on us, or as creatures for whom rights comparable to our own are claimed. The simultaneous satisfaction of such imperatives is impossible; and the priority assigned by individuals can only vary. So one sees in the historical record of the resolutions of the conflicts, patterns expressing the full range of variations of nationality, historical period and personal character and experience.

It is, indeed, an area of human debate where the role of the individual seems to be especially important: Cobbe, Lind-af-Hageby, Coleridge, Paget, Baroness Burdett Coutts, even Klein with his apparent heartlessness, seem in Britain to be genuine prime movers rather than surface markers of already existing forces — a feature perhaps in keeping with the intensely moral nature of the debate. In Germany and Switzerland, it is Baroness von Schwartz, Grysanowski, von Weber and Hermann; in Sweden, Nordvall; in the USA, Caroline Earle White and Bergh versus Keen and Cannon; and in Italy, Frances Cobbe again. Of recent years, it is true, economic factors come to be mentioned, e.g. the profits of the cosmetics or pharmaceutical industries, or the claim that a scientist may practise animal experiment simply to further his career rather than for knowledge or general benefit. But it is still pain and suffering on the one hand and the acquisition of knowledge and understanding on the other that provide the energy in the clash of argument; for both sides, reduction of suffering is claimed, so that the stakes are high; and it involves, at the deepest level, our views of ourselves, of animals and ultimately of all creation.

One virtue of the closer analysis presented by the chapters in this book is the erosion of simplistic ideas. One might expect two simple packages labelled 'anti-vivisection' and 'vivisection', the former accompanied by vegetarianism, preoccupation with rights and anti-farming, the latter stressing the claims of pure curiosity. One finds instead that Bentham, in his famous footnote,[1] not only created the battle cry of today's animal rights movement ('the question is not, Can they *reason*? nor, Can they *talk*? but, Can they *suffer*?'), but also justified killing for food. Frances Cobbe, so trenchant an opponent of experiment on animals, was a meat-eater and did not believe in animal rights.[2] Stephen Coleridge, the leading anti-vivisectionist witness at the 1906 Commission, hardly objected to the practices of agriculture.[3] Charles Darwin could both write:

> You ask my opinion on vivisection. I quite agree that it is justifiable for real investigations on physiology; but not for mere damnable and detestable curiosity. It is a subject that makes me sick with horror, so I will not say another word about it, else I shall not sleep tonight;

and:

> I have long thought physiology one of the greatest of sciences, sure sooner, or more probably later, greatly to benefit mankind; but judging from all other sciences, the benefits will accrue only indirectly in the search for abstract truth. It is certain that physiology can progress only by experiments on living animals. Therefore the proposal to limit research to points of which we can now see the bearing in regard to health &c., I look at as puerile.[4]

So, too, today one finds experimenters varying widely in the experiments they would accept as justifiable.

With issues which touch so many nerves, no easy trend to tidy resolution is likely to be detectable. One might, indeed, be pessimistic, and expect that with rising standards and expectations, the conflict between the demands of research and the demands of animal welfare would become increasingly severe. Indeed a new element has appeared in recent years, hardly discussed in this book, namely the animal activist groups with their varying willingness to practise violence in the furtherance of their aims. This is indeed a subject worthy of study in itself. For those unfamiliar with these groups, the activities of the Animal Liberation Front in the first six months of 1983 are listed by Duffy.[5]

But there are other trends that will deserve study. One major one is that the medical and veterinary gains resulting from animal experiment are now more extensive, clearer and better documented. It is probable that the perception of the significance of this work has also advanced. Of course, it is still possible to argue that these gains were nevertheless won by immoral means, and therefore such work is still not to be tolerated. But the consequences of such an attitude are much clearer.

A second great factor is the major improvements in experimental technology. These allow far more to be learnt from far less severe procedures; anaesthetic and analgesic techniques are far better understood; statistical principle used for the design of experiment increases experimental productivity; the role of cell, tissue and organ culture steadily advances; non-invasive methods, and earlier detection of effects, progress. Likewise, the care of animals, the techniques of husbandry, have greatly improved. So, even if the standards of what could be viewed as minor discomfort or suffering have also risen, and the issue is no longer simply that of pain, yet, for those involved in these arguments who are not absolutists, areas of compromise become practicable. Hampson's review of the legal practices now current in various parts of the world shows the start of this general process.[6] If one compares it with some of the passionate past debates, it may be that, despite the intrusion of violence, a new phase is beginning.

But there is one aspect in modern trends that is not clear: what is it that is looked for in the long run? The animal experimenter, perhaps, simply looks to the day, still far away, when animal experiment will be redundant, and other practices under fully humane control, but when otherwise the relation of man to animal will be the same. The animal welfare advocate seeks to go further: to abolish the use of animals for food, furs, field-sports or farming, for scientific experiment, as pets, or indeed for any 'exploitation'.

The question arises: what relationship remains, what ultimately is envisaged? Man has far greater power than animals; so that *any* relationship is liable to be, or to be seen as, exploitation. The suggested prohibitions are such that man could not simply take on the role of another animal, pursuing his own ecological welfare. Is the objective, therefore, to be the separation of animals from man — a new form of 'separate development', ecological isolationism, with no domestication or use of animals, and a deliberate destruction of man-animal contacts? It is not a plausible scenario; but the question still remains; what is the relationship of man to animal that we seek to achieve?

Notes

1. Jeremy Bentham, *An Introduction to the Principles of Morals and Legislation*, ed. J.H. Burns and H.L.A. Hart (Methuen, London, 1982), ch. 17, section 4, pp. 282–3.

2. See Elston, Chapter 11.

3. *Royal Commission on Vivisection*, Appendix to Third Report of the Commissioners, Cd. 3757 (HMSO, London, 1907), pp. 197–8.

4. Francis Darwin (ed.), *The Life and Letters of Charles Darwin* (3 vols, Murray, London, 1888), vol. 3, pp. 200–2.

5. Maureen Duffy, *Men and Beasts, an Animal Rights Handbook* (Paladin Books, Granada, London, 1984), pp. 139–47.

6. See Hampson, Chapter 13, this volume.

Index

Note: Sub-entries are in alphabetical order except where chronological order is significant